BRITISH WRITERS

BRITISH WRITERS

Edited under the auspices of the British Council

IAN SCOTT-KILVERT

General Editor

VOLUME VIII

INDEX

CHARLES SCRIBNER'S SONS / NEW YORK

Copyright © 1984 The British Council

Library of Congress Cataloging in Publication Data (Revised for volume 8)

Main entry under title:

British writers.

Includes bibliographies.
CONTENTS: v. 1. William Langland to the English
Bible.—v. 2. Thomas Middleton to George Farquhar.—[etc.]
—v. 8. Index.
1. English literature—History and criticism.
2. English literature—Bio-bibliography. 3. Authors,
English—Biography. I. Scott-Kilvert, Ian. II. Great
Britain. British Council.
PR85.B688   820'.9   78–23483
ISBN 0–684–15798–5 (v.1)   ISBN 0–684–16636–4 (v.5)
ISBN 0–684–16407–8 (v.2)   ISBN 0–684–16637–2 (v.6)
ISBN 0–684–16408–6 (v.3)   ISBN 0–684–16638–0 (v.7)
ISBN 0–684–16635–6 (v.4)   ISBN 0–684–17417–0 (v.8)

1 3 5 7 9 11 13 15 17 19   V/C   20 18 16 14 12 10 8 6 4 2

PRINTED IN THE UNITED STATES OF AMERICA

The paper in this book meets the guidelines for
permanence and durability of the Committee on
Production Guidelines for Book Longevity of the
Council on Library Resources.

Editorial Staff

BRITISH WRITERS

INDEX

All references include volume numbers in **bold-face Roman numerals** and page numbers either in Arabic, to indicate the text of an essay, or in lowercase Roman, to refer to the introduction in a volume. Extended treatment of a subject is indicated by **bold-face page numbers.**

A

Aaron's Rod (Lawrence), **VII:** 90, 94, **106–107**

Abaft the Funnel (Kipling), **VI:** 204

"Abasement of the Northmores, The" (James), **VI:** 69

"Abbé Delille and Walter Landor, The" (Landor), **IV:** 88$_n$, 92–93

Abbey Theatre, **VI:** 212, 218, 307, 309, 316; **VII:** 3, 6, 11

Abbot, The (Scott), **IV:** 39

Abbott, C. C., **V:** 379, 381

Abercrombie, Lascelles, **II:** 247

Abinger Harvest (Forster), **VI:** 411, 412

Abridgement of the History of England, An (Goldsmith), **III:** 191

Abridgement of the Light of Nature Pursued, An (Hazlitt), **IV:** 139

Absalom and Achitophel (Dryden), **II:** 292, 298–299, 304

"Absence" (Thompson), **V:** 444.

"Absent-Minded Beggar, The" (Kipling), **VI:** 203

"Absent-Mindedness in a Parish Choir" (Hardy), **VI:** 22

"Abt Vogler" (Browning), **IV:** 365, 366, 370

Abuses of Conscience, The (Sterne), **III:** 135

Academy (periodical), **VI:** 249

Academy Notes (Ruskin), **V:** 178

Acceptable Sacrifice, The (Bunyan), **II:** 253

Acceptance World, The (Powell), **VII:** 347, 348, 350

Accident (Bennett), **VI:** 250

"According to His Lights" (Galsworthy), **VI:** 276–277

"Account, The" (Cowley), **II:** 197

Account of Corsica, An (Boswell), **III:** 236, 239, 243, 247

Account of the European Settlements in America, An (Burke), **III:** 205

Account of the Growth of Popery and Arbitrary Government, An (Marvell), **II:** 207–208, 219

Account of the Life of Dr. Samuel Johnson . . . by Himself, An (Johnson), **III:** 122

Achilles (Gay), **III:** 55, 66, 67

Achilles in Scyros (Bridges), **VI:** 83

Acis and Galatea (Gay), **III:** 55, 67

A. Couleii Plantarum Libri Duo (Cowley), **II:** 202

Across the Plains (Stevenson), **V:** 389, 396

Actaeon and Diana (Jonson), **I:** 286

acting companies, **I:** 197, 206, 298; see also boys' theaters, Inns of Court

Actions and Reactions (Kipling), **VI:** 204

Acton, John, **IV:** 289, 290; **VI:** 385

Adam Bede (Eliot), **V:** xxii, 2, 191–192, 194, 200

"Ad Amicam" sonnets (Thompson), **V:** 441

Adams, Henry, **VI:** 65

"Adam's Curse" (Yeats), **III:** 184; **VI:** 213

Addison, Joseph, **II:** 195, 200; **III:** 1, 18, 19, **38–53**, 74, 198; **IV:** 278, 281, 282

"Additional Poems" (Housman), **VI:** 161

"Address to the Deil" (Burns), **III:** 315, 317

Address to the Irish People, An (Shelley), **IV:** 208

"Address to the Unco Guid" (Burns), **III:** 319

"Adina" (James), **VI:** 69

Administrator, The (MacNeice) **VII:** 401

Admirable Bashville, The (Barker), **VI:** 113

Admiral Guinea (Stevenson), **V:** 396

1

Adonais (Shelley), **I**: 160; **VI**: 73; **IV**: xviii, 179, 196, 205–206, 207, 208

Adonis and the Alphabet (Huxley), **VII**: 206–207

"Adrian and Bardus" (Gower), **I**: 54

"Advanced Lady, The" (Mansfield), **VII**: 172

Advancement of Learning, The (Bacon), **I**: 261–265; **II**: 149; **IV**: 279

Advantages Proposed by Repealing the Sacramental Test, The (Swift), **III**: 36

"Adventure of Charles Wentworth" (Brontë), **V**: 118–119

Adventures of Caleb Williams, The (Godwin), **III**: 332, 345; **IV**: 173

Adventures of Covent Garden, The (Farquhar), **II**: 352, 354, 364

Adventures of Ferdinand Count Fathom, The (Smollett), see *Ferdinand Count Fathom*

Adventures of Harry Richmond, The (Meredith), **V**: xxiii, 228, 234

Adventures of Peregrine Pickle, The (Smollett), see *Peregrine Pickle*

Adventures of Philip on His Way Through the World, The (Thackeray), **V**: 19, 29, 35, 38

Adventures of Roderick Random, The (Smollett), see *Roderick Random*

Adventures of Sir Launcelot Greaves, The (Smollett), see *Sir Launcelot Greaves*

Adventures of the Black Girl in Her Search for God, The (Shaw), **VI**: 124, 127, 129

Adventures of Ulysses, The (Lamb), **IV**: 85

Advice: A Satire (Smollett), **III**: 152$_n$, 158

Advice to a Daughter (Halifax), **III**: 40

Advice to a Son (Osborne), **II**: 145

Advocateship of Jesus Christ, The (Bunyan), **II**: 253

A. E. Housman (Gow), **VI**: 164

A. E. Housman: A Divided Life (Watson), **VI**: 164

A. E. Housman: An Annotated Handlist (Sparrow), **VI**: 164

Aeneid (tr. Douglas), **III**: 311

Aeneid (tr. Surrey), **I**: 116–119

Aeneids of Virgil, Done into English Verse, The (Morris), **V**: 306

Aeneis (Dryden), **II**: 290, 293, 297, 301

Aeschylus, **IV**: 199

Aesop (Vanbrugh), **II**: 324, 332, 336

"Aesop and Rhodopè" (Landor), **IV**: 94

"Aesthetic Apologia, An" (Betjeman), **VII**: 357–358

Aesthetic movement, **V**: xii, xiii, 342–344, 400–403, 406, 407–408; **VI**: 365; **VII**: 29

"Aesthetic Poetry" (Pater), **V**: 356, 357

Aethiopian History (Heliodorus), **I**: 164

Affair, The (Snow), **VII**: xxi, 324, 329–330

"Affliction" (Herbert), **II**: 125, 127

"Affliction" (Vaughan), **II**: 187–188

"Affliction of Childhood, The" (De Quincey), **IV**: 152–153, 154

African Witch, The (Cary), **VII**: 186

"After a Journey" (Hardy), **VI**: 18

"After Dunkirk" (Lewis), **VII**: 445

"After Long Silence" (Yeats), **VI**: 212

After Many a Summer (Huxley), **VII**: xviii, 205

Aftermath, The (Churchill), **VI**: 359

Afternoon Men (Powell), **VII**: 343–345

After Strange Gods (Eliot), **VI**: 207; **VII**: 153

"Afterthought, An" (Rossetti), **V**: 258

"Afterwards" (Hardy), **VI**: 13, 19

"Against Absence" (Suckling), **II**: 227

"Against Fruition" (Cowley), **II**: 197

"Against Fruition" (Suckling), **II**: 227

Against Venomous Tongues (Skelton), **I**: 90

Agamemnon (Seneca), **II**: 71

Agamemnon, a Tragedy Taken from Aeschylus (Fitz-Gerald), **IV**: 349, 353

Agamemnon of Aeschylus, The (tr. Browning), **IV**: 358–359, 374

Agamemnon of Aeschylus, The (tr. MacNeice), **VII**: 408–409

Agents and Patients (Powell), **VII**: 345–346

Age of Anxiety, The (Auden), **VII**: 379, 388, 389–390

Age of Bronze, The (Byron), **IV**: xviii, 193

Age of Indiscretion, The (Davis), **V**: 394

Age of Shakespeare, The (Swinburne), **V**: 333

Aglaura (Suckling), **II**: 226, 238

Agnes Grey (Brontë), **V:** xx, 129–130, 132, 134–135, 140–141, 153

"Agnes Lahens" (Moore), **VI:** 98

agnostic rationalism, **VI:** 210

Agnostic's Apology, An (Stephen), **VI:** 289

"Ah, what avails the sceptred race" (Landor), **IV:** 88

Aids to Reflection (Coleridge), **IV:** 53, 56

Aiken, Conrad, **VII:** 149, 179

Ainger, Alfred, **IV:** 254, 267

Ainsworth, Harrison, **IV:** 311; **V:** 47

"Aire and Angels" (Donne), **II:** 197

Aissa Saved (Cary), **VII:** 185

"Akbar's Bridge" (Kipling), **VI:** 201

Akerman, Rudolph, **V:** 111

Alamanni, Luigi, **I:** 110–111

Alamein to Zem-Zem (Douglas), **VII:** xxii, 441

Alarcos (Disraeli), **IV:** 306, 308

Alaric at Rome (Arnold), **V:** 216

Alastor (Shelley), **III:** 330, 338; **IV:** xvii, 195, 198, 208, 217

"Albergo Empedocle" (Forster), **VI:** 399, 412

"Albinus and Rosemund" (Gower), **I:** 53–54

Albion and Albanius (Dryden), **II:** 305

"Albion & Marina" (Brontë), **V:** 110

Album Verses (Lamb), **IV:** 83, 85

Alcazar (Peele), see *Battle of Alcazar, The*

Alcestis (Euripides), **IV:** 358

Alchemist, The (Jonson), **I:** 304–341, 342; **II:** 4, 48

"Alchemist in the City, The" (Hopkins), **V:** 362

Aldington, Richard, **VI:** 416; **VII:** xvi, 36, 121

Aldiss, Brian, **III:** 341, 345

Aldous Huxley (Brander), **VII:** 208

Alexander, Peter, **I:** 300$_n$, 326

Alexander, William (earl of Stirling), **I:** 218; **II:** 80

"Alexander and Zenobia" (Brontë), **V:** 115

Alexander Pope (Sitwell), **VII:** 138–139

Alexander Pope (Stephen), **V:** 289

Alexander Pope as Critic and Humanist (Warren), **II:** 332$_n$

Alexander's Feast: Or the Power of Musique (Dryden), **II:** 200, 300, 304

Alexandria: A History and Guide (Forster), **VI:** 408, 412

"Alfieri and Salomon the Florentine Jew" (Landor), **IV:** 91

Alfred Lord Tennyson: A Memoir (Tennyson), **IV:** 324, 338

Algernon Charles Swinburne (Thomas), **VI:** 424

Alice in Wonderland (Carroll), see *Alice's Adventures in Wonderland*

Alice's Adventures in Wonderland (Carroll), **V:** xxiii, 261–265, **266–269**, 270–273

Alice's Adventures Under Ground (Carroll), **V:** 266, 273; see *Alice's Adventures in Wonderland*

"Alicia's Diary" (Hardy), **VI:** 22

Alien (Foster), **III:** 345

"Alien Corn, The" (Maugham), **VI:** 370, 374

"All blue and bright, in glorious light" (Brontë), **V:** 115

"All Day It Has Rained" (Lewis), **VII:** 445

allegory, **IV:** 46

Allen, John, **IV:** 341, 349–350, 352

Allen, Walter Ernest, **V:** 219; **VI:** 257; **VII:** xvii, xxxvii, 71, 343

Allestree, Richard, **III:** 82

"All Flesh" (Thompson), **V:** 442

All Fools (Chapman), **I:** 235, 238, 244

All for Love (Dryden), **II:** 295–296, 305

All for Love (Southey), **IV:** 71

All My Eyes See: The Visual World of G. M. Hopkins (ed. Thornton), **V:** 377$_n$, 379$_n$, 382

Allott, Kenneth, **IV:** 236; **VI:** xi, xxvii, 218

Allott, Miriam, **IV:** x, xxiv, 223$_n$, 224, 234, 236; **V:** x, 218

All Ovid's Elegies (Marlowe), **I:** 280, 291, 293

"All philosophers, who find" (Swift), **IV:** 160

All Quiet on the Western Front (Remarque), **VII:** xvi

All Religions Are One (Blake), **III:** 292, 307

"All Saints: Martyrs" (Rossetti), **V:** 255

All's Well That Ends Well (Shakespeare), **I:** 313, 318

All the Conspirators (Isherwood), **VII:** 310

"All the hills and vales along" (Sorley), **VI:** 421–422

All the Year Round (periodical), **V:** 42

"Allusion to the Tenth Satire of the Second Book of Horace" (Rochester), **II:** 259

Almayer's Folly (Conrad), **VI:** 135–136, 148

"Aloe, The" (Mansfield), **VII:** 173–174

Alone (Douglas), **VI:** 293, 294, 297, 304, 305

Alpers, Antony, **VII:** 176

"Alphabetical Catalogue of Names . . . and Other Material Things Mentioned in These Pastorals, An" (Gay), **III:** 56

"Alps in Winter, The" (Stephen), **V:** 282

Alroy (Disraeli), **IV:** 296, 297, 308

"Al Som de l'Escalina" (Eliot), **VII:** 152

"Altar, The" (Herbert), **II:** 128

"Altar of the Dead, The" (James), **VI:** 69

Alton, R. E., **I:** 285

Alton Locke (Kingsley), **V:** vii, xxi, 2, 4; **VI:** 240

Alvarez, A., **II:** 125*n*

Amadis of Gaul (tr. Southey), **IV:** 71

Amateur Emigrant, The (Stevenson), **V:** 389, 396

Amazing Marriage, The (Meredith), **V:** 227, 232, 233, 234

Ambarvalia: Poems by T. Burbidge and A. H. Clough, **V:** 159–160, 161, 170

Ambassadors, The (James), **VI:** 55, **57–59**

"Amber Bead, The" (Herrick), **II:** 106

Amberley, Lady, **V:** 129

Amboyna (Dryden), **II:** 305

Amelia (Fielding), **III:** 102–103, 105

"Amen" (Rossetti), **V:** 256

Amendments of Mr. Collier's False and Imperfect Citations (Congreve), **II:** 339, 340, 350

America. A Prophecy (Blake), **III:** 300, 302, 307

America I Presume (Lewis), **VII:** 77

American, The (James), **VI:** 24, **28–29,** 39, 67

American Notes (Dickens), **V:** 42, 54, 55, 71

American Scene, The (James), **VI:** 54, **62–64,** 67

American Senator, The (Trollope), **V:** 100, 102

American Visitor, An (Cary), **VII:** 186

"Ametas and Thestylis Making Hay-Ropes" (Marvell), **II:** 211

Aminta (Tasso), **II:** 49

"Amir's Homily, The" (Kipling), **VI:** 201

"Among All Lovely Things My Love Had Been" (Wordsworth), **IV:** 21

"Among School Children" (Yeats), **VI:** 211, 217

Amores (tr. Marlowe), **I:** 276, 290

Amoretti and Epithalamion (Spenser), **I:** 124, 128–131

"Amos Barton" (Eliot), **V:** 190

Amours de Voyage (Clough), **V:** xxii, 155, 156, 158, 159, 161–163, 165, 166–168, 170

Amphytrion: or, the Two Sosias (Dryden), **II:** 296, 305

"Ample Garden, The" (Graves), **VII:** 269

Amusements Serious and Comical (Brown), **III:** 41

"Amy Foster" (Conrad), **VI:** 134, 148

Anacreontiques (Johnson), **II:** 198

"Anactoria" (Swinburne), **V:** 319–320, 321

"Anarchist, An" (Conrad), **VI:** 148

Anatomy of Exchange-Alley, The (Defoe), **III:** 13

Anatomy of Frustration, The (Wells), **VI:** 228

Anatomy of Melancholy (Burton), **II:** 88, 106, 108; **IV:** 219

Ancient and English Versions of the Bible (Isaacs), **I:** 385

Ancient Lights (Ford), **VI:** 319, 320

"Ancient Mariner, The" (Coleridge), **III:** 330, 338; **IV:** viii, ix, 42, 44–48, 54, 55

"Ancient Sage, The" (Tennyson), **IV:** 329

"Ancient to Ancients, An" (Hardy), **VI:** 13

"And country life I praise" (Bridges), **VI:** 75

Anderson, Sherwood, **VII:** 75

Anderton, Basil, **II:** 154, 157

"Andrea del Sarto" (Browning), **IV:** 357, 361, 366

Andrea of Hungary, and Giovanna of Naples (Landor), **IV:** 100

"Andrey Satchel and the Parson and Clerk" (Hardy), **VI:** 22

Androcles and the Lion (Shaw), **VI:** 116, 124, 129

"Andromeda" (Hopkins), **V:** 370, 376

Andromeda Liberata (Chapman), **I:** 235, 254

And What if the Pretender Should Come? (Defoe), **III:** 13

Anecdotes (Spence), **II:** 261

Anecdotes of Johnson (Piozzi), **III:** 246

Anecdotes . . . of Mr. Pope . . . by the Rev. Joseph Spence (ed. Singer), **III:** 69, 78

Angel Pavement (Priestley), **VII:** xviii, 211, 216–217

Anglicanism, **I:** 178–184, 362–364; 375

Anglo-Italian Review, **VI:** 294

Angrian chronicles (Brontë), **V:** 110–111, 120–121, 122, 124–125, 126, 135

Animadversions upon the Remonstrants Defence Against Smectymnuus (Milton), **II:** 175

Animal Farm (Orwell), **VII:** xx, 273, 278, 283–284

Anima Poetae: From the Unpublished Notebooks (Coleridge), **IV:** 56

Animated Nature (Goldsmith), see *History of the Earth . . .*

"Anna, Lady Braxby" (Hardy), **VI:** 22

Annan, Noel, **V:** 284, 290

Anna of the Five Towns (Bennett), **VI:** xiii, 248, 249, 252, 253, 266

Anne Brontë (Gérin), **V:** 153

"Anne Killigrew" (Dryden), **II:** 303

Anne of Geierstein (Scott), **IV:** 39

Anniversaries (Donne), **I:** 361–362, 364, 367

Annotations of Scottish Songs by Burns (Cook), **III:** 322

Annual Register (periodical), **III:** 194, 205

Annus Domini (Rossetti), **V:** 260

Annus Mirabilis: The Year of Wonder (Dryden), **II:** 292, 304

Ann Veronica: A Modern Love Story (Wells), **VI:** 227, 238

"Another Grace for a Child" (Herrick), **II:** 114

"Ansell" (Forster), **VI:** 398

Anstey, Christopher, **III:** 155

"Answer, The" (Wycherley), **II:** 322

Answer to a Paper Called "A Memorial of the Poor Inhabitants" (Swift), **III:** 35

Answer to a Question That No Body Thinks of, An (Defoe), **III:** 13

"Answer to Davenant" (Hobbes), **II:** 256$_n$

"Ant, The" (Lovelace), **II:** 231

Ant and the Nightingale or Father Hubburd's Tales, The (Middleton), **II:** 3

"Anthem for Doomed Youth" (Owen), **VI:** 443, 447, 448, 452

"Anthem of Earth, An" (Thompson), **V:** 448

Anthology of War Poetry, An (ed. Nichols), **VI:** 419

Anthony Trollope: A Critical Study (Cockshut), **V:** 98, 103

Antic Hay (Huxley), **VII:** 198, 201–202

"Anti-Christ, or the Reunion of Christendom (Chesterton), **VI:** 340–341

Anticipations of the Reaction of Mechanical and Scientific Progress upon Human Life and Thought (Wells), **VI:** 227, 240

Anti-Coningsby (Disraeli), **IV:** 308

Antigua, Penny, Puce (Graves), **VII:** 259

Antiquarian Prejudice (Betjeman), **VII:** 358, 359

Antiquary, The (Scott), **IV:** xvii, 28, 32–33, 37, 39

anti-Semitism, **VI:** 288

Anti-Thelyphthora (Cowper), **III:** 220

Antonio and Mellida (Marston), **II:** 27–28, 40

Antonio's Revenge (Marston), **II:** 27–29, 36, 40

Antony and Cleopatra (Sedley), **II:** 263, 271

Antony and Cleopatra (Shakespeare), **I:** 318, 319–320; **II:** 70; **III:** 22

Antony and Octavius. Scenes for the Study (Landor), **IV:** 100

"Antwerp" (Ford), **VI:** 323, 416

"Any Saint" (Thompson), **V:** 444

Anything for a Quiet Life (Middleton and Webster), **II:** 21, 69, 83, 85

Apes of God, The (Lewis), **VII:** xv, 35, 71, 73, 74, 77, 79

Aphorisms on Man (Lavater), **III:** 298

Aphrodite in Aulis (Moore), **VI:** 88, 95, 99

Apocalypse (Lawrence), **VII:** 91

"Apollo and the Fates" (Browning), **IV:** 366

"Apollo in Picardy" (Pater), **V:** 355, 356

"Apollonius of Tyre" (Gower), **I:** 53

"Apologia pro Poemate Meo" (Owen), **VI:** 452

Apologie for Poetry (Sidney), see *Defence of Poesie, The*

Apologie for the Royal Party, An: . . . . By a Lover of Peace and of His Country (Evelyn), **II:** 287

Apology Against a Pamphlet Call'd A Modest Confutation of the Animadversions upon the Remonstrant Against Smectymnuus, An (Milton), **II:** 175

"Apology for Plainspeaking, An" (Stephen), **V:** 284

Apology for the Bible (Watson), **III:** 301

Apology for the Life of Mrs. Shamela Andrews, An (Fielding), see *Shamela*

Apology for the Voyage to Guiana (Ralegh), **I:** 153

Apophthegms (Bacon), **I:** 264, 273

"Apostasy, The" (Traherne), **II:** 191

Apostle, The (Moore), **VI:** 88, 96, 99

Apostles, the (Cambridge Society), **IV:** 331; **V:** 278 **VI:** 399

"Apparition of His Mistresse Calling Him to Elizium, The" (Herrick), **II:** 113

Appeal from the New to the Old Whigs, An (Burke), **III:** 205

Appeal to England, An (Swinburne), **V:** 332

Appeal to Honour and Justice, An (Defoe), **III:** 4, 13

Appeal to the Clergy of the Church of Scotland, An (Stevenson), **V:** 395

"Appius and Virginia" (Gower), **I:** 55

Appius and Virginia (R.B.), **I:** 216

Appius and Virginia (Webster), **II:** 68, 83, 85

Applebee, John, **III:** 7

Apple Cart, The: A Political Extravaganza (Shaw), **VI:** 118, 120, 125–126, 127, 129

"Apple Tree, The" (Galsworthy), **VI:** 276

"Apple Tree, The" (Mansfield), **VII:** 173

"Appraisal, An" (Compton-Burnett), **VII:** 59

Appreciations (Pater), **V:** 338, 339, 341, 351–352, 353–356

April Love (Hughes), **V:** 294

"Apron of Flowers, The" (Herrick), **II:** 110

Apropos of Dolores (Wells), **VI:** 240

"A Propos of *Lady Chatterley's Lover*" (Lawrence), **IV:** 106; **VII:** 91

"Arabella" (Thackeray), **V:** 24

Arabian Nights, The, **III:** 327, 335, 336

"Arab Love Song" (Thompson), **V:** 442, 445, 449

"Aramantha" (Lovelace), **II:** 230, 231

Aran Islands, The (Synge), **VI:** 308–309

Aratra Pentelici (Ruskin), **V:** 184

Arbuthnot, John, **III:** 19, 34, 60

"Arcades" (Milton), **II:** 159

Arcadia (Sidney), **I:** 161, 163–169, 173, 317; **II:** 48, 53–54; **III:** 95

Arcadian Rhetorike (Fraunce), **I:** 164

Arcadian style, **I:** 164–166

Archer, William, **II:** 79, 358, 363, 364 **V:** 103, 104, 113

Architectural Review (periodical), **VII:** 356, 358

Architecture in Britain: 1530–1830 (Reynolds), **II:** 336

Architecture, Industry and Wealth (Morris), **V:** 306

"Arctic Summer" (Forster), **VI:** 406

Arden of Feversham (Kyd), **I:** 212, 213, 218–219

"Ardour and Memory" (Rossetti), **V:** 243

Ardours and Endurances (Nichols), **VI:** 423

Areopagitica (Milton), **II:** 163, 164, 169, 174, 175; **IV:** 279

Aretina (Mackenzie), **III:** 95

"Argonauts of the Air, The" (Wells), **VI:** 244

"Argument of His Book, The" (Herrick), **II:** 110

Argument Shewing that a Standing Army . . . Is Not Inconsistent with a Free Government, An (Defoe), **III:** 12

Argument . . . that the Abolishing of Christianity . . . May . . . be Attended with some Inconveniences, An (Swift), **III:** 26, 35

Ariadne Florentina (Ruskin), **V:** 184

Ariel Poems (Eliot), **VII:** 152

Aristophanes, **V:** 227

Aristophanes' Apology (Browning), **IV:** 358, 367, 370, 374

"Armada, The" (Macaulay), **IV:** 283, 291

Arms and the Covenant (Churchill), **VI:** 356

Arms and the Man (Shaw), **VI:** 104, 110, 120

Armstrong, Isobel Mair, **V:** xi, xxvii, 339, 375

Armstrong, William, **VII:** xviii, xxxvii

Arnold, Matthew, **IV:** 359; **V:** viii–xi, 14, 156–158, 160, **203–218**, 283, 285, 289, 342, 352–353; works, **III:** 23, 174, 277; **V:** 206–215; literary

Arnold, Matthew (Cont.)
    criticism, I: 42–43; III: 68, 277; IV: 220, 234, 323, 371; V: 160, 165–169, 352, 408
Arnold, Thomas, V: 155–156, 157, 165, 207, 208, 277, 284, 349
Arnold Bennett (Lafourcade), VI: 268
Arnold Bennett (Pound), VI: 247, 268
Arnold Bennett (Swinnerton), VI: 268
Arnold Bennett: A Biography (Drabble), VI: 247, 253, 268
Arnold Bennett: A Last Word (Swinnerton), VI: 268
Arnold Bennett and H. G. Wells: A Record of a Personal and Literary Friendship (ed. Wilson), VI: 246, 267
Arnold Bennett in Love (ed. and trans. Beardmore and Beardmore), VI: 251, 268
Arnold Bennett: The "Evening Standard" Years (ed. Mylett), VI: 265$_n$, 266
Arraignment of London, The (Daborne and Tourneur), II: 37
Arraignment of Paris (Peele), I: 197–200
"Arrest of Oscar Wilde at the Cadogan Hotel, The" (Betjeman), VII: 356, 365–366
Arrow of Gold, A (Conrad), VI: 134, 144, 147
art, function of, VI: 189–192; VII: 75–76
"Art and Morality" (Stephen), V: 286
Art and Reality (Cary), VII: 186
"Arthur Snatchfold" (Forster), VI: 411
Articles of Charge Against Hastings (Burke), III: 205
"Articles of Inquiry Concerning Heavy and Light" (Bacon), I: 261
"Artistic Temperament of Stephen Carey, The" (Maugham), VI: 373
"Artists, The" (Thackeray), V: 22, 37
Art of Angling, The (Barker), II: 131
Art of Being Ruled, The (Lewis), VII: 72, 75, 76
Art of English Poetry, The (Puttenham), I: 94, 146, 214
Art of Fiction, The (James), VI: 46, 67
Art of Fiction, The (Kipling), VI: 204
"Art of Fiction, The" (Woolf), VII: 21, 22
Art of Love, The (Ovid), I: 237–238

Art of Sinking in Poetry, The (Pope), IV: 187
Art of the Novel, The (James), VI: 67
arts and crafts movement, VI: 166, 167–168, 169–170
Arts and Crafts Movement, The (Naylor), VI: 168
Ascent of F6, The (Auden and Isherwood), VII: 312, 380, 383, 385
Ashenden (Maugham), VI: 371
Ashford, Daisy, V: 111, 262
Ashley, Lord, see Shaftesbury, seventh earl of
Ash-Wednesday (Eliot), VII: 144, 150, 151–152
Asimov, Isaac, III: 341
"As kingfishers catch fire" (Hopkins), V: 371
"Ask Me No More" (Tennyson), IV: 334
"Asleep" (Owen), VI: 455
Asolando (Browning), IV: 359, 365, 374
Aspects of E. M. Forster (Stallybrass), VI: 413
Aspects of the Novel (Forster), V: 229; VI: 397, 411, 412; VII: 21, 22
Aspern Papers, The (James), VI: 38, **46–48**
Asquith, Herbert, VI: 417
Asquith, Raymond, VI: 417, 428
"Ass, The" (Vaughan), II: 186
"Assault, The" (Nichols), VI: 419
Assignation, The, or Love in a Nunnery (Dryden), II: 305
"Astarte Syriaca" (Rossetti), V: 238, 240
"As the Team's Head-Brass" (Thomas), VI: 425
Astraea Redux. A Poem on the Happy Restoration . . . of . . . Charles the Second (Dryden), II: 292, 304
"Astronomy" (Housman), VI: 161
Astrophel (collection), I: 160
Astrophel and Other Poems (Swinburne), V: 333
Astrophel and Stella (Sidney), I: 161, 169–173
Astrophel. A Pastoral Elegy (Spenser), I: 126; IV: 205
As You Like It (Shakespeare), I: 278, 312; III: 117
"At a Calvary near the Ancre" (Owen), VI: 450, 451
Atalanta in Calydon (Swinburne), IV: 90; V: xxiii, 309, 313, 318, **321–324**, 331, 332; VII: 134
"At Castle Boterel" (Hardy), VI: 18
"Atheism" (Bacon), III: 39

Atheist's Tragedy, The (Tourneur), **II:** 29, 33, 36, 37, **38–40,** 41, 70

Athenaeum (periodical), **IV:** 252, 254, 262, 310, 315; **V:** 32, 134; **VI:** 167, 234, 375; **VII:** 32

Athenian Mercury (newspaper), **III:** 41

"At Isella" (James), **VI:** 69

At Lady Molly's (Powell), **VII:** 348

Atlantic Monthly (periodical), **VI:** 29, 33

Atlas (periodical), **V:** 144

"At Lehmann's" (Mansfield), **VII:** 172, 173

atomic age, **VII:** 137

"At Senlis Once" (Blunden), **VI:** 428

"Attack" (Sassoon), **VI:** 431

Attempt to Describe Hafod, An (Cumberland), **IV:** 47

Atterbury, Francis, **III:** 23

"At the Bay" (Mansfield), **VII:** 175, 177, 179, 180

"At the British War Cemetery, Bayeux" (Causley), **VII:** 448

"At the End of the Passage" (Kipling), **VI:** 173–175, 183, 184, 193

"At the Grave of Henry James" (Auden), **VII:** 380

"At the Great Wall of China" (Blunden), **VI:** 429

"At the 'Mermaid' " (Browning), **IV:** 359

Attlee, Clement, **VI:** 358

"Aubade" (Sitwell), **VII:** 131

Aubrey, John, **I:** 260; **II:** 45, 46, 205–206, 226, 233

Auden, W. H., **I:** 92; **IV:** 106, 208; **V:** 46; **VI:** 160, 208; **VII:** xii, xviii, xix–xx, 153, **379–399,** 403, 407

"Audley Court" (Tennyson), **IV:** 326$_n$

"Auguries of Innocence" (Blake), **III:** 300

Augustan Ages, The (Elton), **III:** 51$_n$

Augustans and Romantics (Butt and Dyson), **III:** 51$_n$

Augusta Triumphans: or, The Way to Make London the Most Flourishing City . . . (Defoe), **III:** 14

"August 1914" (Rosenberg), **VI:** 434

Augustus Does His Bit (Shaw), **VI:** 120

"Auld Lang Syne" (Burns), **III:** 321

Ault, Norman, **III:** 69, 78

Aunt Judy's (periodical), **V:** 271

Aureng-Zebe (Dryden), **II:** 295, 305

Aurora Leigh (Browning), **IV:** xxi, 311, 312, 314–315, 316–318, 321

Ausonius, **II:** 108, 185

Austen, Alfred, **V:** 439

Austen, Jane, **III:** 90, 283, 335–336, 345; **IV:** xi, xiv, xvii, 30, **101–124; V:** 51

Austen-Leigh, J. E., **III:** 90

Australia and New Zealand (Trollope), **V:** 102

Authorized Version of the Bible, see King James Version

"Author of 'Beltraffio,' The" (James), **VI:** 69

Author's Apology, The (Bunyan), **II:** 246$_n$

Author's Farce, The (Fielding), **III:** 105

"Author Upon Himself, The" (Swift), **III:** 19, 32

Autobiographies (Yeats), **V:** 301, 304, 306, 404; **VI:** 317

"Autobiographies, The" (James), **VI:** 65

"Autobiography" (MacNeice), **VII:** 401

Autobiography (Russell), **VII:** 90

Autobiography, An (Trevelyan), **VI:** 383, 386, 388

Autobiography, An (Trollope), **V:** 89, 90–93, 96, 101, 102

Autobiography and Other Essays, An (Trevelyan), **VI:** 383

Autobiography of Edward Gibbon, The (ed. Smeaton), **III:** 229$_n$

"Autumnall, The" (Donne), **II:** 118

Autumn Journal (MacNeice), **VII:** 412

"Autumn 1942" (Fuller), **VII:** 430–431

Autumn Sequel (MacNeice), **VII:** 407, 412, 415

avant-garde literature, **VII:** xii, xvi, 17

Ave (Moore), **VI:** 99

"Ave Atque Vale" (Swinburne), **V:** 314, 327

"Ave Imperatrix" (Kipling), **VI:** 201

Aveling, Edward, **VI:** 102

"Avising the bright beams of those fair eyes" (Wyatt), **I:** 110

Avowals (Moore), **VI:** 97–98, 99

"Awake, my heart, to be loved" (Bridges), **VI:** 74, 77

Awakened Conscience, The (Dixon Hunt), **VI:** 167

Awakening Conscience, The (Hunt), **V:** 45, 51, 240

Awkward Age, The (James), **VI:** 45, 56, 67

Ayala's Angel (Trollope), **V:** 100, 102

Aylott & Jones (publishers), **V:** 131

B

"Baa, Baa Black Sheep" (Kipling), **VI:** 166

Babees Book, The (Early English Poems and Treatises on Manners and Meals in Olden Time) (ed. Furnival), **I:** 22, 26

Babes in the Darkling Wood (Wells), **VI:** 228

Babylon Hotel (Bennett), see *Grand Babylon Hotel, The*

"Baby's cradle with no baby in it, A" (Rossetti), **V:** 255

Back to Methuselah (Shaw), **VI: 121–122,** 124

Bacon, Francis, **I: 257–274; II:** 149, 196; **III:** 39; **IV:** 138, 278, 279; annotated list of works, **I:** 271–273

"Bad Five Minutes in the Alps, A" (Stephen), **V:** 283

Bagehot, Walter, **IV:** 289, 291; **V:** xxiii, 156, 165, 170, 205, 212

"Bagpipe Music" (MacNeice), **VII:** 413

Bailey, Benjamin, **IV:** 224, 229, 230, 232–233

Baillie, Alexander, **V:** 368, 374, 375, 379

Baines, Jocelyn, **VI:** 133–134

Baird, Julian, **V:** 316, 317, 318, 335

"Baite, The" (Donne), **IV:** 327

Balaustion's Adventure (Browning), **IV:** 358, 374

"Balder Dead" (Arnold), **V:** 209, 216

Baldwin, Stanley, **VI:** 353, 355

Bale, John, **I:** 1, 3

Balfour, Arthur, **VI:** 226, 241, 353

Balfour, Graham, **V:** 393, 397

Balin or the Knight with Two Swords (Malory), **I:** 79

ballad, **VI:** 338

Ballad at Dead Men's Bay, The (Swinburne), **V:** 332

ballade, **I:** 106–107

Ballade du temps jadis (Villon), **VI:** 254

Ballade of Truthful Charles, The, and Other Poems (Swinburne), **V:** 333

Ballade on an Ale-Seller (Lydgate), **I:** 92

"Ballad of Bouillabaisse" (Thackeray), **V:** 19

"Ballad of Death, A" (Swinburne), **V:** 316, 317–318

Ballad of Jan Van Hunks, The (Rossetti), **V:** 238, 244, 245

"Ballad of Life, A" (Swinburne), **V:** 317, 318

Ballad of Reading Gaol, The (Wilde), **V:** xxvi, 417–418, 419

"Ballad of the Investiture 1969, A" (Betjeman, **VII:** 372

"Ballad of the Three Spectres" (Gurney), **VI:** 426

"Ballad of the White Horse, The" (Chesterton), **VI:** 338–339, 341

"Ballad of Villon and Fat Madge, The" (tr. Swinburne), **V:** 327

Ballads (Stevenson), **V:** 396

Ballads (Thackeray), **V:** 38

Ballads and Lyrical Pieces (Scott), **IV:** 38

Ballads and Other Poems (Tennyson), **IV:** 338

Ballads and Poems of Tragic Life (Meredith), **V:** 224, 234

Ballads and Sonnets (Rossetti), **V:** xxiv, 238, 244, 245

Ballads of the English Border (Swinburne), **V:** 333

"Ballad upon a Wedding, A" (Suckling), **II:** 228–229

Ball and the Cross, The (Chesterton), **VI:** 338

Ballard, J. G., **III:** 341

ballette, **I:** 106–107

Balzac, Honoré de, **III:** 334, 339, 345; **IV:** 153$_n$; **V:** xvi, xviii, xix–xxi, 17, 429

Bancroft, John, **II:** 305

Banks, John, **II:** 305

Barbara, pseud. of Arnold Bennett

"Barbara of the House of Grebe" (Hardy), **VI:** 22

Barbauld, Anna Laetitia, **III:** 88, 93

"Barber Cox and the Cutting of His Comb" (Thackeray), **V:** 21, 37

Barcellona: or, The Spanish Expedition under . . . Charles, Earl of Peterborough (Farquhar), **II:** 353, 355, 364

Barchester Towers (Trollope), **V:** xxii, 93, 101

"Bard, The" (Gray), **III:** 140–141

"Bards of Passion . . ." (Keats), **IV:** 221

Barker, Sir Ernest, **III:** 196

Barker, Granville, see Granville Barker, Harley

Barker, Thomas, **II:** 131

Barker's Delight (Barker), see *Art of Angling, The*

Barksted, William, **II:** 31

Barnaby Rudge (Dickens), **V:** 42, 54, 55, 66, 71

Barnes, William, **VI:** 2

"Barnfloor and Winepress" (Hopkins), **V:** 381

Barrack-Room Ballads (Kipling), **VI:** 203, 204

Barren Fig Tree, The: or, The Doom . . . of the Fruitless Professor (Bunyan), **II:** 253

Barrett, Eaton Stannard, **III:** 335

Barrie, J. M., **V:** 388, 392; **VI:** 265, 273, 280

Barry Lyndon (Thackeray), **V:** 24, 28, 32, 38

Barsetshire novels (Trollope), **V:** 92–96, 98, 101

Bartas, Guillaume du, **II:** 138

Bartholomew Fair (Jonson), **I:** 228, 243, 324, 340, 342–343; **II:** 3

Bartlett, Phyllis, **V:** x, xxvii

Barton, Bernard, **IV:** 341, 342, 343, 350

"Base Details" (Sassoon), **VI:** 430

Basil Seal Rides Again (Waugh), **VII:** 290

Bateson, F. W., **IV:** 217, 323$_n$, 339

Bath (Sitwell), **VII:** 127

Bath Chronicle (periodical), **III:** 262

Bathurst, Lord, **III:** 33

"Bathurst, Mrs." (Kipling), **VI:** 193–194

Battenhouse, Roy, **I:** 282

"Batter my heart, three person'd God" (Donne), **I:** 367–368; **II:** 122

Battiscombe, Georgina, **V:** xii, xxvii, 260

Battle of Alcazar, The (Peele), **I:** 205, 206

"Battle of Blenheim, The" (Southey), **IV:** 58, 67–68

Battle of Life, The (Dickens), **V:** 71

Battle of Marathon, The (Browning), **IV:** 310, 321

Battle of the Books, The (Swift), **III:** 17, 23, 35

Baucis and Philemon (Swift), **III:** 35

Baudelaire, Charles, **III:** 337, 338; **IV:** 153; **V:** xiii, xviii, xxii–xxiii, 310–318, 327, 329, 404, 405, 409, 411

Bay (Lawrence), **VII:** 118

Bayly, Lewis, **II:** 241

Beach, J. W., **V:** 221$_n$, 234

Beachcroft, T. O., **VII:** xxii

"Beach of Falesá, The" (Stevenson), **V:** 396

Beaconsfield, Lord, see Disraeli, Benjamin

Beardsley, Aubrey, **V:** 318$_n$, 412, 413

"Beast in the Jungle, The" (James), **VI:** 55, 64, 69

Beasts' Confession to the Priest, The (Swift), **III:** 36

Beattie, James, **IV:** 198

Beatty, David, **VI:** 351

Beau Austin (Stevenson), **V:** 396

Beauchamp's Career (Meredith), **V:** xxiv, 225, 228–230, 231, 234

Beaumont, Francis, **II:** **42–67**, 79, 82, 87

Beaumont, Sir George, **IV:** 3, 12, 21, 22

Beaumont, Joseph, **II:** 180

Beauties of English Poesy, The (ed. Goldsmith), **III:** 191

"Beautiful Lofty Things" (Yeats), **VI:** 216

"Beautiful Young Nymph Going to Bed, A" (Swift), **III:** 32, 36; **VI:** 256

Beauty in a Trance, **II:** 100

Beaux' Strategem, The (Farquhar), **II:** 334, 353, 359–360, 362, 364

"Because of the Dollars" (Conrad), **VI:** 148

Becket (Tennyson), **IV:** 328, 338

Beckford, William, **III:** 327–329, 345; **IV:** xv, 230

Beddoes, Thomas, **V:** 330

Bedford-Row Conspiracy, The (Thackeray), **V:** 21, 37

Bedtime Story (O'Casey), **VII:** 12

Bee (periodical), **III:** 40, 179

Beerbohm, Max, **V:** 252, 390; **VI:** 365, 366

"Before Action" (Hodgson), **VI:** 422

"Before Her Portrait in Youth" (Thompson), **V:** 442

"Before the Mirror" (Swinburne), **V:** 320

"Before the Party" (Maugham), **VI:** 370

Beggar's Bush (Beaumont, Fletcher, Massinger), **II:** 66

Beggar's Opera, The (Gay), **III:** 54, 55, **61–64**, 65–67

"Beggar's Soliloquy, The" (Meredith), **V:** 220

Behind the Green Curtains (O'Casey), **VII:** 11

"Behold, Love, thy power how she despiseth" (Wyatt), **I:** 109

"Being Treated, to Ellinda" (Lovelace), **II:** 231–232

"Beldonald Holbein, The" (James), **VI:** 69

Belin, Mrs., **II:** 305

Bell, Acton, pseud. of Anne Brontë

Bell, Clive, **V:** 345

Bell, Currer, pseud. of Charlotte Brontë

Bell, Ellis, pseud. of Emily Brontë

Bell, Quentin, **VII:** 35

Bell, Robert, **I:** 98

Bell, Vanessa, **VI:** 118

Bellamira or the Mistress (Sedley), **II:** 263

"Belle Heaulmière" (tr. Swinburne), **V:** 327

"Belle of the Ball-Room" (Praed), **V:** 14

Belloc, Hilaire, **VI:** 246, 320, 335, 337, 340, 447; **VII:** xiii

"Bell of Aragon, The" (Collins), **III:** 163

Bells and Pomegranates (Browning), **IV:** 356, 373–374

Belton Estate, The (Trollope), **V:** 100, 101

"Bench of Desolation, The" (James), **VI:** 69

Bender, T. K., **V:** 364–365, 382

Bending of the Bough, The (Moore), **VI:** 87, 95–96, 98

Benlowes, Edward, **II:** 123

Bennett, Arnold, **VI:** xi, xii, xiii, 226, 233$_n$, **247–268**, 275; **VII:** xiv, xxi

Bennett, Joan, **II:** 181, 187, 201, 202; **V:** 199, 201

Benson, A. C., **V:** 133, 151

Bentham, Jeremy, **IV:** xii, xv, 50, 130–133, 278, 295; **V:** viii

Bentley, Clerihew, **IV:** 101

Bentley, E. C., **VI:** 335

Bentley, G. E., Jr., **III:** 289$_n$, 307

Bentley, Richard, **III:** 23

Bentley's Miscellany (periodical), **V:** 42

"Benvolio" (James), **VI:** 69

Beowulf, **I:** 69

Beppo (Byron), **IV:** xvii, 172, 177, **182–184**, 186, 188, 192

Berdoe, Edward, **IV:** 371

Bérénice (Racine), **II:** 98

Bergerac, Cyrano de, see Cyrano de Bergerac

Bergonzi, Bernard, **VII:** xxi, xxxvii

Berkeley, George, **III:** 50

Berlin stories (Isherwood), **VII:** 309, 311–312

"Bermudas" (Marvell), **II:** 208, 210, 211, 217

Bernard, Charles de, **V:** 21

Bernard, Richard, **II:** 246

Bernard Shaw and Mrs. Patrick Campbell: Their Correspondence (ed. Dent), **VI:** 130

Bernard Shaw's Letters to Granville Barker (ed. Purdom), **VI:** 115$_n$, 129

Bernard Shaw's Rhyming Picture Guide . . . (Shaw), **VI:** 130

Bertrams, The (Trollope), **V:** 101

Besant, Annie, **VI:** 103, 249

"Be still, my soul" (Housman), **VI:** 162

Best of Defoe's Review, The (ed. Payne), **III:** 41

"Bestre" (Lewis), **VII:** 77

Bethell, Augusta, **V:** 84

Betjeman, John, **VII:** xxi–xxii, **355–377**

Betrayal of the Left, The (Orwell), **VII:** 284

Betrothed, The (Scott), **IV:** 39

"Better Resurrection, A" (Rossetti), **V:** 254

Between the Acts (Woolf), **VII:** 18, 19, 22, 24, 26

"Beware of Doubleness" (Lydgate), **I:** 64

Beyond Good and Evil (Nietzsche), **IV:** 121; **V:** xxv

Beyond the Mexique Bay (Huxley), **VII:** 201

"Beyond the Pale" (Kipling), **VI:** **178–180**

Biala, Janice, **VI:** 324

"Bianca Among the Nightingales" (Browning), **IV:** 315

Biathanatos (Donne), **I:** 370

Bible, see English Bible

Bibliography of Henry James, A (Edel and Laurence), **VI:** 66

Bickerstaff, Isaac, pseud. of Sir Richard Steele and Joseph Addison

Bildungsroman, **VII:** 95

Bill for the Better Promotion of Oppression on the Sabbath Day, A (Peacock), **IV:** 170

"Binsey Poplars" (Hopkins), **V:** 370, 371

Binyon, Laurence, **VI:** 416, 439

Biographia Literaria (Coleridge), **IV:** xvii, 4, 6, 18, 25, 41, 44–45, 50, 51, 52–53, 56

"Biographical Notice of Ellis and Acton Bell" (Brontë), **V:** 131, 134, 152, 153

"Bird and Beast" (Rossetti), **V:** 258

Birds, The (film), **III:** 343

Birds, Beasts and Flowers (Lawrence), **VII:** 90, 118, 119

"Birds of Paradise" (Rossetti), **V:** 255

Birkenhead, Lord (F. E. Smith), **VI:** 340–341

Birmingham Colony, **VI:** 167

Birrell, A., **II:** 216

"Birth-Bond, The" (Rossetti), **V:** 242

"Birthday, A" (Mansfield), **VII:** 172, 173

"Birthday, A" (Rossetti), **V:** 252

Birth of Manly Virtue, The (Swift), **III:** 35

"Birth of the Squire, The" (Gay), **III:** 58

"Birthplace, The" (James), **VI:** 69

"Bishop Blougram's Apology" (Browning), **IV:** 357, 361, 363

"Bishop Burnet and Humphrey Hardcastle" (Landor), **IV:** 91

"Bishop Orders His Tomb at St. Praxed's Church, The" (Browning), **IV:** 356, 370, 372

Bishop's Bonfire, The (O'Casey), **VII:** xvii, 10

"Bishop's Fool, The" (Lewis), **VII:** 80

Bit o' Love, A (Galsworthy), **VI:** 280

"Black and Tans," **VII:** 2

Black Arrow, The (Stevenson), **V:** 396

Black Book, The (Middleton), **II:** 3

Black Dwarf, The (Scott), **IV:** 39

Blackfriars theater, **I:** 197, 299; **II:** 47–48

"Black Goddess, The" (Graves), **VII:** 261, 270

Black Knight, The (Lydgate), see *Complaint of the Black Knight, The*

"Black Mate, The" (Conrad), **VI:** 135, 148

Black Mischief (Waugh), **VII:** 290, 294–295

Black-out in Gretley (Priestley), **VII:** 212, 217

Blackstone, Bernard, **VII:** xiv, xxxvii

Blackstone, Sir William, **III:** 199

"Black Takes White" (Cameron), **VII:** 426

Blackwood's (periodical), **IV:** xvii, 129, 145, 269–270, 274; **V:** 108–109, 111, 137, 142, 190, 191

Blair, Robert, **III:** 336

Blake, Robert, **IV:** 296, 304, 306–308

Blake, William, **II:** 102, 115, 258; **III:** 174, **288–309,** 336; **IV:** 178; **V:** xiv–xvi, xviii, 244, 316–317, 325, 329–330, 403; **V:** viii, 163; **VI:** viii. **VII:** 23–24

Blake's Chaucer: The Canterbury Pilgrims (Blake), **III:** 307

"Blakesmoor in H—shire" (Lamb), **IV:** 76–77

Blank Cheque, The (Carroll), **V:** 274

blank verse, **VII:** xiii

Blank Verse (Lloyd and Lamb), **IV:** 78, 85

Blast (periodical), **VII:** xiii, 72

Blasting and Bombardiering (Lewis), **VII:** 72, 76, 77

Blatty, William Peter, **III:** 343, 345

Bleak House (Dickens), **IV:** 88; **V:** 4, 42, 47, 53, 54, 55, 59, 62–66, 68, 69, 70, 71

Blenheim (Trevelyan), **VI:** 392–393

"Blessed Among Women" (Swinburne), **V:** 325

"Blessed Are Ye That Sow Beside All Waters": A Lay Sermon (Coleridge), **IV:** 56

"Blessed Damozel, The" (Rossetti), **V:** 236, 239, 315

"Blighters" (Sassoon), **VI:** 430

Blind Beggar of Alexandria, The (Chapman), **I:** 234, 243

Blind Fireworks (MacNeice), **VII:** 411

"Bliss" (Mansfield), **VII:** 174

Bloch, Robert, **III:** 342

Blood, Sweat and Tears (Churchill), **VI:** 349, 361

"Bloody Son, The" (Swinburne), **V:** 321

Bloom, Harold, **III:** 289_n, 307; **V:** 309, 316, 329, 402

Bloomfield, Paul, **IV:** xii, xxiv, 306

Bloomsbury: A House of Lions (Edel), **VII:** 39

Bloomsbury group, **VI:** 372; **VII:** xv, xviii, 17, 33, 34–35, 36, 90, 238

Bloomsbury Group, The (Johnstone), **VI:** 413

Blot in the Scutcheon, A (Browning), **IV:** 374

"Blow, The" (Hardy), **VI:** 17

"Blucher and Sandt" (Landor), **IV:** 92

"Bluebeard's Ghost" (Thackeray), **V:** 24, 38

"Blue bell is the sweetest flower, The" (Brontë), **V:** 134

"bluebook" plays, **VI:** 108

"Blue Closet, The" (Morris), **IV:** 313

Blunden, Edmund, **IV:** xi, xxiv, 86, 210, 254, 267, 316; **VI:** 416, **427–429,** 439, 454; **VII:** xvi

Boas, F. S., **I:** 218, 275

"Bob Robinson's First Love" (Thackeray), **V:** 24, 38

Boccaccio, Giovanni, **II:** 292, 304

"Body's Beauty" (Rossetti), **V:** 237

Body Snatcher, The (Stevenson), **V:** 396

Boehme, Jacob, **IV:** 45

Boer War, **VI:** 335, 351–352

Boethius, **I:** 31, 32; **II:** 185

"Bohemians, The" (Gurney), **VI:** 427

Boiardo, Matteo, **IV:** 231

Boileau, Nicolas, **IV:** 92, 93

Boke of Eneydos, The (Skelton), **I:** 82

Boklund, Gunnar, **II:** 73

Bonduca (Fletcher), **II:** 45, 58, 60, 65

"Bonfire Under a Black Sun" (O'Casey), **VII:** 13

Bonnefon, Jean de, **II:** 108

Boodle, Adelaide, **V:** 391, 393, 397

"Book, The" (Vaughan), **II:** 187

Booke of Balettes, A (Wyatt), **I:** 97

Book for Boys and Girls, A: or, Country Rhimes for Children (Bunyan), **II:** 253

Book of Ahania, The (Blake), **III:** 307

Book of Los, The (Blake), **III:** 307

Book of Nonsense, A (Lear), **V:** xx, 76, 82–83, 87

Book of Sir Lancelot and Queen Guinevere, The (Malory), **I:** 70–71, 77

Book of Snobs, The (Thackeray), **V:** 24–25, 28, 38

Book of the Church, The (Southey), **IV:** 71

Book of the Duchess, The (Chaucer), **I:** 29, 31, 43, 54

Book of Thel, The (Blake), **III:** 302, 307

Book of Urizen, The (Blake), see *First Book of Urizen, The*

Books and Persons: Being Comments on a Past Epoch (Bennett), **VI:** 265, 267

Books Do Furnish a Room (Powell), **VII:** 352

"Books of the Ocean's Love to Cynthia, The" (Ralegh), **I:** 147, 148, 149

Boon (Wells), **VI:** 227, 239–240, 333

Border Antiquities (Scott), **IV:** 38

Border Ballads (Swinburne), **V:** 333

Borderers, The (Wordsworth), **III:** 338; **IV:** 3, 5–6, 25

"Borgia, thou once wert almost too august" (Landor), **IV:** 98

Born in Exile (Gissing), **V:** 425, 428, 429–430, 437

Borough, The (Crabbe), **III:** 273–274, 275, 280, 281, 283–285, 286

Bostonians, The (James), **VI:** **39–41,** 67

Boswell, James, **III:** 54, 107, 110–115, 117, 119–122, **234–251; IV:** xv, xvi, 27, 88$_n$, 280

"Boswell and Rousseau" (Leigh), **III:** 246$_n$

Boswell for the Defence 1769–1774 (ed. Pottle and Wimsatt), **III:** 249

Boswelliana . . . Memoir and Annotations by the Rev. Charles Rogers (Rogers), **III:** 249

Boswell in Extremis 1776–1778 (ed. Pottle and Weis), **III:** 249

Boswell in Holland 1763–1764 (ed. Pottle), **III:** 249

Boswell in Search of a Wife 1766–1769 (ed. Brady and Pottle), **III:** 249

Boswell: Lord of Auchinleck 1778–1782 (ed. Pottle and Reed), **III:** 249

Boswell on the Grand Tour: Germany and Switzerland 1764 (ed. Pottle), **III:** 249

Boswell on the Grand Tour: Italy . . . 1765–1766 (ed. Brady and Pottle), **III:** 249

Boswell's Book of Bad Verse (ed. Werner), **III:** 249

Boswell's London Journal 1762–1763 (ed. Pottle), **III:** 249

Boswell's Notebook, 1776–1777 (Boswell), **III:** 244, 249

Boswell: The Ominous Years 1774–1776 (ed. Pottle and Ryskamp), **III:** 249

"Botany Bay Eclogues" (Southey), **IV:** 60

Bothie of Tober-na-Vuolich, The (Clough), **V:** 155, 156, 158, 159, 161–164, 166, 167, 169, 170

Bothie of Toper-na-Fuosich, The (Clough), **V:** 170

Bothwell (Swinburne), **V:** 314, 330, 331, 332

Botticelli, Sandro, **V:** 345

"Bottle Imp, The" (Stevenson), **V:** 396

Boucicault, Dion, **V:** 415; **VII:** 2

Bouge of Court, The (Skelton), **I:** 83, 84–85

Boughner, D. C., **I:** 186

Boursault, Edme, **II:** 324, 332

Bowen, Stella, **VI:** 324

Bowers, Fredson, **II:** 44

Bowles, Caroline, **IV:** 62, 63

Bowra, C. M., **VI:** 153

Bowra, Maurice, **V:** 252–256, 260

Boyd, H. S., **IV:** 312

Boyer, Abel, **II:** 352

Boy in the Bush, The (Lawrence), **VII:** 114

Boyle, Robert, **III:** 23, 95

boy players, see boys' theaters

boys' theaters, **I:** 197

Bradbrook, M. C., **I:** xi, 292, 329; **II:** 42, 78; **VII:** xiii–xiv, xxxvii, 234

Bradbury, Ray, **III:** 341

Braddon, Mary Elizabeth, **V:** 327

Bradley, A. C., **IV:** 106, 123, 216, 235, 236

Bradley, F. H., **V:** xxi, 212, 217

Bradley, Henry, **VI:** 76

Brady, F., **III:** 249

Brander, Laurence, **IV:** xxiv; **VII:** xxii

Branwell Brontë (Gérin), **V:** 153

Branwell's Blackwood's (periodical), **V:** 109, 123

Branwell's Young Men's (periodical), see *Branwell's Blackwood's*

Brave New World (Huxley), **III:** 341; **VII:** xviii, 200, 204

Brave New World Revisited (Huxley), **VII:** 207

Brawne, Fanny, **IV:** 211, 216–220, 222, 226, 234

Bray, Charles, **V:** 188

Bray, William, **II:** 275, 276, 286

"Break of Day in the Trenches" (Rosenberg), **VI:** 433, 434

Brecht, Bertolt, **II:** 359; **IV:** 183; **VI:** 109, 123

"Bredon Hill" (Housman), **VI:** 158

Brennoralt (Suckling), see *Discontented Colonel, The*

Brett, Raymond Laurence, **IV:** x, xi, xxiv, 57

Bridal of Triermain, The (Scott), **IV:** 38

Bride of Abydos, The (Byron), **IV:** xvii, 172, 174–175, 192; see also Turkish tales

Bride of Frankenstein (film), **III:** 342

Bride of Lammermoor, The (Scott), **IV:** xviii, 30, 36, 39

Brideshead Revisited (Waugh), **VII:** xx–xxi, 290, 299–300

"Bride's Prelude, The" (Rossetti), **V:** 239, 240

"Bridge of Sighs, The" (Hood), **IV:** 252, 261, 264–265

Bridges, Robert, **II:** 160; **V:** xx, 205, 362–368, 370–372, 374, 376–381; **VI:** xv, **71–83,** 203

Brief History of Moscovia . . . , A (Milton), **II:** 176

Brief Lives (Aubrey), **I:** 260

Brief Notes upon a Late Sermon . . . (Milton), **II:** 176

Bright, A. H., **I:** 3

Bright Day (Priestley), **VII:** 209, 218–219

"Bright Star!" (Keats), **IV:** 221

Brissenden, R. F., **III:** 86$_n$

Bristow Merchant, The (Dekker and Ford), **II:** 89, 100

Britain and West Africa (Cary), **VII:** 186

Britannia (periodical), **V:** 144

Britannia Rediviva: A Poem on the Birth of the Prince (Dryden), **II:** 304

"Britannia Victrix" (Bridges), **VI:** 81

"British Church, The" (Herbert), **I:** 189

British History in the Nineteenth Century (Trevelyan), **VI:** 390

British Magazine (periodical), **III:** 149, 179, 188

British Raj, **VI:** 409; **VII:** 276

British Women Go to War (Priestley), **VII:** 212

Briton (Smollett), **III:** 149

Brittain, Vera, **II:** 246

Broadbent, J. B., **II:** 102, 116

"Broad Church, The" (Stephen), **V:** 283

Broken Cistern, The (Dobrée), **V:** 221, 234

Broken Heart, The (Ford), **II:** 89, 92, **93–98,** 99, 100

"Broken Wings, The" (James), **VI:** 69

Brome, Richard, **II:** 87

Brontë, Anne, **IV:** 30; **V:** xviii, xx, xxi, 105, 106, 108, 110, 112–119, 122, 126, **128–130,** 131, 132, **134–135, 140–141,** 145, 150, 153

Brontë, Branwell, **V:** xvii, 13, 105, 106, 108–112, 117–119, 121–124, 126, 130, 131, 135, 141, 145, 150, 153

Brontë, Charlotte, **III:** 338, 344, 345; **IV:** 30, 106, 120; **V:** xvii, xx–xxii, 3, 13–14, 20, 68, 105–107, **108–112,** 113–118, **119–126,** 127, 129, **130–140,** 144, **145–150,** 152, 286

Brontë, Emily, **III:** 333, 338, 344, 345; **IV:** ix, xvii, xx–xxi, 13, 14, 105, 106, 108, 110, **112–117,** 118, 122, **126–128,** 130, 131, **132–135, 141–145,** 147, 150, 152–153, 254

Brontë, Patrick, **V:** 105–108, 109, 122, 146, 151

Brontë Poems (ed. Benson), **V:** 133, 151

Brontës, The, Their Lives, Friendships and Correspondence (ed. Wise and Symington), **V:** 117, 118, 151

Brontë Story, The: A Reconsideration of Mrs. Gaskell's "Life of Charlotte Brontë" (Lane), **V:** 13$_n$, 16

Brontës' Web of Childhood, The (Ratchford), **V:** 151

"Bronze Head, The" (Yeats), **VI:** 217

Brooke, Arthur, **I:** 305

Brooke, Jocelyn, **VII:** xviii, xxxvii

Brooke, Rupert, **VI:** xvi, 416, **419–420,** 439; **VII:** 35

Brooke Kerith, The. A Syrian Story (Moore), **VI:** xii, 88, 89, **93–94,** 99

Brooks, C., **IV:** 323$_n$, 339

"Brooksmith" (James), **VI:** 48, 69

Brophy, Brigid, **IV:** 101

"Brother Fire" (MacNeice), **VII:** 414

Brotherly Love: A Sermon (Swift), **III:** 36

"Brothers" (Hopkins), **V:** 368–369

Brothers and Sisters (Compton-Burnett), **VII:** 61, 66, 67, 69

Brown, Charles, **IV:** 211, 221, 231–233

Brown, E. K., **V:** 211–212, 217

Brown, Ford Madox, **V:** 248

Brown, John, **II:** 245, 253, 254

Brown, Tom, **III:** 41

Browne, Moses, **II:** 142

Browne, Sir Thomas, **II:** 145–157, 185, 345$_n$; **III:** 40

"Brownie" (Gissing), **V:** 437

Browning, Elizabeth Barrett, **IV:** xvi, xix–xxii, **310–322,** 356, 357

Browning, Robert, **IV:** viii, xii, xiii, xix–xxiii, 240, 248, 252, 254, 311–312, 314, 318–319, 352, **354–375;** **V:** xxv, 209, 287, 315, 330; **VI:** 336

Browning: "Men and Women" and Other Poems: A Casebook (ed. Watson), **IV:** 375

Browning's Essay on Chatterton (ed. Smalley), **IV:** 374

Browning's Major Poetry (Jack), **IV:** 375

Browning Society of London, The, **IV:** 371

Brown Owl, The (Ford), **VI:** 320

"Bruno's Revenge" (Carroll), **V:** 270

"Brute, The" (Conrad), **VI:** 148

Brutus (Pope), **III:** 71–72

Bryce, James, **IV:** 289

Bryskett, Lodowick, **I:** 124

Bubble, The (Swift), **III:** 35

Bucer, Martin, **I:** 177

Buchanan, Robert, **V:** 238, 245

Buckhurst, Lord, see Dorset, earl of (Charles Sackville)

Buckingham, duke of (George Villiers), **II:** 206, 255, 294

Buckle, G. E., **IV:** 306–308

"Buckles of Superior Dosset, The" (Galsworthy), **VI:** 270

Bucolic Comedies (Sitwell), **VII:** 131, 132

Budgell, Eustace, **III:** 48

Buffon, Georges, **III:** 189

"Bugler's First Communion, The" (Hopkins), **V:** 368–369

Bullett, Gerald, **V:** 196, 199, 200

"Bull That Thought, The" (Kipling), **VI:** 189, 190

Bulwer-Lytton, Edward, **III:** 340, 345; **IV:** 256, 295, 311; **V:** 22, 47

Bundle of Letters, A (James), **VI:** 67, 69

Bunyan, John, **I:** 16; **II: 240–254; III:** 82; **V:** 27

Buoyant Billions: A Comedy of No Manners in Prose (Shaw), **VI:** 127, 129

Burbidge, Thomas, **V:** 159

Burckhardt, Jakob, **V:** 342

"Burden of Itys, The" (Wilde), **V:** 401

"Burden of Ninevah, The" (Rossetti), **V:** 240, 241

Bürger, Gottfried August, **IV:** 44, 48

Buried Alive (Bennett), **VI:** 250, 252, 257, 266

"Buried Life, The" (Arnold), **V:** 210

Burke, Edmund, **III:** 185, **193–206,** 274; **IV:** xii–xvi, 54, 127, 130, 133, 136–138, 271, 275; **VI:** 356

Burke and Bristol, 1774–1780 (Barker), **III:** 196

"Burleigh" (Macaulay), **IV:** 279

"Burma Casualty" (Lewis), **VII:** 447

Burmann, Peter, **III:** 96

Burmese Days (Orwell), **VII:** 276, 278

Burne-Jones, Edward, **IV:** 346; **V:** 236, 293–296, 302, 318$_n$, 355; **VI:** 166

Byron, George Gordon, Lord, **III:** 329; **IV:** x, xi, 46, 61, 91, 129, 132, 168, **171–194,** 198–199, 202, 206, 215, 281, 299; **V:** 111–112, 247, 324; and Coleridge, **IV:** 46, 48; and Hazlitt, **IV:** 129; and Shelley, **IV:** 159, 172, 176–177, 179, 181, 182, 198–199, 202, 206; and Southey, **IV:** 61, 184–187; literary style, **III:** 336, 337–338; **IV:** viii, ix, xi, 129, 281; **V:** 17, 116; **VII:** xix; see also Byronic hero

"Byron" (Macaulay), **IV:** 281

Byron and the Ruins of Paradise (Gleckner), **IV:** 173, 194

Byronic hero, **IV:** 173–180, 183, 186; **V:** 143

Byronic Hero, The: Types and Prototypes (Thorslev), **IV:** 173, 194

Byron in Italy (Quennell), **IV:** 194

Byron's Conspiracy (Chapman), **I:** 249–251

Byron's Tragedy (Chapman), see *Tragedy of Byron, The*

Byron: The Years of Fame (Quennell), **IV:** 194

"Byzantium" (Yeats), **VI:** 215

C

Cabinet of Dr. Caligari, The (film), **III:** 342

Cadenus and Vanessa (Swift), **III:** 18, 31, 35

Caesar and Cleopatra (Shaw), **VI:** 112

Caesar and Pompey (Chapman), **I:** 252–253

Caesar Borgia (Lee), **II:** 305

Caesar's Fall (Drayton, Middleton, Munday, Webster, et al.), **II:** 68, 85

Caesar's Wife (Maugham), **VI:** 369

Cagliostro, Alessandro di, **III:** 332

Cain (Byron), **IV:** xviii, 173, 177, **178–182,** 193

Cakes and Ale (Maugham), **VI:** 367, 371, 374, 377

Calderón de la Barca, Pedro, **II:** 312$_n$, 313$_n$; **IV:** 206, 342, 349

Caleb Williams (Godwin), see *Adventures of Caleb Williams, The*

Caledonia (Defoe), **III:** 13

Calendar of Modern Letters (periodical), **VII:** 233

"Caliban upon Setebos" (Browning), **IV:** 358, 364, 370, 372

"Calidore" (Keats), **IV:** 214

Caliph's Design, The (Lewis), **VII:** 72, 75$_n$

Called to Be Saints (Rossetti), **V:** 260

Calvin, John, **II:** 241

Cambises (Preston), **I:** 122, 213–214

Cambridge Bibliography of English Literature, **III:** 51, 52

Cambridge University, **VI:** 385–386

Cambyses (Preston), see *Cambises*

Cameron, Norman, **VII:** 421, 422, 426

Cammaerts, Emile, **V:** 262, 274

Camp, The (Sheridan), **III:** 253, 264

Campaign, The (Addison), **III:** 46

Campaspe (Lyly), **I:** 198, 199–200

Campbell, Ian, **IV:** xii, xxiv, 250

Campbell, Joseph, **VII:** 53

Campbell, Roy, **IV:** 320; **VII:** 422, 428

Campensis, Joannes, **I:** 119

"Canacee" (Gower), **I:** 53–54, 55

Canavans, The (Gregory), **VI:** 315

Candida (Shaw), **III:** 263; **VI:** 108, 110–111, 113

Candidate, The (Crabbe), **III:** 286

"Candidate, The" (Gray), **III:** 142

Candide (Voltaire), **IV:** 295

"Candle Indoors, The" (Hopkins), **V:** 370

Canning, George, **IV:** 132, 164

Canon of Thomas Middleton's Plays, The (Lake), **II:** 1, 21

Canterbury Tales, The (Chaucer), **I:** 1, 2, **20–47**

Canticle of the Rose, The (Sitwell), **VII:** xvii, 130, 137

Cantos (Pound), **V:** 317$_n$

Cantos of Mutability (Spenser), **I:** 140

Can You Forgive Her? (Trollope), **V:** 96, 101

"Cap and Bells, The" (Keats), **IV:** 217

Cap, The, and, The Falcon (Tennyson), **IV:** 338

Capell, Edward, **I:** 326

Captain, The (Beaumont and Fletcher), **II:** 65

Captain Brassbound's Conversion (Shaw), **VI:** 110

"Captain Henry Hastings" (Brontë), **V:** 122, 123–124, 135, 138, 151

"Captain Parry" (Hood), **IV:** 267

"Captain Rook and Mr. Pigeon" (Thackeray), **V:** 21, 37

Captains Courageous (Kipling), **VI:** 204

"Captain's Doll, The" (Lawrence), **VII:** 90

Captain Singleton (Defoe), **III:** 8, 13

Captives, The (Gay), **III:** 60–61, 67

Car, Thomas, **II:** 181

Carceri d'invenzione (Piranesi), **III:** 325

Card, The (Bennett), **VI:** 250, 258–259, 266

Cardenio (Fletcher and Shakespeare), **II:** 43, 66, 87

"Careless Lover, The" (Suckling), **II:** 227

Carew, Thomas, **I:** 354; **II:** 222–225, 237

Carey, John, **V:** ix, xxvii, 39, 62, 73

Carlingford, Lord, see Fortescue, Chichester

Carlyle, A. J., **III:** 272$_n$

Carlyle, Jane, **IV:** 239, 240

Carlyle, R. M., **III:** 272$_n$

Carlyle, Thomas, **IV:** xii, 38, 41–42, 70, 231, **238–250,** 266$_n$, 273, 289, 295, 301–302, 311, 324, 341–342; **V:** vii, ix, xii, 3, 5, 165, 182, 213$_n$, 285, 319

Carmen Deo Nostro, Te Decet Hymnus, Sacred Poems, Collected (Crashaw), **II:** 180, 181, 184, 201

Carmen Triumphale, for the Commencement of the Year 1814 (Southey), **IV:** 71

"Carmilla" (Le Fanu), **III:** 340, 345

Carmina V (Herrick), **II:** 108

Carnall, Geoffrey Douglas, **IV:** xxiv, 72, 156

Caroline (Maugham), **VI:** 369

"Caroline Vernon" (Brontë), **V:** 112, 122, 123, 124–125, 138, 151

Carpenter, Edward, **VI:** 407, 408

"Carrickfergus" (MacNeice), **VI:** 401

Carrington, Charles, **VI:** 166

"Carrion Comfort" (Hopkins), **V:** 374

Carroll, Lewis, **V:** xi, xix, xxii, xxvi, 86, 87, **261–275**

Carter, Angela, **III:** 341, 345

Carter, Frederick, **VII:** 114

Cartwright, John, **IV:** 103

Cartwright, William, **II:** 134, 185, 222, 237, 238

Cary, Joyce, **VII:** xvii, **185–196**

Casa Guidi Windows (Browning), **IV:** 311, 314, 318, 321

Casanova's Chinese Restaurant (Powell), **VII:** 348–349

Case, A. E., **III:** 25, 36

Case for African Freedom, The (Cary), **VII:** 186

Case of Conscience Resolved, A (Bunyan), **II:** 253

Case of Elijah, The (Sterne), **III:** 135

Case of General Ople and Lady Camper, The (Meredith), **V:** 230–231, 234

Case of Ireland . . . Stated, The (Molyneux), **III:** 27

Cashel Byron's Profession (Shaw), **VI:** 102, 103, 105–106, 109–110, 113, 129

"Cask of Amontillado, The" (Poe), **III:** 339

"Castaway, The" (Cowper), **III:** 218–219

Castle, The (Kafka), **III:** 340, 345

Castle Corner (Cary), **VII:** 186

Castle-Croquet (Carroll), **V:** 274

Castle Dangerous (Scott), **IV:** 39

Castle of Indolence, The (Thomson), **III:** 162, 163, 171, 172

Castle of Otranto, The (Walpole), **III:** 324, **325–327,** 336, 345; **IV:** 30

Castle Richmond (Trollope), **V:** 101

Castles of Athlin and Dunbayne, The (Radcliffe), **IV:** 35

Casuarina Tree, The (Maugham), **VI:** 370, 371

"Catarina to Camoens" (Browning), **IV:** 314

Catharine and Petruchio, **I:** 327; see *Taming of the Shrew, The*

Catherine (Thackeray), **V:** 22, 24, 28, 37

Cathleen ni Houlihan (Yeats and Gregory), **VI:** 218, 222, 309; **VII:** 4

Catholicism, influence of, **I:** 178–184, 362–364, 369; **VI:** 330; **VII:** 293

Catiline (Jonson), **I:** 345–346

Cato (Addison), **III**: 46

Catriona (Stevenson), **V**: 387, 396

Catullus, **II**: 108; **IV**: 327

Causeries du lundi (Sainte-Beuve), **III**: 226

Causley, Charles, **VII**: 422, 434–435

Caution to Stir Up to Watch Against Sin, A (Bunyan), **II**: 253

Cavafy, C. P., **VI**: 408

Cavalcade (Coward), **VI**: 264

cavalier poets, **II**: 221–239; see Thomas Carew, Richard Lovelace, Sir John Suckling, Edmund Waller; see also William Cartwright, Sir John Denham, Sidney Godolphin, marquess of Montrose, William Habington, Lord Herbert of Cherbury, Thomas Randolph

Cave, Edward, **III**: 107

Cavendish, George, **I**: 114

"Caverns of the Grave I've Seen, The" (Blake), **III**: 305

Caxton, William, **I**: 67, 82

Cayley, Charles Bagot, **V**: 250–251, 253, 259

"Ceix and Alceone" (Gower), **I**: 53–54

Celestial Omnibus, The (Forster), **VI**: 399

Celibate Lives (Moore), **VI**: 95

Celibates (Moore), **VI**: 87, 91, 95

Cellular Pathologie (Virchow), **V**: 348

Celt and Saxon (Meredith), **V**: 234

Celtic Twilight, The, Men and Women, Ghouls and Faeries (Yeats), **VI**: 221

Cenci, The (Shelley), **III**: 338; **IV**: xviii, 202, 208

censorship, **VI**: 273, 411; **VII**: 9, 91

"Centenary of Charles Dickens, The" (Joyce), **V**: 41

Centuries of Meditations (Traherne), **II**: 189$_n$, 190, 192–193, 202

Century of Roundels, A (Swinburne), **V**: 332

"Certain Mercies" (Graves), **VII**: 265

Certain Noble Plays of Japan (Yeats), **VI**: 218

Certain Satires (Marston), **II**: 25

Cervantes, Miguel de, **IV**: 190

Cestus of Aglaia, The (Ruskin), **V**: 180–181, 184

Chabot, Admiral of France (Chapman), **I**: 252–253

Chadourne, Marc, **III**: 329

"Chair that Will sat in, I sat in the best, The" (Fitz-Gerald), **IV**: 341

Chalkhill, John, **II**: 133

Chamberlain, Neville, **VI**: 353, 355–356

"Chambermaid's Second Song, The" (Yeats), **VI**: 215

Chamber Music (Joyce), **VII**: 41, 42

Chambers, E. K., **I**: 299; **II**: 187; **IV**: 41, 57

Chambers, R. W., **I**: 3

Champion (periodical), **III**: 97–98, 105

Chance (Conrad), **VI**: 144, 146

Chances, The (Fletcher), **II**: 65

Chandler, Edmund, **V**: 354, 359

"Changed Man, A" (Hardy), **VI**: 22

Changed Man, A, The Waiting Supper, and Other Tales (Hardy), **VI**: 20, 22

Changeling, The (Middleton and Rowley), **II**: 1, 3, 8, **14–18**, 21, 93

Channel Passage, A, and Other Poems (Swinburne), **V**: 333

Chant of the Celestial Sailors, The (Pater), **V**: 357

"Chant-Pagan" (Kipling), **VI**: 203

Chants for Socialists (Morris), **V**: 306

Chaos and Night (Montherlant), **II**: 99$_n$

"Chaperon, The" (James), **VI**: 69

Chapman, George, **I**: 232–256, 278, 288; **II**: 30, 37, 47, 55, 70, 71, 85; **IV**: 215, 255–256

Chapman, John, **V**: 189

Chapman, R. W., **III**: 249

Chappell, E., **II**: 288

Character and Opinions of Dr. Johnson, The (Swinburne), **V**: 333

Characterismes of Vertues and Vice (Hall), **II**: 81

Characteristicks (Shaftesbury), **III**: 44

"Characteristics" (Carlyle), **IV**: 241

Characteristics: In the Manner of Rochefoucault's Maxims (Hazlitt), **IV**: 132, 139

Character of a Trimmer (Halifax), **III**: 40

"Character of a Virtuous Widow" (Webster), **II**: 77

Character of England, A, as It Was Lately Presented . . . (Evelyn), **II**: 287

"Character of Holland, The" (Marvell), **II:** 211, 219

"Character of Mr. Burke" (Hazlitt), **IV:** 136

Character of Robert Earl of Salisbury, The (Tourneur), **II:** 37, 41

"Characters" (Dickens), **V:** 46

Characters (Theophrastus), **III:** 50

Characters (Webster), **II:** 68, 81

"Characters of Dramatic Writers Contemporary with Shakespeare" (Lamb), **IV:** 79–80

Characters of Shakespeare's Plays (Hazlitt), **I:** 329; **IV:** xvii, 129, 139

Charge Delivered to the Grand Jury, A (Fielding), **III:** 105

"Charge of the Light Brigade, The" (Tennyson), **IV:** xxi, 325

"Charity" (Cowper), **III:** 212

Charles I (Shelley), **IV:** 206

Charles Dickens (Swinburne), **V:** 333

Charles Dickens: A Critical Study (Gissing), **V:** 424, 435, 437

"Charles Lamb" (De Quincey), **IV:** 148

Charles Lamb and His Contemporaries (Blunden), **IV:** 86

"Charles Lamb, to those who know thee justly dear" (Southey), **IV:** 85

Charley Is My Darling (Cary), **VII:** 186, 188, 189, 190–191

"Charlotte Brontë as a Critic of *Wuthering Heights*" (Drew), **V:** 153

Charlotte Brontë, 1816–1916: A Centenary Memorial (ed. Wood), **V:** 152

"Charlotte Brontë in Brussels" (Spielman), **V:** 137_n

Charlotte Brontë: The Evolution of Genius (Gérin), **V:** 111, 152

Chartism (Carlyle), **IV:** xix, 240, 244–245, 249, 250; **V:** viii

Chase, The, and William and Helen (Scott), **IV:** 29, 38

Chastelard (Swinburne), **V:** 313, 330, 331, 332

Chaste Maid in Cheapside, A (Middleton), **II:** 1, 3, **6–8,** 10, 21

Châtiments, Les (Hugo), **V:** 324

Chatterton, Thomas, **IV:** xiv, 228; **V:** 405

Chaucer, Geoffrey, **I:** 2, 15, 16, **19–47,** 49, 60, 67, 126; **II:** 70, 292, 302, 304; **IV:** 189; **V:** 298, 303

"Chearfulness" (Vaughan), **II:** 186

Chekhov, Anton, **VI:** 372

"Cherry-ripe" (Herrick), **II:** 115

Chester, Robert, **I:** 313

Chester Nimmo trilogy (Cary), **VII:** 186, 191, 194–195; see also *Prisoner of Grace, Except the Lord, Not Honour More*

Chesterton, G. K., **IV:** 107; **V:** xxiv, 60, 262, 296, 383, 391, 393, 397; **VI:** 200, 241, 248, **335–345; VII:** xiii

Chettle, Henry, **I:** 276, 296; **II:** 47, 68

"Chief Petty Officer" (Causley), **VII:** 434

Child Christopher and Goldilind the Fair (Morris), **V:** 306

Childe Harold's Pilgrimage (Byron), **III:** 337, 338; **IV:** x, xvii, 172, **175–178,** 180, 181, 188, 192; **V:** 329

"Childe-hood" (Vaughan), **II:** 188, 189, 190

Childermass (Lewis), **VII:** 71, 79, 80–81

"Childe Roland to the Dark Tower Came" (Browning), **IV:** 357; **VI:** 16

"Child in the House, The" (Pater), **V:** 337, 357

Child of the Jago, The (Morrison), **VI:** 365–366

Children of the Chapel (Gordon), **V:** 313

"Children of the Zodiac, The" (Kipling), **VI:** 169, 189, 191–193

Child's Garden of Verses, A (Stevenson), **V:** 385, 387, 395

Child's History of England, A (Dickens), **V:** 71

Chimes, The (Dickens), **V:** 42, 64, 71

"Chimney Sweeper" (Blake), **III:** 297

China. A Revised Reprint of Articles from Titan . . . (De Quincey), **IV:** 155

"Chinese Letters" (Goldsmith), see *Citizen of the World, The*

Chit-chat (periodical), **III:** 50

Chivers, Thomas Holley, **V:** 313

Chloe (Meredith), **V:** 231_n, 234

Choice of Kipling's Prose, A (Maugham), **VI:** 200, 204

Christabel (Coleridge), **II:** 179; **III:** 338; **IV:** ix, xvii, 29, 44, 48–49, 56, 218, 313

Christ a Compleat Saviour in His Intercession (Bunyan), **II:** 253

Christe's Bloody Sweat (Ford), **II:** 88, 100

Christian Behaviour . . . (Bunyan), **II:** 253

Christian Captives, The (Bridges), **VI:** 83

Christian Dialogue, A (Bunyan), **II:** 253

Christian doctrine, influence of, **VI:** 336–337, 339–340, 341–342; **VII:** 187, 242–243; see also Catholicism, Puritanism

Christian Ethicks (Traherne), **II:** 190, 191, 201

Christian Hero, The (Steele), **III:** 43, 44, 53

Christian Morals (Browne), **II:** 149, 153, 154, 156; **III:** 40

Christie, Agatha, **III:** 341

Christina Alberta's Father (Wells), **VI:** 227

Christina Rossetti (Packer), **V:** 251, 252–253, 260

Christina Rossetti: A Divided Life (Battiscombe), **V:** 260

"Christmas Antiphones" (Swinburne), **V:** 325

"Christmas at Sea" (Stevenson), **V:** 396

Christmas at Thompson Hall (Trollope), **V:** 102

Christmas Books (Dickens), **V:** 71

Christmas Carol, A (Dickens), **V:** xx, 42, 56–57, 71

"Christmas Carol, A" (Swinburne), **V:** 315

Christmas Comes But Once a Year (Chettle, Dekker, Heywood, Webster), **II:** 68, 85

Christmas-Eve and Easter-Day (Browning), **IV:** 357, 363, 370, 372, 374

Christmas Holiday (Maugham), **VI:** 377

"Christmas Storms and Sunshine" (Gaskell), **V:** 15

Christopher and His Kind (Isherwood), **VII:** 318

Christopher Columbus (MacNeice), **VII:** 406

"Christopher Marlowe" (Swinburne), **V:** 332

Christopher Marlowe in Relation to Greene, Peele and Lodge (Swinburne), **V:** 333

Christ's Hospital (school), **IV:** xi, 41, 42, 44, 74, 75–77, 84

Christ's Hospital, a Retrospect (Blunden), **IV:** 86

"Christ's Hospital Five-and-Thirty Years Ago" (Lamb), **IV:** 42; **IV:** 42, 76

Christ Stopped at Eboli (Levi), **VI:** 299

"Chronicle, The" (Cowley), **II:** 198

Chronicle Historie of Perkin Warbeck, The (Ford), see *Perkin Warbeck*

chronicle history, **I:** 73

Chronicle of Friendships, A, 1873–1900 (Low), **V:** 393, 397

Chronicle of Queen Fredegond, The (Swinburne), **V:** 333

Chronicle of the Cid (tr. Southey), **IV:** 71

"Chronicle of the Drum, The" (Thackeray), **V:** 17, 38

Chronicles (Hall), **II:** 43

Chronicles of the Canongate (Scott), **IV:** 39

Chroniques (Froissart), **I:** 21

Chrysaor (Landor), **IV:** 96

Church, Dean R. W., **I:** 186

Church and Queen. Five Speeches, 1860–1864 (Disraeli), **IV:** 308

"Churche-Floore, The" (Herbert), **II:** 126

"Churches of Northern France, The" (Morris), **V:** 293, 306

Churchill, Lady Randolph, **VI:** 349

Churchill, Winston, **III:** 27; **VI:** xv, 261, 274, **347–362,** 369, 385, 392; speeches, **VI:** 361

Churchill by His Contemporaries (ed. Eade), **VI:** 351$_n$, 361

"Church-monuments" (Herbert), **II:** 127

"Church Service" (Vaughan), **II:** 187

"Church-warden and the Curate, The" (Tennyson), **IV:** 327

"Church Windows, The" (Herbert), **II:** 127

"Churl and the Bird, The" (Lydgate), **I:** 57

Chymist's Key, The (tr. Vaughan), **II:** 185, 201

Cibber, Colley, **I:** 327; **II:** 314, 324–326, 331, 334, 337

Cicadas, The (Huxley), **VII:** 199

"Cicero and His Brother" (Landor), **IV:** 90, 91

Ciceronianus (Harvey), **I:** 122

Cinkante balades (Gower), **I:** 56

Cinque Ports, The (Ford), **VI:** 238, 332

Cinthio, Giraldi, **I:** 316; **II:** 71

Circe (Davenant), **II:** 305

Circle, The (Maugham), **VI:** 369

Circular Billiards for Two Players (Carroll), **V:** 273

"Circus Animals' Desertion, The" (Yeats), **V:** 349; **VI:** 215

Citation and Examination of William Shakespeare . . . (Landor), **IV:** 100

Citizen of the World, The; or, Letters from a Chinese Philosopher . . . (Goldsmith), **III:** 177, 179, 185, 188–189, 191

"City of Brass, The" (Kipling), **VI:** 203

City Wives' Confederacy, The (Vanbrugh), see *Confederacy, The*

"Civilised, The" (Galsworthy), **VI:** 273, 274, 276

Civilization in the United States (Arnold), **V:** 216

Civilization of the Renaissance in Italy, The (Burckhardt), **V:** 342

Civitatis Amor (Middleton), **II:** 3

Clapham Sect, **IV:** 268; **V:** viii, 277

Clara Florise (Moore), **VI:** 96

Clare, John, **IV:** 260

"Clarel" (Melville), **V:** 211

"Clarice of the Autumn Concerts" (Bennett), **VI:** 266

Clarissa (Richardson), **III:** 80–81, **85–89**, 91, 92, 95; **VI:** 266

"Clarissa": Preface, Hints of Prefaces and Postscripts (ed. Brissenden), **III:** 86$_n$

Clark, Sir George, **IV:** 290

Clark, Kenneth, **III:** 325, 346

Clarke, Charles Cowden, **IV:** 214, 215

Clarke, Herbert E., **V:** 318$_n$

Clarke, Samuel, **II:** 251

Clarkson, Catherine, **IV:** 49

Classical Tradition, The: Greek and Roman Influences on Western Literature (Highet), **II:** 199$_n$

Classic Irish Drama (Armstrong), **VII:** 14

Claude Lorrain's House on the Tiber (Lear), **V:** 77

Claudius novels (Graves), **VII:** xviii, 259

Claudius the God and His Wife Messalina (Graves), **VII:** 259

Claverings, The (Trollope), **V:** 99–100, 101

Clayhanger (Bennett), **VI:** 248, 250, 251, 257–258

Clayhanger series (Bennett), **VI:** xiii, 247, 248, 250, 251, 257–258,

Clayhanger trilogy (Bennett), **VI:** xiii

Clear State of the Case of Elizabeth Canning, A (Fielding), **III:** 105

Cleomenes, the Spartan Hero (Dryden), **II:** 296, 305

"Cleon" (Browning), **IV:** 357, 360, 363

Cleopatra (Daniel), **I:** 162

"Cleopatra" (Swinburne), **V:** 332

Clergyman's Daughter, A (Orwell), **VII:** 274, 278

Clergymen of the Church of England (Trollope), **V:** 101

"clerihew" verse, **VI:** 335

Clerk's Prologue, The (Chaucer), **I:** 29

Clerk's Tale, The (Chaucer), **I:** 34

Cleveland, John, **II:** 123

Clifford, J. L., **III:** 244$_n$

Clifford, W. K., **V:** 409$_n$

Clio: A Muse (Trevelyan), **VI:** 383–384

Clishbotham, Jedidiah, pseud. of Sir Walter Scott

"Clive" (Browning), **IV:** 367

Clodd, Edward, **V:** 429

"Clopton Hall" (Gaskell), **V:** 3

"Clorinda and Damon" (Marvell), **II:** 210, 211

Closing the Ring (Churchill), **VI:** 361

"Cloud, The" (Shelley), **IV:** 196, 204

"Clouds" (Brooke), **VI:** 420

"Cloud's Swan Song, The" (Thompson), **V:** 443

Clough, Arthur Hugh, **IV:** 371; **V:** ix, xi, xviii, xxii, 7, **155–171**, 207, 208$_n$, 209, 211, 212

"Club in an Uproar, A" (Thackeray), **V:** 25

"Coast, The" (Fuller), **VII:** 431

Coat of Varnish, A (Snow), **VII:** 337–338

Cobbett, William, **VI:** 337

Coburn, Kathleen, **IV:** 52, 55–57

Cock-a-Doodle Dandy (O'Casey), **VII:** xviii, 9–10

"Cockcrow" (Herrick), **II:** 114

"Cock-crowing" (Vaughan), **II:** 185

Cockshut, A.O.J., **V:** 98, 100–101, 103

Cocktail Party, The (Eliot), **VII:** 158, 159, 160–161

Coelum Britannicum . . . (Carew), **II:** 222

Coggan, Donald, archbishop of Canterbury, **I:** vi

Cohen, Francis, **IV:** 190

Colasterion: A Reply to a Nameless Answer Against the Doctrine and Discipline of Divorce (Milton), **II:** 175

Colburn, Henry, **IV:** 254, 293; **V:** 135

"Cold, clear, and blue, the morning heaven" (Brontë), **V:** 115

"Cold in the earth" (Brontë), **V:** 114, 133, 134

Colenso, Bishop John William, **V:** 283

Coleridge, Derwent, **IV:** 48–49, 52

Coleridge, Hartley, **IV:** 44; **V:** 105, 125

Coleridge, Samuel Taylor, **III:**338; **IV:**viii–xii, **41–57,** 59, 75–78, 82, 84, 115, 204, 253, 257, 281; **V:** 244; and DeQuincey, **IV:** 143, 144, 150; and Hazlitt, **IV:** 125–130, 133–134, 137, 138; and Peacock, **IV:** 161–162, 167; and Wordsworth, **IV:** 3–4, 6, 15, 128; at Christ's Hospital, **IV:** 75–78, 82; critical works, **II:** 42, 119$_n$, 155, 179, 249–250, 298; **III:** 174, 281, 286; **IV:** 4, 6, 18, 96, 253, 257; literary style, **II:** 154; **III:** 336, 338; **IV:** viii, xi, 18, 180; **V:** 62, 361, 447; Pater's essay in *Appreciations*, **V:** 244, 340–341

"Coleridge" (Mill), **IV:** 50, 56

"Coleridge" (Pater), **V:** 338, 340–341, 403

Coleridge's Miscellaneous Criticism (ed. Raysor), **IV:** 46

Coleridge's Shakespearean Criticism (ed. Raysor), **IV:** 51, 52, 56

"Coleum, or the Origin of Things" (Bacon), **I:** 267

Colin Clout (Skelton), **I:** 84, 86, 87, 91–92

Colin Clout's Come Home Again (Spenser), **I:** 124, 127–128, 146–147

"Collaboration" (James), **VI:** 48, 69

"Collar, The" (Herbert), **II:** 120–121, 216

Collected Essays, Papers, etc. (Bridges), **VI:** 83

Collected Ewart 1933–1980, The (Ewart), **VII:** 423

Collected Letters (Owen), **VI:** 448

Collected Plays (Maugham), **VI:** 367

Collected Poems (Ford), **VI:** 323, 332

Collected Poems of Robert Louis Stevenson (ed. Smith), **V:** 393

Collected Stories (Maugham), **VI:** 370

Collected Verse, The (Carroll), **V:** 270, 273

Collected Works of Izaak Walton (Keynes), **II:** 134

Collection of Meditations and Devotions in Three Parts, A (Traherne), **II:** 191, 201

Collection of Original Poems, A (Boswell), **III:** 247

"College Garden, The" (Bridges), **VI:** 82

Collier, Jeremy, **II:** 303, 325, 331–332, 338, 340, 356; **III:** 44

Collier, John Payne, **I:** 285; **IV:** 52, 56

Collier's Friday Night, A (Lawrence), **VII:** 89, 121

Collingwood, R. G., **VI:** 203

Collingwood, S. D., **V:** 270, 273, 274

Collins, Michael, **VI:** 353

Collins, Phillip, **V:** 46, 73

Collins, Wilkie, **III:** 334, 338, 340, 345; **V:** xxii–xxiii, 42, 62

Collins, William, **II:** 68, 323$_n$; **III: 160–176,** 336; **IV:** 227

Collinson, James, **V:** 249

Colloquies on the Progress and Prospects of Society (Southey), see *Sir Thomas More: or, Colloquies on the Progress . . .*

Colman, George, **IV:** 271

Colombe's Birthday (Browning), **IV:** 374

"Colonel Fantock" (Sitwell), **VII:** 133

Colonel Jack (Defoe), **III:** 5, 6, 7, 8, 13

"Colonel's Lady, The" (Maugham), **VI:** 370

"Colours of Good and Evil" (Bacon), see "Examples of the Colours of Good and Evil"

"Colubriad, The" (Cowper), **III:** 217–218

Colvin, Sidney, **V:** 386, 389–396

Come and Welcome, to Jesus Christ (Bunyan), **II:** 253

comedy, **V:** 224–225; **VI:** 368; see also comedy of manners

Comedy of Errors, The (Shakespeare), **I:** 302, 303, 312, 321

comedy of manners, **IV:** 112–113; **V:** 224

Comical Revenge, The (Etherege), **II:** 266, 267–268, 271

Comic Annual, The (Hood), **IV:** 251, 252, 253–254, 258, 259, 266

Comic Romance of Monsieur Scarron, The (tr. Goldsmith), **III:** 191

Coming of Gabrielle, The (Moore), **VI:** 96, 99

"Coming of the Anglo-Saxons, The" (Trevelyan), **VI:** 393

Coming Up for Air (Orwell), **VII:** 281–282

Commendatory Verses Prefixed to Heywood's Apology for Actors (Webster), **II:** 85

Commendatory Verses Prefixed to . . . Munday's Translation of Palmerin . . . (Webster), **II:** 85

Commentaries of Caesar, The (Trollope), **V:** 102

Commentarius solutus (Bacon), **I:** 263, 272

Commentary on Macaulay's History of England, A (Firth), **IV:** 290, 291

Commentary on "Memoirs of Mr. Fox" (Landor), **IV:** 100

Commentary on the Collected Plays of W. B. Yeats (Jeffares and Knowland), **VI:** 224

Commentary on the Collected Poems of W. B. Yeats (Jeffares), **VI:** 224

Commentary on the Complete Poems of Gerard Manley Hopkins, A (Mariani), **V:** 373_n, 378_n, 382

"Comment on Christmas, A" (Arnold), **V:** 216

Comming of Good Luck, The (Herrick), **II:** 107

"Committee-Man of 'The Terror,' The" (Hardy), **VI:** 22

Common Asphodel, The (Graves), **VII:** 261

Commonplace and Other Short Stories (Rossetti), **V:** 260

Commonplace Book of Robert Herrick, **II:** 103

Common Pursuit (Leavis), **VII:** 234, 246

Common Reader, The (Woolf), **VII:** 22, 28, 32–33

"Commonsense About the War" (Shaw), **VI:** 119, 129

Common Sense of War and Peace, The: World Revolution or War Unending (Wells), **VI:** 245

Commonweal (periodical), **V:** 302

Commonweal, The: A Song for Unionists (Swinburne), **V:** 332

Communication to My Friends, A (Moore), **VI:** 89, 99

Communism, **VI:** 242

Compassion: An Ode (Hardy), **VI:** 20

Compendium of Authentic and Entertaining Voyages, A (Smollett), **IV:** 158

Complaint of Chaucer to His Purse (Chaucer), **I:** 31

Complaint of the Black Knight, The (Lydgate), **I:** 57, 60, 61, 65

Complaint of Venus, The (Chaucer), **I:** 31

Complaints (Spenser), **I:** 124

Compleat Angler, The (Walton) **II:** 131–136, **137–139,** 141–143

Compleat English Gentleman, The (Defoe), **III:** 5, 14

Compleat Gard'ner, The: or, Directions for . . . Fruit-Gardens and Kitchen-Gardens . . . (tr. Evelyn), **II:** 287

Compleat Vindication of the Licensers of the Stage, A (Johnson), **III:** 121

"Complement, The" (Carew), **II:** 223–224

Complete Collection of Genteel and Ingenious Conversation, A (Swift), **III:** 29, 36

Complete English Tradesman, The (Defoe), **III:** 5, 14

Complete History of England . . . (Smollett), **III:** 148, 149, 158

Complete Poems and Fragments of Wilfred Owen, The (Stallworthy), **VI:** 458, 459

Complete Poems of Emily Brontë, The (ed. Hatfield), **V:** 133, 152

Complete Works of John Webster, The (ed. Lucas), **II:** 70_n

Compton-Burnett, Ivy, **VII:** xvii, **59–70**

Comte, Auguste, **V:** 428–429

Comus (Milton), **II:** 50, 159–160, 166, 175

"Concealment, The" (Cowley), **II:** 196

"Conceit Begotten by the Eyes" (Ralegh), **I:** 148, 149

Concept of Nature in Nineteenth-Century Poetry, The (Beach), **V:** 221_n

"Concerning Geffray Teste Noir" (Morris), **V:** 293

Concerning Humour in Comedy (Congreve), **II:** 338, 341, 346, 350

"Concerning the Beautiful" (tr. Taylor), **III:** 291

Concerning the Relations of Great Britain, Spain, and Portugal . . . (Wordsworth), **IV:** 24

"Concert Party: Busseboom" (Blunden), **VI:** 428

Conciones ad Populum (Coleridge), **IV:** 56

Concordance to the Poems of Robert Browning, A (Broughton and Stelter), **IV:** 373

"Conde, Il" (Conrad), **VI:** 148

"Condition of England, The" (Masterman), **VI:** viii, 273

Condition of the Working Class in England in 1844, The (Engels), **IV:** 249

Conduct of the Allies, The (Swift), **III:** 19, 26–27, 35

Confederacy, The (Vanbrugh), **II:** 325, 336

Conference of Pleasure, A (Bacon), **I:** 265, 271

Confessio amantis (Gower), **I:** 48, 49, 50–56, 58, 321

Confession of My Faith, A, . . . (Bunyan), **II:** 253

Confessions of an English Opium-Eater (De Quincey), **III:** 338; **IV:** xviii, 141, 143, 148–149, 150–153, 154, 155

Confessions of an Inquiring Spirit (Coleridge), **IV:** 53, 56

Confessions of a Young Man (Moore), **VI:** 85–86, 87, 89, 91, 96

Confidence (James), **VI:** 67

Confidential Clerk, The (Eliot), **VII:** 161–162

Confines of Criticism, The (Housman), **VI:** 164

Congreve, William, **II:** 269, 289, 302, 304, 325, 336, **338–350,** 352; **III:** 45, 62

Coningsby (Disraeli), **IV:** xii, xx, 294, 300–303, 305, 307, 308; **V:** 4, 22

Conjugal Lewdness: or, Matrimonial Whoredom (Defoe), **III:** 14

Connell, John, **VI:** xv, xxxiii

Connolly, Cyril, **VI:** 363, 371; **VII:** xvi, 37, 138, 310

Connolly, T. L., **V:** 442$_n$, 445, 447, 450, 451

Conquest of Granada by the Spaniards, The (Dryden), **II:** 294, 305

Conrad, Joseph, **VI:** xi, **133–150,** 170, 193, 242, 270, 279–280, 321; **VII:** 122; list of short stories, **VI:** 149–150

Conrad in the Nineteenth Century (Watt), **VI:** 149

Conrad's Prefaces to His Works (Garnett), **VI:** 149

Conscience of the Rich, The (Snow), **VII:** 324, 326–327

"Conscious" (Owen), **VI:** 451

Consider (Rossetti), **V:** 260

Considerations Touching the Likeliest Means to Remove Hirelings out of the Church (Milton), **II:** 176

Consolation of Philosophy (Boethius), **I:** 31

Consolidator, The (Defoe), **III:** 4, 13

Constant Couple, The, or, A Trip to the Jubilee (Farquhar), **II:** 352, 356–357, 364

"Constantine and Silvester" (Gower), **I:** 53–54

Constantine the Great (Lee), **II:** 305

Constant Wife, The (Maugham), **VI:** 369

"Constellation, The" (Vaughan), **II:** 186, 189

Constitutional (periodical), **V:** 19

Constitutional History of England, The (Hallam), **IV:** 283

"Contemplation" (Thompson), **V:** 442, 443

Contemporaries of Shakespeare (Swinburne), **V:** 333

Continual Dew (Betjeman), **VII:** 365

Continuation of the Complete History, A (Smollett), **III:** 148, 149, 158

Contrarini Fleming (Disraeli), **IV:** xix, 292–293, 294, 296–297, 299, 308

Contrary Experience, The (Read), **VI:** 416

Contre-Machiavel (Gentillet), **I:** 283

"Convergence of the Twain, The" (Hardy), **II:** 69; **VI:** 16

Conversations in Ebury Street (Moore), **V:** 129, 153; **VI:** 89, 98, 99

Conversations of James Northcote, Esq., R. A. (Hazlitt), **IV:** 134, 140

Convivio (Dante), **I:** 27

Cook, D., **III:** 322

Cook, Eliza, **IV:** 259, 320

Cook, J. D., **V:** 279

Cooke, W., **III:** 184$_n$

"Coole Park" (Yeats), **VI:** 212

"Coole Park and Ballylee" (Yeats), **VI:** 215

"Cool Web, The" (Graves), **VII:** 266

Cooper, Lettice Ulpha, **V:** x, xxvii, 397, 398

Cooper, William, **VII:** xxi, xxxvii

"Co-ordination" (Forster), **VI:** 399

Copeland, T. W., **III:** 245$_n$, 250

Coppy of a Letter Written to . . . Parliament, A (Suckling), **II:** 238

Corbett, Sir Julian, **I:** 146

"Corinna's Going a-Maying" (Herrick), **II:** 109–110

"Coriolan" (Eliot), **VII:** 152–153, 158

Coriolanus (Shakespeare), **I:** 318; **II:** 70

Corke, Helen, **VII:** 93

"Cornac and His Wife, The" (Lewis), **VII:** 77, 78

Corneille, Pierre, **II:** 261, 270, 271

Cornelia (Kyd), **I:** 162, 220

Cornélie (Garaier), **I:** 220

Cornelius: A Business Affair in Three Transactions (Priestley), **VII:** 224

Cornhill (periodical), **V:** xxii, 1, 20, 279; **VI:** 31

Corno di Bassetto, pseud. of George Bernard Shaw

Cornwall, Barry, **IV:** 311

Cornwallis, Sir William, **III:** 39–40

"Coronet, The" (Marvell), **II:** 113, 211, 216

Coronet for His Mistress Philosophy, A (Chapman), **I:** 234

Correspondence (Flaubert), **V:** 353

Correspondence (Swift), **III:** 24

Correspondence of James Boswell and John Johnston . . . (ed. Walker), **III:** 249

Correspondence . . . of James Boswell Relating to the "Life of Johnson," The (ed. Waingrow), **III:** 249

Correspondence of James Boswell with . . . the Club, The (ed. Fifer), **III:** 249

Corridors of Power (Snow), **VII:** xxvi, 324, 330–331

"Corruption" (Vaughan), **II:** 185, 186, 189

Corsair, The (Byron), **IV:** xvii, 172, 173, 175, 192; see also Turkish tales

Corson, James C., **IV:** 27, 38–40

"Corymbus for Autumn" (Thompson), **V:** 442

Cosmopolitans (Maugham), **VI:** 370

"Cottage Hospital, The" (Betjeman), **VII:** 375

"Cotter's Saturday Night, The" (Burns), **III:** 311, 313, 315, 318

Cottle, Joseph, **IV:** 44, 45, 52, 56, 59

Cotton, Charles, **II:** 131, 134, 137

Coué, Émile, **VI:** 264

Count Belisarius (Graves), **VII:** xviii, 258

Counter-Attack (Sassoon), **VI:** 430, 431

Counterblast (McLuhan), **VII:** 71$_n$

Countess Cathleen, The (Yeats), **VI:** 87

Countess Cathleen and Various Legends and Lyrics, The (Yeats), **VI:** 211, 309

Countess of Pembroke, **I:** 161, 163–169, 218

Countess of Pembroke's Arcadia, The (Sidney), see *Arcadia*

Count Julian (Landor), **IV:** 89, 96, 100

Count Robert of Paris (Scott), **IV:** 39

Country House, The (Galsworthy), **VI:** 271, 272, 273, 275, 278, 282

Country House, The (Vanbrugh), **II:** 325, 333, 336

"Country of the Blind, The" (Wells), **VI:** 234

Country of the Blind, The, and Other Stories (Wells), **VI:** 228, 244

Country-Wife, The (Wycherley), **I:** 243; **II:** 307, 308, **314–318**, 321, 360

Courier (periodical), **IV:** 50

Courte of Venus, The (Wyatt), **I:** 97

"Court of Cupid, The" (Spenser), **I:** 123

Cousine Bette (Balzac), **V:** xx, 17

Cousin Henry (Trollope), **V:** 102

"Cousin Maria" (James), **VI:** 69

Cousin Phillis (Gaskell), **V:** 1, 2, 4, 8, 11, 15

"Cousins, The" (Burne-Jones), **VI:** 167, 169

Covent Garden Journal, The (periodical), **III:** 103–104

Covent-Garden Tragedy, The (Fielding), **III:** 97, 105

Coverdale, Myles, **I:** 377

"Covering End" (James), **VI:** 52, 69

Cowasjee, S., **VII:** 4

Cowell, Edward, **IV:** 342–346

Cowley, Abraham, **II:** 123, 179, **194–200, 202,** 236, 256, 259, 275, 347; **III:** 40, 118

Cowper, William, **II:** 119$_n$, 196, 240; **III:** 173, **207–220,** 282; **IV:** xiv–xvi, 93, 184, 281

"Cowper's Grave" (Browning), **IV:** 312, 313

Cox, Charles Brian, **VI:** xi, xxxiii; **VI:** xi

Coxcomb, The (Beaumont, Fletcher, Massinger), **II:** 66

Coxhead, Elizabeth, **VI:** xiv, xxxiii

"Coxon Fund, The" (James), **VI:** 69

"Cox's Diary" (Thackeray), see "Barber Cox and the Cutting of His Comb"

C. P. Snow (Karl), **VII:** 341

Crabbe, George, **III: 272–287,** 338; **IV:** xv, xvii, 103, 326; **V:** 6; **VI:** 378

Craig, Hardin, **I:** 187, 326

Craig, W. J., **I:** 326

Craigie, Mrs., **VI:** 87

Crane, Stephen, **VI:** 320

Cranford (Gaskell), **V:** xxi, 1–4, 8–10, 11, 14, 15

"Crapy Cornelia" (James), **VI:** 69

Crashaw, Richard, **II:** 90–91, 113, 122, 123, 126, **179–184, 200–201; V:** 325

"Craving for Spring" (Lawrence), **VII:** 118

"Crawford's Consistency" (James), **VI:** 69

Creators of Wonderland (Mespoulet), **V:** 266

Cricket on the Hearth, The (Dickens), **V:** 71

Criminal Case, A (Swinburne), **V:** 333

Crimson in the Tricolour, The (O'Casey), **VII:** 12

"Crinoline" (Thackeray), **V:** 22

Crisis, The, a Sermon (Fielding), **III:** 105

Crisis Examined, The (Disraeli), **IV:** 308

Criterion (periodical), **VI:** 248; **VII:** xv, 143, 165

Critic (periodical), **V:** 134

Critic, The (Sheridan), **III:** 253, **263–266,** 270

Critical and Historical Essays (Macaulay), **IV:** xx, 272, 277, **278–282,** 291

Critical Bibliography of Katherine Mansfield, The (Mantz), **VII:** 182

Critical Essays (Orwell), **VII:** 282

Critical Essays of the Seventeenth Century (Spingarn), **II:** 256$_n$

Critical Essays on George Eliot (Hardy), **V:** 201

Critical Essays on the Poetry of Tennyson (ed. Killham), **IV:** 323$_n$, 338, 339

Critical Observations on the Sixth Book of the Aeneid (Gibbon), **III:** 233

Critical Review (periodical), **III:** 147–148, 149, 179, 188

Critical Strictures on the New Tragedy of Elvira . . . (Boswell, Dempster, Erskine), **III:** 246

Critical Studies of the Works of Charles Dickens (Gissing), **V:** 437

"Critic as Artist, The" (Wilde), **V:** 407, 408, 409

criticism, see literary criticism, social commentary

Criticism on Art: And Sketches of the Picture Galleries of England (Hazlitt), **IV:** 140

Croker, J. W., **IV:** 280

Crome Yellow (Huxley), **VII:** 197, 200

Cromwell (Carlyle), see *Oliver Cromwell's Letters and Speeches*

Cromwell's Army (Firth), **II:** 241

Cronica tripertita (Gower), **I:** 50

Croquet Castles (Carroll), **V:** 274

Cross, John Walter, **V:** 13, 198, 200

Cross, Wilbur L., **III:** 125, 126, 135

"Crossing alone the nighted ferry" (Housman), **VI:** 161

Crotchet Castle (Peacock), **IV:** xix, 165–166, 169, 170

Crowley, Aleister, **VI:** 374

Crowley, Robert, **I:** 1, 3

Crowning Privilege, The (Graves), **VII:** 260, 268

Crown of All Homer's Works, The (Chapman), **I:** 236

Crown of Life, The (Gissing), **V:** 437

Crown of Wild Olive, The (Ruskin), **V:** 184

"Cruelty and Love" (Lawrence), **VII:** 118

Cruelty of a Stepmother, The, **I:** 218

Crux Ansata: An Indictment of the Roman Catholic Church (Wells), **VI:** 242, 244

"Cry of the Children, The" (Browning), **IV:** xx, 313

"Cry of the Human, The" (Browning), **IV:** 313

Cuala Press, **VI:** 221

Cub, at Newmarket, The (Boswell), **III:** 247

Cuckold in Conceit, The (Vanbrugh), **II:** 337

Cuirassiers of the Frontier, The (Graves), **VII:** 267

Culture and Anarchy (Arnold), **III:** 23; **V:** 203, 206, 213, 215, 216

Cumberland, George, **IV:** 47

Cumberland, Richard, **II:** 363; **III:** 257

Cunningham, William, **VI:** 385

"Cupid and Psyche" (tr. Pater), **V:** 351

"Cupid, or the Atom" (Bacon), **I:** 267

Cupid's Revenge (Beaumont and Fletcher), **II:** 46, 65

"Curate's Friend, The" (Forster), **VI:** 399

"Curate's Walk, The" (Thackeray), **V:** 25

Cure for a Cuckold, A (Rowley and Webster), **II:** 69, 83, 85

Curiosissima Curatoria (Carroll), **V:** 274

Curious Fragments (Lamb), **IV:** 79

"Curious if True" (Gaskell), **V:** 15

Curse of Kehama, The (Southey), **IV:** 65, 66, 71, 217

Curse of Minerva, The (Byron), **IV:** 192

Curtis, Anthony, **VI:** xiii, xxxiii, 372

Curtis, L. P., **III:** 124$_n$, 127$_n$

Custom of the Country, The (Fletcher [and Massinger]), **II:** 66, 340

Cymbeline (Shakespeare), **I:** 322

Cymbeline Refinished (Shaw), **VI:** 129

Cynthia's Revels (Jonson), **I:** 346

Cyrano de Bergerac, **III:** 24

"Cyril Tourneur" (Swinburne), **V:** 332

D

Daborne, Robert, **II:** 37, 45

"Daedalus, or the Mechanic" (Bacon), **I:** 267

Daemon of the World, The (Shelley), **IV:** 209

Daffodil Murderer, The (Sassoon), **VI:** 429

Daiches, David, **V:** ix

Daily Graphic (periodical), **VI:** 350

Daily News (periodical), **VI:** 335

Daily Worker (periodical), **VI:** 242

Daisy Miller (James), **VI: 31–32,** 69

Dallas, Eneas Sweetland, **V:** 207

Dampier, William, **III:** 7, 24

"Danac" (Galsworthy), see *Country House, The*

Danby, J. F., **II:** 46, 53, 64

Dance of Death, The, **I:** 15

Dance to the Music of Time, A, novel cycle (Powell), **VII:** xxi, **347–353**

Dancourt, Carton, **II:** 325, 336

Dangerous Corner (Priestley), **VII:** 223

Daniel, Samuel, **I:** 162

Daniel Deronda (Eliot), **V:** xxiv, 190, 197–198, 200

D'Annunzio, Gabriele, **V:** 310

"Danny Deever" (Kipling), **VI:** 203

Dante Alighieri, **II:** 75, 148; **III:** 306; **IV:** 93, 187

Dante and His Circle (Rossetti), **V:** 245

"Dante at Verona" (Rossetti), **V:** 239, 240

"Dantis Tenebrae" (Rossetti), **V:** 243

Danvers, Charles, **IV:** 60

Daphnaida (Spenser), **I:** 124

"Daphne" (Sitwell), **VII:** 133

"Daphnis and Chloe" (Marvell), **II:** 209, 211, 212

Daphnis and Chloë (tr. Moore), **VI:** 89

"Daphnis, an Elegiac Eclogue" (Vaughan), **II:** 185

"Dark Angel, The" (Johnson), **VI:** 211

Dark Flower, The (Galsworthy), **VI:** 274

Dark Lady of the Sonnets, The (Shaw), **VI:** 115, 129

"Darkling Thrush, The" (Hardy), **VI:** 16

Darkness at Noon (Koestler), **V:** 49

Dark Night's Work, A (Gaskell), **V:** 15

Dark Tower, The (MacNeice), **VII:** 407, 408

"Darwin and Divinity" (Stephen), **V:** 284

Das Leben Jesu (tr. Eliot), **V:** 189, 200

Daughter-in-Law, The (Lawrence), **VII:** 119, 121

Daughters and Sons (Compton-Burnett), **VII:** 60, 63, 64–65

"Daughters of the Late Colonel, The" (Mansfield), **VII:** 175, 177, 178

"Daughters of the Vicar" (Lawrence), **VII:** 114

"Daughters of War" (Rosenberg), **VI:** 434

Davenant, Charles, **II:** 305

Davenant, Sir William, **I:** 327; **II:** 87, 185, 196, 259

Davenport, Arnold, **IV:** 227

David and Bethsabe (Peele), **I:** 198, 206–207

"David Balfour" (Stevenson), see *Catriona*

David Copperfield (Dickens), **V:** xxi, 7, 41, 42, 44, 59–62, 63, 67, 71

Davideis (Cowley), **II:** 195, 198, 202

Davidson, John, **V:** 318$_n$

Davie, Donald, **VI:** 220

Davis, Clyde Brion, **V:** 394

Davis, H., **III:** 15$_n$, 35

Davy, Sir Humphrey, **IV:** 200

Dawkins, R. M., **VI:** 295, 303–304

"Dawn on the Somme" (Nichols), **VI:** 419

Dawson, Christopher, **III:** 227

Dawson, W. J., **IV:** 289, 291

"Day Dream, A" (Brontë), **V:** 142

Day Lewis, Cecil, **V:** 220, 234; **VI:** x, xxxiii, 454; **VII:** 382, 410

Daylight on Saturday (Priestley), **VII:** 212, 217–218

"Day of Days, A" (James), **VI:** 69

Day's Work, The (Kipling), **VI:** 204

Deacon Brodie (Stevenson), **V:** 396

"Dead, The" (Brooke), **VI:** 420

"Dead, The" (Joyce), **VII:** xiv, 44–45

"Dead and Alive" (Gissing), **V:** 437

"Dead-Beat, The" (Owen), **VI:** 451, 452

"Dead Love" (Swinburne), **V:** 325, 331, 332

"Dead Man's Dump" (Rosenberg), **VI:** 432, 434

Dealings with the Firm of Dombey and Son . . . (Dickens), see *Dombey and Son*

Dean, L. F., **I:** 269

Dearest Emmie (Hardy), **VI:** 20

De arte graphica (tr. Dryden), **II:** 305

"Death and Doctor Hornbook" (Burns), **III:** 319

"Death and Dying Words of Poor Mailie, The" (Burns), **IV:** 314, 315

"Death by Water" (Eliot), **VII:** 144–145

"Death Clock, The" (Gissing), **V:** 437

"Death in the Desert, A" (Browning), **IV:** 358, 364, 367, 372

"Death of an Old Lady" (MacNeice), **VII:** 401

Death of a Salesman (Miller), **VI:** 286

"Death of Bernard Barton" (FitzGerald), **IV:** 353

Death of Christopher Marlowe, The (Hotson), **I:** 275

Death of Cuchulain, The (Yeats), **VI:** 215, 222

"Death of King George, The" (Betjeman), **VII:** 367

Death of Oenone, The, Akbar's Dream, and Other Poems (Tennyson), **IV:** 338

"Death of Simon Fuge, The" (Bennett), **VI:** 254

Death of Sir John Franklin, The (Swinburne), **V:** 333

"Death of the Duchess, The" (Eliot), **VII:** 150

"Death of the Lion, The" (James), **VI:** 69

"Death of the Rev. George Crabbe" (FitzGerald), **IV:** 353

Death of Wallenstein, The (Coleridge), **IV:** 56

"Death's Chill Between" (Rossetti), **V:** 252

"Death stands above me, whispering low" (Landor), **IV:** 98

"Death the Drummer" (Lewis), **VII:** 79

Death Under Sail (Snow), **VII:** 323

De augmentis scientiarium (Bacon), **I:** 260–261, 264; see also *Advancement of Learning, The*

Debates in Parliament (Johnson), **III:** 108, 122

de Beer, E. S., **II:** 276ₙ, 287

Debits and Credits (Kipling), **VI:** 173, 204

"Debt, The" (Kipling), **VI:** 201

Decadent movement, **V:** 399, 412, 413

Decadents, **VI:** 210, 447; **VII:** 292

Decameron (Boccaccio), **I:** 313

De casibus virorum illustrium (Boccaccio), **I:** 57, 214

"Decay of Lying, The" (Wilde), **V:** 407–408

"Deceased, The" (Douglas), **VII:** 440

Declaration of Rights (Shelley), **IV:** 208

Decline and Fall (Waugh), **VII:** 289–290, 291

Decline and Fall of the Roman Empire, The (Gibbon), **III:** 109, 221, **225–233**

Decorative Art in America: A Lecture (Wilde), **V:** 419

"Dedicatory Letter" (Ford), **VI:** 331

De doctrina christiana (Milton), **II:** 176

Defeat of Youth, The (Huxley), **VII:** 199

"Defence of an Essay of 'Dramatick Poesie' " (Dryden), **II:** 297, 305

Defence of English Commodities, A (Swift), **III:** 35

Defence of Guenevere, The (Morris), **V:** xxii, 293, 305–306, 312

Defence of Poesie, The (Sidney), **I:** 161–163, 169, 170, 173

"Defence of Poetry, A" (Shelley), **IV:** 168–169, 204, 208, 209

Defence of the Doctrine of Justification, A, . . . (Bunyan), **II:** 253

"Definition of Love, The" (Marvell), **II:** 208, 211, 215

Defoe, Daniel, **II:** 325; **III:** **1–14**, 24, 39, 41–42, 50–53, 62, 82; **V:** 288

"Deformed Mistress, The" (Suckling), **II:** 227

Deformed Transformed, The (Byron), **IV:** 193

De genealogia deorum (Boccaccio), **I:** 266

Degeneration (Nordau), **VI:** 107

"De Grey: A Romance" (James), **VI:** 25–26, 69

De Guiana Carmen Epicum (Chapman), **I:** 234

" 'De Gustibus—' " (Browning), **IV:** 356–357

De inventione (Cicero), **I:** 38–39

Deirdre (Yeats), **VI:** 218

"Dejection" (Coleridge), **IV:** 41, 49, 50

Dekker, Thomas, **I:** 68, 69; **II:** 3, 21, 47, 71, 89, 100

de la Mare, Walter, **III:** 340, 345; **V:** 268, 274; **VII:** xiii

"Delay Has Danger" (Crabbe), **III:** 285

Delight (Priestley), **VII:** 212

"Delight in Disorder" (Herrick), **II:** 104

"Demephon and Phillis" (Gower), **I:** 53–54

Demeter, and Other Poems (Tennyson), **IV:** 338

"Demeter and Persephone" (Tennyson) **IV:** 328

"Democracy" (Lawrence), **VII:** 87–88

Demon of Progress in the Arts, The (Lewis), **VII:** 74

Demos (Gissing), **V:** 432–433, 437

Denham, Sir John, **II:** 236, 238

"Deniall" (Herbert), **II:** 127, 128

Denis Duval (Thackeray), **V:** 27, 34, 36, 38

Dennis, John, **II:** 69, 310, 338, 340

Dennis, Nigel, **III:** 23, 37

"Dennis Haggarty's Wife" (Thackeray), **V:** 23–24

"Dennis Shand" (Rossetti), **V:** 239

Denry the Audacious (Bennett), see *Card, The*

Dent, Arthur, **II:** 241, 246

Denzil Quarrier (Gissing), **V:** 437

Departmental Ditties (Kipling), **VI:** 168, 204

De Profundis (Wilde), **V:** 416–417, 418, 419

De Quincey, Thomas, **III:** 338; **IV:** ix, xi–xii, xv, xviii, xxii, 49, 51, 137, **141–156**, 260, 261, 278; **V:** 353

De Quincey Memorials (ed. Japp), **IV:** 144, 155

"De Quincey on 'The Knocking at the Gate'" (Carnall), **IV:** 156

De rerum natura (tr. Evelyn), **II:** 275, 287

Derham, William, **III:** 49

Derry Down Derry, pseud. of Edward Lear

Dervorgilla (Gregory), **VI:** 315

De sapientia veterum (Bacon), **I:** 235, 266–267, 272

"Descent into the Maelstrom, The" (Poe), **III:** 339

"Descent of Odin, The" (Gray), **III:** 141

"Description of a City Shower, A" (Swift), **III:** 30

"Description of an Author's Bedchamber" (Goldsmith), **III:** 184

Description of Antichrist and His Ruin, A (Bunyan), **II:** 253

"Description of the Morning, A" (Swift), **III:** 30

Description of the Scenery of the Lakes in the North of England, A (Wordsworth), **IV:** 25

Description of the Western Islands (Martin), **III:** 117

Descriptive Catalogue of Pictures . . . , A (Blake), **III:** 305, 307

Descriptive Sketches (Wordsworth), **IV:** xv, 1, 2, 4–5, 24

de Selincourt, E., **IV:** 25

"Deserted Garden, The" (Browning), **IV:** 312

Deserted Parks, The (Carroll), **V:** 274

Deserted Village, The (Goldsmith), **III:** 177, 180, 185, 186–187, 191, 277

Desert Highway (Priestley), **VII:** 227–228

Desperate Remedies (Hardy), **VI:** 2, 19–20

"Despite and Still" (Graves), **VII:** 268

"Despondency, an Ode" (Burns), **III:** 315

"Destinie" (Cowley), **II:** 194, 195, 198

"Destiny and a Blue Cloak" (Hardy), **VI:** 20

"Destroyers in the Arctic" (Ross), **VII:** 433

detective fiction, **VI:** 338; **VII:** 323, 337–338, 395

De tranquillitate animi (tr. Wyatt), **I:** 99

"Development" (Browning), **IV:** 365

Development of Christian Doctrine, The (Newman), **V:** 340

"Development of Genius, The" (Browning), **IV:** 310

Devil and the Lady, The (Tennyson), **IV:** 338

Devil of Dowgate, The (Fletcher), **II:** 67

"Devil's Advice to Story-tellers, The" (Graves), **VII:** 259, 263

Devil's Disciple, The (Shaw), **VI:** 104, 105, 110, 112

"Devil's Due, The" (Swinburne), **V:** 332

Devil's Elixir, The (Hoffmann), **III:** 334, 345

Devil's Law-Case, The (Webster), **II:** 68, 82–83, 85

Devils of Loudon, The (Huxley), **VII:** 205–206

Devil's Walk, The (Coleridge and Southey), **IV:** 56

Devil's Walk, The (Shelley), **IV:** 208

Devlin, Christopher, **V:** 372, 373, 381

Devout Trental for Old John Clarke (Skelton), **I:** 86

D. G. Rossetti: A Critical Essay (Ford), **VI**: 332

"D. G. Rossetti as a Translator" (Doughty), **V**: 246

D. H. Lawrence: A Calendar of His Works (Sugar), **VII**: 104, 115, 123

D. H. Lawrence: Novelist (Leavis), **VII**: 101, 234–235, 252–253

Diabolical Principle and the Dithyrambic Spectator (Lewis), **VII**: 72, 76, 83

Dialogue Between the Devil, the Pope, and the Pretender, The (Fielding), **III**: 105

"Dialogue Between the Resolved Soul, and Created Pleasure, A" (Marvell), **II**: 208, 211, 216

"Dialogue Between the Soul and Body, A" (Marvell), **II**: 208, 211, 216

"Dialogue Between the Two Horses, The" (Marvell), **II**: 218

"Dialogue Between Thyrsis and Dorinda, A" (Marvell), **II**: 211

"Dialogue on Dramatic Poetry" (Eliot), **VII**: 157

Diana (Montemayor), **I**: 164, 302

Diana of the Crossways (Meredith), **V**: xxv, 227, 232–233, 234

"Diaphanéité" (Pater), **V**: 345, 348, 356

Diaries of Lewis Carroll, The (ed. Green), **V**: 264, 274

Diarmuid and Grania (Moore and Yeats), **VI**: 87, 96, 99

Diary (Evelyn), **II**: **274–280, 286–287**

Diary (Pepys), **II**: 274, **280–286, 288,** 310

Diary of a Dead Officer (West), **VI**: 423

Diary of a Journey into North Wales . . . , A (Johnson), **III**: 122

Diary of a Madman, The (Gogol), **III**: 345

Diary of a Man of Fifty, The (James), **VI**: 67, 69

Diary of Fanny Burney (Burney), **III**: 243

Diary, Reminiscences and Correspondence of H. Crabb Robinson, The, **IV**: 52, 56, 81

Dickens, Charles, **II**: 42; **III**: 151, 157, 340; **IV**: 27, 34, 38, 88, 240, 241, 247, 251, 252, 259, 295, 306; **V**: viii, ix, 3, 5, 6, 9, 14, 20, 22, **41–74,** 148, 182, 191, 424, 435; **VI**: viii

Dickens and Daughter (Storey), **V**: 72

Dickens and the Twentieth Century (ed. Cross and Pearson), **V**: 63, 73

Dickens from Pickwick to Dombey (Marcus), **V**: 46

"Dickens in Memory" (Gissing), **V**: 437

Dickens: Interviews and Recollections (ed. Collins), **V**: 46

Dickens Theatre, The (Garis), **V**: 70, 73

Dickens the Novelist (Leavis), **VII**: 250–251

Dickinson, Goldsworthy Lowes, **VI**: 398, 399

Dickson, Lovat, **VI**: 239

Dictionary of Madame de Sévigné (FitzGerald and Kerrich), **IV**: 349, 353

Dictionary of National Biography (ed. Stephen and Lee), **V**: xxv, 280–281, 290

Dictionary of the English Language, A (Johnson), **III**: 113–114, 115, 121

"Did any Punishment attend" (Sedley), **II**: 265

Did He Steal It? (Trollope), **V**: 102

Dido, Queen of Carthage (Marlowe), **I**: 278–279, **280–281, 292**

Die Räuber (Schiller), **IV**: xiv, 173

Dierdre of the Sorrows (Synge), **VI**: 310, 313

Die Spanier in Peru (Kotzebue), **III**: 254, 268

"Dietary" (Lydgate), **I**: 58

Differences in Judgement about Water Baptism . . . (Bunyan), **II**: 253

"Difficulties of a Statesman" (Eliot), **VII**: 152–153

"Diffugere Nives" (Housman), **VI**: 155

Dilecta (Ruskin), **V**: 184

Dilke, Charles, **IV**: 254, 262, 306

"Dill Pickle, A" (Mansfield), **VII**: 174

"Dinner at Poplar, A" (Dickens), **V**: 41, 47$_n$

"Dinner in the City, A" (Thackeray), **V**: 25

Diodorus Siculus (tr. Skelton), **I**: 82

"Diogenes and Plato" (Landor), **IV**: 91

Dipsychus (Clough), **V**: 156, 159, 161, 163–165, 167, 211

"Dirce" (Landor), **IV**: 96–97

Directions to Servants (Swift), **III**: 36

"Dirge" (Eliot), **VII**: 150

"Dirge for the New Sunrise" (Sitwell), **VII**: 137

"Dirge of Jephthah's Daughter, The: Sung by the Virgins" (Herrick), **II**: 113

"Disabled" (Owen), **VI:** 447, 451, 452

"Dîs aliter visum; or, Le Byron de nos jours" (Browning), **IV:** 366, 369

Disappointment, The (Southern), **II:** 305

"Discharge, The" (Herbert), **II:** 127

Discontented Colonel, The (Suckling), **II:** 238

Discourse of Civil Life (Bryskett), **I:** 124

Discourse of the Building of the House of God, A (Bunyan), **II:** 253

Discourse of the Contests and Dissensions between the Nobles and the Commons in Athens and Rome (Swift), **III:** 17, 35

Discourse on Pastoral Poetry, A (Pope), **III:** 56

Discourse on Satire (Dryden), **II:** 297

Discourse on the Love of Our Country (Price), **IV:** 126

Discourse on the Pindarique Ode, A (Congreve), **II:** 346–347

Discourse on 2 Corinthians, i, 9 . . . , A (Crabbe), **III:** 286

Discourses by Way of Essays (Cowley), **III:** 40

Discourses in America (Arnold), **V:** 216

Discourse upon Comedy, A (Farquhar), **II:** 332, 355

Discourse upon the Pharisee and the Publicane, A (Bunyan), **II:** 253

Discoveries (Jonson), **I:** 270

Discovery of Guiana, The (Ralegh), **I:** 145, 146, 149, 151–153

Discovery of the Future, The (Wells), **VI:** 244

"Disdaine Returned" (Carew), **II:** 225

Disenchantment (Montague), **VII:** 421

Disraeli, Benjamin, **IV:** xii, xvi, xviii, xix, xx, xxiii, 271, 288, **292–309; V:** viii, x, xxiv, 2, 22; **VII:** xxi

Disraeli (Blake), **IV:** 307, 308

"Dissatisfaction" (Traherne), **II:** 192

Dissenters, **II:** 2–4

"Distracted Preacher, The" (Hardy), **VI:** 22

"Distraction" (Vaughan), **II:** 188

Distress'd Wife, The (Gay), **III:** 67

"Disturber of the Traffic, The" (Kipling), **VI:** 169, **170–172**

Divine and Moral Songs for Children (Watts), **III:** 299

Divine Comedy, The (Dante), **II:** 148; **III:** 306; **IV:** 93, 187, 229

"Divine Judgments" (Blake), **III:** 300

Divine Poems (Waller), **II:** 238

"Divine Wrath and Mercy" (Blake), **III:** 300

"Division, The" (Hardy), **VI:** 17

Dixon, Richard Watson, **V:** 362–365, 371, 372, 377, 379; **VI:** 76, 83, 167

Dixon Hunt, John, **VI:** 167

"Dizzy" (Strachey), **IV:** 292

Dobell, Sydney, **IV:** 310; **V:** 144–145

Dobrée, Bonamy, **II:** 362, 364; **III:** 33, 51, 53; **V:** 221, 234; **VI:** xi, 200–203; **VII:** xxii

Doctor, The (Southey), **IV:** 67$_n$, 71

Doctor Birch and His Young Friends (Thackeray), **V:** 38

Doctor Faustus (film), **III:** 344

Doctor Faustus (Marlowe), **I:** 212, 279–280, **287–290**

Dr. Goldsmith's Roman History Abridged by Himself . . . (Goldsmith), **III:** 191

Dr. Jekyll and Mr. Hyde (Stevenson), see *Strange Case of Dr. Jekyll and Mr. Hyde, The*

Doctors' Delusions, Crude Criminology, and Sham Education (Shaw), **VI:** 129

Doctor's Dilemma, The (Shaw), **VI:** xv, 116, 129

"Doctor's Legend, The" (Hardy), **VI:** 20

Doctor Thorne (Trollope), **V:** xxii, 93, 101

"Dr. Woolacott" (Forster), **VI:** 406

Dr. Wortle's School (Trollope), **V:** 100, 102

Doctrine and Discipline of Divorce . . . , The (Milton) **II:** 175

"Doctrine of Scattered Occasions, The" (Bacon), **I:** 261

Doctrine of the Law and Grace Unfolded, The (Bunyan), **II:** 253

Dodge, Mabel, **VII:** 109

Dodgson, Charles Lutwidge, see Carroll, Lewis

"Does It Matter?" (Sassoon), **VI:** 430

"Dog and the Waterlily, The" (Cowper), **III:** 220

Dog Beneath the Skin, The (Auden and Isherwood), **VII:** 312, 380, 385

Doktor Faustus (Mann), **III:** 344

Dolben, Digby Mackworth, **VI:** 72, 75

Doll's House, A (Ibsen), **IV:** xxiii, 118–119; **V:** xxiv; **VI:** ix, 111

"Doll's House, The" (Mansfield), **VII:** 175

Dolores (Compton-Burnett), **VII:** 59, 68

"Dolores" (Swinburne), **V:** 313, 320–321

"Dolorida" (Swinburne), **V:** 332

Dombey and Son (Dickens), **IV:** 34; **V:** xxi, 42, 44, 47, 53, 57–59, 70, 71

"Domicilium" (Hardy), **VI:** 14

Don Fernando (Maugham), **VI:** 371

"Dong with a Luminous Nose, The" (Lear), **V:** 85

Don Juan (Byron), **I:** 291; **II:** 102$_n$; **IV:** xvii, 171, 172, 173, 178, 183, 184, 185, **187–191,** 192

Donne, John, **I:** **352–369; II:** 102, 113, 114, 118, 121–124, 126–128, 132, 134–138, 140–143, 147, 185, 196, 197, 209, 215, 221, 222, 226; **IV:** 327

Donne, William Bodham, **IV:** 340, 344, 351

Donnelly, M. C., **V:** 427, 438

Donohue, J. W., **III:** 268

Don Quixote (Cervantes), **II:** 49; **IV:** 190; **V:** 46

Don Quixote in England (Fielding), **III:** 105

Don Sebastian, King of Portugal (Dryden), **II:** 305

"Doom of the Griffiths, The" (Gaskell), **V:** 15

Doom of Youth, The (Lewis), **VII:** 72

"Door in the Wall, The" (Wells), **VI:** 235, 244

Dorando, A Spanish Tale (Boswell), **III:** 247

Dorian Gray (Wilde), see *Picture of Dorian Gray, The*

"Dorinda's sparkling Wit, and Eyes" (Dorset), **II:** 262

Dorothy Wordsworth (Selincourt), **IV:** 143

Dorset, earl of (Charles Sackville), **II:** 255, **261–263,** 266, 268, 270–271

Dorset Farm Laborer Past and Present, The, (Hardy), **VI:** 20

Dostoevsky: The Making of a Novelist (Simmons), **V:** 46

Double-Dealer, The (Congreve), **II:** 338, 341–342, 350

Double Falsehood, The (Theobald), **II:** 66, 87

Double Marriage, The (Fletcher and Massinger), **II:** 66

Doublets: A Word-Puzzle (Carroll), **V:** 273

"Double Vision of Michael Robartes, The" (Yeats), **VI:** 217

Doughty, Oswald, **V:** xi, xxvii, 246, 297$_n$, 307

Douglas, Lord Alfred, **V:** 411, 416–417, 420

Douglas, Gavin, **I:** 116–118; **III:** 311

Douglas, Keith, **VII:** xxii, 422, **440–444**

Douglas, Norman, **VI:** **293–305**

Douglas Cause, The (Boswell), **III:** 247

Douglas Jerrold's Weekly (periodical), **V:** 144

"Dover" (Auden), **VII:** 379

Do What You Will (Huxley), **VII:** 201

"Down" (Graves), **VII:** 264

Down and Out in Paris and London (Orwell), **VII:** xx, 275, 277

"Down by the Sally-Garden" (Yeats), **VII:** 368

Downfall and Death of King Oedipus, The (FitzGerald), **IV:** 353

Downs, Brian, **III:** 84, 93

"Downs, The" (Bridges), **VI:** 78

Down There on a Visit (Isherwood), **VII:** 315–316

Dowson, Ernest, **V:** 441; **VI:** 210

Doyle, Arthur Conan, **III:** 341, 345

"Do you remember me? or are you proud?" (Landor), **IV:** 99

Drabble, Margaret, **VI:** 247, 253, 268

Dracula (film), **III:** 342

Dracula (Stoker), **III:** 334, 342, 345

Drafts and Fragments of Verse (Collins), **II:** 323$_n$

Dragon of the Apocalypse (Carter), **VII:** 114

Drake, Nathan, **III:** 51

Drama in Muslin, A (Moore), **VI:** 86, 89, **90–91,** 98

"Drama of Exile, A" (Browning), **IV:** 313

Dramatic Character in the English Romantic Age (Donohue), **III:** 268$_n$

Dramatic Idyls (Browning), **IV:** xxiii, 358, 374; **V:** xxiv

dramatic lyric, **VI:** 217

Dramatic Lyrics (Browning), **IV:** xx, 374

dramatic monologue, **IV:** 359–362

Dramatic Romances and Lyrics (Browning), **IV:** 374

Dramatic Works of Richard Brinsley Sheridan, The (ed. Price), **III:** 258

Dramatis Personae (Browning), **IV:** xxii, 358, 364, 374

Dramatis Personae (Yeats), **VI:** 317

Drapier's Letters, The (Swift), **III:** 20$_n$, 28, 31, 35

Drayton, Michael, **I:** 196, 278; **II:** 68, 134, 138

"Dread of Height, The" (Thompson), **V:** 444

"Dream, The" (Galsworthy), **VI:** 280

"Dream-Fugue" (De Quincey), **IV:** 153–154

"Dreaming Spires" (Campbell), **VII:** 430

Dream of Destiny, A (Bennett), **VI:** 262

"Dream of Eugene Aram, the Murderer, The" (Hood), **IV:** 256, 261–262, 264, 267

Dream of John Ball, A (Morris), **V:** 301, 302–303, 305, 306

Dream of Scipio, The (Cicero), **IV:** 189

Dream of the Rood, The, **I:** 11

"Dreams" (Spenser), **I:** 123

"Dreams Old and Nascent" (Lawrence), **VII:** 118

"Dream-Tryst" (Thompson), **V:** 444

Drebbel, Cornelius, **I:** 268

"Dressing" (Vaughan), **II:** 186

Drew, Philip, **IV:** xiii, xxiv, 375

"Drinking" (Cowley), **II:** 198

"Drink to Me Only *with Thine Eyes*" (Jonson), **I:** 346; **VI:** 16

"Drummer Hodge" (Housman), **VI:** 161

Drummond of Hawthornden, William, **I:** 328, 349

Drums of Father Ned, The (O'Casey), **VII:** 10–11

Drums Under the Windows (O'Casey), **VII:** 9, 12

Drunken Sailor, The (Cary), **VII:** 186, 191

Dry Salvages, The (Eliot), **V:** 241; **VII:** 143, 144, 152, 154, 155

Dryden, John, **I:** 176, 327, 328, 341, 349; **II:** 166–167, 195, 198, 200, **289–306,** 325, 338, 340, 348, 350, 352, 354–355; **III:** 40, 47, 68, 73–74, 118; **IV:** 93, 196, 287; **V:** 376

Dryden, John, the younger, **II:** 305

Du Bellay, Joachim, **I:** 126; **V:** 345

Dubliners (Joyce), **VII:** xiv, 41, 43–45, 47–52; critical studies, **VII:** 57

"Duchess of Hamptonshire, The" (Hardy), **VI:** 22

Duchess of Malfi, The (Webster), **II:** 68, 70–73, **76–78,** 79, 81, 82, 84, 85

Duchess of Padua, The (Wilde), **V:** 419

"Duel, The" (Conrad), **VI:** 148

"Duel of the Crabs, The" (Dorset), **II:** 271

Duenna, The (Sheridan), **III:** 253, 257, 259–261, 270

Due Preparations for the Plague (Defoe), **III:** 13

Dugdale, Florence Emily, **VI:** 17$_n$

Dugdale, Sir William, **II:** 274

Dugmore, C. W., **I:** 177$_n$

Dujardin, Edouard, **VI:** 87

Duke of Gandia, The (Swinburne), **V:** 333

Duke of Guise, The (Dryden), **II:** 305

Duke's Children, The (Trollope), **V:** 96, 99, 101, 102

"Duke's Reappearance, The" (Hardy), **VI:** 22

"Dulce et Decorum Est" (Owen), **VI:** 448, 451

"Dull London" (Lawrence), **VII:** 94, 116, 121

"Dulwich Gallery, The" (Hazlitt), **IV:** 135–136

Dumas *père*, Alexandre, **III:** 332, 334, 339

du Maurier, Daphne, **III:** 343

du Maurier, George, **V:** 403

"Dumnesse" (Traherne), **II:** 189

Dunbar, William, **I:** 23

Dunciad, The (Pope), **II:** 259, 311; **III:** 73, 77, 95; **IV:** 187

Dunciad of Today, The; and, The Modern Aesop (Disraeli), **IV:** 308

Dun Cow, The (Lander), **IV:** 100

Dun Emer Press, **VI:** 221

Dunn, Nell, **VI:** 271

Dunne, John William, **VII:** 209, 210

Dunsany, Lord Edward, **III:** 340

Duns Scotus, John, **V:** 363, 370, 371

"Duns Scotus's Oxford" (Hopkins), **V:** 363, 367, 370

Dunton, John, **III:** 41

Dupee, F. W., **VI:** 31, 45

"Duriesdyke" (Swinburne), **V:** 333

"During Wind and Rain" (Hardy), **VI:** 17

Dutch Courtesan, The (Marston), **II:** 30, 40

"Duty—that's to say complying" (Clough), **V:** 160

Dyer, Sir Edward, **I:** 123

Dyer, John, **IV:** 199

Dyer's Hand, The, and Other Essays (Auden), **V:** 46; **VII:** 394, 395

Dyet of Poland, The (Defoe), **III:** 13

"Dying Swan, The" (Tennyson), **IV:** 329

"Dykes, The" (Kipling), **VI:** 203

Dynamics of a Particle, The (Carroll), **V:** 274

Dynasts, The: A Drama of the Napoleonic Wars (Hardy), **VI:** 6–7, **10–12**

Dyson, A. E., **III:** 51

dystopian literature, **VII:** xx; see also utopian literature

"Dyvers thy death doo dyverslye bemone" (Surrey), **I:** 115

E

Eagle's Nest, The (Ruskin), **V:** 184

Earle, John, **IV:** 286

"Earl Robert" (Swinburne), **V:** 333

Early Essays (Eliot), **V:** 200

Early Italian Poets, The (Rossetti), **V:** 245

Early Kings of Norway, The (Carlyle), **IV:** 250

Earthly Paradise, The (Morris), **V:** xxiii, **296–299,** 302, 304, 306

Earths in Our Solar System (Swedenborg), **III:** 297

"East Coker" (Eliot), **II:** 173; **VII:** 154, 155

"Easter" (Herbert), **II:** 128

"Easter Day" (Crashaw), **II:** 183

"Easter Day, Naples, 1849" (Clough), **V:** 165

"Easter Day II" (Clough), **V:** 159

Easter Greeting for Every Child Who Loves "Alice," An (Carroll), **V:** 273

"Easter Hymn" (Housman), **VI:** 161

Eastern Front, The (Churchill), **VI:** 359

"Easter 1916" (Yeats), **VI:** 219, 220

Eastern Tales (Voltaire), **III:** 327

Easter Rebellion of 1916, **VI:** 212; **VII:** 3

"Easter Wings" (Herbert), **II:** 128

"East London" (Arnold), **V:** 209

East of Suez (Maugham), **VI:** 369

Eastward Ho! (Chapman, Jonson, Marston), **I:** 234, 254; **II:** 30, 40

Eaton, H. A., **IV:** 142$_n$, 155, 156

Ebb-Tide, The (Stevenson), **V:** 384, 387, 390, 396

Ecce Ancilla Domini! (Rossetti), **V:** 236, 248

Ecclesiastical Polity (Hooker), **II:** 147

Ecclesiastical Sonnets (Wordsworth), **IV:** 22, 25

"Echo from Willowwood, An" (Rossetti), **V:** 259

"Eclogue for Christmas, An" (MacNeice), **VII:** 416

Eclogues (Vergil), **III:** 222$_n$

Ecstasy, The (Donne), **I:** 238, 355, 358

Edel, Leon, **VI:** 49, 55

"Eden" (Traherne), **II:** 189

Eden End (Priestley), **VII:** 224

Edinburgh: Picturesque Notes (Stevenson), **V:** 395

Edinburgh Review (periodical), **III:** 276, 285; **IV:** xvi, 129, 145, 269–270, 272, 278

Edith Sitwell (Bowra), **VII:** 141

Editor's Tales, An (Trollope), **V:** 102

Education and the University (Leavis), **VII:** 238, 241

"Education of Otis Yeere, The" (Kipling), **VI:** 183, 184

Edward I (Peele), **I:** 205–206, 208

Edward II (Marlowe), **I:** 278, **286–287**

Edward III (anon.), **V:** 328

Edwardian materialism, **VII:** xii

Edward Lear in Greece (Lear), **V:** 87

Edward Lear's Indian Journal (ed. Murphy), **V:** 78, 79, 87

Edwards, H.L.R., **I:** 87

"Edwin and Angelina: A Ballad" (Goldsmith), **III:** 185, 191

Edwin Drood (Dickens), **V:** xxiii, 42, 69, 72

"Edwin Morris" (Tennyson), **IV:** 326$_n$

Egan, Pierce, **IV:** 260$_n$

Egoist, The (Meredith), **V:** x, xxiv, 227, 230–232, 234

"Egypt" (Fraser), **VII:** 425

Eight Dramas of Calderón (tr. FitzGerald), **IV:** 353

Eighteen-Eighties, The (ed. de la Mare), **V:** 268, 274

"Eight o'clock" (Housman), **VI:** 160

Eight or Nine Wise Words about Letter-Writing (Carroll), **V:** 273

ΕΙΚΟΝΟΚΛΑΣΤΗΣ: . . . (Milton), **II:** 175

Ekblad, Inga Stina, **II:** 77, 86

Elder Brother, The (Fletcher and Massinger), **II:** 66

Elders and Betters (Compton-Burnett), **VII:** 63, 66

Elder Statesman, The (Eliot), **VII:** 161, 162

Eldest Son, The (Galsworthy), **VI:** 269, 287

Election, An (Swinburne), **V:** 332

Elections to the Hebdomadal Council, The (Carroll), **V:** 274

"Elegiac Stanzas, Suggested by a Picture of Peele Castle . . ." (Wordsworth), **IV:** 21–22

"Elegie, An. Princesse Katherine" (Lovelace), **II:** 230

Elegies (Donne), **I:** 360–361

Elegies (Johannes Secundus), **II:** 108

Elegies for the Dead in Cyrenaica (Henderson), **VII:** 425

"Elegie upon the Death of . . . Dr. John Donne" (Carew), **II:** 223

"Elegy in April and September" (Owen), **VI:** 453

"Elegy on Dead Fashion" (Sitwell), **VII:** 133

Elegy on Dicky and Dolly, An (Swift), **III:** 36

Elegy on Dr. Donne, An (Walton), **II:** 136

"Elegy on Marlowe's Untimely Death" (Nashe), **I:** 278

"Elegy on the Death of a Mad Dog" (Goldsmith), **III:** 184

Elegy on the Death of an Amiable Young Lady . . . , An (Boswell), **III:** 247

Elegy on the Usurper O. C., An (Dryden), **II:** 304

"Elegy to the Memory of an Unfortunate Lady" (Pope), **III:** 70, 288

Elegy upon the Death of My Lord Francis Villiers, An (Marvell), **II:** 219

"Elegy Written in a Country Churchyard" (Gray), **III:** 119, 137, **138–139**, 144–145

Elementary, The (Mulcaster), **I:** 122

Elements of Drawing, The (Ruskin), **V:** 184

Elements of Perspective, The (Ruskin), **V:** 184

Eleonora: A Panegyrical Poem (Dryden), **II:** 304

Elia, pseud. of Charles Lamb

"Elinor and Marianne" (Austen), see *Sense and Sensibility*

Eliot, George, **III:** 157; **IV:** 238, 323; **V:** ix–x, xviii, xxii–xxiv, 2, 6, 7, 14, 45, 52, 56, 57, 63, 66, 67, **187–201**, 212; **VI:** 23

Eliot, T. S., **II:** 148; **IV:** 271; **V:** xxv, 241, 309, 402; **VII:** xii–xiii, xv, 34, **143–170**; and Matthew Arnold, **V:** 204, 205–206, 210, 215; and Yeats, **VI:** 207, 208; influence on modern literature, **I:** 98; **VII:** xii–xiii, xv, 34, 143–144, 153–154, 165–166; list of collected essays, **VII:** 169–170; literary criticism, **I:** 232, 275, 280; **II:** 16, 42, 83, 179, 196, 204, 208, 219; **III:** 51, 305; **IV:** 195, 234; **V:** 204–206, 210, 215, 310, 367; **VI:** 207, 226; **VII:** 162–165; style, **II:** 173; **IV:** 323, 329; in drama, **VII:** 157–162; in poetry, **VII:** 144–157

Elizabethan blank verse, **I:** 280, 298

Elizabeth and Her German Garden (Forster), **VI:** 406

Elizabethan drama, **I:** 198, 206–207, 212–228, 298, 336

Elizabethan Drama and Shakespeare's Early Plays (Talbert), **I:** 224

Elizabethan lyric verse, **I:** 97–98, 291; **VII:** 41

Elizabethan tragedy, **I:** 212–229, 284; **II:** 78–79

Elizabeth Cooper (Moore), **VI:** 96, 99

"Elizas, The" (Gurney), **VI:** 425

"Ellen Orford" (Crabbe), **III:** 281

Ellen Terry and Bernard Shaw, a Correspondence (ed. St. John), **VI:** 130

Ellis, Havelock, **I:** 281

Ellis-Fermor, U. M., **I:** 284, 292

El maestro de danzar (Calderón), **II:** 313$_n$

"Elm Tree, The" (Hood), **IV:** 261–262, 264

"Eloisa to Abelard" (Pope), **III:** 70, 75–76, 77; **V:** 319, 321

Eloquence of the British Senate, The (Hazlitt), **IV:** 130, 139

Elton, Oliver, **III:** 51

Emancipated, The (Gissing), **V:** 437

Embarrassments (James), **VI:** 49, 67

Emerson, Ralph Waldo, **IV:** xx, 54, 81, 240; **V:** xxv

E. M. Forster: A Study (Trilling), **VI:** 413

E. M. Forster: A Tribute, with Selections from His Writings on India (Natwar-Singh), **VI:** 413

E. M. Forster: The Critical Heritage (ed. Gardner), **VI:** 413

Emilia in England (Meredith), see *Sandra Belloni*

Emily Brontë: A Biography (Gérin), **V:** 153

Eminent Victorians (Strachey), **V:** 13, 157, 170

Emma (Austen), **IV:** xvii, 108, 109, 111, 112, 113, 114, 115, 117, 119, 120, 122; **VI:** 106

Emma (Brontë), **V:** 151, 152

Empedocles on Etna (Arnold), **IV:** 231; **V:** xxi, 206, 207, 209, 210, 211, 216

"Emperor Alexander and Capo d'Istria" (Landor), **IV:** 92

"Emperor and the Little Girl, The" (Shaw), **VI:** 120

Empson, William, **I:** 282; **II:** 124, 130; **V:** 367, 381

Empty Purse, The (Meredith), **V:** 223, 234

"Enallos and Cymodameia" (Landor), **IV:** 96

Enchafèd Flood, The (Auden), **VII:** 380, 394

Enchanted Isle, The (Dryden), **I:** 327

Enchantress, The, and Other Poems (Browning), **IV:** 321

"End, The" (Owen), **VI:** 449

Endiomion (Lyly), **I:** 202

End of a War, The (Read), **VI:** 436, 437

End of the Beginning, The (O'Casey), **VII:** 12

End of the Chapter (Galsworthy), **VI:** 275, 282

"End of the Tether, The" (Conrad), **VI:** 148

Ends and Means (Huxley), **VII:** xvii, 205

Endymion (Disraeli), **IV:** xxiii, 294, 295, 296, 306, 307, 308; **V:** xxiv

"Endymion" (Keats), **III:** 174, 338; **IV:** x, xvii, 205, 211, 214, 216–217, 218, 222–224, 227, 229, 230, 233, 235

Enemies of Promise (Connolly), **VI:** 363

"Enemy Dead, The" (Gutteridge), **VII:** 433

"Enemy Interlude" (Lewis), **VII:** 71

Enemy of the People, An (Ibsen), **VI:** ix

Enemy of the Stars, The (Lewis), **VII:** 72, 73, 74–75

England and the Italian Question (Arnold), **V:** 216

England in the Age of Wycliffe (Trevelyan), **VI:** 385–386

"England, My England" (Lawrence), **VII:** xv, 114

England, My England, and Other Stories (Lawrence), **VII:** 114

"England's Answer" (Kipling), **VI:** 192

England's Helicon, **I:** 291

England's Pleasant Land (Forster), **VI:** 411

England Under Queen Anne (Trevelyan), **VI: 391–393**

England Under the Stuarts (Trevelyan), **VI:** 386

England Your England (Orwell), **VII:** 282

English Bards and Scotch Reviewers (Byron), **IV:** x, xvi, 129, 171, 192

English Bible, **I: 370–388;** list of versions, **I:** 387

English Comic Characters, The (Priestley), **VII:** 211

English Eccentrics, The (Sitwell), **VII:** 127

English Folk-Songs (ed. Barrett), **V:** 263$_n$

English Historical Review, **VI:** 387

English Hours (James), **VI:** 46, 67

English Humour (Priestley), **VII:** 213

English Humourists of the Eighteenth Century, The (Thackeray), **III:** 124, 146$_n$; **V:** 20, 31, 38

English Journey (Priestley), **VII:** 212, 213–214

English Literature and Society in the Eighteenth Century (Stephen), **III:** 41; **V:** 290

English Literature, 1815–1832 (ed. Jack), **IV:** 40, 140

English Literature in Our Time and the University (Leavis), **VII:** 169, 235, 236–237, 253

"English Mail-Coach, The" (De Quincey), **IV:** 149, 153, 155

Englishman (periodical), **III:** 7, 50, 53

"Englishman in Italy, The" (Browning), **IV:** 368

Englishman Looks at the World, An (Wells), **VI:** 244

"Englishmen and Italians" (Trevelyan), **V:** 227; **VI:** 388$_n$

English Men of Letters series, **VI:** 336

English Mirror, The (Whetstone), **I:** 282

English Novel, The (Ford), **VI:** 322, 332

English Novel, The: A Short Critical History (Allen), **V:** 219

English People, The (Orwell), **VII:** 282

English Poems (Blunden), **VI:** 429

"English Poet, An" (Pater), **V:** 356, 357

English Poetry (Bateson), **IV:** 217, 323$_n$, 339

English Poetry and the English Language (Leavis), **VII:** 234

English Poetry of the First World War (Owen), **VI:** 453

English Poets (Browning), **IV:** 321

English Prisons Under Local Government (Webb), **VI:** 129

English Renaissance drama, **I:** 191–192

"English Renaissance of Art, The" (Wilde), **V:** 403–404

English Review (periodical), **VI:** xi–xii, 294, 323–324; **VII:** 89

English Revolution, 1688–1689 (Trevelyan), **VI:** 391

"English School, An" (Kipling), **VI:** 201

English Seamen (Southey and Bell), **IV:** 71

English Social History: A Survey of Six Centuries (Trevelyan), **VI:** xv, 393–394

English Songs of Italian Freedom (Trevelyan), **V:** 227

English symbolist tradition, see symbolism

English Town in the Last Hundred Years (Betjeman), **VII:** 360

English Traits (Emerson), **IV:** 54

English Utilitarians, The (Stephen), **V:** 279, 288–289

Enoch Arden (Tennyson), **IV:** xxii, 388; **V:** 6_n

Enough Is as Good as a Feast (Wager), **I:** 213

Enquiry Concerning Political Justice, An (Godwin), **IV:** xv, 181

Enquiry into the Causes of the Late Increase of Robbers (Fielding), **III:** 104

Enquiry into the Occasional Conformity of Dissenters . . . , An (Defoe), **III:** 12

Enquiry into the Present State of Polite Learning in Europe, An (Goldsmith), **III:** 179, 191

"Enter a Dragoon" (Hardy), **VI:** 22

Entertainment (Middleton), **II:** 3

"Entreating of Sorrow" (Ralegh), **I:** 147–148

"Eolian Harp, The" (Coleridge), **IV:** 46

Epicoene (Jonson), **I:** 339, 341

"Epicure, The" (Cowley), **II:** 198

"Epicurus, Leontion and Ternissa" (Landor), **IV:** 94, 96–97

epigram, **IV:** 96–99

Epigram CXX (Jonson), **I:** 347

Epigrammatum sacrorum liber (Crashaw), **II:** 179, 201

Epilogue (Graves), **VII:** 261

Epilogue to the Satires (Pope), **III:** 74, 78

"Epipsychidion" (Shelley), **IV:** xviii, 204, 208; **VI:** 401

Epistles to the King and Duke (Wycherley), **II:** 321

Epistle to a Canary (Browning), **IV:** 321

Epistle to a Lady . . ., An (Swift), **III:** 36

Epistle to Augustus (Pope), **II:** 196

Epistle to Cobham, An (Pope), see *Moral Essays*

"Epistle to Davie" (Burns), **III:** 316

Epistle to Dr. Arbuthnot (Pope), **III:** 71, 74–75, 78

"Epistle to Henry Reynolds" (Drayton), **I:** 196

Epistle to Her Grace Henrietta . . . , An (Gay), **III:** 67

"Epistle to John Hamilton Reynolds" (Keats), **IV:** 221

Epistle to . . . Lord Carteret, An (Swift), **III:** 35

"Epistle to Mr. Dryden, An, . . ." (Wycherley), **II:** 322

Epistle to the . . . Earl of Burlington, An (Pope), see *Moral Essays*

Epistle upon an Epistle, An (Swift), **III:** 35

Epistola adversus Jovinianum (St. Jerome), **I:** 35

Epitaphium Damonis (Milton), **II:** 175

"Epitaph on a Jacobite" (Macaulay), **IV:** 283

"Epitaph on an Army of Mercenaries" (Housman), **VI:** 161, 415–416

Epitaph on George Moore (Morgan), **VI:** 86

"Epitaph on the Admirable Dramaticke Poet, W. Shakespeare, An" (Milton), **II:** 175

"Epitaph on the Lady Mary Villers" (Carew), **II:** 224

"Epithalamion" (Hopkins), **V:** 376, 377

Epithalamion (Spenser), **I:** 130–131; see also *Amoretti and Epithalamion*

"Epithalamion for Gloucester" (Lydgate), **I:** 58

"Epithalamion Thamesis" (Spenser), **I:** 123

Epping Hunt, The (Hood), **IV:** 256, 257, 267

Erdman, D. V., **III:** 289_n, 307

Erechtheus (Swinburne), **V:** 314, 331, 332

Eros and Psyche (Bridges), **VI:** 83

"Erotion" (Swinburne), **V:** 320

Erskine, Andrew, **III**: 247

Escape (Galsworthy), **VI**: 275, 287

"Escaped Cock, The" (Lawrence), **VII**: 91, 115

"Escorial, The" (Hopkins), **V**: 361

espionage stories, **VI**: 367; **VII**: 217

Essais (Montaigne), **III**: 39

Essai sur l'étude de la littérature (Gibbon), **III**: 222, 223

Essay Concerning Human Understanding (Locke), **III**: 22

"Essay Concerning Humour in Comedy, An" (Congreve), see *Concerning Humour in Comedy*

Essayes (Cornwallis), **III**: 39

Essay of Dramatick Poesy (Dryden), **I**: 328, 349; **II**: 301, 302, 305; **III**: 40

"Essay on *Burmese Days*" (Orwell), **VII**: 276

"Essay on Christianity, An" (Shelley), **IV**: 199, 209

Essay on Comedy and the Uses of the Comic Spirit, An (Meredith), **V**: 224–225, 234

Essay on Criticism, An (Pope), **II**: 197; **III**: 68, 72, 77

Essay on Man, An (Pope), **III**: 72, 76, 77–78, 280

Essay on Mind, An (Browning), **IV**: 310, 316, 321

"Essay on Percy Bysshe Shelley, An" (Browning), **IV**: 357, 366, 374

Essay on the Dramatic Poetry of the Last Age (Dryden), **I**: 328

Essay on the External Use of Water . . . , An (Smollett), **III**: 158

Essay on the First Book of T. Lucretius Carus de Rerum Natura, An (Evelyn), see *De rerum natura*

Essay on the Genius and Writings of Pope (Warton), **III**: 170$_n$

Essay on the Genius of George Cruikshank, An (Thackeray), **V**: 37

Essay on the History and Reality of Apparitions, An (Defoe), **III**: 14

Essay on the Idea of Comedy (Meredith), **I**: 201–202

Essay on the Lives and Works of Our Uneducated Poets (Southey), **IV**: 71

Essay on the Principle of Population (Malthus), **IV**: xvi, 127

Essay on the Principles of Human Action, An (Hazlitt), **IV**: 128, 139

Essay on the Theatre: Or, A Comparison Between the Laughing and Sentimental Comedy (Goldsmith), **III**: 187, 256

Essay on the Theory of the Earth (Cuvier), **IV**: 181

Essays (Bacon), **I**: 258, 259, 260, 271; **III**: 39

Essays (Goldsmith), **III**: 180

Essays and Leaves from a Note-book (Eliot), **V**: 200

Essays and Reviews (Newman), **V**: 340

Essays and Studies (Swinburne), **V**: 298, 332

Essays From "The Guardian" (Pater), **V**: 357

Essays Illustrative of The Tatler (Drake), **III**: 51

Essays in Criticism (Arnold), **III**: 277; **V**: xxiii, 203, 204–205, 212, 213, 214, 215, 216

Essays in Divinity (Donne), **I**: 353, 360, 363

Essays in London and Elsewhere (James), **VI**: 49, 67

Essays in Verse and Prose (Cowley), **II**: 195

Essays, Moral and Political (Southey), **IV**: 71

Essays of Elia (Lamb), **IV**: xviii, 73, 74, 75, 76, 82–83, 85

Essays of Five Decades (Priestley), **VII**: 212

Essays on Freethinking and Plainspeaking (Stephen), **V**: 283, 289

Essays on His Own Times (Coleridge), **IV**: 56

Essays, Theological and Literary (Hutton), **V**: 157, 170

Essay Towards an Abridgement of the English History, An (Burke), **III**: 205

Essay upon Projects, An (Defoe), **III**: 12

Essence of Christianity, The (tr. Eliot), **V**: 200

Essence of the Douglas Cause, The (Boswell), **III**: 247

Esther Waters (Moore), **VI**: ix, xii, 87, 89, 91–92, 96, 98

Eternal Moment, The (Forster), **VI**: 399, 400

Etherege, Sir George, **II**: 255, 256, **266–269, 271,** 305

Etherege and the Seventeenth-Century Comedy of Manners (Underwood), **II**: 256$_n$

Ethical Characters (Theophrastus), **II**: 68

Ethics of the Dust, The (Ruskin), **V**: 180, 184

Etruscan Places (Lawrence), **VII**: 116, 117

Euclid and His Modern Rivals (Carroll), **V**: 264, 274

Eugene Aram (Bulwer-Lytton), **IV**: 256; **V**: 22, 46

"Eugene Aram" (Hood), see "Dream of Eugene Aram, the Murderer, The"

"Eugene Pickering" (James), **VI:** 69

Eugenia (Chapman), **I:** 236, 240

Eugenius Philalethes, pseud. of Thomas Vaughan

Euphranor: A Dialogue on Youth (FitzGerald), **IV:** 344, 353

Euphues and His England (Lyly), **I:** 194, 195–196

Euphues, the Anatomy of Wit (Lyly), **I:** 165, 193–196

euphuism, **I:** 165–166, 196, 209

Euripides, **IV:** 358; **V:** 321–324

"Europe" (James), **VI:** 69

Europeans, The (James), **VI:** 29–31

Europe. A Prophecy (Blake), **III:** 302, 307

"Eurydice" (Sitwell), **VII:** 136–137

Eurydice, a Farce (Fielding), **III:** 105

Eustace Diamonds, The (Trollope), **V:** xxiv, 96, 98, 101, 102

Evan Harrington (Meredith), **V:** xxii, 227, 234

Evans, Abel, **II:** 335

Evans, G. Blakemore, **I:** 326

Evans, Marian, see Eliot, George

"Eve" (Rossetti), **V:** 258

Evelina (Burney), **III:** 90, 91; **IV:** 279

"Eveline" (Joyce), **VII:** 44

Evelyn, John, **II:** 194, 196, **273–280, 286–287**

Evelyn Innes (Moore), **VI:** 87, 92

Evening (Macaulay), **IV:** 290

Evening's Love, An, or the Mock Astrologer (Dryden), **II:** 305

Evening Standard (periodical), **VI:** 247, 252, 265

Evening Walk, An (Wordsworth), **IV:** xv, 2, 4–5, 24

"Even So" (Rossetti), **V:** 242

"Even Such Is Time" (Ralegh), **I:** 148–149

"Eve of St. Agnes, The" (Keats), **III:** 338; **IV:** viii, xviii, 212, 216–219, 231, 235; **V:** 352

Eve of Saint John, The (Scott), **IV:** 38

"Eve of St. Mark, The" (Keats), **IV:** 212, 216, 218, 220, 226

"Ever drifting down the stream" (Carroll), **V:** 270

"Everlasting Gospel" (Blake), **III:** 304

Everlasting Man, The (Chesterton), **VI:** 341–342

Everlasting Spell, The: A Study of Keats and His Friends (Richardson), **IV:** 236

"Ever mine hap is slack and slow in coming" (Wyatt), **I:** 110

Every-Body's Business, Is No-Body's Business (Defoe), **III:** 13–14

Everybody's Political What's What? (Shaw), **VI:** 125, 129

Everyman, **II:** 70

Everyman in His Humour (Jonson), **I:** 336–337

Every Man out of His Humour (Jonson), **I:** 336–337, 338–340; **II:** 24, 27

"Everything that is born must die" (Rossetti), **V:** 254

Eve's Ransom (Gissing), **V:** 437

Evidences of Christianity (Paley), **IV:** 144

Evolution and Poetic Belief (Roppen), **V:** 221$_n$

Ewart, Gavin, **VII:** 422, 423–424

Examen Poeticum (ed. Dryden), **II:** 290, 291, 301, 305

Examination of Certain Abuses, An (Swift), **III:** 36

Examiner (periodical), **III:** 19, 26, 35, 39; **IV:** 129

"Example of a Treatise on Universal Justice or the Fountains of Equity" (Bacon), **I:** 261

"Examples of Antitheses" (Bacon), **I:** 261

"Examples of the Colours of Good and Evil" (Bacon), **I:** 261, 264

Examples of the Interposition of Providence in . . . Murder (Fielding), **III:** 105

"Excellent New Ballad, An" (Montrose), **II:** 236–237

Except the Lord (Cary), **VII:** 186, 194–195

Excursion, The (Wordsworth), **IV:** xvii, 5, 22–24, 95, 129, 214, 230, 233

"Execution of Cornelius Vane, The" (Read), **VI:** 436

"Exhortation" (Shelley), **IV:** 196

Exiles (Joyce), **VII:** 42–43

existentialism, **VI:** 228

Exorcist, The (film), **III:** 343, 345

Expedition of Humphrey Clinker, The (Smollett), see
 Humphrey Clinker
Expedition of Orsua and the Crimes of Aquirre, The
 (Southey), **IV:** 71
"Experience with Images" (MacNeice), **VII:** 401,
 414, 419
Experiment, The (Defoe), **III:** 13
Experimental Drama (Armstrong), **VII:** 14
Experiment in Autobiography (Wells), **V:** 426–427, 429,
 438; **VI:** xi, 225, 320, 333
Experiments (Douglas), **VI:** 296, 305
Explorations (Knights), **II:** 123
Exposition of the First Ten Chapters of Genesis, An (Bun-
 yan), **II:** 253
Expostulation (Jonson), **I:** 243
"Expostulation and Reply" (Wordsworth), **IV:** 7
"Exposure" (Owen), **VI:** 446, 450, 452, 455, 457
Exposure of Luxury, The: Radical Themes in Thackeray
 (Hardy), **V:** 39
expressionism, **VII:** 7
"Exstasie, The" (Donne), **II:** 197
"Extempore Effusion on the Death of the Ettrick
 Shepherd" (Wordsworth), **IV:** 73
Eye for an Eye, An (Trollope), **V:** 102
Eyeless in Gaza (Huxley), **II:** 173; **VII:** 204–205
"Eye of Allah, The" (Kipling), **VI:** 169, 190–191
"Eyes and Tears" (Marvell), **II:** 209, 211
Eyes of Asia, The (Kipling), **VI:** 204

F

Faber, Geoffrey, **III:** 66, 67
Fabian Essays in Socialism (Shaw), **VI:** 129
Fabian Freeway (Martin), **VI:** 242
Fabian Socialism, **VI:** 226, 241–242, 273
Fabian Society, **VI:** 102
"Fable of the Widow and Her Cat, A" (Swift), **III:**
 27, 31
Fables (Dryden), **II:** 293, 301, 304; **III:** 40; **IV:** 287
Fables (Gay), **III:** 59, 67

Fables (Stevenson), **V:** 396
Façade (Sitwell and Walton), **VII:** xv, xvii, 128, 130,
 131$_n$, 132
Face of the Deep, The (Rossetti), **V:** 260
"Faces, The" (James), **VI:** 69
Faerie Queen, The (Spenser), **I:** 121, 123, 124, **131–
 141**, 266; **II:** 50; **IV:** 59, 198, 213; **V:** 142
"Faery Song, A" (Yeats), **VI:** 211
"Failure, A" (Thackeray), **V:** 18
"Fair Ines" (Hood), **IV:** 255
Fair Maid of the Inn, The (Ford, Massinger, Webster),
 II: 66, 69, 83, 85
Fair Quarrel, A (Middleton and Rowley), **II:** 1, 3, 21
"Fair Singer, The" (Marvell), **II:** 211
Fairy and Folk Tales of the Irish Peasantry (ed. Yeats),
 VI: 222
Fairy Knight, The (Dekker and Ford), **II:** 89, 100
"Faith" (Herbert), **II:** 127
Faithful Friends, The, **II:** 67
Faithful Narrative of . . . Habbakkuk Hilding, A (Smol-
 lett), **III:** 158
"Faithfulness of GOD in the Promises, The" (Blake),
 III: 300
Faithful Shepherdess, The (Fletcher), **II:** 45, 46, **49–52,**
 53, 62, 65, 82
"Faithless Nelly Gray" (Hood), **IV:** 257
"Faithless Sally Brown" (Hood), **IV:** 257
"Faith on Trial, A" (Meredith), **V:** 222
"Falk" (Conrad), **VI:** 148
"Fallen Majesty" (Yeats), **VI:** 216
"Fallen Yew, A" (Thompson), **V:** 442
Fall of Hyperion, The (Keats), **IV:** xi, 211–213, 220,
 227–231, 234, 235
Fall of Princes, The (Lydgate), **I:** 57, 58, 59, 64
Fall of Robespierre, The (Coleridge and Southey), **IV:**
 55
"Fall of the House of Usher, The" (Poe), **III:** 339
False Alarm, The (Johnson), **III:** 121
False Friend, The (Vanbrugh), **II:** 325, 333, 336
"False Morality of the Lady Novelists, The" (Greg),
 V: 7
False One, The (Fletcher and Massinger), **II:** 43, 66

"False though she be to me and love" (Congreve), **II:** 269

Fame's Memoriall, or the Earle of Devonshire Deceased (Ford), **II:** 100

Familiar and Courtly Letters Written by Monsieur Voiture (ed. Boyer), **II:** 352, 364

Familiar Letters (Richardson), **III:** 81, 83, 92

Familiar Letters (Rochester), **II:** 270

Familiar Studies of Men and Books (Stevenson), **V:** 395

Family and a Fortune, A (Compton-Burnett), **VII:** 60, 61, 62, 63, 66

Family Instructor, The (Defoe), **III:** 13, 82

Family of Love, The (Dekker and Middleton), **II:** 3, 21

Family Reunion, The (Eliot), **VII:** 146, 151, 154, 158, 160

Famous History of Sir Thomas Wyat, The (Webster), **II:** 85

Famous Tragedy of the Queen of Cornwall . . . , The (Hardy), **VI:** 20

Famous Victories of Henry V, The, **I:** 308–309

Fan, The: A Poem (Gay), **III:** 67

Fancies, Chaste and Noble, The (Ford), **II:** 89, 91–92, 99, 100

"Fancy" (Keats), **IV:** 221

Fancy and Imagination (Brett), **IV:** 57

Fanfare for Elizabeth (Sitwell), **VII:** 127

"Fanny and Annie" (Lawrence), **VII:** 90, 114, 115

Fanny Brawne: A Biography (Richardson), **IV:** 236

Fanny's First Play (Shaw), **VI:** 115, 116, 117, 129

Fanshawe, Sir Richard, **II:** 49, 222, 237

Fantasia of the Unconscious (Lawrence), **VII:** 122

fantasy fiction, **VI:** 228–235, 338, 399

"Fare Thee Well" (Byron), **IV:** 192

"Farewell, A" (Arnold), **V:** 216

"Farewell to Angria" (Brontë), **V:** 125

"Farewell to Essay-Writing, A" (Hazlitt), **IV:** 135

Farewell to Military Profession (Rich), **I:** 312

"Farewell to Tobacco" (Lamb), **IV:** 81

"Far—Far—Away" (Tennyson), **IV:** 330

Farfetched Fables (Shaw), **VI:** 125, 126

Far from the Madding Crowd (Hardy), **VI:** 1, 5–6

Farina (Meredith), **V:** 225, 234

"Farmer's Ingle, The" (Fergusson), **III:** 318

Farnham, William, **I:** 214

Farquhar, George, **II:** 334–335, **351–365**

Farther Adventures of Robinson Crusoe, The (Defoe), **III:** 13

Farthing Hall (Walpole and Priestley), **VII:** 211

Fascinating Foundling, The (Shaw), **VI:** 129

Fascism, **VII:** 106

"Fashionable Authoress, The" (Thackeray), **V:** 22, 37

Fashionable Lover, The (Cumberland), **III:** 257

Fasti (Ovid), **II:** 110$_n$

"Fatal Boots, The" (Thackeray), **V:** 21, 37

"Fatal Sisters, The" (Gray), **III:** 141

"Fat Contributor Papers, The" (Thackeray), **V:** 25, 38

Fate of Homo Sapiens, The (Wells), **VI:** 228

"Fates, The" (Owen), **VI:** 449

Father and His Fate, A (Compton-Burnett), **VII:** 61, 63

"Father and Lover" (Rossetti), **V:** 260

Father Brown stories (Chesterton), **VI:** 338

Father Damien (Stevenson), **V:** 383, 390, 396

Fathers, The; or, The Good-Natur'd Man (Fielding), **III:** 98, 105

Faulkner, Charles, **VI:** 167

Faust (Goethe), **III:** 344; **IV:** xvi, xix, 179

"Faustine" (Swinburne), **V:** 320

Fawkes, F., **III:** 170$_n$

Fawn, The (Marston), **II,** 30, 40

"Fear" (Collins), **III:** 166, 171, 336

Fears in Solitude . . . (Coleridge), **IV:** 55

Feast of Bacchus, The (Bridges), **VI:** 83

"Feast of Famine, The" (Stevenson), **V:** 396

Feeding the Mind (Carroll), **V:** 274

"Félise" (Swinburne), **V:** 321

Felix Holt, the Radical, **V:** xxiii, 195–196, 199, 200

"Felix Randal" (Hopkins), **V:** 368–369, 371

"Fellow-Townsmen" (Hardy), **VI:** 22

"Female God, The" (Rosenberg), **VI:** 432

"Female Vagrant, The" (Wordsworth), **IV:** 5

feminism, **VII:** 23, 27, 91, 97

Fénelon, François, **III:** 95, 99

Fenwick, Isabella, **IV:** 2

Ferdinand Count Fathom (Smollett), **III:** 153, 158

Fergusson, Robert, **III:** 312–313, 316, 317, 318

Ferishtah's Fancies (Browning), **IV:** 359, 374

Fernandez, Ramon, **V:** 225–226

Ferrex and Porrex (Norton and Sackville), see *Gorboduc*

Festival at Farbridge (Priestley), **VII:** 219–210

"Festubert: The Old German Line" (Blunden), **VI:** 428

Feuerbach, Ludwig, **IV:** 364

"Feuille d'Album" (Mansfield), **VII:** 174

"Few Crusted Characters, A" (Hardy), **VI:** 20, 22

Few Late Chrysanthemums, A (Betjeman), **VII:** 369–371

Few Sighs from Hell, A (Bunyan), **II:** 253

Fichte, Johann Gottlieb, **V:** 348

Ficino (philosopher), **I:** 237

Fiction and the Reading Public (Leavis), **VII:** 233, 234

"Fiddler of the Reels, The" (Hardy), **VI:** 22

Field, Isobel, **V:** 393, 397

Field, Nathaniel, **II:** 45, 66, 67

Fielding, Henry, **II:** 273; **III:** 62, 84, **94–106**, 148, 150; **IV:** 106, 189; **V:** 52, 287

Fielding, K. J., **V:** 43, 72

Field of Waterloo, The (Scott), **IV:** 38

Fifer, C. N., **III:** 249

Fifine at the Fair (Browning), **IV:** 358, 367, 374

"Fifth Philosopher's Song" (Huxley), **VII:** 199

Fifth Queen, The (Ford), **VI:** 324

Fifth Queen Crowned, The (Ford), **VI:** 325, 326

Fifty Years of English Literature, 1900–1950 (Scott-James), **VI:** 21

Fight for Barbara, The (Lawrence), **VII:** 120

"Fight to a Finish" (Sassoon), **VI:** 430

"Figure in the Carpet, The" (James), **VI:** 69

Filibusters in Barbary (Lewis), **VII:** 83

Fille du Policeman (Swinburne), **V:** 325, 333

Filostrato (Boccaccio), **I:** 30

Finden's Byron Beauties (Finden), **V:** 111

Findlater, Richard, **VII:** 8

Finer Grain, The (James), **VI:** 67

Finnegan's Wake (Joyce), **VII:** 42, 46, 52–54; critical studies, **VII:** 58

Firbank, Ronald, **VII:** 132, 200

First and Last Loves (Betjeman), **VII:** 357, 358, 359

First & Last Things (Wells), **VI:** 244

First Anniversary, The (Donne), **I:** 188, 356

"First Anniversary of the Government under O.C., The" (Marvell), **II:** 210, 211

First Book of Urizen, The (Blake), **III:** 299, 300, 306, 307

"First Countess of Wessex, The" (Hardy), **VI:** 22

First Folio (Shakespeare), **I:** 299, 324, 325

First Hundred Years of Thomas Hardy, The (Weber), **VI:** 19

"First Impressions" (Austen), see *Pride and Prejudice*

First Lady Chatterley, The (Lawrence), **VII:** 111–112

First Men in the Moon, The (Wells), **VI:** 229, 234, 244

First Ode of the Second Book of Horace Paraphras'd, The (Swift), **III:** 35

First Satire (Wyatt), **I:** 111

First Satire of the Second Book of Horace, Imitated, The (Pope), **III:** 234

First World War, see World War I

Firth, Sir Charles Harding, **II:** 241; **III:** 25, 36; **IV:** 289, 290, 291

"Fish" (Lawrence), **VII:** 119

"Fisherman, The" (Yeats), **VI:** 214

"Fitz-Boodle Papers, The" (Thackeray), **V:** 38

FitzGerald, Edward, **IV:** xvii, xxii, xxiii, 310, **340–353; V:** xxv

Fitzgerald, Percy, **III:** 125, 135

Five Metaphysical Poets (Bennett), **II:** 181, 202

Five Nations, The (Kipling), **VI:** 204

Five Novelettes by Charlotte Brontë (ed. Gérin), **V:** 151

"Five Students, The" (Hardy), **VI:** 17

Five Tales (Galsworthy), **VI:** 276

Five Uncollected Essays of Matthew Arnold (ed. Allott), **V:** 216

Fixed Period, The (Trollope), **V:** 102

"Flaming Heart Upon the Book and Picture of the Seraphicall Saint Teresa, The" (Crashaw), **II:** 182

"Flaming sighs that boil within my breast, The" (Wyatt), **I:** 109–110

Flatman, Thomas, **II:** 133

Flaubert, Gustave, **V:** xviii–xxiv, 340, 353, 429

Flea, The (Donne), **I:** 355

"Fleckno, an English Priest at Rome" (Marvell), **II:** 211

Fleshly School of Poetry, The (Buchanan), **V:** 238, 245

Fletcher, Ian, **V:** xii, xiii, xxvii, 359

Fletcher, John, **II:** **42–67**, 79, 82, 87–88, 90, 91, 93, 185, 305, 340, 357, 359

Fletcher, Phineas, **II:** 138

Fletcher, Thomas, **II:** 21

Fleurs du Mal (Baudelaire), **V:** xxii, 316, 329, 411

Fleurs du Mal (Swinburne), **V:** 329, 331, 333

"Flickerbridge" (James), **VI:** 69

"Flight of the Duchess, The" (Browning), **IV:** 356, 361, 368

Flood, A (Moore), **VI:** 99

Floor Games (Wells), **VI:** 227

"Florent" (Gower), **I:** 55

Flores Solitudinis (Vaughan), **II:** 185, 201

Floud, Peter, **V:** 296, 307

"Flower, The" (Herbert), **II:** 119n, 125

Flowering Rifle (Campbell), **VII:** 428

Flowering Wilderness (Galsworthy), **VI:** 275, 282

Flower of Courtesy (Lydgate), **I:** 57, 60, 62

Flowers of Passion (Moore), **VI:** 85, 98

Flurried Years, The (Hunt), **VI:** 333

"Fly, The" (Blake), **III:** 295–296

"Fly, The" (Mansfield), **VII:** 176

Flying Inn, The (Chesterton), **VI:** 340

Foe-Farrell (Quiller-Couch), **V:** 384

folk history, **VI:** 315

folklore, **VI:** 307

Folly of Industry, The (Wycherley), **II:** 322

Fontaine amoureuse, **I:** 33

"Food of the Dead" (Graves), **VII:** 269

Foote, Samuel, **III:** 253; **V:** 261

Footnote to History, A: Eight Years of Trouble in Samoa (Stevenson), **V:** 396

"For All We Have and Are" (Kipling), **VI:** 415

"Force That Through the Green Fuse Drives the Flower, The" (Thomas), **II:** 156

For Children: The Gates of Paradise (Blake), **III:** 307

"For Conscience' Sake" (Hardy), **VI:** 22

Ford, Charles, **III:** 33, 34

Ford, Ford Madox, **VI:** 145–146, 238, **319–333**, 416, 439; **VII:** xi, xv, xxi, 89

Ford, John, **II:** 57, 69, 83, 85, **87–101**

"Fordham Castle" (James), **VI:** 69

Ford Madox Ford: Letters (ed. Ludwig), **VI:** 332

Foreigners, The (Tutchin), **III:** 3

Forest, The (Galsworthy), **VI:** 276, 287

Foresters, The (Tennyson), **IV:** 328, 338

Forewords and Afterwords (Auden), **VII:** 394

"Forget not yet" (Wyatt), **I:** 106

"Forgiveness, A" (Browning), **IV:** 360

Formalism, **VII:** 242, 243

Forrest, James F., **II:** 245n

"Forsaken Garden, A" (Swinburne), **V:** 314, 327

Fors Clavigera (Ruskin), **V:** 174, 181, 184

For Services Rendered (Maugham), **VI:** 368

Forster, E. M., **IV:** 302, 306; **V:** xxiv, 208, 229, 230; **VI:** xii, 365, **397–413**; **VII:** xi, xv, 18, 21, 34, 35, 122, 144

Forster, John, **IV:** 87, 89, 95, 99, 100, 240; **V:** 47, 72

Forsyte Saga, The (Galsworthy), **VI:** xiii, 269, 272, 274; see also *Man of Property, The;* "Indian Summer of a Forsyte"; *In Chancery; Awakening; To Let*

Fortescue, Chichester, **V:** 76–83, 85

"For the Fallen" (Binyon), **VI:** 416; **VII:** 448

For the Sexes: The Gates of Paradise (Blake), **III:** 307

For the Time Being (Auden), **VII:** 379

Fortnightly Review (periodical), **V:** 279, 338

"For to Admire" (Kipling), **VI:** 203

Fortunate Mistress, The: or, A History of . . . Mademoiselle de Beleau . . . (Defoe), **III:** 13

Fortunes and Misfortunes of the Famous Moll Flanders, The (Defoe), see *Moll Flanders*

Fortunes of Falstaff, The (Wilson), **III:** 116n

Fortunes of Nigel, The (Scott), **IV:** 30, 35, 37, 39

Foster, A. D., **III:** 345

"Found" (Rossetti), **V:** 240

"Foundation of the Kingdom of Angria" (Brontë), V: 110–111

Fountains in the Sand (Douglas), VI: 294, 297, 299, 300, 305

Four Ages of Poetry, The (Peacock), IV: 168–169, 170

Foure-footed Beastes (Topsel), II: 137

Four Georges, The (Thackeray), V: 20, 34–35, 38

Four Hymns (Spenser), I: 124

Four Lectures (Trollope), V: 102

"Four Meetings" (James), VI: 69

Four Plays (Stevenson and Henley), V: 396

Four Plays for Dancers (Yeats), VI: 218

Four Prentices of London with the Conquest of Jerusalem (Heywood), II: 48

Four Quartets (Eliot), VII: 143, 148, 153–157; see also "Burnt Norton," "The Dry Salvages," "East Coker," "Little Gidding"

"14 November 1973" (Betjeman), VII: 372

Fourteenth Century Verse and Prose (Sisam), I: 20, 21

Four Zoas, The (Blake), III: 300, 302–303, 307

Fowler, Alastair, I: 237

Fowler, H. W., VI: 76

Fox, Caroline, IV: 54

Fox, George, IV: 45

"Fox, The" (Lawrence), VII: 90, 91

"Fox Trot" (Sitwell), VII: 131

"Fragment" (Brooke), VI: 421

Fragmenta Aurea (Suckling), II: 238

"Fragment of a Greek Tragedy" (Housman), VI: 156

"Fragoletta" (Swinburne), V: 320

"Frail as thy love, the flowers were dead" (Peacock), IV: 157

"Fra Lippo Lippi" (Browning), IV: 357, 361, 369

Framley Parsonage (Trollope), V: xxii, 93, 101

"France, an Ode" (Coleridge), IV: 55

"France, December 1870" (Meredith), V: 223

"Frances" (Brontë), V: 132

Francillon, R. E., V: 83

Francis, G. H., IV: 270

Francis, P., III: 249

"Francis Beaumont" (Swinburne), V: 332

Franck, Richard, II: 131–132

Frankenstein (Shelley), III: 329–331, 341, 342, 345

Frankenstein Un-bound (Aldiss), III: 341, 345

"Frank Fane: A Ballad" (Swinburne), V: 332

Franklin's Tale, The (Chaucer), I: 23

Fra Rupert: The Last Part of a Trilogy (Landor), IV: 100

Fraser, G. S., VI: xiv, xxxiii; VII: xviii, 422, 425, 443

Fraser's (periodical), IV: 259; V: 19, 22, 111, 142

"Frater Ave atque Vale" (Tennyson), IV: 327, 336

Fraternity (Galsworthy), VI: 274, 278, 279–280, 285

"Frau Brechenmacher Attends a Wedding" (Mansfield), VII: 172

"Frau Fischer" (Mansfield), VII: 172

Fraunce, Abraham, I: 122, 164

Frazer, Sir James, V: 204

Free and Offenceless Justification of a Lately Published and Most Maliciously Misinterpreted Poem Entitled "Andromeda Liberata," A (Chapman), I: 254

Free-Holder (periodical), III: 51, 53

Free-Holders Plea against . . . Elections of Parliament-Men, The (Defoe), III: 12

Freelands, The (Galsworthy), VI: 279

Free Thoughts on Public Affairs (Hazlitt), IV: 139

free trade movement, VI: 389

free verse, VII: xiii, 159

French Eton, A (Arnold), V: 206, 216

French Gardiner, The: Instructing How to Cultivate All Sorts of Fruit-Trees . . . (tr. Evelyn), II: 287

French Lyrics (Swinburne), V: 333

French Poets and Novelists (James), VI: 67

French Revolution, The (Blake), III: 307

French Revolution, The (Carlyle), IV: xii, xix, 240, 243, 245, 249, 250

Frere, John Hookham, IV: 182–183

"Freya of the Seven Isles" (Conrad), VI: 148

Friar Bacon and Friar Bungay (Greene), II: 3

Friar's Tale, The (Chaucer), I: 30

"Friday, or The Dirge" (Gay), III: 56

Friedman, A., III: 178, 190

Friend (periodical), IV: 50, 55, 56

"Friendly Epistle to Mrs. Fry, A" (Hood), IV: 257, 267

Friendship's Garland (Arnold), **V:** 206, 213*ₙ*, 215, 216

"Friends of the Friends, The" (James), **VI:** 69

Froissart, Jean, **I:** 21

Frolic and the Gentle, The (Ward), **IV:** 86

From a View to a Death (Powell), **VII:** 345, 353

"From My Diary. July 1914" (Owen), **VI:** 446

"From Sorrow Sorrow Yet is Born" (Tennyson), **IV:** 329

From the Four Winds (Galsworthy), **VI:** 276

"From the Greek" (Landor), **IV:** 98

"From the Night of Forebeing" (Thompson), **V:** 443, 448

"From Tuscan cam my ladies worthi race" (Surrey), **I:** 114

Frost, Robert, **VI:** 424

"Frost at Midnight" (Coleridge), **IV:** 41, 44, 55

Frost in the Flower, The (O'Casey), **VII:** 12

Froude, James Anthony, **IV:** 238, 240, 250, 324; **V:** 278, 287

Frozen Deep, The (Collins), **V:** 42

"Fruit" (Betjeman), **VII:** 373

Fry, Christopher, **IV:** 318

Fry, Roger, **VII:** xii, 34

Fugitive, The (Galsworthy), **VI:** 283

Fugitive Pieces (Byron), **IV:** 192

Fulbecke, William, **I:** 218

Fulford, William, **VI:** 167

Fuller, Roy, **VII:** 422, 428–431

Fuller, Thomas, **I:** 178; **II:** 45

Full Moon in March, A (Yeats), **VI:** 222

Fumifugium: or The Inconvenience of Aer and Smoak . . . (Evelyn), **II:** 287

"Function of Criticism at the Present Time, The" (Arnold), **V:** 204–205, 212, 213

Funeral, The (Steele), **II:** 359

"Funeral Poem Upon the Death of . . . Sir Francis Vere, A," **II:** 37, 41

Furbank, P. N., **VI:** 397

Furetière, Antoine, **II:** 354

Furness, H. H., **I:** 326

Furnivall, F. J., **VI:** 102

"Fust and His Friends" (Browning), **IV:** 366

"Futility" (Owen), **VI:** 453, 455

"Future, The" (Arnold), **V:** 210

Future in America, The: A Search after Reality (Wells), **VI:** 244

"Futurity" (Browning), **IV:** 313

Fyvel, T. R., **VII:** 284

G

"Gabrielle de Bergerac" (James), **VI:** 67, 69

Gadfly, The (Voynich), **VI:** 107

Gaelic League, **VI:** 87; **VII:** 1

Gager, William, **I:** 193

Galileo (Brecht), **IV:** 182

Galland, Antoine, **III:** 327

Gallathea (Lyly), **I:** 200–202

"Gallery, The" (Marvell), **II:** 211

Galsworthy, Ada, **VI:** 271, 272, 273, 274, 282

Galsworthy, John, **V:** xxii, 270*ₙ*; **VI:** ix, xiii, 133, 260, **269–291**; **VII:** xii, xiv

Galsworthy the Man (Sauter), **VI:** 284

Galt, John, **IV:** 35

Game at Chess, A (Middleton), **II:** 1, 2, 3, **18–21**

Game of Logic, The (Carroll), **V:** 273

Gaol Gate, The (Gregory), **VI:** 315

"Garden, The" (Cowley), **II:** 194

"Garden, The" (Marvell), **II:** 208, 210, 211, 212, 213–214

"Gardener, The" (Kipling), **VI:** 197

Gardeners and Astronomers (Sitwell), **VII:** 138

"Gardener's Daughter, The" (Tennyson), **IV:** 326

"Garden in September, The" (Bridges), **VI:** 78

Garden of Cyrus, The (Browne), **II:** 148, **150–153**, 154, 155, 156

"Garden of Eros, The" (Wilde), **V:** 401, 402

"Garden of Proserpine, The" (Swinburne), **V:** 320, 321

Garden Party, The (Mansfield), **VII:** xv, 171, 177

Gardiner, S. R., **I:** 146

Gardner, Helen, **II:** 121, 129

Gardner, Philip, **VI:** xii, xxxiii

Gareth and Lynette (Tennyson), **IV:** 338

Garibaldi and the Making of Italy (Trevelyan), **VI:** 388–389

Garibaldi and the Thousand (Trevelyan), **VI:** 388–389

Garibaldi's Defence of the Roman Republic (Trevelyan), **VI:** xv, **387–389**, 394

Garis, Robert, **V:** 49–50, 70, 73

Garland of Laurel, The (Skelton), **I:** 81, 82, 90, 93–94

Garner, Ross, **II:** 186

Garnett, Edward, **VI:** 135, 149, 273, 277, 278, 283, 366, 373; **VII:** xiv, 89

Garnier, Robert, **I:** 218

Garrick, David, **I:** 327

Garrod, H. W., **III:** 170$_n$, 176

Gascoigne, George, **I:** 215–216, 298

Gaskell, Elizabeth, **IV:** 241, 248; **V:** viii, x, xvi, xxi–xxiii, **1–16,** 108, 116, 122, 137, 147–150; **VI:** viii

Gaskill, William, **II:** 6

"Gaspar Ruiz" (Conrad), **VI:** 148

Gaston de Latour (Pater), **V:** 318$_n$, 357

Gates of Paradise, The (Blake), see *For Children: The Gates of Paradise; For the Sexes: The Gates of Paradise*

Gates of Wrath, The (Bennett), **VI:** 249

Gathering Storm, The (Churchill), **VI:** 361

Gatty, Margaret, **V:** 270

Gaunt, William, **VI:** 169

Gautier, Théophile, **IV:** 153$_n$; **V:** 320$_n$, 346, 404, 410–411

Gay, John, **II:** 348; **III:** 19, 24, 44, **54–67,** 74

Gayton, Edward, **I:** 279

G. B. Shaw (Chesterton), **VI:** 130

Gebir (Landor), **IV:** xvi, 88, 95, 99, 100, 217

Gebirus, poema (Landor), **IV:** 99–100

Gem (periodical), **IV:** 252

"Gemini" (Kipling), **VI:** 184

"General, The" (Sassoon), **VI:** 430

General Grant: An Estimate (Arnold), **V:** 216

General History of Discoveries . . . in Useful Arts, A (Defoe), **III:** 14

General History of the Robberies and Murders of . . . Pyrates, A (Defoe), **III:** 13

General History of the Turkes (Knolles), **III:** 108

General Inventorie of the History of France (Brimeston), **I:** 249

General Prologue, The (Chaucer), **I:** 23, 26, 27–28, 38–40

"Genesis" (Swinburne), **V:** 325

Geneva (Shaw), **VI:** 125, 127–128, 129

Genius of the Thames, The (Peacock), **IV:** 169

Gentleman Dancing-Master, The (Wycherley), **II:** 308, 309, **313–314,** 321

Gentleman in the Parlour, The (Maugham), **VI:** 371

Gentleman's Magazine (periodical), **III:** 107

Gentleman Usher, The (Chapman), **I:** 244–245

Geoffrey de Vinsauf, **I:** 23, 39–40, 59

Geography and History of England, The (Goldsmith), **III:** 191

George, Henry, **VI:** 102

George Bernard Shaw (Chesterton), **VI:** 344

George Crabbe and His Times (Huchon), **III:** 273$_n$

George Eliot (Stephen), **V:** 289

George Eliot: Her Life and Books (Bullet), **V:** 196, 200–201

George Eliot's Life as Related in Her Letters and Journals (ed. Cross), **V:** 13, 200

George Gissing: Grave Comedian (Donnelly), **V:** 427$_n$, 438

George Moore: L'homme et l'oeuvre (Noël), **VI:** 98, 99

George Orwell (Fyvel), **VII:** 287

George Passant (Snow), **VII:** 324, 325–326

George Silverman's Explanation (Dickens), **V:** 72

Georgianism, **VI:** xvi

Georgian Poetry 1911–1912 (ed. Marsh), **VI:** 416, 419, 420, 453; **VII:** xvi

Georgian poets, **VI:** 416, 453, 454; **VII:** xiii, 199, 260

"Georgina's Reasons" (James), **VI:** 69

Gerard Manley Hopkins: A Critical Symposium (Kenyon Critics), **V:** 382

Gerard Manley Hopkins: The Classical Background . . . (Bender), **V:** 364–365, 382

Gérin, Winifred, **V:** x, xxvii, 111, 151, 152, 153

Germ (periodical), **V:** xxi, 235–236, 249

"Gerontion" (Eliot), **VII:** 144, 146–147, 152

Gesta Romanorum, **I:** 52, 53

Getting Married (Shaw), **VI:** 115, 117–118

"Geve place ye lovers" (Surrey), **I:** 120

Ghastly Good Taste (Betjeman), **VII:** 357, 361

Ghost of Lucrece, The (Middleton), **II:** 3

Giaour, The (Byron), **III:** 338; **IV:** xvii, 172, 173–174, 180, 192; see also Turkish tales (Byron)

Gibbon, Edward, **III:** 109, **221–233**; **IV:** xiv, xvi, 93, 284; **V:** 425; **VI:** 347, 353, 383, 390$_n$

Gibbons, Brian, **I:** 281

Gibson, W. W., **VI:** 416

Gide, André, **V:** xxiii, 402

Gifford, William, **II:** 96; **IV:** 133

"Gigolo and Gigolette" (Maugham), **VI:** 370

Gilbert, Elliott, **VI:** 194

"Gilbert" (Brontë), **V:** 131–132

Gil Blas (tr. Smollett), **III:** 150

Gilfillan, George, **I:** 98

"Gilles de Retz" (Keyes), **VII:** 437

Gillman, James, **IV:** 48–49, 50, 56

Gil Perez, the Gallician (tr. FitzGerald), **IV:** 344

Gilpin, William, **IV:** 36, 37

Gilson, Étienne, **VI:** 341

"Giorgione" (Pater), **V:** 345, 348, 353

Giorgione da Castelfranco, **V:** 345, 348

"Gipsy Vans" (Kipling), **VI:** 193, 196

"Giraffes, The" (Fuller), **VII:** 430

Girlhood of Mary Virgin, The (Rossetti), **V:** 236, 248, 249

Gisborne, John, **IV:** 206

Gismond of Salerne (Wilmot), **I:** 216

Gissing, George, **V:** xiii, xxii, xxv–xxvi, 69, **423–438**; **VI:** 365

"Give Her a Pattern" (Lawrence), **II:** 330$_n$

"Given Heart, The" (Cowley), **II:** 197

Giving Alms No Charity . . . (Defoe), **III:** 13

Glanvill, Joseph, **II:** 275

Glass Town chronicles (Brontës), **V:** 110–111

Gleanings from the Menagerie and Aviary at Knowsley Hall (Lear), **V:** 76, 87

Gleckner, R. F., **IV:** 173, 194

Glen, Heather, **III:** 297

Glimpse of Reality, The (Shaw), **VI:** 129

Glorious First of June, The, **III:** 266

"Glory of Women" (Sassoon), **VI:** 430

G. M. Trevelyan (Moorman), **VI:** 396

gnomic moralizing poem, **I:** 57

"Goal of Valerius" (Bacon), **I:** 263

"Goblin Market" (Rossetti), **V:** 250, 256–258,

Goblin Market and Other Poems (Rossetti), **V:** xxii, 250, 260

Goblins, The (Suckling), **II:** 226

God and His Gifts, A (Compton-Burnett), **VII:** 60, 64, 65

God and the Bible (Arnold), **V:** 216

Godber, Joyce, **II:** 243, 254

"God! How I Hate You, You Young Cheerful Men (West), **VI:** 423

Godman, Stanley, **V:** 271, 274

"God Moves in a Mysterious Way" (Cowper), **III:** 210

Godolphin, Sidney, **II:** 237, 238, 271

"God's Eternity" (Blake), **III:** 300

"God's Grandeur" (Hopkins), **V:** 366

"God's Judgement on a Wicked Bishop" (Southey), **IV:** 67

God's Revenge Against Murder (Reynolds), **II:** 14

God the Invisible King (Wells), **VI:** 227

Godwin, E. W., **V:** 404

Godwin, Mary Wollstonecraft, see Shelley, Mary Wollstonecraft

Godwin, Mary Wollstonecraft, see Wollstonecraft, Mary

Godwin, William, **III:** 329, 330, 332, 340, 345; **IV:** xv, 3, 43, 127, 173, 181, 195–197

Goethe, Johann Wolfgang von, **III:** 344; **IV:** xiv–xix, 179, 240, 245, 249; **V:** 214, 343, 344, 402

Goethe's Faust (MacNeice), **VII:** 408–410

Gogol, Nikolai, **III:** 340, 345

"Going, The" (Hardy), **VI:** 18

"Going to See a Man Hanged" (Thackeray), **V:** 23, 37

Gold Coast Customs (Sitwell), **VII:** xvii, 132, 133–134

Golden Book of St. John Chrysostom, The, Concerning the Education of Children (tr. Evelyn), **II:** 275, 287

Golden Bough, The (Frazer), **V:** 204

Golden Bowl, The (James), **VI:** 53, 55, **60–62,** 67

Golden Echo, The (Garnett), **VI:** 333

"Golden Hair" (Owen), **VI:** 449

Golden Labyrinth, The (Knight), **IV:** 328$_n$, 339

Golden Lion of Granpère, The (Trollope), **V:** 102

Golden Mean, The (Ford), **II:** 88, 100

Golden Targe, The (Dunbar), **I:** 23

Golden Treasury, The (Palgrave), **II:** 208; **IV:** xxii, 196, 337

Golding, Arthur, **I:** 161

Goldring, Douglas, **VI:** 324, 419

Goldsmith, Oliver, **II:** 362, 363; **III:** 40, 110, 149, 165, 173, **177–192,** 256, 277, 278

Goldsworthy Lowes Dickinson (Forster), **VI:** 411

Gollancz, Victor, **VII:** xix, 279, 381

"Go, Lovely Rose!" (Waller), **II:** 234

Gondal literature (Brontë), **V:** 113–117, 133, 142

Gondal Poems (Brontë), **V:** 152

Gondal's Queen (Ratchford), **V:** 133, 152

Gondibert (Davenant), **II:** 196, 259

Gonne, Maud, **VI:** 207, 210, 211, 212

"Good-bye in fear, good-bye in sorrow" (Rossetti), **V:** 255

Goodbye to All That (Graves), **VI:** xvi; **VII:** xviii, 257, 258

Goodbye to Berlin (Isherwood), **VII:** xx

Good Companions, The (Priestley), **VII:** xviii, 209, 211, 215–216

"Good Counsel to a Young Maid" (Carew), **II:** 224

"Good Friday" (Herbert), **II:** 128

"Good Friday: Rex Tragicus, or Christ Going to His Crosse" (Herrick), **II:** 114

Good Friday, 1613 (Donne), **I:** 368

Good Kipling, The (Gilbert), **VI:** 194

"Good ladies ye that have" (Surrey), **I:** 120

"Good-Morrow, The" (Donne), **II:** 197

Good Natur'd Man, The (Goldsmith), **III:** 111, 180, 187, 191

Good News for the Vilest of Men: or, A Help for Despairing Souls (Bunyan), **II:** 253

Good Soldier, The (Ford), **VI:** 49; **VI:** 319, 323, **327–328,** 329

"Goose Fair" (Lawrence), **VII:** 114

Go, Piteous Heart (Skelton), **I:** 83

Gorboduc (Norton and Sackville), **I:** 161–162, 214–216

Gordon, D. J., **I:** 237, 239

Gordon, Ian Alistair, **VII:** xvii, xxxvii

Gordon, Mary, **V:** 312, 313, 315–316, 330

Gosse, Edmund, **II:** 354, 361, 363, 364; **V:** 311, 313, 334, 392, 395

Gosson, Stephen, **I:** 161

Gothic architecture, **V:** 176–177, 178

Gothic Architecture (Morris), **V:** 306

Gothic fiction, **III:** **324–346;** **IV:** 110, 111; **V:** 142–143

Gothic novel, **III:** **324–346**

Gothic Revival, The (Clark), **III:** 325, 346

Gower, John, **I:** 20, 41, **48–56,** 57, 321

Grace Abounding to the Chief of Sinners (Bunyan), **II:** 240, 241, 243–245, 250, 253

Grace Darling (Swinburne), **V:** 333

"Grace of the Way" (Thompson), **V:** 442

Graham, James, see Montrose, marquess of

"Grammarian's Funeral, A" (Browning), **IV:** 357, 361, 366

Grammar of Assent, The (Newman), **V:** 340

Grand Alliance, The (Churchill), **VI:** 361

Grand Babylon Hotel, The (Bennett), **VI:** 249, 253, 262, 266

Grania (Gregory), **VI:** 316

Grant, Duncan, **VI:** 118

Granville Barker, Harley, **I:** 329; **VI:** ix, 104, 113, 273

"Gratiana Dancing and Singing" (Lovelace), **II:** 230

"Grave by the Handpost, The" (Hardy), **VI:** 22

Graves, Robert, **I:** 94; **VI:** xvi, 207, 211, 219, 419; **VII:** xvi, xviii–xx, **257–272**

Gray, Thomas, **II**: 200; **III**: 118, 119, **136–145**, 173, 294, 325

Great Adventure, The (Bennett), **VI**: 250, 266; see also *Buried Alive*

Great Catherine (Shaw), **VI**: 119

Great Contemporaries (Churchill), **VI**: 354, 356

Great Depression, **VII**: xix

"Greater Love" (Owen), **VI**: 450

Great Expectations (Dickens), **V**: xxii, 42, 60, 63, 66–68, 72

Great Favourite, The, or the Duke of Lerma (Howard), **II**: 100

"Great Good Place, The" (James), **VI**: 69

Great Hoggarty Diamond, The (Thackeray), **V**: 21, 38

Great Instauration, The (Bacon), **I**: 259, 272

Great Law of Subordination Consider'd, The (Defoe), **III**: 13

"Great men have been among us" (Wordsworth), **II**: 208

Greatness of the Soul, A, . . . (Bunyan), **II**: 253

Great Short Stories of Detection, Mystery and Horror (ed. Sayers), **III**: 341

"Great Spirits Now on Earth Are Sojourning . . ." (Keats), **IV**: 214

Great Trade Route (Ford), **VI**: 324

Great Tradition, The (Leavis), **VI**: 68, 149; **VII**: 234, **248–251**

"Great Unknown, The" (Hood), **IV**: 267

Greber, Giacomo, **II**: 325

Grecian History, The (Goldsmith), **III**: 181, 191

Greek Christian Poets, The, and the English Poets (Browning), **IV**: 321

Greek idyll, **IV**: 326

Greek Studies (Pater), **V**: 355, 357

Green, Joseph Henry, **IV**: 57

Green, Roger Lancelyn, **V**: 265$_n$, 273, 274

Green Crow, The (O'Casey), **VII**: 13

Greene, Graham, **VI**: 329, 370; **VII**: xii

Greene, Robert, **I**: 165, 220, 275, 286, 296, 322; **II**: 3

"Green Geese" (Sitwell), **VII**: 131

"Green, Green Is Aghir" (Cameron), **VII**: 426

Green Helmet, The (Yeats), **VI**: 222

"Green Hills of Africa" (Fuller), **VII**: 429, 432

Greenlees, Ian Gordon, **VI**: xxxiii

Green Song (Sitwell), **VII**: 132, 135, 136

"Green Tea" (Le Fanu), **III**: 340, 345

"Greenwich—Whitebait" (Thackeray), **V**: 38

Greenwood, Edward Baker, **VII**: xix, xxxvii

Greenwood, Frederick, **V**: 1

Greg, W. R., **V**: 5, 7, 15

Greg, W. W., **I**: 279

Gregory, Lady Augusta, **VI**: 210, 218, **307–312**, **314–316**, 317–318; **VII**: 1, 3, 42

Gregory, Sir Richard, **VI**: 233

Greiffenhagen, Maurice, **VI**: 91

"Grenadier" (Housman), **VI**: 160

Grenfell, Julian, **VI**: xvi, 417–418, 420

"Gretchen" (Gissing), **V**: 437

Greville, Fulke, **I**: 160, 164

Greybeards at Play (Chesterton), **VI**: 336

Grey Eminence (Huxley), **VII**: 205

Grey of Fallodon (Trevelyan), **VI**: 383, 391

"Grey Woman, The" (Gaskell), **V**: 15

"Grief" (Browning), **IV**: 313, 318

"Grief on the Death of Prince Henry, A" (Tourneur), **II**: 37, 41

Grierson, Herbert J. C., **II**: 121, 130, 196, 200, 202, 258

Grigson, Geoffrey, **IV**: 47; **VII**: xvi

Grim Smile of the Five Towns, The (Bennett), **VI**: 250, 253–254

Groatsworth of Wit, A (Greene), **I**: 275, 276

Grosskurth, Phyllis, **V**: xxvii

Grote, George, **IV**: 289

Group of Noble Dames, A (Hardy), **VI**: 20, 22

"Growing Old" (Arnold), **V**: 203

Growth of Love, The (Bridges), **VI**: 81, 83

Gryffydh, Jane, **IV**: 159

Gryll Grange (Peacock), **IV**: xxii, 166–167, 170

Grylls, R. Glynn, **V**: 247, 260; **VII**: xvii, xxxviii

Guardian (periodical), **III**: 46, 49, 50

Guardian, The (Cowley), **II**: 194, 202

Guarini, Guarino, **II**: 49–50

Guide Through the District of the Lakes in the North of England, A (Wordsworth), **IV:** 25

Guide to Kulchur (Pound), **VI:** 333

Guido della Colonna, **I:** 57

Guild of St. George, The, **V:** 182

Guillaume de Deguilleville, **I:** 57

Guillaume de Lorris, **I:** 71

"Guilt and Sorrow" (Wordsworth), **IV:** 5, 45

"Guinevere" (Tennyson), **IV:** 336–337, 338

Guise, The (Marlowe), see *Massacre at Paris, The*

Guise, The (Webster), **II:** 68, 85

Gulliver's Travels (Swift), **II:** 261; **III:** 11, 20, **23–26,** 28, 35; **VI:** 121–122

Gurney, Ivor, **VI:** 416, **425–427**

Gutch, J. M., **IV:** 78, 81

Gutteridge, Bernard, **VII:** 422, 432–433

Guy Domville (James), **VI:** 39

Guy Mannering (Scott), **IV:** xvii, 31–32, 38

Guy of Warwick (Lydgate), **I:** 58

Gypsies Metamorphos'd (Jonson), **II:** 111$_n$

"Gyrtt in my giltetesse gowne" (Surrey), **I:** 115

H

Habington, William, **II:** 222, 237, 238

"Habit of Perfection, The" (Hopkins), **V:** 362, 381

"Hag, The" (Herrick), **II:** 111

Ha! Ha! Among the Trumpets (Lewis), **VII:** 447, 448

Haight, Gordon, **V:** 199, 200, 201

Hail and Farewell (Moore), **VI:** xii, 85, 88, 97, 99

Hakluyt, Richard, **I:** 150, 267; **III:** 7

"Half-a-Crown's Worth of Cheap Knowledge" (Thackeray), **V:** 22, 37

Halidon Hill (Scott), **IV:** 39

Halifax, marquess of, **III:** 38, 39, 40, 46

Hall, Edward, **II:** 43

Hall, Joseph, **II:** 25–26, 81; **IV:** 286

Hall, Radcliffe, **VI:** 411

Hallam, Arthur, **IV:** 234, 235, 328–336, 338

Hallam, Henry, **IV:** 283

Haller, Albrecht von, **III:** 88

Hall of Healing (O'Casey), **VII:** 11–12

"Hallowe'en" (Burns), **III:** 315

"Hamadryad, The" (Landor), **IV:** 96

Hamilton, Sir George Rostrevor, **IV:** xxiv

Hamlet (early version), **I:** 212, 221, 315

Hamlet (Shakespeare), **I:** 188, 280, 313, 315–316; **II:** 29, 36, 71, 75, 84; **III:** 170, 234; **V:** 328

Hammerton, Sir John, **V:** 393, 397

Hampden, John, **V:** 393, 395

"Hand and Soul" (Rossetti), **V:** 236, 320

Handful of Dust, A (Waugh), **VII:** xx, 294, 295–297

Hand of Ethelberta, The: A Comedy in Chapters (Hardy), **VI:** 4, 6, 20

"Handsome Heart, The" (Hopkins), **V:** 368–369

"Hanging, A" (Powell), **VII:** 276

Hanging Judge, The (Stevenson), **V:** 396

"Happily Ever After" (Huxley), **VII:** 199–200

"Happiness" (Owen), **VI:** 449, 458

"Happinesse to Hospitalitie, or a Hearty Wish to Good House-keeping" (Herrick), **II:** 111

"Happy old man, whose worth all mankind knows" (Flatman), **II:** 133

Happy Pair, The (Sedley), **II:** 266, 271

"Happy Prince, The" (Wilde), **V:** 406, 419

Hard Times (Dickens), **IV:** 247; **V:** viii, xxi, 4, 42, 47, 59, 63–64, 68, 70, 71

Hardy, Barbara, **V:** ix, xxviii, 39, 73, 201

Hardy, G. H., **VII:** 239–240

Hardy, Thomas, **II:** 69; **III:** 278; **V:** xx–xxvi, 144, 279, 429; **VI:** x, **1–22,** 253, 377; **VII:** xvi; list of short stories, **VI:** 22

Hardy of Wessex (Weber), **VI:** 21

Hare, J. C., **IV:** 54

Harington, Sir John, **I:** 131

"Hark, My Soul! It Is the Lord" (Cowper), **III:** 210

"Hark! the Dog's Howl" (Tennyson), **IV:** 332

Harlot's House, The (Wilde), **V:** 410, 418, 419

Harold (Tennyson), **IV:** 328, 338

Harold the Dauntless (Scott), **IV:** 39

Harriot, Thomas, **I:** 277, 278

Harris, Frank, **VI:** 102

Harris, Joseph, II: 305

Harrison, Frederic, V: 428–429

Harry Heathcote of Gangoil (Trollope), V: 102

"Harry Ploughman" (Hopkins), V: 376–377

Hartley, David, IV: 43, 45, 50, 165

Harvest Festival, The (O'Casey), VII: 12

Harvey, Christopher, II: 138

Harvey, Gabriel, I: 122–123, 125; II: 25

Harvey, T.W.J., V: 63, 199, 201

Harvey, William, I: 264

Hastings, Warren, IV: xv–xvi, 271, 278

"Has Your Soul Slipped" (Owen), VI: 446

Hatfield, C. W., V: 133, 151, 152, 153

Haunch of Venison, The (Goldsmith), III: 191

Haunted and the Haunters, The (Bulwer-Lytton), III: 340, 345

"Haunted House, The" (Graves), VII: 263

"Haunted House, The" (Hood), IV: 261, 262

Haunted Man and the Ghost's Bargain, The (Dickens), V: 71

"Haunter, The" (Hardy), VI: 18

Haunter of the Dark, The . . . (Lovecraft), III: 345

Hawes, Stephen, I: 49, 81

Hawkins, Sir John, II: 143

Hawkins, Lewis Weldon, VI: 85

Hawthorne, Nathaniel, III: 339, 345; VI: 27, 33–34

Hawthorne (James), VI: 33–34, 67

Haxton, Gerald, VI: 369

Haydon, Benjamin, IV: 214, 227, 312

"Haystack in the Floods, The" (Morris), V: 293

Hayter, Alethea, III: 338, 346; IV: xxiv–xxv, 57, 322

Hazard, Paul, III: 72

Hazlitt, William, I: 121, 164; II: 153, 332, 333, 337, 343, 346, 349, 354, 361, 363, 364; III: 68, 70, 76, 78, 165, 276–277; IV: ix, xi, xiv, xvii–xix, 38, 39, 41, 50, **125–140**, 217

Headlong Hall (Peacock), IV: xvii, **160–163**, 164, 165, 168, 169

Health and Holiness (Thompson), V: 450, 451

Hearing Secret Harmonies (Powell), VII: 352, 353

"Hears not my Phillis, how the Birds" (Sedley), II: 264

Heartbreak House (Shaw), V: 423; VI: viii, xv, 118, **120–121,** 127, 129

"Heart Knoweth Its Own Bitterness, The" (Rossetti), V: 253–254

Heart of Darkness (Conrad), VI: 135, **136–139,** 172

"Heart of John Middleton, The" (Gaskell), V: 15

Heart of Mid-Lothian, The (Scott), IV: xvii, 30, 31, 33–34, 35, 36, 39; V: 5

"Heart's Chill Between" (Rossetti), V: 249, 252

"Heart, II, The" (Thompson), V: 443

"Heather Ale" (Stevenson), V: 396

Heather Field, The (Martyn), VI: 87, 95

Heaven and Earth (Byron), IV: 178, 193

Heavenly Foot-man, The (Bunyan), II: 246, 253

Hebrew Melodies, Ancient and Modern . . . (Byron), IV: 192

Hecatommitthi (Cinthio), I: 316

Heine, Heinrich, IV: xviii, 296

Heinemann, William, VII: 91

He Knew He Was Right (Trollope), V: 98, 99, 102

"Hélas" (Wilde), V: 401

Helena (Waugh), VII: 292, 293–294, 301

hell, VI: 175

Hellas (Shelley), IV: xviii, 206, 208

Hellenics, The (Landor), IV: 96, 100

Héloïse and Abélard (Moore), VI: xii, 88, 89, **94–95,** 99

Hemans, Felicia, IV: 311

"Hendecasyllabics" (Swinburne), V: 321

"Hendecasyllabics" (Tennyson), IV: 327–328

Henderson, Hamish, VII: 422, 425–426

Henderson, Hubert, VII: 35

Henderson, Philip, V: xii, xviii, 335

Henderson, T. F., IV: 290_n

Hengist, King of Kent (or *The Mayor of Quinborough*) (Middleton), II: 3, 21

Henley, William Ernest, V: 386, 389, 391–392; VI: 159

Henn, T. R., VI: 220

"Henrietta Marr" (Moore), VI: 87

Henrietta Temple (Disraeli), **IV:** xix, 293, 298–299, 307, 308

"Henrik Ibsen" (James), **VI:** 49

Henry II (Bancroft), **II:** 305

Henry IV (Shakespeare), **I:** 308–309, 320

Henry V (Shakespeare), **I:** 309; **V:** 383

Henry VI's Triumphal Entry into London (Lydgate), **I:** 58

Henry VI trilogy (Shakespeare) **I:** 286, 299–300, 309

Henry VIII (Shakespeare), **I:** 324; **II:** 43, 66, 87; **V:** 328

"Henry VIII and Ann Boleyn" (Landor), **IV:** 92

Henry Esmond (Thackeray), see *History of Henry Esmond, Esq. . . . , The*

Henry for Hugh (Ford), **VI:** 331

Henry James (ed. Tanner), **VI:** 68

"Henry Purcell" (Hopkins), **V:** 370–371

Henry Vaughan: Experience and the Tradition (Garner), **II:** 186$_n$

Henslowe, Philip, **I:** 228, 235, 284; **II:** 3, 25, 68

Herakles (Euripides), **IV:** 358

Herbert, Edward, pseud. of John Hamilton Reynolds

Herbert, Edward, see Herbert of Cherbury, Lord

Herbert, George, **II:** 113, **117–130,** 133, 134, 137, 138, 140–142, 184, 187, 216, 221

Herbert of Cherbury, Lord, **II:** 117–118, 222, 237, 238

Hercules Oetaeus (Seneca), **I:** 248

Heretics (Chesterton), **VI:** 204, 336–337

"He Revisits His First School" (Hardy), **VI:** 17

Heritage and Its History, A (Compton-Burnett), **VII:** 60, 61, 65

"Hermaphroditus" (Swinburne), **V:** 320

Hermetical Physick . . . Englished (tr. Vaughan), **II:** 185, 201

Hermeticists, **I:** 237

Hermit of Marlow, the, pseud. of Percy Bysshe Shelley

"Hero" (Rossetti), **V:** 260

"Hero and Leander" (Hood), **IV:** 255–256, 267

Hero and Leander (Marlowe), **I:** 234, 237–240, 276, 278, 280, 288, **290–291,** 292

Hero and Leander, in Burlesque (Wycherley), **II:** 321

"Hero as King, The" (Carlyle), **IV:** 245, 246

Heroes and Hero-Worship (Carlyle), **IV:** xx, 240, 244–246, 249, 250, 341

Heroic Idylls, with Additional Poems (Landor), **IV:** 100

"Heroic Stanzas" (Dryden), **II:** 292

Heroine, The: Or The Adventures of Cherubina (Barrett), **III:** 335

Herrick, Robert, **II: 102–116,** 121

Herself Surprised (Cary), **VII:** 186, 188, 191–192

"Hertha" (Swinburne), **V:** 325

Her Triumph (Jonson), **I:** 347

"Hervé Riel" (Browning), **IV:** 367

Herzog, Werner, **IV:** 180

"He saw my heart's woe" (Brontë), **V:** 132

"Hesperia" (Swinburne), **V:** 320, 321

Hesperides, The (Herrick), **II:** 102, 103, 104, 106, 110, 112, 115, 116

"He Thinks of His Past Greatness . . . When a Part of the Constellations of Heaven" (Yeats), **VI:** 211

"He thought he saw a Banker's Clerk" (Carroll), **V:** 270

Heylyn, Peter, **I:** 169

Heywood, Jasper, **I:** 215

Heywood, Thomas, **II:** 19, 47, 48, 68, 83

H. G. Wells and His Critics (Raknem), **VI:** 228, 245, 246

H.G. Wells: His Turbulent Life and Times (Dickson), **VI:** 246

H. G. Wells: The Critical Heritage (ed. Parrinder), **VI:** 246

Hibberd, Dominic, **VI:** xvi, xxxiii

Hide and Seek (Swinburne), **V:** 334

Higden, Ranulf, **I:** 22

Higher Schools and Universities in Germany (Arnold), **V:** 216

Highet, Gilbert, **II:** 199

Highland Widow, The (Scott), **IV:** 39

"High Life in Verdopolis" (Brontë), **V:** 135

"High wavering heather . . ." (Brontë), **V:** 113

Hilda Lessways (Bennett), **VI:** 258

Hill, G. B., **III:** 233, 234$_n$

Hill of Devi, The (Forster), **VI:** 397, 408, 411

"Hill of Venus, The" (Morris), **V:** 298

Hind, The, and the Panther (Dryden), **II:** 291, 292, 299–300, 304

Hinge of Faith, The (Churchill), **VI:** 361

Hinman, Charlton, **I:** 326–327

Hints Towards the Formation of a More Comprehensive Theory of Life (Coleridge), **IV:** 56

Hippolytus (Euripides), **V:** 322, 324

"His Age, Dedicated to his Peculiar Friend, M. John Wickes" (Herrick), **II:** 112

"His Fare-well to Sack" (Herrick), **II:** 111

"His Letanie, to the Holy Spirit" (Herrick), **II:** 114

His Majesties Declaration Defended (Dryden), **II:** 305

His Majesty Preserved . . . Dictated to Samuel Pepys by the King . . . (ed. Rees-Mogg), **II:** 288

His Noble Numbers (Herrick), **II:** 102, 103, 112, 114, 115, 116

"His Returne to London" (Herrick), **II:** 103

Historia naturalis et experimentalis (Bacon), **I:** 259, 273

Historia regis Henrici Septimi (André), **I:** 270

Historical Account of the Theatre in Europe, An (Riccoboni), **II:** 348

historical novel, **VI:** 325, 326

Historical Register, The (Fielding), **III:** 97, 98, 105

Historical Relation of the Island of Ceylon, An (Knox), **III:** 7

historical writing, **III:** 225–232; **IV:** 283–290; **VI:** 347, 383, 385; see also literary history, military history, social history

history, see historical writing, literary history, military history, social history

"History" (Macaulay), **IV:** 284

History and Adventures of an Atom, The (Smollett), **III:** 149–150, 158

History and Remarkable Life of . . . Col. Jack (Defoe), see *Colonel Jack*

History of a Good Warm Watch-Coat, The (Sterne), see *Political Romance, A*

"History of Angria" (Brontë), **V:** 110–111, 118

History of Antonio and Mellida, The (Marston), see *Antonio and Mellida*

History of a Six Weeks' Tour Through a Part of France . . . (Shelley and Shelley), **IV:** 208

History of Brazil (Southey), **IV:** 68, 71

History of Britain . . . , The (Milton), **II:** 176

History of British India, The, (Mill), **V:** 288

History of England (Hume), **III:** 148; **IV:** 273

History of England (Macaulay), **II:** 255

History of England, An (Goldsmith), **III:** 180, 181, 189, 191

History of England, The (Trevelyan), **VI:** xv, 390–391, 393

History of England from the Accession of James II, The (Macaulay), **IV:** xx, 272, 273, 280, 282, **283–290,** 291

History of English Thought in the Eighteenth Century (Stephen), **V:** 280, 288, 289

History of Frederick the Great, The (Carlyle), **IV:** xxi, 240, 246, 249, 250

History of Friar Francis, The, **I:** 218

History of Henry Esmond, Esq. . . . , The (Thackeray), **V:** xxi, 20, **31–33,** 38

History of Madan, The (Beaumont), **II:** 67

History of Mr. Polly, The (Wells), **VI:** xii, 225, 238–239

History of My Own Times (Burnet), **III:** 39

History of Pendennis, The (Thackeray), **V:** xxi, **28–31,** 33, 35, 38; **VI:** 354

History of Rasselas Prince of Abyssina, The (Johnson), **III:** 112–113, 121; **IV:** 47

History of Samuel Titmarsh and the Great Hoggarty Diamond, The (Thackeray), see *Great Hoggarty Diamond, The*

History of Sir Charles Grandison, The (Richardson), see *Sir Charles Grandison*

History of the Adventures of Joseph Andrews . . . , The (Fielding), see *Joseph Andrews*

"History of the Boswell Papers" (Pottle), **III:** 240$_n$

History of the Church of Scotland (Spottiswoode), **II:** 142

History of the Earth, and Animated Nature, An (Goldsmith), **III:** 180, 181, 189–190, 191

History of the English-Speaking Peoples, A (Churchill), **VI:** 356

History of the Four Last Years of Queen Anne, The (Swift), **III:** 27, 36

"History of the Hardcomes, The" (Hardy), **VI:** 22

History of the Italian Renaissance (Symonds), **V:** 83

History of the Kentish Petition, The (Defoe), **III:** 12

History of the League, The (tr. Dryden), **II:** 305

"History of the Next French Revolution, The" (Thackeray), **V:** 38

History of the Peninsular War (Southey), **IV:** 58, 63, 71; **V:** 109

History of the Pyrates, The (Defoe), **III:** 13

History of the Reign of Henry the Seventh, The (Bacon), **I:** 259, 269, 270, 272

History of the Royal Society of London (Sprat), **II:** 196; **III:** 29

History of the Union of Great Britain, The (Defoe), **III:** 4, 13

History of the Wars of . . . Charles XII . . . , The (Defoe), **III:** 13

"History of the Winds" (Bacon), **I:** 263

History of the World, The (Ralegh), **I:** 145, 146, 149, 153–157

History of Titus Andronicus, The, **I:** 305

History of Tom Jones, a Foundling, The (Fielding), see *Tom Jones*

History of Van's House, The, **II:** 335

Histriomastix (Prynne), **II:** 339

Histriomastix: or The Player Whipt (Marston), **II:** 27, 28, 40

Hitchcock, Alfred, **III:** 342–343

Hitherto Unpublished Poems and Stories . . . (Browning), **IV:** 321

Hoare, D. M., **V:** 299, 306

Hobbes, John Oliver, pseud. of Mrs. Craigie

Hobbes, Thomas, **II:** 190, 196, 256, 294; **III:** 22; **IV:** 121, 138

Hoccleve, Thomas, **I:** 49

"Hock-Cart, or Harvest Home, The" (Herrick), **II:** 110–111

Hodder, E., **IV:** 62$_n$

Hodgson, W. N., **VI:** 422, 423

Hoffman, Calvin, **I:** 277

Hoffman, Heinrich, **I:** 25

Hoffmann, E.T.A., **III:** 333, 334, 345

Hogarth Press, **VII:** xv, 17, 34

Hogg, James, **IV:** xvii, 73

Hogg, Thomas Jefferson, **IV:** 196, 198, 209

Hoggart, Richard, **VII:** xx, xxxviii

Holiday Romance (Dickens), **V:** 72

Hollis, Maurice Christopher, **VI:** xxxiii

Holloway, John, **VII:** 82

"Hollow Men, The" (Eliot), **VII:** 150–151, 158

Hollow's Mill (Brontë), see *Shirley*

"Holy Baptisme I" (Herbert), **II:** 128

Holy City, The: or, The New Jerusalem (Bunyan), **II:** 253

"Holy-Cross Day" (Browning), **IV:** 367

"Holy Fair, The" (Burns), **III:** 311, 315, 317

Holy Grail, The, and Other Poems (Tennyson), **IV:** 338

"Holyhead, September 25, 1717" (Swift), **III:** 32

Holy Life, the Beauty of Christianity, A (Bunyan), **II:** 253

"Holy Scriptures" (Vaughan), **II:** 187

Holy Sinner, The (Mann), **II:** 97$_n$

Holy Sonnets (Donne), **I:** 362, 366, 367

Holy War, The: Made by Shaddai . . . (Bunyan), **II:** 246, 250, 251–252, 253

"Holy Willie's Prayer" (Burns), **III:** 311, 313, 319

Homage to Catalonia (Orwell), **VII:** 275, 280–281

Homage to Clio (Auden), **VII:** 392

Home and Beauty (Maugham), **VI:** 368–369

"Home at Grasmere" (Wordsworth), **IV:** 3, 23–24

Homecomings (Snow), **VII:** xxi, 324, 329, 335

Home Letters (Disraeli), **IV:** 296, 308

Homer, **I:** 236; **II:** 304, 347; **III:** 217, 220; **IV:** 204, 215

Homeric Hymns (tr. Chapman), **I:** 236

Home Rule, see Irish Home Rule

"Home Thoughts from Abroad" (Browning), **IV:** 356

Home University Library, **VI:** 337, 391

homosexuality, **V:** 312; **VI:** 365, 397, 398–399, 407–408, 410–412; **VII:** 103, 309, 318

Hone, Joseph, **VI:** 88

Hone, William, **IV:** 255

Honest Man's Fortune, The (Field, Fletcher, Massinger), **II:** 66

Honest Whore, The (Dekker and Middleton), **II:** 3, 21, 89

"Honourable Laura, The" (Hardy), **VI:** 22

Honour of the Garter, The (Peele), **I:** 205

Honour Triumphant, or the Peeres Challenge (Ford), **II:** 88, 100

Hood, Thomas, **IV:** xvi, xx, **251–267**, 311

Hood's (periodical), **IV:** 252, 261, 263, 264

"Hood's Literary Reminiscences" (Blunden), **IV:** 267

Hood's Own (Hood), **IV:** 251–252, 253, 254, 266

Hook, Theodore, **IV:** 254

Hooker, Richard, **I:** **176–190**, 362; **II:** 133, 137, 140–142, 147

"Hope" (Cowper), **III:** 212

Hopes and Fears for Art (Morris), **V:** 301, 306

Hopkins, Gerard Manley, **II:** 123, 181; **IV:** xx; **V:** ix, xi, xxv, 53, 205, 210, 261, 309–310, 338, **361–382**; **VI:** 75, 83

Hopkins (MacKenzie), **V:** 375$_n$, 382

Hopkinson, Sir Tom, **VII:** xx, xxxviii

Horace, **II:** 108, 112, 199, 200, 265, 292, 300, 309, 347; **IV:** 327

"Horatian Ode . . . , An" (Marvell), **II:** 204, 208, 209, 210, 211, 216–217

"Horatius" (Macaulay), **IV:** 282

Horestes (Pickering), **I:** 213, 216–218

Horne, Richard Hengist, **IV:** 312, 321, 322

Hornet (periodical), **VI:** 102

Horniman, Annie, **VI:** 309; **VII:** 1

"Horns Away" (Lydgate), **I:** 64

"Horse Dealer's Daughter, The" (Lawrence), **VII:** 114

"Horse, Goose and Sheep, The" (Lydgate), **I:** 57

Horse's Mouth, The (Cary), **VII:** 186, 188, 191, 192, 193–194

Hoskins, John, **I:** 165–166, 167

"Hospital Barge" (Owen), **VI:** 454

Hotson, Leslie, **I:** 275, 276

Hough, Graham, **IV:** 323$_n$, 339; **V:** 355, 359

Houghton, Lord, see Monckton Milnes, Richard

Hound of Death, The (Christie), **III:** 341

"Hound of Heaven, The" (Thompson), **V:** 445–447, 449, 450

Hound of the Baskervilles, The (Doyle), **III:** 341, 342, 345

"Hour and the Ghost, The" (Rossetti), **V:** 256

Hours in a Library (Stephen), **V:** 279, 285, 286, 287, 289

Hours of Idleness (Byron), **IV:** xvi, 192

House, Humphry, **IV:** 167

"House" (Browning), **IV:** 359

House and Its Head, A (Compton-Burnett), **VII:** 61

House by the Churchyard, The (Le Fanu), **III:** 340, 345

Household Words (periodical), **V:** xxi, 3, 42

House of Children, A (Cary), **VII:** 186, 187, 189

"House of Christmas, The" (Chesterton), **VI:** 344

House of Cobwebs, The (Gissing), **V:** 437

House of Fame, The (Chaucer), **I:** 23, 30

House of Life, The (Rossetti), **V:** 237, 238, 241, 242, 243, 244, 245

House of Pomegranates, A (Wilde), **V:** 419

House of the Seven Gables, The (Hawthorne), **III:** 339, 345

House on the Beach, The (Meredith), **V:** 230–231, 234

Housman, A. E., **III:** 68, 70; **V:** xxii, xxvi, 311; **VI:** ix, xv–xvi, **151–164**, 415

Housman, Laurence, **V:** 402, 420

Housman: 1897–1936 (Richards), **VI:** 164

How About Europe? (Douglas), **VI:** 295, 305

Howard, Henry, earl of Surrey, see Surrey, Henry Howard, earl of

Howard, R., **V:** 418

Howard, Sir Robert, **II:** 100

Howards End (Forster), **VI:** viii, xii, 397, 398, 401, **404–406,** 407

Howarth, R. G., **II:** 69

Howe, Irving, **VI:** 41

Howells, William Dean, **VI:** 23, 29, 33

How He Lied to Her Husband (Shaw), **VI:** 129

"How I Became a Socialist" (Orwell), **VII:** 276–277

"How It Strikes a Contemporary" (Browning), **IV:** 354, 367, 373

Howitt, William, **IV:** 212

How Lisa Loved the King (Eliot), **V:** 200

"How Many Bards" (Keats), **IV:** 215

"How Sleep the Brave" (Collins), **III:** 166

"How Sweet the Name of Jesus Sounds" (Newton), **III:** 210

How the "Mastiffs" Went to Iceland (Trollope), **V:** 102

" 'How They Brought the Good News from Ghent to Aix (16—)' " (Browning), **IV:** 356, 361

How to Become an Author (Bennett), **VI:** 264

"How to Kill" (Douglas), **VII:** 443

How to Live on 24 Hours a Day (Bennett), **VI:** 264

How to Read (Pound), **VII:** 235

How to Settle the Irish Question (Shaw), **VI:** 119, 129

"How to Teach Reading" (Leavis), **VII:** 235, 248

"How would the ogling sparks despise" (Etherege), **II:** 268

Huchon, René, **III:** 273$_n$

Hudibras (Butler), **II:** 145

Hudson, Derek, **V:** xi, xxviii, 263, 274

Hudson, W. H., **V:** 429

Hueffer, Ford, see Ford, Ford Madox

Hueffer, Ford Madox, see Ford, Ford Madox

Hughes, Arthur, **V:** 294

Hughes, John, **I:** 121, 122; **III:** 40

Hughes, Thomas, **I:** 218; **V:** xxii, 170

Hughes, Willie, **V:** 405

Hugh Selwyn Mauberley (Pound), **VI:** 417; **VII:** xvi

Hugo, Victor, **III:** 334; **V:** xxii, xxv, 22, 320

Hugo (Bennett), **VI:** 249

Hulme, T. E., **VI:** 416

"Human Abstract, The" (Blake), **III:** 296

Human Age, The (Lewis), **VII:** 80

human ecology, **VI:** 241

"Humanitad" (Wilde), **V:** 401–402

Human Machine, The (Bennett), **VI:** 250

Human Odds and Ends (Gissing), **V:** 437

"Human Seasons, The" (Keats), **IV:** 232

Human Shows, Far Phantasies, Songs and Trifles (Hardy), **VI:** 20

"Humble Petition of Frances Harris" (Swift), **III:** 30–31

Hume, David, **III:** 148; **IV:** xiv, 138, 145, 273, 288; **V:** 288, 343

Humorous Day's Mirth, A (Chapman), **I:** 243, 244

Humorous Lieutenant, The (Fletcher), **II:** 45, 60–61, 65, 359

Humours of the Court (Bridges), **VI:** 83

Humphrey Clinker (Smollett), **III:** 147, 150, **155–157**, 158

Hunt, John, **IV:** 129, 132

Hunt, Leigh, **II:** 332, 355, 357, 359, 363; **IV:** ix, 80, 104, 129, 132, 163, 172, 198, 202, 205–206, 209, 212–217, 230, 306

Hunt, Violet, **VI:** 324

Hunt, William Holman, **V:** 45, 77–78, 235, 236, 240

Hunted Down (Dickens), **VI:** 66, 72

Hunter, G. K., **I:** 165; **II:** 29, 41

Hunting of Cupid, The (Peele), **I:** 205

Hunting of the Snark, The (Carroll), **V:** 270, 272, 273

Hunting Sketches (Trollope), **V:** 101

Huntley, F. L., **II:** 152, 157

"Huntsman, The" (Lowbury), **VII:** 431–432

Hurd, Michael, **VI:** 427

Hurd, Richard, **I:** 122

"Hurrahing in Harvest" (Hopkins), **V:** 366, 367, 368

"Husband and Wife" (Rossetti), **V:** 259

Husband His Own Cuckold, The (Dryden the younger), **II:** 305

Hussey, Maurice, **II:** 250, 254

Hutchinson, F. E., **II:** 121, 123, 126, 129

Hutchinson, Sara, **IV:** 15, 49, 50, 54

Hutton, James, **IV:** 200

Hutton, R. H., **V:** 157–158, 168, 170

Huxley, Aldous, **II:** 105, 173; **III:** 341; **IV:** 303; **V:** xxii, 53; **VII:** xii, xvii–xviii, 79, **197–208**

Huxley, Thomas, **V:** xxii, 182, 284

Hyacinth Halvey (Gregory), **VI:** 315, 316

Hyde, Douglas, **VI:** 307; **VII:** 1

Hyde-Lees, George, **VI:** 213

Hydriotaphia (Browne), **II:** **150–153**, 154, 155, 156

Hygiasticon (Lessius), **II:** 181$_n$

Hymenaei (Jonson), **I:** 239

"Hymne of the Nativity, A" (Crashaw), **II:** 180, 183

"Hymn of Apollo" (Shelley), **II:** 200; **IV:** 203

Hymn of Nature, A (Bridges), **VI:** 81

Hymns (Spenser), **I:** 131

Hymns Ancient and Modern (Betjeman), **VII:** 363–364

"Hymn to Adversity" (Gray), **III:** 137

Hymn to Christ on the Cross (Chapman), **I:** 241–242

"Hymn to Colour" (Meredith), **V:** 222

Hymn to Diana (Jonson), **I:** 346

"Hymn to God, my God, in my sickness" (Donne), **I:** 368; **II:** 114

Hymn to Harmony, A (Congreve), **II:** 350

"Hymn to Intellectual Beauty" (Shelley), **IV:** 198

"Hymn. To Light" (Cowley), **II:** 198, 200, 259

"Hymn to Mercury" (Shelley), **IV:** 196, 204

"Hymn to Pan" (Keats), **IV:** 216, 217, 222

"Hymn to the Name and Honor of the Admirable Sainte Teresa, A" (Crashaw), **II:** 179, 182

Hymn to the Pillory, A (Defoe), **III:** 13

"Hymn to the Sun" (Hood), **IV:** 255

"Hymn to the Winds" (du Bellay), **V:** 345

"Hymn to Venus" (Shelley), **IV:** 209

Hymnus in Cynthiam (Chapman), **I:** 240

Hyperion (Keats), **IV:** 95, 204, 211, 212, 213, **227–231**, 235; **VI:** 455

Hypnerstomachia (Colonna), **I:** 134

Hypochondriack, The (Boswell), **III:** 237, 240, 243, 248

I

"I abide and abide and better abide" (Wyatt), **I:** 108, 109

I Am a Camera (Isherwood), **VII:** 311

Ian Hamilton's March (Churchill), **VI:** 351

"Ianthe" poems (Landor), **IV:** 88, 89, 92, 99

Ibrahim (Scudéry), **III:** 95

Ibsen, Henrik, **IV:** 118; **V:** xxiii–xxvi, 414; **VI:** viii–ix, 104, 110, 269

I Can Remember Robert Louis Stevenson (ed. Masson), **V:** 393, 397

"I care not if I live" (Bridges), **VI:** 81

Icelandic journals (Morris), **V:** 299, 300–301, 307

I, Claudius (Graves), **VII:** 259

I Crossed the Minch (MacNeice), **VII:** 403, 411

Ideal Husband, An (Wilde), **V:** 414–415, 419

idealism, **VI:** 23

Ideals in Ireland (ed. Lady Gregory), **VI:** 98

Idea of Christian Society, The (Eliot), **VII:** 153

Idea of Comedy, The, and the Uses of the Comic Spirit (Meredith), see *Essay on Comedy and the Uses of the Comic Spirit*

Idea of the Perfection of Painting, An (tr. Evelyn), **II:** 287

Ideas of Good and Evil (Yeats), **V:** 301, 306

"I dined with a Jew" (Macaulay), **IV:** 283

Idiocy of Idealism, The (Levy), **VI:** 303

"Idiot Boy, The" (Wordsworth), **IV:** 7, 11

"Idiots, The" (Conrad), **VI:** 148

Idleness of Business, The: A Satyr . . . (Wycherley), see *Folly of Industry, The*

Idler (periodical), **III:** 111–112, 121

Idyllia heroica decem (Landor), **IV:** 100

Idylls of the King (Tennyson), **IV:** xxii, 328, 336–337, 338

"If by Dull Rhymes Our English Must be Chained . . ." (Keats), **IV:** 221

"I find no peace and all my war is done" (Wyatt), **I:** 110

"If in the world there be more woe" (Wyatt), **I:** 104

If I Were Four and Twenty: Swedenborg, Mediums and Desolate Places (Yeats), **VI:** 222

"If This Were Faith" (Stevenson), **V:** 385

"I have loved and so doth she" (Wyatt), **I:** 102

"I heard an Angel singing" (Blake), **III:** 296

I Knock at the Door (O'Casey), **VII:** 12

"I know a Bank Whereon the Wild Thyme Grows" (Shakespeare), **IV:** 222

Il cortegiano (Castiglione), **I:** 265

"I lead a life unpleasant" (Wyatt), **I:** 104

Iliad (tr. Pope), **III:** 77

Iliad, The (tr. Cowper), **III:** 220

I Live Under a Black Sun (Sitwell), **VII:** 127, 135, 139

Ill Beginning Has a Good End, An, and a Bad Beginning May Have a Good End, **II:** 89, 100

"I'll come when thou art saddest" (Brontë), **V:** 127

Illustrated Excursions in Italy (Lear), **V:** 77, 79, 87

Illustrated London News (periodical), **VI:** 337

Illustrations of Latin Lyrical Metres (Clough), **V:** 170

Illustrations of the Family of Psittacidae, or Parrots (Lear), **V:** 76, 79, 87

"I Look into My Glass" (Hardy), **VI:** 16

"I love all beauteous things" (Bridges), **VI:** 72

Il pastor fido (Guarini), **II:** 49–50

Il pecorone (Fiorentino), **I:** 310

"Il Penseroso" (Milton), **II:** 158–159; **III:** 211$_n$; **IV:** 14–15

Image Men, The (Priestley), **VII:** 209, 210, 218, 221–223

Imaginary Conversations (Landor), **IV:** xviii, 87, 88, 89, **90–94,** 96–97, 99, 100

Imaginary Conversations of Greeks and Romans (Landor), **IV:** 100

Imaginary Portraits (Pater), **V:** 339, 340, 348–349, 355, 356

"Imaginative Woman, An" (Hardy), **VI:** 22

imagism, **VI:** xvi, 416; **VII:** xiii

"I'm happiest when most away" (Brontë), **V:** 116

"Imitation of Spenser" (Keats), **IV:** 213

Imitation of the Sixth Satire of the Second Book of Horace, An (Swift), **III:** 36

Imitations of Horace (Pope), **II:** 298; **III:** 77

Immaturity (Shaw), **VI:** 105

Immorality and Profaneness of the English Stage, A (Collier), see *Short View of the Immorality . . . , A*

Immorality, Debauchery and Prophaneness (Meriton), **II:** 340

Immortal Dickens, The (Gissing), **V:** 437

"Imperial Elegy, An" (Owen), **VI:** 448

imperialism, **VI:** 165–166, 168, 175–180, 183–184, 335, 355, 409; **VII:** 186, 276

Imperial Palace (Bennett), **VI:** xiii, 247, 250, 251, 262–263

Importance of Being Earnest, The (Wilde), **V:** xxvi, 415–416, 419

Importance of the Guardian Considered, The (Swift), **III:** 35

Impossible Thing, An: A Tale (Congreve), **II:** 350

Impressions and Opinions (Moore), **VI:** 87

Impressions of America (Wilde), **V:** 419

Impressions of Theophrastus Such (Eliot), **V:** 198, 200

Imprisonment (Shaw), **VI:** 129

In a Free State (Naipaul), **VII:** xx

In a German Pension (Mansfield), **VII:** 171, 172–173

In a Glass Darkly (Le Fanu), **III:** 345

"In an Artist's Studio" (Rossetti), **V:** 249

"In Broken Images" (Graves), **VII:** 267

Inca of Perusalem, The (Shaw), **VI:** 120

In Chancery (Galsworthy), **VI:** 274

"Inchcape Rock, The" (Southey), **IV:** 58

"Incident in the Life of Mr. George Crookhill" (Hardy), **VI:** 22

Inclinations (Sackville-West), **VII:** 70

Incognita; or, Love and Duty Reconcil'd (Congreve), **II:** 338, 346

Inconstant, The, or, The Way to Win Him (Farquhar), **II:** 352–353, 357, 362, 364

Incredulity of Father Brown, The (Chesterton), **VI:** 338

"In Deep and Solemn Dreams" (Tennyson), **IV:** 329

"In Defence of Milton" (Leavis), **VII:** 246

Independent Labour Party, **VII:** 280

Independent Review (periodical), **VI:** 399

Independent Theatre Society, **VI:** 104

Index to "In Memoriam," An (ed. Carroll), **V:** 274

Index to the Private Papers of James Boswell . . . (ed. Pottle et al.), **III:** 249

Indian Education Minutes . . . , The (Macaulay), **IV:** 291

Indian Emperour or the Conquest of Mexico . . . , The, Being the Sequel to the Indian Queen (Dryden), **II:** 290, 294, 305

Indian Journal (Lear), see *Edward Lear's Indian Journal*

Indian Queen, The (Dryden), **II:** 305

"Indian Serenade, The" (Shelley), **IV:** 195, 203

"Indian Summer of a Forsyte" (Galsworthy), **VI:** 274, 276, 283

Indiscretion in the Life of an Heiress, An (Hardy), **VI:** 20

"Induction" (Sackville), **I:** 169

Induction, The (Field), **II:** 66

"In dungeons dark I cannot sing" (Brontë), **V:** 115–116

Inebriety (Crabbe), **III:** 274, 278–279, 286

"I never shall love the snow again" (Bridges), **VI:** 77

In Excited Reverie: A Centenary Tribute to William Butler Yeats, 1865–1939 (Ed. Jeffares and Cross), **VI:** 224

"Infancy" (Crabbe), **III:** 273, 281

"Inferior Religions" (Lewis), **VII:** 77

Infernal Desire Machine of Dr. Hoffman, The (Carter), **III:** 345

Infernal Marriage, The (Disraeli), **IV:** 297, 299, 308

"In Flanders Fields" (McCrae), **VI:** 434

Influence of the Roman Censorship on the Morals of the People, The (Swinburne), **V:** 333

"Informer, The" (Conrad), **VI:** 148

Ingannati: The Deceived . . . and Aelia Laelia Crispis (Peacock), **IV:** 170

Inge, William Ralph, **VI:** 344

In Good King Charles's Golden Days (Shaw), **VI:** 125, 127, 129

Inheritors, The (Conrad and Ford), **VI:** 321, 332

Inheritors, The: An Extravagant Story (Conrad and Ford), **VI:** 146, 148

Inishfallen, Fare Thee Well (O'Casey), **VII:** 4, 12

Inland Voyage, An (Stevenson), **V:** 386, 395

"In Memoriam (Easter, 1915)" (Thomas), **VI:** 424–425

In Memorium (Tennyson), **IV:** xxi, 234, 248, 292, 310, 313, 323, 325–328, 330, 333–338, 371; **V:** 285, 455

"In Memory of Eva Gore-Booth and Con Markiewicz" (Yeats), **VI:** 217

"In Memory of Sigmund Freud" (Auden), **VII:** 379

"In Memory of W. B. Yeats" (Auden), **VI:** 208

"In My Own Album" (Lamb), **IV:** 83

Inn Album, The (Browning), **IV:** 358, 367, 369–370, 374

Inner Temple, Gentlemen of the, **I:** 214

Innocence of Father Brown, The (Chesterton), **VI:** 338

"Inn of the Two Witches, The" (Conrad), **VI:** 148

Inns of Court, **I:** 212–213, 298; see Elizabethan drama

In Our Infancy (Corke), **VII:** 93

In Parenthesis (Jones), **VI:** xvi, 437–438

"In Praise of Lessius His Rule of Health" (Crashaw), **II:** 181$_n$

"In Praise of Limestone" (Auden), **VII:** 390, 391

"In Procession" (Graves), **VII:** 264

Inquiry into the Nature & Causes of the Wealth of Nations (Smith), **IV:** xiv, 145

Insatiate Countess, The (Barsted and Marston), **II:** 31, 40

"Insensibility" (Owen), **VI:** 453, 455

Inside the Whale (Orwell), **VII:** 282

In Single Strictness (Moore), **VI:** 87, 95, 99

"Installation Ode" (Gray), **III:** 142

Instead of Trees (Priestley), **VII:** 209–210

Instructions Concerning Erecting of a Liberty (tr. Evelyn), **II:** 287

Instructions for the Ignorant (Bunyan), **II:** 253

"Instructions to a Painter . . ." (Waller), **II:** 233

"Intellectual Felicity" (Boswell), **III:** 237

Intelligencer (journal), **III:** 35

Intelligent Woman's Guide to Socialism and Capitalism, The (Shaw), **VI:** 116, 125

"In Tenebris II" (Hardy), **VI:** 14

Intentions (Wilde), **V:** 407, 419

interior monologue, **VII:** 174, 178; see also stream of consciousness

"Interloper, The" (Hardy), **VI:** 17

"Interlopers at the Knapp" (Hardy), **VI:** 22

"Interlude, An" (Swinburne), **V:** 321

"Intermediate Sex, The" (Carpenter), **VI:** 407

"International Episode, An" (James), **VI:** 69

internationalism, **VI:** 241$_n$; **VII:** 229

In the Beginning (Douglas), **VI:** 303, 304, 305

In the Cage (James), **VI:** 67, 69

In the Days of the Comet (Wells), **VI:** 227, 237, 244

"In the Garden at Swainston" (Tennyson), **IV:** 336

"In the Great Metropolis" (Clough), **V:** 164

In the Green Tree (Lewis), **VII:** 447

"In the House of Suddhoo" (Kipling), **VI:** 170

"In the rude age when science was not so rife" (Surrey), **I:** 115–116

"In the Same Boat" (Kipling), **VI:** 193

In the Seven Woods (Yeats), **VI:** 213, 222

In the South Seas (Stevenson), **V:** 396

In the Twilight (Swinburne), **V:** 333

In the Year of Jubilee (Gissing), **V:** 437

"Intimate World of Ivy Compton-Burnett, The" (Karl), **VII:** 70

"Intimations of Immortality . . ." (Wordsworth), see "Ode. Intimations of Immortality from Recollections of Early Childhood"

"In Time of Absence" (Graves), **VII:** 270

Into Battle (Churchill), **VI:** 356

"Into Battle" (Grenfell), **VI:** 418

In Touch with the Infinite (Betjeman), **VII:** 365

Intriguing Chambermaid, The (Fielding), **III:** 105

Introductory Lecture (Housman), **VI:** 164

Intruder, The (Hardy), **VI:** 20

Invective against Jonson, The (Chapman), **I:** 243

"Inversnaid" (Hopkins), **V:** 368, 372

Invisible Man, The: A Grotesque Romance (Wells), **VI:** 226, 232–233, 244

"Invitation, The" (Shelley), **IV:** 196

"Invocation" (Sitwell), **VII:** 136

In Wicklow, West Kerry, and Connemara (Synge), **VI:** 309, 317

Ion (Plato), **IV:** 48

Iphigenia (Peele), **I:** 198

"Iphis and Araxarathen" (Gower), **I:** 53–54

I promessi sposi (Manzoni), **III:** 334

"Ireland" (Swift), **III:** 31

Ireland's Abbey Theatre (Robinson), **VI:** 317

Ireland Since the Rising (Coogan), **VII:** 9

Ireland's Literary Renaissance (Boyd), **VI:** 316

"I Remember" (Hood), **IV:** 255

Irene: A Tragedy (Fielding), **III:** 109, 121

Irish Drama, The (Malone), **VI:** 316

Irish Dramatic Movement, The (Ellis-Fermor), **VI:** 317

Irish dramatic revival, **VI:** xiv, 207, 218, 307–310; **VII:** 3

Irish Essays and Others (Arnold), **V:** 216

Irish Free State, **VI:** 207; **VII:** 2

Irish Home Rule, **VI:** ix, 119; see also Irish nationalism

Irish Impressions (Chesterton), **VI:** 345

Irish literary renaissance, **VI:** xiv, 207, 218, 307–310; **VII:** 1

Irish Literary Theatre, **VI:** 87, 88, 218, 309; **VII:** 1

Irish National Dramatic Company, **VI:** 88

Irish nationalism, **VI:** 212–214, 309–310; **VII:** 1

Irish Republican Brotherhood, **VII:** 1

Irish Sketch Book, The (Thackeray), **V:** 25, 38

Irrational Knot, The (Shaw), **VI:** 102, 103, 105, 129

Irving, Washington, **III:** 54

Isabel Clarendon (Gissing), **V:** 437

"Isabella" (Keats), **IV:** xviii, 216, 217–218, 235

Is He Popenjoy? (Trollope), **V:** 100, 102

Isherwood, Christopher, **VII:** xx, **309–320**

Island (Huxley), **VII:** xviii, 206

Island, The (Byron), **IV:** xviii, 173, 193

"Islanders, The" (Kipling), **VI:** 169, 203

Island in the Moon, An (Blake), **III:** 290, 292

Island Nights' Entertainments (Stevenson), **V:** 387, 396

Island of Dr. Moreau, The (Wells), **VI:** 230–231

Island Pharisees, The (Galsworthy), **VI:** 271, 273, 274, 277, 281

Island Princess, The (Fletcher), **II:** 45, 60, 65

Isle of Man, The (Bernard), **II:** 246

"Isle of Voices, The" (Stevenson), **V:** 396

"Isobel's Child" (Browning), **IV:** 313

"Isopes Fabules" (Lydgate), **I:** 57

Israel's Hope Encouraged (Bunyan), **II:** 253

"I Stood Tip-toe" (Keats), **IV:** 214, 216

"I strove with none" (Landor), **IV:** 98

Italian, The (Radcliffe), **III:** 331–332, 335, 337, 345; **IV:** 173

Italian Hours (James), **VI:** 43, 67

Italian Mother, The, and Other Poems (Swinburne), **V:** 333

Italics of Walter Savage Landor, The (Landor), **IV:** 100

"Italio, Io Ti Saluto" (Rossetti), **V:** 250

"Italy and the World" (Browning), **IV:** 318

"It is a beauteous evening, calm and free" (Wordsworth), **IV:** 22

"I took my heart in my hand" (Rossetti), **V:** 252

It's an Old Country (Priestley), **VII:** 211

"It Was Upon a Lammas Night" (Burns), **III:** 315

"Itylus" (Swinburne), **V:** 319

Ivanhoe (Scott), **IV:** xviii, 31, 34, 39

"I've Thirty Months" (Synge), **VI:** 314

Ivory Tower, The (James), **VI:** 64, 65

"Ivry: A Song of the Huguenots" (Macaulay), **IV:** 283, 291

Ivy Compton-Burnett (Iprigg), **VII:** 70

"Ivy Day in the Committee Room" (Joyce), **VII:** 44, 45

"I wake and feel the fell of dark" (Hopkins), **V:** 374$_n$, 375

"I Wandered Lonely as a Cloud" (Wordsworth), **IV:** 22

"I will not let thee go" (Bridges), **VI:** 74, 77

I Will Pray with the Spirit (Bunyan), **II:** 253

"I will write" (Graves), **VII:** 269

"I would be a bird" (Bridges), **VI:** 81–82

Ixion in Heaven (Disraeli), **IV:** 297, 299, 308

J

"Jabberwocky" (Carroll), **V:** 265

Jack, Ian Robert James, **II:** 298; **III:** 125$_n$; **IV:** xi, xxv, 40, 140, 236, 373, 375

Jackdaw, The (Gregory), **VI:** 315

Jack Drum's Entertainment (Marston), **II:** 27, 40

Jackson, T. A., **V:** 51

Jack Straw (Maugham), **VI:** 368

Jacob, Giles, **II:** 348

Jacobite's Journal, The (Fielding), **III:** 105

Jacob's Room (Woolf), **VII:** 18, 20, 26–27, 38

Jacta Alea Est (Wilde), **V:** 400

Jaggard, William, **I:** 307

James, Henry, **II:** 42; **III:** 334, 340, 345; **IV:** 35, 107, 319, 323, 369, 371, 372; **V:** x, xx, xxiv–xxvi, 2, 48, 51, 70, 95, 97, 98, 102, 191, 199, 205, 210, 295, 384, 390–392; **VI:** x–xi, 5, **23–69**, 227, 236, 239, 266, 320, 322; list of short stories and novellas, **VI:** 69

James, M. R., **III:** 340

James, Richard, **II:** 102

James, William, **V:** xxv, 272; **VI:** 24

James Joyce and the Making of "Ulysses" (Budgen) **VII:** 56

"James Lee's Wife" (Browning), **IV:** 367, 369

Jane Austen's Literary Manuscripts (ed. Southam), **IV:** 124

Jane Austen: The Critical Heritage (ed. Southam), **IV:** 122, 124

Jane Eyre (Brontë), **III:** 338, 344, 345; **V:** xx, 106, 108, 112, 124, 135, **137–140**, 145, 147, 148, 152; **VII:** 101

"Janeites, The" (Kipling), **IV:** 106

"Jane's Marriage" (Kipling), **IV:** 106, 109

"Janet's Repentance" (Eliot), **V:** 190–191

Janowitz, Haas, **III:** 342

Japp, A. H., **IV:** 144$_n$, 155

Jarrell, Randall, **VI:** 165, 194, 200

"Jason and Medea" (Gower), **I:** 54, 56

J. B. Priestley, the Dramatist (Lloyd-Evans), **VII:** 223, 231

Jeames's Diary, or, Sudden Wealth (Thackeray), **V:** 38

Jean de Meung, **I:** 49

Jeffares, Alexander Norman, **VI:** xxxiii–xxxiv, 98, 221

Jefferson, D. W., **III:** 182, 183

Jeffrey, Francis, **III:** 276, 285; **IV:** 31, 39, 60, 72, 129, 269

Jeffrey, Sara, **IV:** 225

"Je ne parle pas Français" (Mansfield), **VII:** 174, 177

Jenkin, Fleeming, **V:** 386

"Jenny" (Rossetti), **V:** 240

Jerrold, Douglas, **V:** 19

Jerrold, W. C., **IV:** 252, 254, 267

"Jersey Villas" (James), **III:** 69

Jerusalem (Blake), **III:** 303, 304–305, 307; **V:** xvi, 330

Jerusalem Sinner Saved (Bunyan), see *Good News for the Vilest of Men*

Jesting Pilate (Huxley), **VII:** 201

Jeweller of Amsterdam, The (Field, Fletcher, Massinger), **II:** 67

Jew of Malta, The (Marlowe), **I:** 212, 280, **282–285,** 310

"Jews, The" (Vaughan), **II:** 189

Jew Süss (Feuchtwanger), **VI:** 265

Jitta's Atonement (Shaw), **VI:** 129

J. M. Synge and the Irish Dramatic Movement (Bickley), **VI:** 317

"Joachim au Bellay" (Pater), **V:** 344

Joan and Peter (Wells), **VI:** 240

Joannis Miltonii pro se defensio . . . (Milton), **II:** 176

Joan of Arc (Southey), **IV:** 59, 60, 63–64, 71

Job (biblical book), **III:** 307

Jocasta (Gascoigne), **I:** 215–216

Jocelyn (Galsworthy), **VI:** 277

"Jochanan Hakkadosh" (Browning), **IV:** 365

Jocoseria (Browning), **IV:** 359, 374

"Johannes Agricola in Meditation" (Browning), **IV:** 360

Johannes Secundus, **II:** 108

John Bull's Other Island (Shaw), **VI:** 112, **113–115**

John Caldigate (Trollope), **V:** 102

"John Fletcher" (Swinburne), **V:** 332

John Gabriel Borkman (Ibsen), **VI:** 110

"John Galsworthy" (Lawrence), **VI:** 275–276, 290

John Galsworthy (Mottram), **VI:** 271, 275, 290

"John Galsworthy, An Appreciation" (Conrad), **VI:** 290

"John Gilpin" (Cowper), **III:** 212, 220

John Keats: A Reassessment (ed. Muir), **IV:** 219, 227, 236

John Keats: His Life and Writings (Bush), **IV:** 224, 236

John M. Synge (Masefield), **VI:** 317

"John Norton" (Moore), **VI:** 98

"John Ruskin" (Proust), **V:** 183

John Ruskin: The Portrait of a Prophet (Quennell), **V:** 185

John Sherman and Dhoya (Yeats), **VI:** 221

Johnson, Edgar, **IV:** 27, 40; **V:** 60, 72

Johnson, James, **III:** 320, 322

Johnson, Lionel, **VI:** 3, 210, 211

Johnson, Samuel, **III:** 54, 96, **107–123,** 127, 151, 275; **IV:** xiv, xv, 27, 31, 34, 88$_n$, 101, 138, 268, 299; **V:** 9, 281, 287; **VI:** 363; and Boswell, **III:** 234, 235, 238, 239, 243–249; and Collins, **III:** 160, 163, 164, 171, 173; and Crabbe, **III:** 280–282; and Goldsmith, **III:** 177, 180, 181, 189; dictionary, **III:** 113–116; **V:** 281, 434; literary criticism, **I:** 326; **II:** 123, 173, 197, 200, 259, 263, 293, 301, 347; **III:** 11, 88, 94, 139, 257, 275; **IV:** 101; on Addison and Steele, **III:** 39, 42, 44, 49, 51

Johnson over Jordan (Priestley), **VII:** 226–227

John Thomas and Lady Jane (Lawrence), **VII:** 111–112

John Woodvil (Lamb), **IV:** 78–79, 85

Jolly Beggars, The (Burns), **III:** 319–320

Jonathan Swift (Stephen), **V:** 289

Jonathan Wild (Fielding), **III:** 99, 103, 105, 150

Jones, David, **VI:** xvi, 436, **437–439**

Jones, Henry Arthur, **VI:** 367, 376

Jonson, Ben, **I:** 228, 234–235, 270, **335–351;** **II:** 3, 4, 24, 25, 27, 28, 30, 45, 47, 48, 55, 65, 79, 87, 104, 108, 110, 111$_n$, 115, 118, 141, 199, 221–223; **IV:** 35, 327; **V:** 46, 56

Joseph Andrews (Fielding), **III:** 94, 95, 96, 99–100, 101, 105

Joseph Conrad (Baines), **VI:** 133–134

Joseph Conrad (Ford), **VI:** 321, 322

Joseph Conrad (Walpole), **VI:** 149

Joseph Conrad: A Personal Reminiscence (Ford), **VI:** 149

Joseph Conrad: The Modern Imagination (Cox), **VI:** 149

"Joseph Grimaldi" (Hood), **IV:** 267

"Joseph Yates' Temptation" (Gissing), **V:** 437

journal, as a literary form, **II:** 5–6

Journal (Mansfield), **VII:** 181, 182

Journal, 1825–32 (Scott), **IV:** 39

Journalism for Women: A Practical Guide (Bennett), **VI:** 264, 266

Journal of a Dublin Lady, The (Swift), **III:** 35

Journal of a Landscape Painter in Corsica (Lear), **V:** 87

Journal of a Tour in Scotland in 1819 (Southey), **IV:** 71

Journal of a Tour in the Netherlands in the Autumn of 1815 (Southey), **IV:** 71

Journal of a Tour to the Hebrides, The (Boswell), **III:** 117, 234$_n$, 235, 243, 245, 248, 249

Journal of a Voyage to Lisbon, The (Fielding), **III:** 104, 105

"Journal of My Jaunt, Harvest 1762" (Boswell), **III:** 241–242

Journal of the Plague Year, A (Defoe), **III:** 5–6, 8, 13

Journals and Papers of Gerard Manley Hopkins, The (ed. House and Storey), **V:** 362, 363, 371, 378–379, 381

Journals of a Landscape Painter in Albania etc. (Lear), **V:** 77, 79–80, 87

Journals of a Landscape Painter in Southern Calabria . . . (Lear), **V:** 77, 79, 87

Journals of a Residence in Portugal, 1800–1801, and a Visit to France, 1838 (Southey), **IV:** 71

Journals of Arnold Bennett (Bennett), **VI:** 265, 267

Journal to Eliza, The (Sterne), **III:** 125, 126, 132, 135

Journal to Stella (Swift), **II:** 335; **III:** 32–33, 34

Journey from Cornhill to Grand Cairo, A (Thackeray), see *Notes of a Journey from Cornhill to Grand Cairo*

"Journey of John Gilpin, The" (Cowper), see "John Gilpin"

"Journey of the Magi, The" (Eliot), **VII:** 152

Journey Through France (Piozzi), **III:** 134

Journey to a War (Auden and Isherwood), **VII:** 312

"Journey to Bruges, The" (Mansfield), **VII:** 172

Journey to London, A (Vanbrugh), **II:** 326, 333–334, 336

Journey to the Hebrides (Johnson), **IV:** 281

Journey to the Western Islands of Scotland, A (Johnson), **III:** 117, 121

Jowett, Benjamin, **V:** 278, 284, 285, 312, 338, 400

Joy (Galsworthy), **VI:** 269, 285

Joyce, James, **IV:** 189; **V:** xxv, 41; **VII:** xii, xiv, 18, 41–58; bibliography and critical studies, **VII:** 54–58

Joyce, Jeremiah, **V:** 174$_n$

Jude the Obscure (Hardy), **VI:** 4, 5, 7, 8, 9

Judgement of Martin Bucer . . . , The (Milton), **II:** 175

Judgement of Paris, The (Congreve), **II:** 347, 350

"Judging Distances" (Reed), **VII:** 422

Judith (Bennett), **VI:** 267

Jugement du roi de Behaingne, **I:** 32

"Juggling Jerry" (Meredith), **V:** 220

"Julia" (Brontë), **V:** 122, 151

"Julia Bride" (James), **VI:** 67, 69

"Julian and Maddalo" (Shelley), **IV:** 182, 201–202

Juliana of Norwich, **I:** 20

"Julian M. & A. G. Rochelle" (Brontë), **V:** 133

"Julia's Churching, or Purification" (Herrick), **II:** 112

Julius Caesar (Shakespeare), **I:** 313, 314–315

Jump-to-Glory Jane (Meredith), **V:** 234

"June Bracken and Heather" (Tennyson), **IV:** 336

"Jungle, The" (Lewis), **VII:** 447

Jungle Books, The (Kipling), **VI:** 188, 199

Juno and the Paycock (O'Casey), **VII:** xviii, 4–5, 6, 11

Jure Divino (Defoe), **III:** 4, 13

Jusserand, Jean, **I:** 98

Justice (Galsworthy), **VI:** xiii, 269, 273–274, 286–287

Just So Stories for Little Children (Kipling), **VI:** 188, 204

Juvenal, **II:** 30, 292, 347, 348; **III:** 42; **IV:** 188

"J.W. 51B A Convoy" (Ross), **VII:** 434

K

Kafka, Franz, **III:** 340, 345

Kain, Saul, pseud. of Siegfried Sassoon

Kalendarium Hortense (Evelyn), **II**: 287

Kangaroo (Lawrence), **VII**: 90, **107–109**, 119

Kant, Immanuel, **IV**: xiv, 50, 52, 145

"Karain: A Memory" (Conrad), **VI**: 148

Karl, Frederick R., **VI**: 135, 149

"Karshish" (Browning), **IV**: 357, 360, 363

Katchen's Caprices (Trollope), **V**: 101

Katherine Mansfield (Alpers), **VII**: 183

Kathleen and Frank (Isherwood), **VII**: 316–317

Kathleen Listens In (O'Casey), **VII**: 12

Kavanagh, Julia, **IV**: 108, 122

Keats, John, **II**: 102, 122, 192, 200; **III**: 174, 337, 338; **IV**: viii–xii, 81, 95, 129, 178, 196, 198, 204–205, **211–237,** 255, 284, 316, 323, 332, 349, 355; **V**: 173, 361, 401, 403

Keats and the Mirror of Art (Jack), **IV**: 236

Keats Circle, The: Letters and Papers . . . (Rollins), **IV**: 231, 232, 235

Keats's Publisher: A Memoir of John Taylor (Blunden), **IV**: 236

Keats: The Critical Heritage (ed. Matthews), **IV**: 237

Keble, John, **V**: xix, 252

"Keen, Fitful Gusts" (Keats), **IV**: 215

Keep the Aspidistra Flying (Orwell), **VII**: 275, 278–279

"Keep the Home Fires Burning" (Novello), **VI**: 435

Keeton, G. W., **IV**: 286

Kellys and the O'Kellys, The (Trollope), **V**: 101

Kelmscott Press, publishers, **V**: xxv, 302

Kelsall, Malcolm Miles, **IV**: x, xxv

Kelvin, Norman, **V**: 221, 234

Kemble, Fanny, **IV**: 340, 350–351

Kenilworth (Scott), **IV**: xviii, 39

Kenner, Hugh, **VI**: 323

Kenyon, Frederic, **IV**: 312, 321

Kenyon, John, **IV**: 311, 356

Kept in the Dark (Trollope), **V**: 102

Kermode, Frank, **I**: 237; **V**: 344, 355, 359, 412, 420; **VI**: 147, 208

Kettle, Thomas, **VI**: 336

Keyes, Sidney, **VII**: xxii, 422, **433–440**

Keynes, G. L., **II**: 134; **III**: 289$_n$, 307, 308, 309

Kickleburys on the Rhine, The (Thackeray), **V**: 38

Kidnapped (Stevenson), **V**: 383, 384, 387, 395

Killham, John, **IV**: 323$_n$, 338, 339; **VII**: 248–249

Kiltartan History Book, The (Gregory), **VI**: 318

Kiltartan Molière, The (Gregory), **VI**: 316, 318

Kiltartan Poetry Book, The (Gregory), **VI**: 318

Kilvert, Francis, **V**: 269

Kim (Kipling), **VI**: 166, 168, 169, **185–189**

"Kind Ghosts, The" (Owen), **VI**: 447, 455, 457

Kind Keeper, The: Or, Mr Limberham (Dryden), **II**: 294, 305

Kindly Ones, The (Powell), **VII**: 344, 347, 348, 349, 350

King, Francis Henry, **VII**: xx, xxxviii

King, Henry, **II**: 121, 221

King, S., **III**: 345

King, T., **II**: 336

King and No King, A (Beaumont and Fletcher), **II**: 43, 45, 52, 54, 57–58, 65

King Arthur; or, the British Worthy (Dryden), **II**: 294, 296, 305

"King Arthur's Tomb" (Morris), **V**: 293

"Kingdom of God, The" (Thompson), **V**: 449–450

"King James I and Isaac Casaubon" (Landor), **IV**: 92

King James Version of the Bible, **I**: 370, 377–380

King John (Shakespeare), **I**: 286, 301

King Lear (Shakespeare), **I**: 316–317; **II**: 69; **III**: 116, 295; **IV**: 232

King of Pirates, The . . . (Defoe), **III**: 13

King of the Golden River, The; or The Black Brothers (Ruskin), **V**: 184

Kingsland, W. G., **IV**: 371

Kingsley, Charles, **IV**: 195; **V**: viii, xxi, 2, 4, 283; **VI**: 266

King Stephen (Keats), **IV**: 231

"King's Tragedy, The" (Rossetti), **V**: 238, 244

King Victor and King Charles (Browning), **IV**: 373

Kinsayder, W., pseud. of John Marston

Kinsella, Thomas, **VI:** 220

Kinsley, James, **III:** 310$_n$ 322

Kipling, Rudyard, **IV:** 106, 109; **V:** xxiii–xxvi; **VI:** ix, xi, xv, **165–206**, 415; **VII:** 33; poetry, **VI:** 200–203; list of short stories, **VI:** 205–206

Kipling and the Critics (Gilbert), **VI:** 195$_n$

Kipling: Realist and Fabulist (Dobrée), **VI:** xi, 200–203, 205

Kipps (Wells), **VI:** xii

Kipps: The Story of a Simple Soul (Wells), **VI:** 225, 236–237

Kirk, Russell, **IV:** 276

Kirkpatrick, T. P. C., **III:** 180$_n$

"Kiss, The" (Sassoon), **VI:** 429

Kitchener, Field Marshall Lord, **VI:** 351

Kittredge, G. L., **I:** 326

Klosterheim (De Quincey), **IV:** 149, 155

"Kneeshaw Goes to War" (Read), **VI:** 437

Knight, G. W., **IV:** 328$_n$, 339

knightly romance, **I:** 68–72, 73–79

Knight of the Burning Pestle, The (Beaumont), **II:** 45, 46, **48–49**, 62, 65

"Knight of the Cart, The" (Malory), **I:** 70

Knights, L. C., **II:** 123, 126, 130

Knights of Malta, The (Field, Fletcher, Massinger), **II:** 66

Knight's Tale, The (Chaucer), **I:** 21, 23, 30, 31, 40

Knight with the Two Swords, The (Malory), **I:** 73

Knoblock, Edward, **VI:** 263, 267; **VII:** 223

Knolles, Richard, **III:** 108

Knowles, Sheridan, **IV:** 311

Knox, Robert, **III:** 7

Koestler, Arthur, **V:** 49

"Kosciusko and Poniatowski" (Landor), **IV:** 92

Kotzebue, August von, **III:** 254, 268

"Kraken, The" (Tennyson), **IV:** 329; **VI:** 16

Krutch, J. W., **III:** 246

"Kubla Khan" (Coleridge), **IV:** ix, xvii, 44, 46–48, 56; **V:** 272, 447

Kyd, Thomas, **I:** 162, **212–231**, 277, 278, 291; **II:** 25, 28, 74

L

"La Belle Dame Sans Merci" (Keats), **IV:** 216, 219, 235, 313

Labels (Waugh), **VII:** 292–293

Laburnum Grove (Priestley), **VII:** 224

La Chapelle, Jean de, **II:** 358

Ladies Triall, The (Ford), see *Lady's Trial, The*

Ladies Whose Bright Eyes (Ford), **VI:** 327

Lady Anna (Trollope), **V:** 102

"Lady Barbarina" (James), **VI:** 69

"Ladybird, The" (Lawrence), **VII:** 115

Lady Chatterley's Lover (Lawrence), **VII:** 87, 88, 91, **110–113**

"Lady Delavoy" (James), **VI:** 69

Lady Frederick (Maugham), **VI:** 367–368

"Lady Geraldine's Courtship" (Browning), **IV:** 311

Lady Gregory, **VI:** xiv

Lady Gregory: A Literary Portrait (Coxhead), **VI:** 318

Lady Icenway, The" (Hardy), **VI:** 22

Lady Jane (Chettle, Dekker, Heywood, Webster), **II:** 68

Lady Maisie's Bairn and Other Poems (Swinburne), **V:** 333

"Lady Mottisfont" (Hardy), **VI:** 22

Lady of Launay, The (Trollope), **V:** 102

Lady of May, The (Sidney), **I:** 161

"Lady of Shalott, The" (Tennyson), **IV:** xix, 231, 313, 329, 331–332

Lady of the Lake, The (Scott), **IV:** xvii, 29, 38

"Lady Penelope, The" (Hardy), **VI:** 22

"Lady's Dream, The" (Hood), **IV:** 261, 264

"Lady's Dressing Room, The" (Swift), **III:** 32

Lady's Magazine (periodical), **III:** 179

"Lady's Maid, The" (Mansfield), **VII:** 174–175

Lady's Pictorial (periodical), **VI:** 87, 91

Lady's Trial, The (Ford), **II:** 89, 91, 99, 100

Lady Susan (Austen), **IV:** 108, 109, 122

Lady Windermere's Fan (Wilde), **V:** xxvi, 412, 413–414, 419

"Lady with the Dog, The" (Chekhov), **V:** 241

"La Fontaine and La Rochefoucault" (Landor), **IV:** 91

Lafourcade, Georges, **VI:** 247, 256, 259, 260, 262, 263, 268

"Lagoon, The" (Conrad), **VI:** 136, 148

Lake, David J., **II:** 1, 2, 21

Lake, The (Moore), **VI:** xii, 88, 89, 92–93, 98

"Lake Isle of Innisfree, The" (Yeats), **VI:** 207, 211

Lake poets, **IV:** ix; **VI:** 73; see also Samuel Taylor Coleridge, Robert Southey, William Wordsworth

"L'Allegro" (Milton), **II:** 158–159; **IV:** 199

La maison de campagne (Dancourt), **II:** 325

Lamb, Charles, **II:** 80, 86, 119$_n$, 143, 153, 256, 340, 361, 363, 364; **IV:** xi, xiv, xvi, xviii, xix, 41, 42, **73–86,** 128, 135, 137, 148, 252–253, 255, 257, 259, 260, 320, 341, 349; **V:** 328

Lamb, John, **IV:** 74, 77, 84

Lamb, Mary, **IV:** xvi, 77–78, 80, 83–84, 128, 135

Lament of Tasso, The (Byron), **IV:** 192

Lamia (Keats), **III:** 338; **IV:** xviii, 216, 217, 219–220, 231, 235

Lamia, Isabella, The Eve of St. Agnes, and Other Poems (Keats), **IV:** xviii, 211, 235

Lamp and the Lute, The (Dobrée), **VI:** 204

Lancelot and Guinevere (Malory), **I:** 70–71, 77

Lancelot du Laik, **I:** 73

Lancelot, The Death of Rudel, and Other Poems (Swinburne), **V:** 333

"Lancer" (Housman), **VI:** 160

Landleaguers, The (Trollope), **V:** 102

Land of Heart's Desire, The (Yeats), **VI:** 221

Land of Promise, The (Maugham), **VI:** 369

Landon, Letitia, **IV:** 311

Landor, Walter Savage, **II:** 293; **III:** 139; **IV:** xiv, xvi, xviii, xix, xxii, **87–100,** 252, 254, 356; **V:** 320

"Landscape Painter, A" (James), **VI:** 69

Landseer, Edwin, **V:** 175

Lane, Margaret, **V:** 13$_n$, 16

Lang, Andrew, **V:** 392–393, 395 **VI:** 158

Lang, C. Y., **V:** 334, 335

Langland, William, **I:** vii, **1–18**

Language, Truth and Logic (Ayer), **VII:** 240

Lannering, Jan, **III:** 52

"Lantern Bearers, The" (Stevenson), **V:** 385

"Lantern out of Doors, The" (Hopkins), **V:** 380

"La Nuit Blanche" (Kipling), **VI:** 193

Laodicean, A, or, The Castle of the De Stancys (Hardy), **VI:** 4–5, 20

Laon and Cynthia (Shelley), **IV:** 195, 196, 198, 208; see also *Revolt of Islam, The*

La parisienne (Becque), **VI:** 369

Lara (Byron), **IV:** xvii, 172, 173, 175, 192; see also Turkish tales

"Lark Ascending, The" (Meredith), **V:** 221, 223

"Lars Porsena of Clusium" (Macaulay), **IV:** 282

Lars Porsena, or the Future of Swearing and Improper Language (Graves), **VII:** 259–260

La Saisiaz (Browning), **IV:** 359, 364–365, 374

La Soeur de la Reine (Swinburne), **V:** 325, 333

Last and the First, The (Compton-Burnett), **VII:** 59, 61, 67

Last Chronicle of Barset, The (Trollope), **II:** 173; **V:** xxiii, 93–95, 101

"Last Confession, A" (Rossetti), **V:** 240–241

Last Days of Lord Byron, The (Parry), **IV:** 191, 193

Last Essays (Conrad), **VI:** 148

Last Essays of Elia, The (Lamb), **IV:** xix, 76–77, 82–83, 85

Last Essays on Church and Religion (Arnold), **V:** 212, 216

Last Fight of the Revenge at Sea, The (Ralegh), **I:** 145, 149–150

Last Fruit off the Old Tree, The (Landor), **IV:** 100

"Last Instructions to a Painter, The" (Marvell), **II:** 217–218

Last Poems (Browning), **IV:** 312, 315, 357, 321

Last Poems (Housman), **VI:** 157, 158, 160, 161, 162, 164

Last Poems (Meredith), **V:** 234

Last Poems (Yeats), **VI:** 214

Last Poems and Two Plays (Yeats), **VI:** 213

Last Post (Ford), **VI:** 319, 330–331

Last Pre-Raphaelite, The: A Record of the Life and Writings of Ford Madox Ford (Goldring), **VI:** 333

La strage degli innocenti (Marino), **II:** 183

Last Things (Snow), **VII:** xxi, 324, 332–333

"Last Tournament, The" (Tennyson), **V:** 327

Last Words of Thomas Carlyle, The (Carlyle), **IV:** 250

Late Harvest (Douglas), **VI:** 300, 302–303, 305, 333

Late Murder in Whitechapel, The, or Keep the Widow Waking, see *Late Murder of the Son . . .*

Late Murder of the Son Upon the Mother, A, or Keep the Widow Waking (Dekker, Ford, Rowley, Webster), **II:** 85–86, 89, 100

"Later Poems" (Bridges), **VI:** 78, 83

"Latest Decalogue, The" (Clough), **V:** 155

Latin and Italian Poems of Milton (tr. Cowper), **III:** 220

Latin hexameter, **IV:** 185

La traicion busca el castigo (Rojas Zorilla), **II:** 325

Latter-Day Pamphlets (Carlyle), **IV:** xxi, 240, 247–248, 249, 250

"Laud and Praise made for our Sovereign Lord the King" (Skelton), **I:** 88–89

Laughable Lyrics (Lear), **V:** 78, 85, 87

Laugh and Lie Down (Swinburne), **V:** 312, 332

Laugh and Lie Down, or The World's Folly (Tourneur), **II:** 37

Laughing Anne (Conrad), **VI:** 148

Laughter in the Next Room (Sitwell), **VII:** 130, 135

"Laus Veneris" (Swinburne), **IV:** 346; **V:** 316, 318, 320, 327, 346

L'Autre monde on les états et empires de la lune (Cyrano de Bergerac), **III:** 24

Lavater, J. C., **III:** 298

La Vendée: An Historical Romance (Trollope), **V:** 101

La vida de la Santa Madre Teresa de Jesus, **II:** 182

La vida es sueño (Calderón), **IV:** 349

La vie de Fénelon (Ramsay), **III:** 99

Law, William, **IV:** 45

Law Against Lovers, The (Davenant), **I:** 327

Law Hill poems (Brontë), **V:** 126–128

Lawrence, D. H., **II:** 330; **IV:** 106, 119, 120, 195; **V:** xxv, 6, 47; **VI:** 235, 243, 248, 259, 275–276, 283, 363, 409, 416; **VII:** xii, xiv–xvi, 18, 75, **87–126,** 201, 203–204, 215

Lawrence, Frieda, **VII:** 90, 111

Lawrence, T. E., **VI:** 207, 408

"Lawrence, of virtuous father virtuous son" (Milton), **II:** 163

Laws of Candy, The, **II:** 67

Layamon, **I:** 72

Lay Morals and Other Papers (Stevenson), **V:** 396

Lay of Lilies, A, and Other Poems (Swinburne), **V:** 333

"Lay of the Brown Rosary, The" (Browning), **IV:** 313

"Lay of the Labourer, The" (Hood), **IV:** 252, 261, 265–266

Lay of the Last Minstrel, The (Scott), **IV:** xvi, 29, 38, 48, 218

"Lay of the Laureate" (Southey), **IV:** 61, 71

Lays of Ancient Rome (Macaulay), **IV:** xx, 272, 282–283, 290–291

Lazy Tour of Two Idle Apprentices, The (Dickens), **V:** 72

"Leaden Echo and the Golden Echo, The" (Hopkins), **V:** 371

Leader (periodical), **V:** 189

"Leaning Tower, The" (Woolf), **VII:** 26

Lear, Edward, **V:** xi, xvii, xv, xxv, **75–87,** 262

Lear Coloured Bird Book for Children, The (Lear), **V:** 86, 87

Lear in Sicily (ed. Proby), **V:** 87

Lear in the Original (ed. Liebert), **V:** 87

Learned Comment upon Dr. Hare's Excellent Sermon, A (Swift), **III:** 35

"Leave-Taking, A" (Swinburne), **V:** 319

"Leaving Barra" (MacNeice), **VI:** 411–412

Leavis, F. R., **II:** 254, 258, 271; **III:** 68, 78; **IV:** 227, 323, 338, 339; **V:** 195, 199, 201, 237, 309, 355, 375, 381, 382; **VI:** 13; **VII:** xvi, xix, 72–73, 88, 101, 102, **233–256**

Leavis, Q. D., **II:** 250; **V:** 286, 290; **VI:** 377; **VII:** 233, 238, 250

"Le christianisme" (Owen), **VI:** 445, 450

Lecky, William, **IV:** 289

L'École des femmes (Molière), **II:** 314

L'École des maris (Molière), **II:** 314

Lectures Chiefly on the Dramatic Literature of the Age of Elizabeth (Hazlitt), **IV:** xviii, 125, 129–130, 139

Lectures on Architecture and Paintings (Ruskin), **V:** 184

Lectures on Art (Ruskin), **V:** 184

Lectures on Justification (Newman), **II:** 243$_n$

Lectures on Shakespeare (Coleridge), **IV:** xvii, 52, 56

Lectures on the English Comic Writers (Hazlitt), **IV:** xviii, 129–130, 131, 136, 139

Lectures on the English Poets (Hazlitt), **IV:** xvii, 41, 129–130, 139

"Leda and the Swan" (Yeats), **V:** 345

Le dépit amoureux (Molière), **II:** 325, 336

Lee, George John Vandeleur, **VI:** 101

Lee, J., **II:** 336

Lee, Nathaniel, **II:** 305

Lee, Sidney, **V:** 280

Leech, Clifford, **II:** 44, 49, 52, 60, 62, 64, 70, 86, 90$_n$, 100

Leech, John, **IV:** 258

Le Fanu, Sheridan, **III:** 333, 340, 342, 343, 345

Left Book Club, **VII:** xix, 279, 381

Le Gallienne, Richard, **V:** 412, 413

Legend of Good Women, The (Chaucer), **I:** 24, 31, 38

Legend of Jubal, The, and Other Poems (Eliot), **V:** 200

Legend of Montrose, A (Scott), **IV:** xviii, 35, 39

Legend of the Rhine, A (Thackeray), **V:** 38

Legendre's Elements of Geometry (Carlyle), **IV:** 250

Legends of Angria (ed. Ratchford), **V:** 112

"Legion Club, The" (Swift), **III:** 21, 31

Legion's Memorial to the House of Commons (Defoe), **III:** 12

Legislation (Ruskin), **V:** 178

Legouis, Pierre, **II:** 207, 209, 218, 219, 220

Lehmann, John Frederick, **VII:** xvii, xxxviii

Leigh, R. A., **III:** 246$_n$

Leigh Hunt's Examiner Examined (Blunden), **IV:** 236

Leila, A Tale (Browning), **IV:** 321

"Leisure" (Lamb), **IV:** 83

"Leith Races" (Fergusson), **III:** 317

Leland, John, **I:** 113

Le misanthrope (Molière), **II:** 318

Lemon, Mark, **IV:** 263

"Leonardo Da Vinci" (Pater), **V:** 345–347, 348

"Lepanto" (Chesterton), **VI:** 340

"Leper, The" (Swinburne), **V:** 315

Le roman bourgeois (Furetière), **II:** 354

Le Sage, Alain René, **II:** 325, **III:** 150

Les aventures de Télémaque (Fénelon), **III:** 95, 99

Lesbia Brandon (Swinburne), **V:** 313, 325, 326–327, 332

Les bourgeoises à la mode (Dancourt), **II:** 325, 336

Les carrosses d'Orleans (La Chapelle), **II:** 358

Les fables d'Ésope (Boursault), **II:** 324

Leslie Stephen (MacCarthy), **V:** 284, 290

Leslie Stephen and Matthew Arnold as Critics of Wordsworth (Wilson), **V:** 287, 290

Leslie Stephen: Cambridge Critic (Leavis), **VII:** 238

Leslie Stephen: His Thought and Character in Relation to His Time (Annan), **V:** 284–285, 290

"Les Noyades" (Swinburne), **V:** 319, 320

"Lesser Arts, The" (Morris), **V:** 291, 301

Lessing, Gotthold Ephraim, **IV:** 53

Lessius, **II:** 181$_n$

"Lesson of the Master, The" (James), **VI:** 48, 67, 69

Lessons of the War (Reed), **VII:** 422

L'Estrange, Sir Robert, **III:** 41

"Les Vaches" (Clough), **V:** 168

Lethaby, W. R., **V:** 291, 296, 306

"Letter, The" (Brontë), **V:** 132

Letter, The (Maugham), **VI:** 369

Letter and Spirit: Notes on the Commandments (Rossetti), **V:** 260

Letterbook of Sir George Etherege, The (ed. Rosenfeld), **II:** 271

Letter . . . Concerning the Sacramental Test, A (Swift), **III:** 35

Letter from a Member . . . in Ireland to a Member . . . in England, A (Defoe), **III:** 18

Letter from Amsterdam to a Friend in England, A, **II:** 206

"Letter from Artemiza . . . to Chloë . . . , A" (Rochester), **II:** 260, 270

Letter . . . in Vindication of His Conduct with Regard to the Affairs of Ireland, A (Burke), **III:** 205

Letter of Advice to a Young Poet, A (Swift), **III:** 35

Letter of Thanks . . . to the . . . Bishop of S. Asaph, A (Swift), **III:** 35

Letter . . . on the Conduct of the Minority in Parliament, A (Burke), **III:** 205

Letters (Coleridge), **II:** 119ₙ

Letters Addressed to Lord Liverpool, and the Parliament . . . (Landor), **IV:** 100

Letters and Journals (Byron), **IV:** 185, 193

Letters and Journals of Lord Byron, with Notices of His Life, by T. Moore (Moore), **IV:** 193, 281; **V:** 116

Letters and Passages from . . . Clarissa (Richardson), **III:** 92

Letters and Private Papers of W. M. Thackeray (ed. Ray), **V:** 37, 140

Letters and Works of Lady Mary Wortley Montagu, **II:** 326ₙ

Letters from a Citizen of the World (Goldsmith), see *Citizen of the World, The*

Letters from England: By Don Manuel Alvarez Espriella (Southey), **IV:** 60, 68–69, 71

Letters from Iceland (Auden and MacNeice), **VII:** 403

Letters from John Galsworthy (ed. Garnett), **VI:** 290

Letters from the Lake Poets to D. Stuart (ed. Coleridge), **IV:** 144

Letters from W. S. Landor to R. W. Emerson (Landor), **IV:** 100

Letters of a Conservative, The (Landor), **IV:** 100

"Letters of an Englishman" (Brontë), **V:** 111

Letters of an Old Playgoer (Arnold), **V:** 216

Letters of Charles Lamb, **II:** 119ₙ

Letters of Charles Lamb . . . , The (ed. Lucas), **IV:** 84, 86

Letters of Elizabeth Barrett Browning (ed. Kenyon), **IV:** 312, 321

Letters of G. M. Hopkins to Robert Bridges (ed. Abbott), **VI:** 83

Letters of James Boswell . . . (ed. Francis), **III:** 249

Letters of James Boswell (ed. Tinker), **III:** 234ₙ, 249

Letters of Laurence Stern (ed. Curtis), **III:** 124ₙ

Letters of Matthew Arnold, 1848–1888 (ed. Russell), **V:** 205, 206, 208, 211, 216

Letters of Mrs. Gaskell, The (ed. Chapell and Pollard), **V:** 108, 137, 151

Letters of Robert Browning and Elizabeth Barrett, 1845–46, **IV:** 318–319, 320, 321

Letters of Runnymede (Disraeli), **IV:** 298, 308

Letters of State, Written by Mr. John Milton . . . (Milton), **II:** 176

Letters of Walter Savage Landor, Private and Public (ed. Wheeler), **IV:** 89, 98, 100

Letters of W. B. Yeats (ed. Wade), **VII:** 134

Letters of William and Dorothy Wordsworth (ed. Selincourt), **IV:** 11, 25

Letters of Wit, Politicks and Morality, **II:** 352, 364

Letters on Several Occasions (Dennis), **II:** 338

Letters to a Young Gentleman . . . (Swift), **III:** 29

"Letters to a Young Man" (De Quincey), **IV:** 146

Letters to the Sheriffs of Bristol . . . (Burke), **III:** 205

Letters with a Chapter of Biography, The (Sorley), **VI:** 421

Letters Written During a Short Residence in Spain and Portugal (Southey), **IV:** 71

Letters Written to and for Particular Friends (Richardson), see *Familiar Letters*

Letter . . . to a Country Gentleman . . . , A (Swift), **III:** 35

Letter to a Friend, A (Browne), **II:** 153, 156

Letter . . . to a Gentleman Designing for Holy Orders, A (Swift), **III:** 35

Letter to a Member of the National Assembly, A (Burke), **III:** 205

Letter to a Noble Lord (Burke), **IV:** 127

Letter to a Peer of Ireland on the Penal Laws (Burke), **III:** 205

Letter to John Murray, Esq., "Touching" Lord Nugent (Southey), **IV:** 71

"Letter to Lord Byron" (Auden), **IV:** 106

Letter to Lord Ellenborough, A (Shelley), **IV:** 208

"Letter to Maria Gisborne" (Shelley), **IV:** 204

Letter to Mr. Harding the Printer, A (Swift), **III:** 35

Letter to Robert MacQueen Lord Braxfield . . . , A (Boswell), **III:** 248

Letter to Samuel Whitbread (Malthus), **IV:** 127

"Letter to Sara Hutchinson" (Coleridge), **IV:** 15

Letter to Sir Hercules Langrishe on . . . the Roman Catholics . . . , A (Burke), **III:** 205

"Letter to the Bishop of Llandaff" (Wordsworth), **IV:** 2

Letter to the Noble Lord on the Attacks Made upon Him . . . in the House of Lords, A (Burke), **III:** 205

Letter to the People of Scotland, on . . . the Articles of the Union, A (Boswell), **III:** 248

Letter to the People of Scotland, on the Present State of the Nation, A (Boswell), **III:** 248

Letter to the Shop-Keepers . . . of Ireland, A (Swift), **III:** 28, 35

Letter to the Whole People of Ireland, A (Swift), **III:** 35

Letter to Viscount Cobham, A (Congreve), **II:** 350

Letter to . . . Viscount Molesworth, A (Swift), **III:** 35

Letter to William Gifford, Esq., A (Hazlitt), **IV:** 139

Letter to William Smith, Esq., MP, A (Southey), **IV:** 71

Letter Writers, The (Fielding), **III:** 97, 105

Letter Written to a Gentleman in the Country, A . . . (Milton), **II:** 176

"Let the Brothels of Paris be opened" (Blake), **III:** 299

Let the People Sing (Priestley), **VII:** 217

Leviathan (Hobbes), **II:** 190; **III:** 22; **IV:** 138

Levin, Harry, **I:** 288, 292

Levin, Ira, **III:** 343

Levin, Richard, **II:** 4, 23

Lewes, George Henry, **IV:** 101, 122; **V:** 137, 189–190, 192, 198

Lewis, Alun, **VII:** xxii, 422, **444–448**

Lewis, C. Day, see Day Lewis, Cecil

Lewis, Cecil Day, see Day Lewis, Cecil

Lewis, C. S., **I:** 81, 95, 117; **III:** 51; **V:** 301, 306; **VII:** 356

Lewis, Matthew, **III:** 331, 332–333, 336, 340, 343, 345

Lewis, Wyndham, **VI:** 118, 216, 247, 322; **VII:** xii, xv, 35, 41, 45, 49, 50, **71–85**

"Lewis Carroll" (de la Mare), **V:** 268, 274

Lewis Carroll (Hudson), **V:** 262–263, 274

Lewis Eliot stories (Snow), **VII:** 322; see *Strangers and Brothers* cycle

Lewis Seymour and Some Women (Moore), **VI:** 86, 89–90, 98, 99

"Liar, The" (James), **VI:** 69

"Libbie Marsh's Three Eras" (Gaskell), **V:** 15

Libel on D[octor] D[elany], A (Swift), **III:** 35

Liberal (periodical), **IV:** 132, 172

liberal humanism, **VI:** 387, 411

Liber Amoris (Hazlitt), **IV:** 128, 131–132, 133, 139

Liber niger (Edward IV), **I:** 25, 44

"Liberty" (Collins), **III:** 166, 172

Library, The (Crabbe), **III:** 274, 280, 286

"Licorice Fields at Pontefract, The" (Betjeman), **VII:** 368

"Lie, The" (Ralegh), **I:** 148

Life, Adventures, and Pyracies of . . . Captain Singleton, The (Defoe), see *Captain Singleton*

Life and Adventures of Martin Chuzzlewit, The (Dickens), see *Martin Chuzzlewit*

Life and Adventures of Nicholas Nickleby, The (Dickens), see *Nicholas Nickleby*

Life and Art (Hardy), **VI:** 20

"Life and Character of Dean Swift, The" (Swift), **III:** 23, 32, 36

Life and Correspondence of Robert Southey, The (Southey), **IV:** 62, 72

Life and Correspondence of Thomas Arnold, The (Stanley), **V:** 13

Life and Death of Jason, The (Morris), **V:** 296, 297, 298, 304, 306

Life and Death of Mr. Badman, The (Bunyan), **II:** 242, 248, 250–251, 253

"Life and Fame" (Cowley), **II:** 196

Life and Labours of Blessed John Baptist De La Salle, The (Thompson), **V:** 450, 451

Life and Letters, The (Macaulay), **IV:** 270–271, 284, 291

Life and Letters of John Galsworthy, The (Marrot), **V:** 270; **VI:** 287

Life and Letters of Leslie Stephen, The (Maitland), **V:** 277, 290

Life and Opinions of Tristram Shandy, Gentleman, The (Sterne), see *Tristram Shandy*

"Life and Poetry of Keats, The" (Masson), **IV:** 212, 235

Life and Strange Surprizing Adventures of Robinson Crusoe . . . , The (Defoe), see *Robinson Crusoe*

Life and Times of Laurence Sterne, The (Cross), **III:** 125

"Life and Writings of Addison" (Macaulay), **IV:** 282

"Life in a Love" (Browning), **IV:** 365

Life in Greece from Homer to Menander (Mahafty), **V:** 400

Life in London (Egan), **IV:** 260

Life in Manchester (Gaskell), **V:** 15

Life, Letters, and Literary Remains of John Keats (Milnes), **IV:** 211, 235, 351

Life of Addison (Johnson), **III:** 42

Life of Alexander Pope (Ruffhead), **III:** 69_n, 71

Life of Algernon Charles Swinburne, The (Gosse), **V:** 311, 334

Life of Benjamin Disraeli, Earl of Beaconsfield, The (Monypenny and Buckle), **IV:** 292, 295, 300, 307, 308

Life of . . . Bolingbroke, The (Goldsmith), **III:** 189, 191

Life of Charlotte Brontë, The (Gaskell), **V:** xxii, 1–2, 3, 13–14, 15, 108, 122

Life of Christina Rossetti, The (Sanders), **V:** 250, 260

Life of Cicero, The (Trollope), **V:** 102

Life of Collins (Johnson), **III:** 164, 171

Life of Crabbe (Crabbe), **III:** 272

Life of Dr. Donne, The (Walton), **II:** 132, 136, 140, 141, 142

Life of Dr. Robert Sanderson, The (Walton), **II:** 133, 135, 136–137, 140, 142

Life of Dryden, The (Scott), **IV:** 38

Life of George Moore, The (Horne), **VI:** 87, 96, 99

Life of Henry Fawcett, The (Stephen), **V:** 289

Life of John Bright, The (Trevelyan), **VI:** 389

Life of John Hales, The (Walton), **II:** 136

Life of Johnson, The (Boswell), **I:** 30; **III:** 54, 114_n, 115, 120, 234, 238, 239, 243–248; **IV:** xv, 280

Life of John Sterling (Carlyle), **IV:** 41–42, 240, 249, 250

Life of Katherine Mansfield, The (Mantz and Murry), **VII:** 183

"Life of Ma Parker" (Mansfield), **VII:** 175, 177

Life of Mrs. Godolphin, The (Evelyn), **II:** 275, 287

"Life of Mrs. Radcliffe" (Scott), **IV:** 35

Life of Mrs. Robert Louis Stevenson, The (Sanchez), **V:** 393, 397

Life of Mr. George Herbert, The (Walton), **II:** 119–120, 133, 140, 142, 143

Life of Mr. Jonathan Wild the Great, The (Fielding), see *Jonathan Wild*

Life of Mr. Richard Hooker, The (Walton), **II:** 133, 134, 135, 140–143

Life of Mr. Richard Savage (Johnson), **III:** 108, 121

Life of Napoleon, The (Scott), **IV:** 38

Life of Napoleon Bonaparte, The (Hazlitt), **IV:** 135, 140

Life of Nelson, The (Southey), **IV:** xvii, 58, 69, 71, 280

Life of Our Lady, The (Lydgate), **I:** 22, 57, 65–66

Life of Richard Nash, The (Goldsmith), **III:** 189, 191

Life of Robert Louis Stevenson, The (Balfour), **V:** 393, 397

Life of Robert Louis Stevenson, The (Masson), **V:** 393, 397

Life of Rudyard Kipling, The (Carrington), **VI:** 166

Life of Saint Albion, The (Lydgate), **I:** 57

Life of Saint Cecilia, The (Chaucer), **I:** 31

Life of Saint Edmund, The (Lydgate), **I:** 57

Life of St. Francis Xavier, The (tr. Dryden), **II:** 305

Life of Samuel Johnson, The (Boswell), see *Life of Johnson, The*

Life of Schiller (Carlyle), **IV:** 241, 249, 250

Life of Sir Henry Wotton, The (Walton), **II:** 133, 141, 142, 143

Life of Sir James Fitzjames Stephen, The (Stephen), **V:** 289

Life of Sterling (Carlyle), see *Life of John Sterling*

"Life of the Emperor Julius" (Brontë), **V:** 113

Life of the Rev. Andrew Bell, The (Southey and Southey), **IV:** 71

Life of the Seventh Earl of Shaftesbury (Hodder), **IV:** 62

Life of Thomas Hardy (Hardy), **VI:** 14–15

"Life of Thomas Parnell" (Goldsmith), **III:** 189

Life of Wesley, The (Southey), **IV:** 68, 71

Life of William Morris, The (Mackail), **V:** 294, 297, 306

Life's Handicap (Kipling), **VI:** 204

Life's Little Ironies (Hardy), **VI:** 20, 22

Life's Morning, A (Gissing), **V:** 437

"Life to Come, The" (Forster), **VI:** 411

"Lifted Veil, The" (Eliot), **V:** 198

Light and the Dark, The (Snow), **VII:** 324, 327

Light for Them That Sit in Darkness . . . (Bunyan), **II:** 253

"Light Man, A" (James), **VI:** 25, 69

"Light Shining Out of Darkness" (Cowper), **III:** 211

Light That Failed, The (Kipling), **VI:** 166, 169, 189–190, 204

light verse, **VI:** 335

"Light Woman, A" (Browning), **IV:** 369

Lilian (Bennett), **VI:** 250, 259–260

"Lilly in a Christal, The" (Herrick), **II:** 104

"Lily Adair" (Chivers), **V:** 313

Limbo (Huxley), **VII:** 199, 200

limerick, **V:** 76, 82–83, 86

Lincolnshire poems (Tennyson), **IV:** 327, 336

Linda Tressel (Trollope), **V:** 102

Linden Tree, The (Priestley), **VII:** 209, 228–229

Line of Life, A (Ford), **II:** 88, 100

"Lines Composed a Few Miles Above Tintern Abbey" (Wordsworth), **IV:** ix, 3, 7, 8, 9–10, 11, 44, 198, 215, 233

"Lines Composed in a Wood on a Windy Day" (Brontë), **V:** 132

"Lines Composed While Climbing the Left Ascent of Brockley Combe" (Coleridge), **IV:** 43–44

"Lines for Cuscuscaraway . . ." (Eliot), **VII:** 163

"Lines on the Loss of the *Titanic*" (Hardy), **VI:** 16

"Lines Written Among the Euganean Hills" (Shelley), **IV:** 199

"Lines Written in the Bay of Lerici" (Shelley), **IV:** 206

"linnet in the rocky dells, The" (Brontë), **V:** 115

Lion and the Fox, The (Lewis), **VII:** 72, 74, 82

Lion and the Unicorn, The (Orwell), **VII:** 282

Lions and Shadows (Isherwood), **VII:** 310, 312

Litanies de Satan (Baudelaire), **V:** 310

"Litany, A" (Swinburne), **V:** 320

literary criticism, **VI:** 163, 265–266; **VII:** xiii, 22, 32–34, 157, 162–165, 235–236

"Literary Criticism and Philosophy: A Reply" (Leavis), **VII:** 241–242

Literary Criticisms by Francis Thompson (ed. Connolly), **V:** 450, 451

literary history, **VII:** 234

Literary Reminiscences (Hood), **IV:** 252, 253, 254, 259–260, 266

Literary Studies (Bagehot), **V:** 156, 170

Literary Taste: How to Form It (Bennett), **VI:** 266

Literature and Dogma (Arnold), **V:** xxiv, 203, 212, 216

"Literature and the Irish Language" (Moore), **VI:** 98

Literature and Western Man (Priestley), **VII:** 209, 214–215

Literature at Nurse, or Circulating Morals (Moore), **VI:** 90, 98

"Little and a lone green lane" (Brontë), **V:** 112–113

"Little Boy Lost, The" (Blake), **III:** 292

Little Dinner at Timmins's, A (Thackeray), **V:** 24, 38

Little Dorrit (Dickens), **V:** xxii, 41, 42, 47, 55, 63, 64–66, 68, 69, 70, 72

Little Dream, The (Galsworthy), **VI:** 274

Little French Lawyer, The (Fletcher and Massinger), **II:** 66

"Little Ghost Who Died for Love, The" (Sitwell), **VII:** 133

"Little Gidding" (Eliot), **VII:** 154, 155, 156

Little Girl, The (Mansfield), **VII:** 171

Little Tour in France, A (James), **VI:** 45–46, 67

"Little Travels and Roadside Sketches" (Thackeray), **V:** 38

Little Wars: A Game for Boys (Wells), **VI:** 227, 244

"Little While, A" (Rossetti), **V:** 242

"Little while, a little while, A," (Brontë), **V:** 127–128

"Lively sparks that issue from those eyes, The" (Wyatt), **I:** 109

"Liverpool Address, A" (Arnold), **V:** 213, 216

Lives, The (Walton), **II:** 131, 134–137, 139, **140–143;** see also individual works: *Life of Dr. Donne, Life of Dr. Robert Sanderson, Life of Mr. George Herbert, Life of Mr. Richard Hooker, Life of Sir Henry Wotton*

Lives of the British Admirals (Southey and Bell), **IV:** 71

Lives of the English Poets, The (Johnson), **II:** 259; **III:** 118–119, 122, 160, 173, 189

Lives of the 'Lustrious: A Dictionary of Irrational Biography (Stephen and Lee), **V:** 290

Lives of the Novelists (Scott), **III:** 146$_n$; **IV:** 38, 39

Lives of the Poets, The (Johnson), see *Lives of the English Poets, The*

Living Novel, The (Pritchett), **IV:** 306

Living Principle, The (Leaves), **VII:** 237

Liza of Lambeth (Maugham), **VI:** 364–365

"Lizzie Leigh" (Gaskell), **V:** 3, 15

Lloyd, Charles, **IV:** 78

Lloyd George, David, **VI:** 264, 340, 352, 353; **VII:** 2

Lobo, Jeronimo, **III:** 107, 112

Locke, John, **III:** 22; **IV:** 169

Lockhart, J. G., **IV:** 27, 30, 34, 36, 38, 39, 294; **V:** 140

"Locksley Hall" (Tennyson), **IV:** 325, 333, 334–335

"Locksley Hall Sixty Years After" (Tennyson), **IV:** 328, 338

"Lock up, fair lids, the treasure of my heart" (Sidney), **I:** 169

Lodge, Thomas, **I:** 306, 312

"Lodging for the Night, A" (Stevenson), **V:** 384, 395

Loftis, John, **III:** 255, 271

Logan, Annie R. M., **VI:** 23

"Logical Ballad of Home Rule, A" (Swinburne), **V:** 332

Logic of Political Economy, The (De Quincey), **IV:** 155

"Lois the Witch" (Gaskell), **V:** 15

Lombroso, Cesare, **V:** 272

Londinium Redivivum (Evelyn), **II:** 287

"London" (Blake), **III:** 294, 295

"London" (Johnson), **III:** 57, 108, 114, 121

London Assurance (Boucicault), **V:** 415

"London by Lamplight" (Meredith), **V:** 219

"London hast thou accusèd me" (Surrey), **I:** 113, 116

London Journal 1762–1763 (Boswell), **III:** 239, 240, 242

London Life, A (James), **VI:** 67, 69

London Magazine (periodical), **III:** 263; **IV:** xviii, 252, 253, 257, 260; **V:** 386

London Mercury (periodical), **VII:** 211

"London Snow" (Bridges), **VI:** 78

London Spy (periodical), **III:** 41

London Street Games (Douglas), **VI:** 304, 305

London to Ladysmith via Preforia (Churchill), **VI:** 351

London Tradesmen (Trollope), **V:** 102

"Long ages past" (Owen), **VI:** 448

Longest Day, The (Clough), **V:** 170

Longest Journey, The (Forster), **VI:** 398, **401–403,** 407

"Longstaff's Marriage" (James), **VI:** 69

"Long Story, A" (Gray), **III:** 140

Lonsdale, R., **III:** 142$_n$, 144

Looking Back (Douglas), **VI:** 304, 305

Looking Back (Maugham), **VI:** 365

"Looking Back" (Vaughan), **II:** 185, 188

Look, Stranger! (Auden), **VII:** xix, 384

Look! We Have Come Through! (Lawrence), **VII:** 127

"Loose Saraband, A" (Lovelace), **II:** 232

Lopez, Bernard, **VI:** 85

"Lord Arthur Savile's Crime" (Wilde), **V:** 405, 419

"Lord Beaupre" (James), **VI:** 69

"Lord Carlisle on Pope" (De Quincey), **IV:** 146

Lord Chancellor Jeffreys and the Stuart Cause (Keeton), **IV:** 286

Lord George Bentinck (Disraeli), **IV:** 303, 308

Lord Grey of the Reform Bill (Trevelyan), **VI:** 389–390

Lord Jim (Conrad), **VI:** 134, **139–140,** 148

"Lord of Ennerdale The" (Scott) **IV:** 31

"Lord of the Dynamos" (Wells), **VI:** 235

Lord of the Isles, The (Scott), **IV:** 39

Lord Ormont and His Aminta (Meredith), **V:** 226, 232, 233, 234

Lord Palmerston (Trollope), **V:** 102

Lord Raingo (Bennett), **VI:** 250, 252, 261–262

Lord Randolph Churchill (Churchill), **VI:** 352

Lord Scales (Swinburne), **V:** 333

Lord Soulis (Swinburne), **V:** 333

"Loss of the Eurydice, The" (Hopkins), **V:** 369–370, 379

Lost Childhood, The, and Other Essays (Greene), **VI:** 333

"Lost Days" (Rossetti), **V:** 243

Lost Empires (Priestley), **VII:** 220–221

Lost Girl, The (Lawrence), **VII:** 90, **104–106**

"Lost Leader, The" (Browning), **IV:** 356

"Lost Legion, The" (Kipling), **VI:** 193

"Lost Mistress, The" (Browning), **IV:** 369

Lothair (Disraeli), **IV:** xxiii, 294, 296, 304, 306, 307, 308

Lotta Schmidt (Trollope), **V:** 101

Lottery, The (Fielding), **III:** 105

"Lotus-Eaters, The" (Tennyson), **IV:** xix; **V:** ix

"Loud without the wind was roaring" (Brontë), **V:** 127

"Louisa Pallant" (James), **VI:** 69

Love Among the Artists (Shaw), **VI:** 103, 105, 106, 129

"Love Among the Haystacks" (Lawrence), **VII:** 115

"Love Among the Ruins" (Browning), **IV:** 357, 369

Love Among the Ruins (Waugh), **VII:** 302

Love and a Bottle (Farquhar), **II:** 352, 356, 364

Love and Business (Farquhar), **II:** 352, 355, 364

"Love and Debt Alike Troublesome" (Suckling), **II:** 227

Love and Freindship [*sic*] *and Other Early Works* (Austen), **IV:** 122

"Love and Life" (Cowley), **II:** 197, 198

"Love and Life" (Rochester), **II:** 258

Love and Mr. Lewisham (Wells), **VI:** 235–236, 244

Love and Truth (Walton), **II:** 134, 143

Lovecraft, H. P., **III:** 340, 343, 345

"Love Declared" (Thompson), **V:** 442

Loved One, The (Waugh), **VII:** 301

Love for Love (Congreve), **II:** 324, 338, 342–343, 350

"Love from the North" (Rossetti), **V:** 259

"Love in a Valley" (Betjeman), **VII:** 366

Love in a Wood; or, St. James's Park (Wycherley), **II:** 308, 309, **311–313,** 321

"Love in Dian's Lap" (Thompson), **V:** 441

Love in Idleness (Nicholls), **IV:** 98$_n$

Love in Several Masques (Fielding), **III:** 96, 105

"Love in the Valley" (Meredith), **V:** 219–220

"Love Is Dead" (Betjeman), **VII:** 359–360

Love is Enough (Morris), **V:** 299$_n$, 306

Lovelace, Richard, **II:** 222, **229–232**

Lovel the Widower (Thackeray), **V:** 35, 37, 38

Lover (periodical), **III:** 50, 53

Lover's Assistant, The (Fielding), see *Ovid's Art of Love Paraphrased*

"Lover's Complaint, A," **I:** 307

"Lovers How They Come and Part" (Herrick), **II:** 107

"Lover's Journey, The" (Crabbe), **III:** 282–283

Lover's Melancholy, The (Ford), **II:** 88–91, 100

"Lovers of Orelay, The" (Moore), **VI:** 96

Lover's Progress, The (Fletcher and Massinger), **II:** 66

Lovers' Quarrels . . . (King), **II:** 336

"Lovers' Rock, The" (Southey), **IV:** 66

Lover's Tale, The (Tennyson), **IV:** 338

Love's Catechism Compiled by the Author of The Recruiting Officer (Farquhar), **II:** 364

Love's Cross Currents (Swinburne), **V:** 313, 323, 325–326, 330, 333

Love's Cure (Beaumont, Fletcher, Massinger), **II:** 66

Love's Labour's Lost (Shakespeare), **I:** 303–304

Love's Last Shift (Cibber), **II:** 324, 326

Love's Martyr (Chester), **I:** 313

Love's Metamorphosis (Lyly), **I:** 202

"Love's Nocturn" (Rossetti), **V:** 241

Loves of Amos and Laura, The (S. P.), **II:** 132

Loves of Ergasto, The (Greber), **II:** 325

"Love Song of Har Dyal, The" (Kipling), **VI:** 202

"Love Song of J. Alfred Prufrock, The" (Eliot), **V:** 163; **VII:** 144

"Love's Philosophy" (Shelley), **IV:** 203

Love's Pilgrimage (Beaumont and Fletcher), **II:** 65

Love's Riddle (Cowley), **II:** 194, 202

Love's Sacrifice (Ford), **II:** 88, 89, 92, 96, 97, 99, 100

"Love's Siege" (Suckling), **II:** 226–227

"Love still has something of the Sea" (Sedley); **II:** 264

"Love that doth raine and live within my thought" (Surrey), **I:** 115

"Love III" (Herbert), **II:** 129

Love Triumphant: Or, Nature Will Prevail (Dryden), **II:** 305

Low, Will, **V:** 393, 397

"Low Barometer" (Bridges), **VI:** 80

Lowbury, Edward, **VII:** 422, 431–432

Lowell, James Russell, **I:** 121

Lowes, J. L., **IV:** 47, 57

Loyal Brother, The (Southern), **II:** 305

Loyal General, The (Tate), **II:** 305

Loyal Subject, The (Fletcher), **II:** 45, 65

Loyalties (Galsworthy), **VI:** xiii, 275, 287

Lucas, E. V., **IV:** 74, 76$_n$, 84, 85, 86

Lucas, F. L., **II:** 69, 70$_n$, 80, 83, 85

Lucasta (Lovelace), **II:** 238

Lucian, **III:** 24

Lucie-Smith, Edward, **IV:** 372, 373

Luck of Barry Lyndon, The (Thackeray), see *Barry Lyndon*

"Lucrece" (Gower), **I:** 54

Lucretia Borgia: The Chronicle of Tebaldeo Tebaldei (Swinburne), **V:** 325, 333

Lucretius, **II:** 275, 292, 300, 301; **IV:** 316

"Lucy" poems (Wordsworth), **IV:** 3, 18; **V:** 11

"Lui et Elles" (Moore), **VI:** 87

"Lullaby" (Auden), **VII:** 383, 398

"Lullaby" (Sitwell), **VII:** 135

"Lullaby for Jumbo" (Sitwell), **VII:** 132

Luria: and a Soul's Tragedy (Browning), **IV:** 374

"Lycidas" (Milton), **II:** 160–161, 164, 165, 168, 169, 175; **III:** 118–119, 120; **IV:** 205; **VI:** 73

"Lycus, the Centaur" (Hood), **IV:** 256, 267

Lydgate, John, **I:** 22, 49, **57–66**

Lyell, Sir Charles, **IV:** 325

Lyly, John, **I: 191–211**, 303

Lyrical Ballads (Wordsworth and Coleridge), **III:** 174, 336; **IV:** viii, ix, x, xvi, 3, 4, 5, **6–11**, 18, 24, 44–45, 55, 77, 111, 138–139, 142

Lyttelton, George, **III:** 118

Lyttleton, Dame Edith, **VII:** 32

M

Mabinogion, **I:** 73

"McAndrew's Hymn" (Kipling), **VI:** 202

Macaulay, Rose, **VII:** 37

Macaulay, Thomas Babington, **II:** 240, 241, 254, 255, 307; **III:** 51, 53, 72; **IV:** xii, xvi, xx, xxii, 101, 122, **268–291**, 295; **V:** viii; **VI:** 347, 353, 383, 392

Macbeth (Shakespeare), **I:** 317–318, 327; **II:** 97, 281; **IV:** 79–80, 188; **V:** 375

MacCarthy, Desmond, **V:** 284, 286, 290; **VI:** 363, 385; **VII:** 32

MacDermots of Ballycloran, The (Trollope), **V:** 101

MacDiarmid, Hugh, **III:** 310

Macdonald, George, **V:** 266

Macdonald, Mary, **V:** 266, 272

Mac Flecknoe or a Satyre Upon the . . . Poet, T. S. (Dryden), **II:** 299, 304

McGann, Jerome J., **V:** 314, 335

Machiavelli, Niccolò, **II:** 71, 72; **IV:** 279

"Machine Stops; The" (Forster), **VI:** 399

Mackail, J. W., **V:** 294, 296, 297, 306

Mackay, M. E., **V:** 223, 234

Mackenzie, Compton, **VII:** 278

Mackenzie, Sir George, **III:** 95

Mackenzie, Henry, **III:** 87; **IV:** 79

MacKenzie, Jean, **VI:** 227, 243

MacKenzie, Norman, **V:** 374$_n$, 375$_n$, 381, 382; **VI:** 227, 243

"Mackery End, in Hertfordshire" (Lamb), **IV:** 83

MacLaren, Moray, **V:** 393, 398

McLeehan, Marshall, **IV:** 323$_n$, 338, 339

Maclure, Millar, **I:** 291

Macmillan's (periodical), **VI:** 351

MacNeice, Louis, **VII:** 153, 382, 385, **401–418**

Macpherson, James, **III:** 336

Macready, William Charles, **I:** 327

Madagascar: or, Robert Drury's Journal (Defoe), **III:** 14

Madame Bovary (Flaubert), **V:** xxii, 429

"Madame de Mauves" (James), **VI:** 69

Madan, Falconer, **V:** 264, 274

Mademoiselle de Maupin (Gautier), **V:** 320$_n$

Madge, Charles, **VII:** xix

Mad Islands, The (MacNeice), **VII:** 405, 407

Mad Lover, The (Fletcher), **II:** 45, 55, 65

"Mad Maids Song, The" (Herrick), **II:** 112

"Mad Mullinix and Timothy" (Swift), **III:** 31

Madoc (Southey), **IV:** 63, 64–65, 71

Madonna of the Future and Other Tales, The (James), **VI:** 67, 69

"Madonna of the Trenches, A" (Kipling), **VI:** 193, **194–196**

Madras House, The (Shaw), **VI:** 118

Mad Soldier's Song (Hardy), **VI:** 11

Mad World, My Masters, A (Middleton), **II:** 3, 4, 21

Magic (Chesterton), **VI:** 340

Magician, The (Maugham), **VI:** 374

Magic Toyshop, The (Carter), **III:** 345

Maginn, William, **V:** 19

Magnificence (Skelton), **I:** 90

Magnusson, Erika, **V:** 299, 300, 306

Mahafty, John Pentland, **V:** 400, 401

"Mahratta Ghats, The" (Lewis), **VII:** 446–447

Maid in the Mill, The (Fletcher and Rowley), **II:** 66

Maid in Waiting (Galsworthy), **VI:** 275

Maid Marian (Peacock), **IV:** xviii, 167–168, 170

Maid of Bath, The (Foote), **III:** 253

Maid's Tragedy, The (Beaumont and Fletcher), **II:** 44, 45, **54–57**, 58, 60, 65

Maid's Tragedy, Alter'd, The (Waller), **II:** 238

"Maim'd Debauchee, The" (Rochester), **II:** 259–260

Maitland, F. W., **V:** 277, 290; **VI:** 385

Maitland, Thomas, pseud. of Algernon Charles Swinburne

Major Barbara (Shaw), **VI:** xv, 102, 108, **113–115**, 124

Major Political Essays (Shaw), **VI:** 129

Major Victorian Poets, The: Reconsiderations (Armstrong), **IV:** 339

Making of an Immortal, The (Moore), **VI:** 96, 99

Malcontent, The (Marston), **II:** 27, 30, **31–33**, 36, 40, 68

Malcontents, The (Snow), **VII:** 336–337

Malign Fiesta (Lewis), **VII:** 72, 80

Malone, Edmond, **I:** 326

Malory, Sir Thomas, **I: 67–80; IV:** 336, 337

Malraux, André, **VI:** 240

"Maltese Cat, The" (Kipling), **VI:** 200

Malthus, Thomas, **IV:** xvi, 127, 133

"Man" (Vaughan) **II:** 186, 188

Manalive (Chesterton), **VI:** 340

Mañanas de abril y mayo (Calderón), **II:** 312$_n$

Man and Superman (Shaw), **IV:** 161

Man and Superman: A Comedy and a Philosophy (Shaw), **VI: 112–113**, 114, 127, 129

Man and Time (Priestley), **VII:** 213

"Manchester Marriage, The" (Gaskell), **V:** 6$_n$, 14, 15

Manchester School, **VI:** 389

Manciple's Prologue, The (Chaucer), **I:** 24

Manciple's Tale, The (Chaucer), **I:** 55

Man Could Stand Up, A (Ford), **VI:** 319, 329

Man Does, Woman Is (Graves), **VII:** 268

Manfred (Byron), **III:** 338; **IV:** xvii, 172, 173, 177, **178–182**, 192

Man from the North, A (Bennett), **VI:** 248, 253

Manifold, John, **VII:** 422, 426–427

Manin and the Venetian Revolution of 1848 (Trevelyan), **VI:** 389

Mankind in the Making (Wells), **VI:** 227, 236

Manly, J. M., **I:** 1

Mann, Thomas, **II:** 97; **III:** 344

Mannerly Margery Milk and Ale (Skelton), **I:** 83

Manner of the World Nowadays, The (Skelton), **I:** 89

Manners, Mrs. Horace, pseud. of Algernon Charles Swinburne

"Manners, The" (Collins), **III:** 161, 162, 166, 171

Manning, Cardinal, **V:** 181

Man of Destiny, The (Shaw), **VI:** 112

Man of Devon, A (Galsworthy), **VI:** 277

Man of Honour, A (Maugham), **VI:** 367, 368

Man of Law's Tale, The (Chaucer), **I:** 24, 34, 43, 51, 57

Man of Mode, The, or, Sir Fopling Flutter (Etherege), **II:** 256, 266, 271, 305

Man of Property, A (Galsworthy), **VI:** 271, 272, 273, 274, 275, 276, 278, 282–283

Man of Property, The (Galsworthy), **VI:** xiii

Man of Quality, A (Lee), **II:** 336

Manservant and Maidservant (Compton-Burnett), **VII:** 62, 63, 67

Mansfield, Katherine, **IV:** 106; **VI:** 375; **VII:** xv, xvii, **171–184,** 314; list of short stories, **VII:** 183–184

Mansfield Park (Austen), **IV:** xvii, 102–103, 108, 109, 111, 112, 115–119, 122

Mantz, Ruth, **VII:** 176

"Manus Animam Pinxit" (Thompson), **V:** 442

"Man was Made to Mourn, a Dirge" (Burns), **III:** 315

"Man Who Could Work Miracles, The" (Wells), **VI:** 235

"Man Who Died, The" (Lawrence), **VII:** 115

"Man Who Loved Islands, The" (Lawrence), **VII:** 115

Man Who Was Thursday, The (Chesterton), **VI:** 338

"Man with a Past, The" (Hardy), **VI:** 17

"Man Without a Temperament, The" (Mansfield), **VII:** 174, 177

Manzoni, Alessandro, **III:** 334

Map, Walter, **I:** 35

Map of Verona, A (Reed), **VII:** 423

Mapp Showing . . . Salvation and Damnation, A (Bunyan), **II:** 253

Marble Faun, The (Hawthorne), **VI:** 27

"Marchese Pallavicini and Walter Landor" (Landor), **IV:** 90

Marching Soldier (Cary), **VII:** 186

"Marchioness of Stonehenge, The" (Hardy), **VI:** 22

March of Literature, The (Ford), **VI:** 321, 322, 324

Marcus, S., **V:** 46, 73

Margin Released (Priestley), **VII:** 209, 210, 211

Margoliouth, H. M., **II:** 214$_n$, 219

"Mariana" (Tennyson), **IV:** 329, 331

"Mariana in the South" (Tennyson), **IV:** 329, 331

Marian hymn, **I:** 57, 60, 65–66

Mariani, Paul L., **V:** 373$_n$, 378, 382

Marianne Thornton (Forster), **VI:** 397, 411

Mari Magno (Clough), **V:** 159, 168

Marino, Giambattista, **II:** 180, 183

Marino Faliero (Swinburne), **V:** 332

Marino Faliero, Doge of Venice (Byron), **IV:** xviii, 178–179, 193

Marion Fay (Trollope), **V:** 102

Marius the Epicurean (Pater), **V:** xxv, 339, 348, **349–351,** 354, 355, 356, 411

Marjorie, **VI:** 249; pseud. of Arnold Bennett

"Markheim" (Stevenson), **V:** 395

"Mark of the Beast, The" (Kipling), **VI:** 183, 193

Marlborough: His Life and Times (Churchill), **VI:** 354–355

Marlowe, Christopher, **I:** 212, 228–229, **275–294,** 336; **II:** 69, 138; **III:** 344; **IV:** 255, 327

Marlowe and His Circle (Boas), **I:** 275, 293

Marlowe and the Early Shakespeare (Wilson), **I:** 286

Marmion (Scott), **IV:** xvi, 29, 30, 38, 129

Marmor Norfolciense (Johnson), **III:** 121

Marprelate controversy, **I:** 179, 204

Marriage A-la-Mode (Dryden), **II:** 293, 296, 305

Marriage of Heaven and Hell, The (Blake), **III:** 289, 297–298, 304, 307; **V:** xv, 329–330, 331

Marriage of Monna Lisa, The (Swinburne), **V:** 333

"Marriage of Tirzah and Ahirad, The" (Macaulay), **IV:** 283

Married Life (Bennett), see *Plain Man and His Wife, The*

Married Man, The (Lawrence), **VII:** 120

"Married Man's Story, A" (Mansfield), **VII:** 174

Marsh, Edward, **VI:** 416, 419, 420, 425, 430, 432, 452; **VII:** xvi

Marshall, William, **II:** 141

Marston, John, **I:** 234, 238, 340; **II:** 4, **24–33,** 34–37, 40–41, 47, 68, 72

Marston, Philip, **V:** 245

Marston, R. B., **II:** 131

Martial, **II:** 104, 265

Martin, John, **V:** 110

Martin, L. C., **II:** 183, 184*n*, 200

Martin, Martin, **III:** 117

Martin Chuzzlewit (Dickens), **V:** xx, 42, 47, 54–56, 58, 59, 68, 71

Martineau, Harriet, **IV:** 311; **V:** 125–126, 146

Martin Luther (Lopez and Moore), **VI:** 85, 95, 98

Martyn, Edward, **VI:** 309

"Martyrs' Song" (Rossetti), **V:** 256

Martz, Louis, **V:** 366, 382

Marvell, Andrew, **II:** 113, 121, 123, 166, 195–199, **204–220,** 255, 261

Marwick, A., **IV:** 290, 291

Marwood, Arthur, **VI:** 323, 331

Marxism, **VI:** 242 **VII:** xix, 8, 242–243, 384

Mary Barton (Gaskell), **V:** viii, x, xxi, 1, 2, 4–5, 6, 15

" 'Mary Gloster,' The" (Kipling), **VI:** 202

Mary Gresley (Trollope), **V:** 101

"Mary Postgate" (Kipling), **VI:** 197, 206

"Mary Queen of Scots" (Swinburne), **V:** 332

Mary Stuart (Swinburne), **V:** 330, 332

"Mary the Cook-Maid's Letter . . ." (Swift), **III:** 31

"Masculine Birth of Time, The" (Bacon), **I:** 263

Masefield, John, **VI:** 429; **VII:** xii, xiii

Mason, William, **III:** 141, 142, 145

masque, **I:** 344

"Masque of Anarchy, The" (Shelley), **IV:** xviii, 202–203, 206, 208

Masque of Queenes (Jonson), **II:** 111*n*

Massacre at Paris, The (Marlowe), **I:** 249, 276, 279–280, **285–286**

Mass and the English Reformers, The (Dugmore), **I:** 177*n*

Massinger, Philip, **II:** 44, 45, 50, 66–67, 69, 83, 87

Masson, David, **IV:** 212, 235

Masson, Rosaline, **V:** 393, 397

Master, The (Brontë), see *Professor, The*

Master Humphrey's Clock (Dickens), **V:** 42, 53–54, 71

"Master John Horseleigh, Knight" (Hardy), **VI:** 22

Masterman, C. F. G., **VI:** viii, 320

Master of Ballantrae, The (Stevenson), **V:** 383–384, 387, 396

Masters, The (Snow), **VII:** xxi, 324, 327–328, 330

"Match, The" (Marvell), **II:** 211

"Mater Dolorosa" (Swinburne), **V:** 325

"materialist" school, **VII:** xiv, xviii

Materials for a Description of Capri (Douglas), **VI:** 305

"Mater Triumphalis" (Swinburne), **V:** 325

"Matres Dolorosae" (Bridges), **VI:** 81

"Mattens" (Herbert), **II:** 127

"Matter of Fact, A" (Kipling), **VI:** 193

Matthew Arnold (ed. Allott), **V:** 218

Matthew Arnold: A Study in Conflict (Brown), **V:** 211–212, 217

Matthew Arnold: A Symposium (ed. Allott), **V:** 218

Matthews, Geoffrey Maurice, **IV:** x, xxv, 207, 208, 209, 237

Matthews, William, **I:** 68

Matthiessen, F. O., **V:** 204

Matthieu de Vendôme, **I:** 23, 39–40

Maturin, Charles, **III:** 327, 331, 333–334, 336, 345

Maud (Tennyson), **IV:** xxi, 325, 328, 330–331, 333–336, 337, 338; **VI:** 420

Maude: A Story for Girls (Rossetti), **V:** 260

"Maud-Evelyn" (James), **VI:** 69

Maugham, Syrie, **VI:** 369

Maugham, W. Somerset, **VI:** xi, xiii, 200, **363–381;** **VII:** 318–319; list of short stories and sketches, **VI:** 379–381

Maumbury Ring (Hardy), **VI:** 20

Maupassant, Guy de, **III:** 340

Maurice, Frederick D., **IV:** 54; **V:** xxi, 284, 285

Maurice (Forster), **VI:** xii, 397, **407–408,** 412

May Day (Chapman), **I:** 244

"May Day Song for North Oxford" (Betjeman), **VII:** 356

Mayer, Carl, **III:** 342

"Mayfly" (MacNeice), **VII:** 411

Mayo, Robert, **IV:** ix

Mayor of Casterbridge, The: The Life and Death of a Man of Character (Hardy), **VI:** 3, 5, 7, 8, 9–10, 20

Mazeppa (Byron), **IV:** xvii, 173, 192

Mazzini, Giuseppi, **V:** 313, 314, 324, 325

"Meaning of the Wild Body, The" (Lewis), **VII:** 77

Measure for Measure (Shakespeare), **I:** 313–314, 327; **II:** 30, 70, 168; **V:** 341, 351

Medal, The: A Satyre Against Sedition (Dryden), **II:** 299, 304

Medea (Seneca), **II:** 71

medieval epic, **I:** 69

Medieval Heritage of Elizabethan Tragedy (Farnham), **I:** 214

Meditations Collected from the Sacred Books . . . (Richardson), **III:** 92

"Meditations in Time of Civil War" (Yeats), **V:** 317; **VII:** 24

Meditations of Daniel Defoe, The (Defoe), **III:** 12

Meditation upon a Broom-Stick, A (Swift), **III:** 35

Mediterranean Scenes (Bennett), **VI:** 264, 267

Medwin, Thomas, **IV:** 196, 209

Meeting By the River, A (Isherwood), **VII:** 317

"Melancholia" (Bridges), **VI:** 80

"Melancholy" (Bridges), **VI:** 80

"Melancholy Hussar of the German Legion, The" (Hardy), **VI:** 20, 22

Melchiori, Giorgio, **VI:** 208

Meleager (Euripides), **V:** 322, 323

Melincourt (Peacock), **IV:** xvii, 162, 163–164, 165, 168, 170

Melmoth Reconciled (Balzac), **III:** 334, 339

Melmoth the Wanderer (Maturin), **III:** 327, 333–334, 335, 345

Melville, Herman, **IV:** 97; **V:** xvii, xx–xxi, xxv, 211; **VI:** 363

"Memoir" (Scott), **IV:** 28, 30, 35–36, 39

Mémoire justificatif etc. (Gibbon), **III:** 233

Mémoires littéraires de la Grande Bretagne (periodical), **III:** 233

"Memoir of Bernard Barton" (FitzGerald), **IV:** 353

"Memoir of Cowper: An Autobiography" (ed. Quinlan), **III:** 220

"Memoir" of Fleeming Jenkin (Stevenson), **V:** 386, 395

Memoir of Jane Austen (Austen-Leigh), **III:** 90

Memoir of the Bobotes (Cary), **VII:** 185

Memoirs (Temple), **III:** 19

Memoirs of a Cavalier, The (Defoe), **III:** 6, 13; **VI:** 353, 359

Memoirs of a Midget (de la Mare), **III:** 340, 345

Memoirs of a Physician, The (Dumas *père*), **III:** 332

Memoirs of a Protestant, The (tr. Goldsmith), **III:** 191

Memoirs of Barry Lyndon, Esq., The (Thackeray), see *Barry Lyndon*

Memoirs of Himself (Stevenson), **V:** 396

"Memoirs of James Boswell, Esq." (Boswell), **III:** 248

Memoirs of Jonathan Swift (Scott), **IV:** 38

Memoirs of Martin Scriblerus, **III:** 24, 77

"Memoirs of M. de Voltaire" (Goldsmith), **III:** 189

Memoirs of My Dead Life (Moore), **VI:** 87, 88, 95, 96, 97, 98–99

"Memoirs of Percy Bysshe Shelley" (Peacock), **IV:** 158, 169, 170

Memoirs of the Late Thomas Holcroft . . . (Hazlitt), **IV:** 128, 139

Memoirs of the Life of Edward Gibbon, The (ed. Hill), **III:** 221$_n$, 233

Memoirs of the Life of Sir Walter Scott, Bart. (Lockhart), **IV:** 27, 30, 34, 35–36, 39

Memoirs of the Navy (Pepys), **II:** 281, 288

Memoirs Relating to . . . Queen Anne's Ministry (Swift), **III:** 27

"Memorabilia" (Browning), **IV:** 354–355, 357

Memorable Masque of the Middle Temple and Lincoln's Inn, The (Chapman), **I:** 235

Memorial, The (Isherwood), **VII:** 205, 310–311

"Memorial for the City" (Auden), **VII:** 388, 393

Memorials of a Tour on the Continent (Wordsworth), **IV:** 24–25

Memorials of Edward Burne-Jones (Burne-Jones), **V:** 295–296, 306

"Memorials of Gormandising" (Thackeray), **V:** 23, 24, 38

Memorials of Thomas Hood (Hood and Broderip), **IV:** 251, 261, 267

Memorials of Two Sisters, Susanna and Catherine Winkworth (ed. Shaen), **V:** 149

Memories and Portraits (Stevenson), **V:** 390, 395

Memories of Vailiona (Osborne and Strong), **V:** 393, 397

Men and Wives (Compton-Burnett), **VII:** 64, 65, 66–67

Men and Women (Browning), **IV:** xiii, xxi, 357, 363, 374

Menaphon (Greene), **I:** 165

Men at Arms (Waugh), **VII:** 304; see also *Sword of Honour* trilogy

Men Like Gods (Wells), **VI:** 226, 240, 244; **VII:** 204

Men's Wives (Thackeray), **V:** 23, 35, 38

"Mental Cases" (Owen), **VI:** 456, 457

Mental Efficiency (Bennett), **VI:** 250, 266

"Men Who March Away" (Hardy), **VI:** 415, 421

Men Without Art (Lewis), **VII:** 72, 76

Merchant of Venice, The (Shakespeare), **I:** 310

Merchant's Tale, The (Chaucer), **I:** 36, 41–42

"Mercy" (Collins), **III:** 166

Mere Accident, A (Moore), **VI:** 86, 91

Meredith, George, **II:** 104, 342, 345; **IV:** 160; **V:** x, xviii, xxii–xxvi, **219–234**, 244, 432; **VI:** 2

Meredith, H. O., **VI:** 399

Meredith (Sassoon), **V:** 219, 234

Meredith et la France (Mackay), **V:** 223, 234

"Mere Interlude, A" (Hardy), **VI:** 22

Meres, Francis, **I:** 212, 234, 296, 307

Merie Tales, The, **I:** 83, 93

Meriton, George, **II:** 340

"Merlin and the Gleam" (Tennyson), **IV:** 329

Mermaid, Dragon, Fiend (Graves), **VII:** 264

Merope (Arnold), **V:** 209, 216

Merry England (periodical), **V:** 440

Merry-Go-Round, The (Lawrence), **VII:** 120

Merry-Go-Round, The (Maugham), **VI:** 372

Merry Jests of George Peele, The, **I:** 194

Merry Men, The, and Other Tales and Fables (Stevenson), **V:** 395

Merry Wives of Windsor, The (Shakespeare), **I:** 295, 311; **III:** 117

Mespoulet, M., **V:** 266

Messages (Fernandez), **V:** 225–226

"Messdick" (Ross), **VII:** 433

Metamorphoses (Ovid), **III:** 54; **V:** 321

Metamorphosis (Kafka), **III:** 340, 345

Metamorphosis of Pygmalion's Image (Marston), **I:** 238; **II:** 25, 40

metaphysical poetry, **II:** 208

metaphysical poets, **II:** 121, 123, 170, **179–203**; see also Abraham Cowley, Richard Crashaw, John Donne, George Herbert, Andrew Marvell, Thomas Traherne, Henry Vaughan

meter, **VII:** xii, 136

"Methinks the poor Town has been troubled too long" (Dorset), **II:** 262

Metrical Tales and Other Poems (Southey), **IV:** 71

Meynell, Wilfred, **V:** 440, 451

"Michael" (Wordsworth), **IV:** 8, 18–19

Michaelmas Term (Middleton), **II:** 3, 4, 21

Michael Robartes and the Dancer (Yeats), **VI:** 217

Michelet, Jules, **V:** 346

Microcosmography (Earle), **IV:** 286

Micro-Cynicon, Six Snarling Satires (Middleton), **II:** 2–3

Midas (Lyly), **I:** 198, 202, 203

Middlemarch (Eliot), **III:** 157; **V:** ix–x, xxiv, 196–197, 200

"Middle of a War" (Fuller), **VII:** 429

Middleton, D., **V:** 253

Middleton, Thomas, **II:** **1–23,** 30, 33, 68–70, 72, 83, 85, 93, 100; **IV:** 79

"Middle Years, The" (James), **VI:** 69

Middle Years, The (James), **VI:** 65, 69

Midnight on the Desert (Priestley), **VII:** 209, 212

"Midnight Skaters, The" (Blunden), **VI:** 429

"Midsummer Holiday, A, and Other Poems" (Swinburne), **V:** 332

Midsummer Night's Dream, A (Shakespeare), **I:** 304–305, 311–312; **II:** 51, 281

Mid-Victorian Memories (Francillon), **V:** 83

Mightier Than the Sword (Ford), **VI:** 320–321

Mighty and Their Full, The (Compton-Burnett), **VII:** 61, 62

Mighty Magician, The (FitzGerald), **IV:** 353

Mike Fletcher (Moore), **VI:** 87, 91

"Mildred Lawson" (Moore), **VI:** 98

Milestones (Bennett), **VI:** 250, 263, 264

Milford, H., **III:** 208$_n$

Military Memoirs of Capt. George Carleton, The (Defoe), **III:** 14

Military Philosophers, The (Powell), **VII:** 349

Mill, James, **IV:** 159; **V:** 288

Mill, John Stuart, **IV:** 50, 56, 246, 355; **V:** xxi–xxii, xxiv, 182, 279, 288, 343

Millais, John Everett, **V:** 235, 236, 379

Miller, Arthur, **VI:** 286

Miller, J. Hillis, **VI:** 147

"Miller's Daughter, The" (Tennyson), **IV:** 326,

Miller's Tale, The (Chaucer), **I:** 37

Millionairess, The (Shaw), **VI:** 102, 127

Mill on the Floss, The (Eliot), **V:** xxii, 14, 192–194, 200

Mills, C. M., pseud. of Elizabeth Gaskell

Milnes, Richard Monckton (Lord Houghton), see Monckton Milnes, Richard

Milton, John, **II:** 50–52, 113, **158–178**, 195, 196, 198, 199, 205, 206, 236, 302; **III:** 43, 118–119, 167$_n$, 211$_n$, 220, 302; **IV:** 9, 11–12, 14, 22, 23, 93, 95, 185, 186, 200, 205, 229, 269, 278, 279, 352; **V:** 365–366

Milton (Blake), **III:** 303–304, 307; **V:** xvi, 330

"Milton" (Macaulay), **IV:** 278, 279

Milton (Meredith), **V:** 234

Milton's Prosody (Bridges), **VI:** 83

"Mina Laury" (Brontë), **V:** 122, 123, 149, 151

Mind at the End of Its Tether (Wells), **VI:** xiii; **VI:** 228, 242

"Mine old dear enemy, my froward master" (Wyatt), **I:** 105

"Miners" (Owen), **VI:** 452, 454

Minor Poems of Robert Southey; The (Southey), **IV:** 71

Minstrel, The (Beattie), **IV:** 198

Minstrelsy of the Scottish Border (ed. Scott), **IV:** 29, 39

Minutes of the Negotiations of Monsr. Mesnager, . . . (Defoe), **III:** 13

"Mirabeau" (Macaulay), **IV:** 278

"Miracle Cure" (Lowbury), **VII:** 432

Mirèio (Mistral), **V:** 219

Mirour de l'omme (Gower), **I:** 48, 49

Mirror for Magistrates, The, **I:** 162, 214

Mirror of the Sea, The: Memories and Impressions (Conrad), **VI:** 134, 148

Mirrour or Looking-Glasse Both for Saints and Sinners, A (Clarke), **II:** 251

Misadventures of John Nicholson, The (Stevenson), **V:** 396

Misalliance (Shaw), **VI:** xv, 115, 117, 118, 120, 129

Miscellanea (Temple), **III:** 40

Miscellaneous Essays (St. Évremond), **III:** 47

Miscellaneous Observations on the Tragedy of Macbeth (Johnson), **III:** 108, 116, 121

Miscellaneous Poems (Marvell), **II:** 207

Miscellaneous Studies (Pater), **V:** 348, 357

Miscellaneous Works of the Duke of Buckingham, **II:** 268

Miscellaneous Works . . . with Memoirs of His Life (Gibbon), **III:** 233

Miscellanies (Cowley), **II:** 198

Miscellanies (Pope and Swift), **II:** 335

Miscellanies (Swinburne), **V:** 332

Miscellanies, Aesthetic and Literary . . . (Coleridge), **IV:** 56

Miscellanies; A Serious Address to the People of Great Britain (Fielding), **III:** 105

Miscellany (Tonson), **III:** 69

Miscellany Poems (Wycherley), **II:** 321

Miscellany Tracts (Browne), **II:** 156

Mischmasch (Carroll), **V:** 274

Miser, The (Fielding), **III:** 105

"Miserie" (Herbert), **II:** 128–129

Miseries of War, The (Ralegh), **I:** 158

Misfortunes of Arthur, The (Hughes), **I:** 218

Misfortunes of Elphin, The (Peacock), **IV:** xviii, 163, 167–168, 170

Mishan, E. J., **VI:** 240

"Misplaced Attachment of Mr. John Dounce, The" (Dickens), **V:** 46

"Miss Brill" (Mansfield), **VII:** 175

"Miss Gunton of Poughkeepsie" (James), **VI:** 69

"Miss Kilmansegg and Her Precious Leg" (Hood), **IV:** 258–259

Miss Lucy in Town (Fielding), **III:** 105

Miss Mackenzie (Trollope), **V:** 101

"Miss Tickletoby's Lectures on English History" (Thackeray), **V:** 38

Mrs. Browning: A Poet's Work and Its Setting (Hayter), **IV:** 322

Mrs. Craddock (Maugham), **VI:** 367

Mrs. Dalloway (Woolf), **VI:** 275, 279; **VII:** xv, 18, 21, 24, 28–29

Mrs. Dot (Maugham), **VI:** 368

Mrs. Fisher, or the Future of Humour (Graves), **VII:** 259–260

"Mrs. Jaypher found a wafer" (Lear), **V:** 86

Mrs. Leicester's School (Lamb and Lamb), **IV:** 80, 85

"Mrs. Medwin" (James), **VI:** 69

"Mrs. Nelly's Complaint," **II:** 268

Mrs. Perkins's Ball (Thackeray), **V:** 24, 38

"Mrs. Temperley" (James), **VI:** 69

Mrs. Warren's Profession (Shaw), **V:** 413; **VI:** 108, 109

Mistake, The (Vanbrugh), **II:** 325, 333, 336

Mistakes, The (Harris), **II:** 305

"Mr. and Mrs. Dove" (Mansfield), **VII:** 180

"Mr. and Mrs. Frank Berry" (Thackeray), **V:** 23

"Mr Apollinax" (Eliot), **VII:** 144

Mr. Bennett and Mrs. Brown (Woolf), **VI:** 247, 267, 275, 290; **VII:** xiv, xv

"Mr. Bodkin" (Hood), **IV:** 267

Mr. Britling Sees It Through (Wells), **VI:** 227, 240

"Mr. Brown's Letters to a Young Man About Town" (Thackeray), **V:** 38

Mr. Bunyan's Last Sermon (Bunyan), **II:** 253

Mr. C[olli]n's Discourse of Free-Thinking (Swift), **III:** 35

"Mr. Crabbe—Mr. Campbell" (Hazlitt), **III:** 276

"Mr Eliot's Sunday Morning Service" (Eliot), **VII:** 145

"Mr. Gilfil's Love Story" (Eliot), **V:** 190

"Mr. Graham" (Hood), **IV:** 267

Mr. H——— (Lamb), **IV:** 80–81, 85

"Mr. Harrison's Confessions" (Gaskell), **V:** 14, 15

Mr. John Milton's Character of the Long Parliament and Assembly of Divines . . . (Milton), **II:** 176

Mister Johnson (Cary), **VII:** 186, 187, 189, 190–191

"Mr. Know-All" (Maugham), **VI:** 370

Mr. Macaulay's Character of the Clergy in the Latter Part of the Seventeenth Century Considered (Babington), **IV:** 291

"Mr. Norris and I" (Isherwood), **VII:** 311–312

Mr. Norris Changes Trains (Isherwood), **VII:** xx, 311–312

Mr. Polly (Wells), see *History of Mr. Polly, The*

Mr. Pope's Welcome from Greece (Gay), **II:** 348

Mr. Prohack (Bennett), **VI:** 260, 267

"Mr. Reginald Peacock's Day" (Mansfield), **VII:** 174

"Mr. Robert Herricke His Farewell unto Poetrie" (Herrick), **II:** 112

"Mr. Robert Montgomery's Poems" (Macaulay), **IV:** 280

Mr. Scarborough's Family (Trollope), **V:** 98, 102

"Mr. Sludge 'the Medium' " (Browning), **IV:** 358, 368

Mr. Smirke: or, The Divine in Mode (Marvell), **II:** 219

Mr. Waller's Speech in the Painted Chamber (Waller), **II:** 238

Mr. Weston's Good Wine (Powys), **VII:** 21

"Mr. Whistler's Ten O'Clock" (Wilde), **V:** 407

Mistral, Frédéric, **V:** 219

Mistress, The (Cowley), **II:** 194, 198, 202, 236

"Mistress of Vision, The" (Thompson), **V:** 447–448

Mist's Weekly Journal (newspaper), **III:** 4

Mitford, Mary Russell, **IV:** 311, 312

Mitford, Nancy, **VII:** 290

Mithridates (Lee), **II:** 305

Mixed Essays (Arnold), **V:** 213$_n$, 216

Mob, The (Galsworthy), **VI:** 280, 288

Moby Dick (Melville), **VI:** 363

Mock Doctor, The (Fielding), **III:** 105

Mock-Mourners, The: . . . Elegy on King William (Defoe), **III:** 12

Mock Speech from the Throne (Marvell), **II:** 207

"Model Prisons" (Carlyle), **IV:** 247

Modern Comedy, A (Galsworthy), **VI:** 270, 275

Modern Fiction (Woolf), **VII:** xiv

Modern Husband, The (Fielding), **III:** 105

modernism, **VI:** 275

Modernism and Romance (Scott-James), **VI:** 21

"Modern Love" (Meredith), **V:** 220, 234, 244

Modern Love, and Poems of the English Roadside . . . (Meredith), **V:** xxii, 220, 234

Modern Lover, A (Moore), **VI:** 86, 89, 98

modern movement, **V:** 309; **VI:** xvi, 314; **VII:** xi–xiii, xv–xvi

Modern Movement, The: 100 Key Books from England, France, and America, 1880–1950 (Connolly), **VI:** 371

modern novelists, **VII:** xv, 18

Modern Painters (Ruskin), **V:** xx, 175–176, 180, 184, 282

Modern Painting (Moore), **VI:** 87

Modern Poetry: A Personal Essay (MacNeice), **VII:** 403, 404, 410

Modern Utopia, A (Wells), **VI:** 227, 234, 241, 244

"Modern Warning, The" (James), **VI:** 48, 69

Modest Proposal, A (Swift), **III:** 21, 28, 29, 35

"Moestitiae Encomium" (Thompson), **V:** 450

Moffatt, James, **I:** 382–383

Mohocks, The (Gay), **III:** 60, 67

Molière (Jean Baptiste Poquelin), **II:** 314, 318, 325, 336, 337, 350; **V:** 224

Moll Flanders (Defoe), **III:** 5, 6, 7, 8, 9, 13, 95

Molyneux, William, **III:** 27

Moments of Being (Woolf), **VII:** 33

Moments of Vision, and Miscellaneous Verses (Hardy), **VI:** 20

Monastery, The (Scott), **IV:** xviii, 39

Monckton Milnes, Richard (Lord Houghton), **IV:** 211, 234, 235, 251, 252, 254, 302, 351; **V:** 312, 313, 334

"Monday, or The Squabble" (Gay), **III:** 56

Monday or Tuesday (Woolf), **VII:** 20, 21, 38

Monk, The (Lewis), **III:** 332–333, 335, 345

Monks and the Giants, The (Frere), see *Whistlecraft*

Monks of St. Mark, The (Peacock), **IV:** 158, 169

Monk's Prologue, The (Chaucer), **II:** 70

Monk's Tale, The (Chaucer), **I:** 31

Monk's Tale, The (Lydgate), **I:** 57

"Monna Innominata" (Rossetti), **V:** 251

Monody on the Death of the Right Hon. R. B. Sheridan . . . (Byron), **IV:** 192

Monro, Harold, **VI:** 448

Monsieur de Pourceaugnac (Molière), **II:** 325, 337, 339, 347, 350

Monsieur d'Olive (Chapman), **I:** 244–245

Monsieur Thomas (Fletcher), **II:** 45, 61, 65

Monstre Gai (Lewis), **VII:** 72, 80

Montagu, Lady Mary Wortley, **II:** 326

Montague, John, **VI:** 220

Montaigne, Michel Eyquem de, **II:** 25, 30, 80, 104, 108, 146; **III:** 39

"Mont Blanc" (Shelley), **IV:** 198

Montemayor, Jorge de, **I:** 164, 302

Montgomery, Robert, **IV:** 280

Month (periodical), **V:** 365, 379

Montherlant, Henry de, **II:** 99$_n$

Monthly Review (periodical), **III:** 147, 188

Montrose, marquess of, **II:** 222, 236–237, 238

Monumental Column, A. Erected to . . . Prince of Wales (Webster), **II:** 68, 85

"Monuments of Honour" (Webster), **II:** 68, 85

Monypenny, W. F., **IV:** 292, 295, 300, 307, 308

Moon and Sixpence, The (Maugham), **VI:** xiii, 365, 374, **375–376**

"Moonlight Night on the Port" (Keyes), **VII:** 439

Moonstone, The (Collins), **III:** 340, 345

Moorcock, Michael, **III:** 341

Moore, George, **IV:** 102; **V:** xxi, xxvi, 129, 153; **VI:** xii, **85–99**, 207, 239, 270, 365

Moore, John Robert, **III:** 1, 12

Moore, Marianne, **IV:** 6

Moore, Thomas, **IV:** xvi, 193, 205; **V:** 116

"Moore's Life of Lord Byron" (Macaulay), **IV:** 281–282

Moorland Cottage, The (Gaskell), **V:** 14, 15

Moorman, Mary, **IV:** 4, 25

Moral and Political Lecture, A (Coleridge), **IV:** 56

Moral Epistle, Respectfully Dedicated to Earl Stanhope (Landor), **IV:** 99

Moral Essays (Pope), **III:** 74–75, 77, 78

"Morality and the Novel" (Lawrence), **VII:** 87

"Mora Montravers" (James), **VI:** 69

More, Hannah, **IV:** 269

More, Paul Elmer, **II:** 152

More, Sir Thomas, **III:** 24; **IV:** 69

More Dissemblers Besides Women (Middleton), **II:** 3, 21

More New Arabian Nights: The Dynamiter (Stevenson), **V:** 395

More Nonsense, Pictures, Rhymes, Botany (Lear), **V:** 78, 87

More Poems (Housman), **VI:** 152, 157, 161–162

More Reformation: A Satyr upon Himself . . . (Defoe), **III:** 13

More Short-Ways with the Dissenters (Defoe), **III:** 13

More Women than Men (Compton-Burnett), **VII:** 61–62

Morgan, Margery M., **VI:** xiii, xiv–xv, xxxiv

Morgann, Maurice, **IV:** xiv, 168

Morgante Maggiore (Pulci), **IV:** 182

Morison, James Augustus Cotter, **IV:** 289, 291

Morley, Frank, **IV:** 79, 86

Morley, John, **VI:** 2, 157, 336

Morley, Lord John, **III:** 201, 205; **IV:** 289, 291; **V:** 279, 280, 284, 290, 313, 334

Morning Chronicle, The (periodical), **IV:** 43, 128, 129; **V:** 41

"Morning, Midday, and Evening Sacrifice" (Hopkins), **V:** 370

Morning Post (periodical), **III:** 269; **VI:** 351

Mornings in Mexico (Lawrence), **VII:** 116, 117

"Morning Sun" (MacNeice), **VII:** 411

"Morning-watch, The" (Vaughan), **II:** 187

Morrell, Sir Charles, **V:** 111

Morrell, Ottoline, **VII:** 103

Morris, Margaret, **VI:** 274

Morris, May, **V:** 298, 301, 305

Morris, William, **IV:** 218; **V:** ix, xi, xii, xix, xxii–xxvi, 236–238, **291–307**, 312, 365, 401, 409; **VI:** 103, 167–168, 283

Morris & Co., **V:** 295, 296, 302

Morrison, Arthur, **VI:** 365–366

"Morris's Life and Death of Jason" (Swinburne), **V:** 298

Mortal Coils (Huxley), **VII:** 200

Morte Arthur, Le, **I:** 72, 73

Morte Darthur, Le (Malory), **I:** 67, 68–79; **V:** 294

"Morte d'Arthur" (Tennyson), **IV:** xx, 332–334, 336

"Mortification" (Herbert), **II:** 127

Mosada, a Dramatic Poem (Yeats), **VI:** 221

Moseley, Humphrey, **II:** 89

Moses (Rosenberg), **VI:** 433

"Mosquito" (Lawrence), **VII:** 119

"Most Extraordinary Case, A" (James), **VI:** 69

Most Piteous Tale of the Morte Arthur Saunz Guerdon, The (Malory), **I:** 72, 77

Mother and Son (Compton-Burnett), **VII:** 64, 65, 68–69

Mother Bombie (Lyly), **I:** 203–204

"Mother Country" (Rossetti), **V:** 255

Mother Courage (Brecht), **VI:** 123

Mother Hubberd's Tale (Spenser), **I:** 124, 131

Motteux, Pierre, **II:** 352, 353

Mountain Town in France, A (Stevenson), **V:** 396

Mount of Olives, The: or Solitary Devotions . . . (Vaughan), **II:** 185, 201

Mount Zion (Betjeman), **VII:** 364

"Mourning" (Marvell), **II:** 209, 212

Mourning Bride, The (Congreve), **II:** 338, 347, 350

Mourning Muse of Alexis, The: A Pastoral (Congreve), **II:** 350

"Mower to the Glo-Worms, The" (Marvell), **II:** 209

"Mowgli's Brothers" (Kipling), **VI:** 199

Moxon, Edward, **IV:** 83, 86, 252

M. Prudhomme at the International Exhibition (Swinburne), **V:** 333

Much Ado About Nothing (Shakespeare), **I:** 310–311, 327

Muggeridge, Malcolm, **VI:** 356; **VII:** 276

Muiopotmos (Spenser), **I:** 124

Muir, Edwin, **I:** 247; **IV:** 27, 40

Muir, K., **IV:** 219, 236

Mulberry Garden, The (Sedley), **II:** 263–264, 271

Mulcaster, Richard, **I:** 122

Müller, Max, **V:** 203

Mummer's Wife, A (Moore), **VI:** xii, 86, 90, 98

"Mundus and Paulina" (Gower), **I:** 53–54

Mundus Muliebris: or, The Ladies-Dressing Room Unlock'd (Evelyn), **II:** 287

Munera Pulveris (Ruskin), **V:** 184

"Municipal Gallery Revisited, The" (Yeats), **VI:** 216

Munnings, Sir Alfred, **VI:** 210

"Murder Considered as One of the Fine Arts" (De Quincey), **IV:** 149–150

Murder in the Cathedral (Eliot), **VII:** 153, 157, 159

murder mystery, see detective fiction

Murder of John Brewer, The (Kyd), **I:** 218

Murder of the Man Who Was Shakespeare, The (Hoffman), **I:** 277

Murderous Michael, **I:** 218

"Murders in the Rue Morgue, The" (Poe), **III:** 339

Murdoch, Iris, **III:** 341, 345; **VI:** 372

Murnau, F. W., **III:** 342

Murphy, Richard, **VI:** 220

Murray, Gilbert, **VI:** 153, 273, 274

Murray, Sir James, **III:** 113

Murray, John, **IV:** 182, 188, 190, 193, 294

Murry, John Middleton, **III:** 68; **VI:** 207, 375, 446; **VII:** 37, 106, 173–174, 181–182

"Muse, The" (Cowley), **II:** 195, 200

"Muse Among the Motors, A" (Kipling), **VI:** 202

"Musée des Beaux Arts" (Auden), **VII:** 379, 385–386

"Muses Dirge, The" (James), **II:** 102

"Museum" (MacNeice), **VII:** 412

"Music" (Owen), **VI:** 449

"Musical Instrument, A" (Browning), **IV:** 315

Music: An Ode (Swinburne), **V:** 333

Music at Night (Priestley), **VII:** 225–226

Music Cure, The (Shaw), **VI:** 129

Musicks Duell (Crashaw), **II:** 90–91

Music of Time, The (Powell), **VII:** 343

Music of Time novel cycle (Powell), see *Dance to the Music of Time, A*

Muslin (Moore), **VI:** 98; see *Drama in Muslin, A*

"My Aged Uncle Arly" (Lear), **V:** 85–86

"My Company" (Read), **VI:** 437

My Darling Dear, My Daisy Flower (Skelton), **I:** 83

My Dear Dorothea: A Practical System of Moral Education for Females (Shaw), **VI:** 109, 130

"My delight and thy delight" (Bridges), **VI:** 77

"My Diary": The Early Years of My Daughter Marianne (Gaskell), **V:** 15

"My Doves" (Browning), **IV:** 313

"My Dream" (Rossetti), **V:** 256

"My Dyet" (Cowley), **II:** 197, 198

My Early Life (Churchill), **VI:** 354

Myers, William Francis, **VII:** xx, xxxviii

"My First Acquaintance with Poets" (Hazlitt), **IV:** 126, 132

"My Friend Bingham" (James), **VI:** 69

"My galley charged with forgetfulness" (Wyatt), **I:** 110

My Guru and His Disciple (Isherwood), **VII:** 318

My Lady Ludlow (Gaskell), **V:** 15

"My Last Duchess" (Browning), **IV:** 356, 360, 372

"My love whose heart is tender said to me" (Rossetti), **V:** 251

"My lute awake!" (Wyatt), **I:** 105–106

"My own heart let me more have pity on" (Hopkins), **V:** 375–376

"My pen take pain a little space" (Wyatt), **I:** 106

Myrick, K. O., **I:** 160, 167

"My Sister's Sleep" (Rossetti), **V:** 239, 240, 242

"My Spectre" (Blake), **V:** 244

"My spirit kisseth thine" (Bridges), **VI:** 77

Mysteries of Udolpho, The (Radcliffe), **III:** 331–332, 335, 345; **IV:** xvi, 111

Mystery of Edwin Drood, The (Dickens), see *Edwin Drood*

Mystery of the Fall (Clough), **V:** 159, 161

Mystery Revealed, The: . . . Containing . . . Testimonials Respecting the . . . Cock Lane Ghost (Goldsmith), **III:** 191

mysticism in literature, **VI:** 209

Mythologiae sive explicationis fabularum (Conti), **I:** 266

"My true love hath my heart, and I have his" (Sidney), **I:** 169

My World as in My Time (Newbolt), **VI:** 75

N

Nadel, G. H., **I:** 269

Naipaul, V. S., **VII:** xx

Naked Warriors (Read), **VI:** 436

Name and Nature of Poetry, The (Housman), **VI:** 157, 162–164

"Naming of Parts" (Reed), **VII:** 422

Nannie's Night Out (O'Casey), **VII:** 11–12

Napier, Macvey, **IV:** 272

Napoleon of Notting Hill, The (Chesterton), **VI:** 335, 338, 343–344

Napoleon III in Italy and Other Poems (Browning), see *Poems Before Congress*

"Narcissus" (Gower), **I:** 53–54

Nares, Edward, **IV:** 280

Narrative of All the Robberies, . . . of John Sheppard, A (Defoe), **III:** 13

Narrow Corner, The (Maugham), **VI:** 375

"Narrow Sea, The" (Graves), **VII:** 270

"Narrow Vessel, A" (Thompson), **V:** 441

Nashe, Thomas, **I:** 114, 123, 171, 199, 221, 278, 279, 281, 288; **II:** 25

Nation (periodical), **VI:** 455

National Observer (periodical), **VI:** 350

National Standard (periodical), **V:** 19

National Tales (Hood), **IV:** 255, 259, 267

national theater, **VI:** 104, 113, 115, 273

National Trust, **VI:** 384, 390

native tradition, **VII:** xvi, xviii

naturalism, **VI:** viii–ix, xiii, 269–270, 285, 366; **VII:** xii, 7, 42, 43

"natural man," **VII:** 94

"Natura Naturans" (Clough), **V:** 159–160

nature, treatment of, **IV:** 171, 173, 184–185, 193, 338, 455–456; **VII:** 92–95

Nature of a Crime, The (Conrad), **VI:** 148

"Nature of Gothic, The" (Ruskin), **V:** 176

Nature of History, The (Marwick), **IV:** 290, 291

"Nature of the Scholar, The" (Fichte), **V:** 348

"Nature That Washt Her Hands in Milk" (Ralegh), **I:** 149

Natwar-Singh, K., **VI:** 408

Naufragium Joculare (Cowley), **II:** 194, 202

Naulahka (Kipling and Balestier), **VI:** 204

Navigation and Commerce (Evelyn), **II:** 287

Naylor, Gillian, **VI:** 168

Nazarene Gospel Restored, The (Graves and Podro), **VII:** 262

Nazism, **VI:** 242

Near and Far (Blunden), **VI:** 428

"Near Lanivet" (Hardy), **VI:** 17

"Near Perigord" (Pound), **V:** 304

Necessity of Atheism, The (Shelley and Hogg), **IV:** xvii, 196, 208

Necessity of Poetry, The (Bridges), **VI:** 75–76, 82, 83

"Ned Bratts" (Browning), **IV:** 370

Needham, Gwendolyn, **V:** 60

"negative method," **VI:** 275–276, 280

Nelson, W., **I:** 86

neo-Christianity, **VII:** 243

Neoplatonism, **IV:** 53

Nerinda (Douglas), **VI:** 300, 305

Nero Part I (Bridges), **VI:** 83

Nero Part II (Bridges), **VI:** 83

Nest of Tigers, A: Edith, Osbert and Sacheverell in Their Times (Lehmann), **VII:** 141

Nether World, The (Gissing), **V:** 424, 437

Nettles (Lawrence), **VII:** 118

"Netty Sargent's Copyhold" (Hardy), **VI:** 22

Neutral Ground (Corke), **VII:** 93

New Age (periodical), **VI:** 247, 265; **VII:** 172

New and Improved Grammar of the English Tongue, A (Hazlitt), **IV:** 139

New and Useful Concordance, A (Bunyan), **II:** 253

New Arabian Nights (Stevenson), **V:** 384$_n$, 386, 395

New Atlantis (Bacon), **I:** 259, 265, 267–269, 273

"New Ballad of Tannhäuser, A" (Davidson), **V:** 318$_n$

New Bath Guide (Anstey), **III:** 155

New Bats in Old Belfries (Betjeman), **VII:** 368–369

New Bearings in English Poetry (Leavis), **V:** 375, 381; **VI:** 21; **VII:** 234, 244–246

New Belfry of Christ Church; The (Carroll), **V:** 274

Newbolt, Henry, **VI:** 75, 417

Newby, T. C., **V:** 140

New Characters . . . of Severall Persons . . . (Webster), **II:** 85

Newcomes, The (Thackeray), **V:** xxii, 18, 19, **28–31,** 35, 38, 69

New Country (ed. Roberts), **VII:** xix, 411

New Criticism, **VII:** 164, 260

New Discovery of an Old Intreague, An (Defoe), **III:** 12

New Dunciad, The (Pope), **III:** 73, 78

Newell, K. B., **VI:** 235, 237

"New England Winter, A" (James), **VI:** 69

New Essays by De Quincey (ed. Tave); **IV:** 155

New Family Instructor, A (Defoe), **III:** 14

New Form of Intermittent Light for Lighthouses, A (Stevenson), **V:** 395

"Newgate" novels, **V:** 22, 47

New Grub Street (Gissing), **V:** xxv, 426, 427, 429, 430, 434–435, 437; **VI:** 377

New Inn; The Noble Gentlemen (Jonson), **II:** 65

New Journey to Paris, A (Swift), **III:** 35

New Light on Piers Plowman (Bright), **I:** 3

New Lives for Old (Snow), **VII:** 323

New Love-Poems (Scott), **IV:** 39

New Machiavelli, The (Wells), **VI:** 226, 239, 244

Newman, F. W., **V:** 208$_n$

Newman, John Henry, **II:** 243; **III:** 46; **IV:** 63, 64; **V:** xi, xxv, 156, 214, 283, 340

New Men, The (Snow), **VII:** xxi, 324, 328–329, 330

New Method of Evaluation as Applied to π, *The* (Carroll), **V:** 274

New Monthly (periodical), **IV:** 252, 254, 258

"New Novel, The" (James), **VI:** xii

New Numbers (periodical), **VI:** 420

New Poems (Arnold), **V:** xxiii, 204, 209, 216

"New Poems" (Bridges), **VI:** 77

New Poems (Thompson), **V:** 444, 446, 451

New Poems by Robert Browning and Elizabeth Barrett Browning (ed. Kenyon), **IV:** 321

New Poems Hitherto Unpublished or Uncollected . . . (Rossetti), **V:** 260

New Review (periodical), **VI:** 136

"News" (Traherne), **II:** 191, 194

News from Nowhere (Morris), **V:** xxv, 291, 301–304, 306, 409

New Signatures (ed. Roberts), **VII:** 411

Newspaper, The (Crabbe), **III:** 275, 286

New Statesman (periodical), **VI:** 119, 250, 371; **VII:** 32

New Testament in Modern English (Phillips), **I:** 383

New Testament in Modern Speech (Weymouth), **I:** 382

Newton, J. F., **IV:** 158

Newton, John, **III:** 210

New Voyage Round the World, A (Dampier), **III:** 7, 24

New Voyage Round the World, A (Defoe), **III:** 5, 13

New Witness (periodical), **VI:** 340, 341

New Worlds for Old (Wells), **VI:** 242

New Writings of William Hazlitt (ed. Howe), **IV:** 140

New Year Letter (Auden), **VII:** 379, 382, 388, 390, 393

"New Year's Burden, A" (Rossetti), **V:** 242

"Next Time, The" (James), **VI:** 69

Nice Valour, The (Fletcher and Middleton), **II:** 21, 66

Nicholas Nickleby (Dickens), **IV:** 69; **V:** xix, 42, 50–53, 54, 71

Nicholls, Bowyer, **IV:** 98

Nichols, Robert, **VI:** 419

Nicoll, Allardyce, **II:** 363

Nietzsche, Friedrich Wilhelm, **IV:** 121, 179

Nigger of the "Narcissus," The (Conrad), **VI:** 136, 137, 148

Nigger Question, The (Carlyle), **IV:** 247, 250

"Night, The" (Vaughan), **II:** 186, 188

Night and Day (Rosenberg), **VI:** 432

Night and Day (Woolf), **VII:** 20, 27

"Night and the Merry Man" (Browning), **IV:** 313

"Nightclub" (MacNeice), **VII:** 414

"Nightmare, A" (Rossetti), **V:** 256

Nightmare Abbey (Peacock), **III:** 336, 345; **IV:** xvii, 158, 162, 164–165, 170, 177

"Night of Frost in May" (Meredith), **V:** 223

"Night Patrol" (West), **VI:** 423

"Nightpiece to Julia, The" (Herrick), **II:** 111

Night Thoughts (Young), **III:** 302, 307

Night Walker, The (Fletcher and Shirley), **II:** 66

"Night Wind, The" (Brontë), **V:** 133, 142

nihilism, **VI:** 147

Nina Balatka (Trollope), **V:** 101

Nine Essays (Housman), **VI:** 164

Nineteen Eighty-four (Orwell), **III:** 341; **VII:** xx, 204, 274, 279–280, 284–285

"1914" (Owen), **VI:** 444

1914 and Other Poems (Brooke), **VI:** 420

1914. Five Sonnets (Brooke), **VI:** 420

"Nineteen Hundred and Nineteen" (Yeats), **VI:** 217

"Nineteenth Century, The" (Thompson), **V:** 442

Nineteenth Century, The: A Dialogue in Utopia (Ellis), **VI:** 241$_n$

Nip in the Air, A (Betjeman), **VII:** 357

Niven, Alastair, **VII:** xiv, xxxviii

No Abolition of Slavery . . . (Boswell), **III:** 248

Noble Jilt, The (Trollope); **V:** 102

Nobleman, The (Tourneur), **II:** 37

Noble Numbers (Herrick), see *His Noble Numbers*

Nocturnal upon S. Lucy's Day, A (Donne), **I:** 358, 359–360; **II:** 128

No Enemy (Ford), **VI:** 324

No Exit (Sartre), **III:** 329, 345

Noh theater, **VI:** 218

"Noli emulari" (Wyatt), **I:** 102

Nollius, **II:** 185, 201

No More Parades (Ford), **VI:** 319, 329

"Nona Vincent" (James), **VI:** 69

Nonconformist tradition, **VII:** 193–194, 196

Nonsense Songs, Stories, Botany and Alphabets (Lear), **V:** 78, 84, 87

Nooks and Byways of Italy, The (Ramage), **VI:** 298

Norman Douglas (Dawkins), **VI:** 303–304

Normyx, pseud. of Norman Douglas

North, Thomas, **I:** 314

North America (Trollope), **V:** 101

North and South (Gaskell), **V:** xxii, 1–6, 8, 15

"North and South, The" (Browning), **IV:** 315

Northanger Abbey (Austen), **III:** 335–336, 345; **IV:** xvii, 103, 104, 107–110, 112–114, 122

Northanger Novels, The (Sadleir), **III:** 335, 346

"Northern Farmer, New Style" (Tennyson), **IV:** 327

"Northern Farmer, Old Style" (Tennyson), **IV:** 327

Northern Memoirs (Franck), **II:** 131

"North Sea" (Keyes), **VII:** 437

Northward Ho! (Dekker, Marston, Webster), **I:** 234–235, 236, 244; **II:** 68, 85

"North Wind, The" (Bridges), **VI:** 80

Norton, Charles Eliot, **IV:** 346; **V:** 3, 9, 299; **VI:** 41

Norton, Thomas, **I:** 214

"Nose, The" (Gogol), **III:** 340, 345

Nosferatu (film), **III:** 342; **IV:** 180

Nostromo (Conrad), **VI:** 140–143

"Not Celia, that I juster am" (Sedley), **II:** 265

Notebook (Maugham), **VI:** 370

Note-Book of Edmund Burke (ed. Somerset), **III:** 205

Notebook on William Shakespeare, A (Sitwell), **VII:** 127, 139, 140

Notebooks of Henry James, The (ed. Matthiessen and Murdock), **VI:** 38

Notebooks of Samuel Taylor Coleridge, The (ed. Coburn), **IV:** 48, 53, 56

Note on Charlotte Brontë, A (Swinburne), **V:** 332

"Note on F. W. Bussell" (Pater), **V:** 356–357

"Note on 'To Autumn,' A" (Davenport), **IV:** 227

Notes and Index to . . . the Letters of Sir Walter Scott (Corson), **IV:** 27, 39

Notes and Observations on "The Empress of Morocco" (Dryden), **II:** 297, 305

Notes and Reviews (James), **V:** 199

Notes by an Oxford Chiel (Carroll), **V:** 274

Notes of a Journey from Cornhill to Grand Cairo (Thackeray), **V:** 25, 37, 38

Notes of a Journey Through France and Italy (Hazlitt), **IV:** 134, 140

Notes of an English Republican on the Muscovite Crusade (Swinburne), **V:** 332

Notes of a Son and Brother (James), **VI:** 59, 65–66

"Notes on Designs of the Old Masters at Florence" (Swinburne), **V:** 329

Notes on English Divines (Coleridge), **IV:** 56

Notes on Joseph Conrad (Symons), **VI:** 149

Notes on Life and Letters (Conrad), **VI:** 67, 148

Notes on Novelists (James), **V:** 384, 392; **VI:** 149

Notes on . . . Pictures Exhibited in the Rooms of the Royal Academy (Ruskin), **V:** 184

Notes on Poems and Reviews (Swinburne), **V:** 316, 329, 332

Notes on Sculptures in Rome and Florence . . . (Shelley), **IV:** 209

"Notes on Technical Matters" (Sitwell), **VII:** 139

Notes on the Construction of Sheep-Folds (Ruskin), **V:** 184

Notes on the Royal Academy Exhibition, 1868 (Swinburne), **V:** 329, 332

Notes on "The Testament of Beauty" (Smith), **VI:** 83

Notes on the Turner Gallery at Marlborough House (Ruskin), **V:** 184

Notes Theological, Political, and Miscellaneous (Coleridge), **IV:** 56

"No, Thank You John" (Rossetti), **V:** 256

Not Honour More (Cary), **VII:** 186, 194–195

Nott, John, **II:** 102

"Nottingham and the Mining Country" (Lawrence), **VII:** 88, 89, 91, 121

Not Without Glory (Scannell), **VII:** 424, 426

novel, development and structure **IV:** 30; **VI:** 321–322; **VII:** 18, 20, 23–25, 34, 49, 98, 103, 122, 188–189, 218, 249–250, 291

novel cycle, **VI:** 324, 328–330; **VII:** 323, 343

"Novelist at Work, The" (Cary), **VII:** 187

Novels of E. M. Forster, The (Woolf), **VI:** 413

Novels of George Eliot, The: A Study in Form (Hardy), **V:** 201

Novels of George Meredith, The, and Some Notes on the English Novel (Sitwell), **V:** 230, 234

Novels Up to Now radio series, **VI:** 372

"November" (Bridges), **VI:** 79–80

Novum organum (Bacon), **I:** 259, 260, 263–264, 272; **IV:** 279

No Wit, No Help Like a Woman's (Middleton), **II:** 3, 21

"No worst, there is none" (Hopkins), **V:** 374

"Now Sleeps the Crimson Petal" (Tennyson), **IV:** 334

Numismata: A Discourse of Medals . . . (Evelyn), **II:** 287

Nun's Priest's Tale, The (Chaucer), **I:** 21

"Nuptiall Song, A, or Epithalamie, on Sir Clipseby Crew and his Lady" (Herrick), **II:** 105, 106

"Nuptials of Attilla, The" (Meredith), **V:** 221

Nursery "Alice," The (Carroll), **V:** 273

Nursery Rhymes (Sitwell), **VII:** 138

"Nurse's Song" (Blake), **III:** 292

Nussey, Ellen, **V:** 108, 109, 113, 117, 118, 126, 152

"Nymph Complaining for the Death of Her Faun, The" (Marvell), **II:** 211, 215–216

"Nympholept, A" (Swinburne), **V:** 328

O

Oak Leaves and Lavender (O'Casey), **VII:** 7, 8

"Obedience" (Herbert), **II:** 126

"Obelisk, The" (Forster), **VI:** 411

"Obermann Once More" (Arnold), **V:** 210

Oberon (Jonson), **I:** 344–345

O'Brien, E. J., **VII:** 176

Obsequies to the Memory of Mr. Edward King (Milton), **II:** 175

Observations on a Late State of the Nation (Burke), **III:** 205

Observations on Macbeth (Johnson), see *Miscellaneous Observations on the Tragedy of Macbeth*

Observations . . . on Squire Foote's Dramatic Entertainment . . . (Boswell), **III:** 247

Observations Relative . . . to Picturesque Beauty . . . [in] the High-Lands of Scotland (Gilpin), **IV:** 36

Observations upon the Articles of Peace with the Irish Rebels . . . (Milton), **II:** 176

Observator (periodical), **III:** 41

O'Casey, Sean, **VI:** xiv, 214, 218, 314–315; **VII:** xviii, **1–15;** list of articles, **VII:** 14–15

Occasional Verses (FitzGerald), **IV:** 353

O'Connor, Monsignor John, **VI:** 338

October (Bridges), **VI:** 81

October and Other Poems (Bridges), **VI:** 83

Odd Women, The (Gissing), **V:** 428, 433–434, 437

Ode, on the Death of Mr. Henry Purcell, An (Dryden), **II:** 304

Ode ad Gustavem regem. Ode ad Gustavem exulem (Landor), **IV:** 100

"Ode: Autumn" (Hood), **IV:** 255

"Ode for Music" (Gray), see "Installation Ode"

"Ode. Intimations of Immortality from Recollections of Early Childhood" (Wordsworth), **IV:** xvi, 21, 22

"Ode on a Distant Prospect of Eton College" (Gray), **III:** 137, 144

"Ode on a Grecian Urn" (Keats), **III:** 174, 337; **IV:** 222–223, 225, 226

"Ode on Indolence" (Keats), **IV:** 221, 225–226

"Ode on Melancholy" (Keats), **III:** 337; **IV:** 224–225

"Ode on Mrs. Arabella Hunt Singing" (Congreve), **II:** 348

"Ode on the Death of Mr. Thomson" (Collins), **III:** 163, 175

"Ode on the Death of Sir H. Morison" (Jonson), **II:** 199

Ode on the Death of the Duke of Wellington (Tennyson), **II:** 200; **IV:** 338

Ode on the Departing Year (Coleridge), **IV:** 55

Ode on the Installation of . . . Prince Albert as Chancellor of . . . Cambridge (Wordsworth), **IV:** 25

"Ode on the Insurrection at Candia" (Swinburne), **V:** 313

Ode on the Intimations of Immortality (Wordsworth), **II:** 189, 200

"Ode on the Pleasure Arising from Vicissitude" (Gray), **III:** 141, 145

"Ode on the Popular Superstitions of the Highlands of Scotland" (Collins), **III:** 163, 171–173, 175

Ode on the Proclamation of the French Republic (Swinburne), **V:** 332

"Ode on the Spring" (Gray), **III:** 137, 295

"Ode Performed in the Senate House at Cambridge" (Gray), **III:** 145

Ode Prefixed to S. Harrison's Arches of Triumph . . . (Webster), **II:** 85

Odes (Gray), **III:** 145

Odes and Addresses to Great People (Hood and Reynolds), **IV:** 253, 257, 267

Odes in Contribution to the Song of French History (Meredith), **V:** 223, 234

Odes on Several Descriptive and Allegorical Subjects (Collins), **III:** 162, 163, 165–166, 175

Odes on the Comic Spirit (Meredith), **V:** 234

Odes to . . . the Emperor of Russia, and . . . the King of Prussia (Southey), **IV:** 71

"Ode to a Lady on the Death of Colonel Ross" (Collins), **III:** 162

"Ode to a Nightingale" (Keats), **II:** 122; **IV:** 212, 221, 222–223, 224, 226

"Ode to Apollo" (Keats), **IV:** 221, 227

"Ode to Duty" (Wordsworth), **II:** 303

"Ode to Evening" (Collins), **III:** 166, 173; **IV:** 227

"Ode to Fear" (Collins), see "Fear"

Ode to Himself (Jonson), **I:** 336

Ode to Independence (Smollett), **III:** 158

"Ode to Liberty" (Shelley), **IV:** 203

"Ode to Master Endymion Porter, Upon his Brothers Death, An" (Herrick), **II:** 112

"Ode to May" (Keats), **IV:** 221, 222

Ode to Mazzini (Swinburne), **V:** 333

"Ode to Memory" (Tennyson), **IV:** 329

"Ode to Mr. Congreve" (Swift), **III:** 30

"Ode to Naples" (Shelley), **II:** 200; **IV:** 195

Ode to Napoleon Buonaparte (Byron), **IV:** 192

"Ode to Pity" (Collins), **III:** 164

"Ode to Psyche" (Keats), **IV:** 221–222

"Ode to Rae Wilson" (Hood), **IV:** 261, 262–263

"Ode to Sir William Temple" (Swift), **III:** 30

"Ode to Sorrow" (Keats), **IV:** 216, 224

"Ode to the Moon" (Hood), **IV:** 255

"Ode to the Setting Sun" (Thompson), **V:** 448, 449

"Ode to the West Wind" (Shelley), **II:** 200; **IV:** xviii, 198, 203

Ode to Tragedy, An (Boswell), **III:** 247

"Ode upon Dr. Harvey" (Cowley), **II:** 196, 198

"Ode: Written at the Beginning of the Year 1746" (Collins), **III:** 169

"Odour of Chrysanthemums" (Lawrence), **VII:** 114

Odyssey (tr. Cowper), **III:** 220

Odyssey (tr. Pope), **III:** 70, 77

Odyssey of Homer, The, done into English Verse (Morris), **V:** 306

Oedipus Tyrannus: or, Swellfoot the Tyrant (Shelley), **IV:** 208

Of Ancient and Modern Learning (Temple), **III:** 23

"Of Democritus and Heraclitus" (Montaigne), **III:** 39

"Of Discourse" (Cornwallis), **III:** 39–40

"Of Divine Love" (Waller), **II:** 235

Of Dramatick Poesie, An Essay (Dryden), see Essay of Dramatick Poesy

Of Education (Milton), **II:** 162–163, 175

"Of Eloquence" (Goldsmith), **III:** 186

"Of English Verse" (Waller), **II:** 233–234

Offer of the Clarendon Trustees, The (Carroll), **V:** 274

Officers and Gentlemen (Waugh), **VII:** 302, 304; see also Sword of Honour trilogy

"Officers Mess" (Ewarts), **VII:** 423

"Of Greatness" (Cowley), **III:** 40

Of Human Bondage (Maugham), **VI:** xiii, 365, 373–374

Of Justification by Imputed Righteousness (Bunyan), **II:** 253

"Oflag Night Piece: Colditz" (Riviere), **VII:** 424

O'Flaherty, V. C. (Shaw), **VI:** 119–120, 129

"Of Liberty" (Cowley), **II:** 198

Of Liberty and Loyalty (Swinburne), **V:** 333

Of Liberty and Servitude (tr. Evelyn), **II:** 287

Of Magnanimity and Chastity (Traherne), **II:** 202

"Of Masques" (Bacon), **I:** 268

"Of My Self" (Cowley), **II:** 195

"Of Nature: Laud and Plaint" (Thompson), **V:** 443

"O! for a Closer Walk with God" (Cowper), **III:** 210

"Of Pacchiarotto" (Browning), **IV:** 366

"Of Pleasing" (Congreve), **II:** 349

"Of Poetry" (Temple), **III:** 23, 190

Of Prelatical Episcopacy . . . (Milton), **II:** 175

Of Reformation Touching Church-Discipline in England (Milton), **II:** 162, 175

Of Style (Hughes), **III:** 40

Of the Characters of Women (Pope), see Moral Essays

Of the Friendship of Amis and Amilie, Done into English (Morris), **V:** 306

Of the House of the Forest of Lebanon (Bunyan), **II:** 253

Of the Lady Mary (Waller), **II:** 238

Of the Law and a Christian (Bunyan), **II:** 253

Of the Laws of Ecclesiastical Polity (Hooker), **I:** 176, 179–190

Of the Trinity and a Christian (Bunyan), **II:** 253

Of the Use of Riches, an Epistle to . . . Bathurst (Pope), see Moral Essays

Of True Greatness (Fielding), **III:** 105

Of True Religion, Haeresie, Schism, Toleration, . . . (Milton), **II:** 176

Ogg, David, **II:** 243

"Oh, dreadful is the check—intense the agony" (Brontë), **V:** 116

"O happy dames, that may embrace" (Surrey), **I:** 115, 120

"Oh! That 'Twere Possible" (Tennyson), **IV:** 330, 332

Oh What a Lovely War (musical), **VI:** 436

"Olalla" (Stevenson), **V:** 395

"O land of Empire, art and love!" (Clough), **V:** 158

Old Adam, The (Bennett), see Regent, The

"Old Andrey's Experience as a Musician" (Hardy), **VI:** 22

Old Batchelour, The (Congreve), **II:** 338, 340–341, 349

"Old Benchers of the Inner Temple, The" (Lamb), **IV:** 74

Old Calabria (Douglas), **VI:** 294, 295–296, 297, 298, 299, 305

"Old Chartist, The" (Meredith), **V:** 220

"Old China" (Lamb), **IV:** 82

"Old Church Tower and the garden wall, The" (Brontë), **V:** 134

Old Curiosity Shop, The (Dickens), **V:** xx, 42, 53, 71

Old Debauchees, The (Fielding), **III:** 105

Old English (Galsworthy), **VI:** 275, 284

Old English Baron, The (Reeve), **III:** 345

"Old Familiar Faces, The" (Lamb), **IV:** 78

Old Fortunatus (Dekker), **II:** 71, 89

Old French Romances, Done into English (Morris), **V:** 306

Old Gang and the New Gang, The (Lewis), **VII:** 83

Oldham, John, **II:** 259

Old Huntsman, The (Sassoon), **VI:** 423, 430, 453

Old Joiner of Aldgate, The (Chapman), **I:** 234, 244

Old Law, The (Middleton, Rowley), **II:** 21

Old Lights for New Chancels (Betjeman), **VII:** 361, 367, 368

Old Man's Love, An (Trollope), **V:** 102

Old Man Taught Wisdom, An (Fielding), **III:** 105

Old Mrs. Chundle (Hardy), **VI:** 20

Old Mortality (Scott), **IV:** 33, 39

Old Mortality club, **V:** 312, 338, 348

"Old Nurse's Story, The" (Gaskell), **V:** 14, 15

Old Possum's Book of Practical Cats (Eliot), **VII:** 167

Old Whig (periodical), **III:** 51, 53

Old Wife's Tale, The (Peele), **I:** 206–208

Old Wives' Tale, The (Bennett), **VI:** xiii, 247, 249, 250, 251, **254–257**

"Old Woman, An" (Sitwell), **VII:** 135–136

"Old Woman of Berkeley, The" (Southey), **IV:** 67

Oley, Barnabas, **II:** 141

Oliver, H. J., **I:** 281

"Oliver Cromwell and Walter Noble" (Landor), **IV:** 92

Oliver Cromwell's Letters and Speeches (Carlyle), **IV:** 240, 244, 246, 249, 250, 342

Oliver Newman (Southey), **IV:** 71

Oliver Twist (Dickens), **V:** xix, 42, 47–50, 51, 55, 56, 66, 71

Olney Hymns (Cowper), **III:** 210, 211, 220

Olor Iscanus . . . (Vaughan), **II:** 185, 201

Oman, Sir Charles, **VI:** 387

"Omar Khayyám" (FitzGerald), **IV:** 353

Omega Workshop, **VI:** 118

Omen, The (film), **III:** 343, 345

Omniana, or, Horae otiosiores (Southey and Coleridge), **IV:** 71

"On a Brede of Divers Colours Woven by Four Ladies" (Waller), **II:** 233

"On a Chalk Mark on the Door" (Thackeray), **V:** 34

On a Chinese Screen (Maugham), **VI:** 371

"On Actors and Acting" (Hazlitt), **IV:** 137

"On a Dead Child" (Bridges), **VI:** 77–78

"On a Drop of Dew" (Marvell), **II:** 211

"On a Girdle" (Waller), **II:** 235

"On a Joke I Once Heard from the Late Thomas Hood" (Thackeray), **IV:** 251–252

"On a Mourner" (Tennyson), **IV:** 332

"On a Prayer Booke Sent to Mrs. M. R." (Crashaw), **II:** 181

"On a Return from Egypt" (Douglas), **VII:** 444

On Baile's Strand (Yeats), **VI:** 218, 309

"Once as me thought Fortune me kissed" (Wyatt), **I:** 102

"On Dryden and Pope" (Hazlitt), **IV:** 217

One Day (Douglas), **VI:** 299, 300, 305

One for the Grave (MacNeice), **VII:** 405, 406, 408

On English Poetry (Graves), **VII:** 260

One of Our Conquerors (Meredith), **V:** 232, 233, 234

"One Sea-side Grave" (Rossetti), **V:** 255

One Thing Is Needful (Bunyan), **II:** 253

"One Viceroy Resigns" (Kipling), **VI:** 202

One-Way Song (Lewis), **VII:** 72, 76

"One Word More" (Browning), **IV:** 357

"On Familiar Style" (Hazlitt), **IV:** 138

"On First Looking into Chapman's Homer" (Keats), **IV:** 214, 215–216

On Forsyte 'Change (Galsworthy), **VI:** 270, 275

"On Greenhow Hill" (Kipling), **VI:** 191

"On Heaven" (Ford), **VI:** 323

"On Her Leaving Town After the Coronation" (Pope), **III:** 76

"On Himself" (Herrick), **II:** 113

On His Grace the Duke of Marlborough (Wycherley), **II:** 322

"On Living to One's-Self" (Hazlitt), **IV:** 137

"Only our love hath no decay:" (Donne), **II:** 221

"On Marriage" (Crashaw), **II:** 180

"On Men and Pictures" (Thackeray), **V:** 37

"On Milton" (De Quincey), **IV:** 146

"On Mr. Milton's 'Paradise Lost' " (Marvell), **II:** 206

"On Not Knowing Greek" (Woolf), **VII:** 35

"On Personal Character" (Hazlitt), **IV:** 136

"On Poetry: A Rhapsody" (Swift), **III:** 30, 36

"On Poetry in General" (Hazlitt), **IV:** 130, 138

"On Preparing to Read Kipling" (Jarrell), **VI:** 195

"On Receiving News of the War" (Rosenberg), **VI:** 432

"On Ribbons" (Thackeray), **V:** 34

"On Seeing the Elgin Marbles" (Keats), **IV:** 212–213, 214

"On Sentimental Comedy" (Goldsmith), see *Essay on the Theatre* . . .

"On Some Characteristics of Modern Poetry" (Hallam), **IV:** 234, 235

"On Some Obscure Poetry" (Landor), **IV:** 98

"On Stella's Birthday, . . . A.D. 1718– " (Swift), **III:** 31

"On Style" (De Quincey), **IV:** 148

"On the Application of Thought to Textual Criticism" (Housman), **VI:** 154, 164

On the Choice of a Profession (Stevenson), **V:** 396

On the Choice of Books (Carlyle), **IV:** 250

"On the City Wall" (Kipling), **VI:** 184

"On the Cliffs" (Swinburne), **V:** 327

On the Constitution of the Church and State (Coleridge), **IV:** 54, 55, 56

"On the Death of Dr. Robert Levet" (Johnson), **III:** 120

"On the Death of General Schomberg . . ." (Farquhar), **II:** 351

"On the Death of Mr. Crashaw" (Cowley), **II:** 198

"On the Death of Mr. William Hervey" (Cowley), **II:** 198

"On the Death of Sir Henry Wootton" (Cowley), **II:** 198

On the Dignity of Man (Mirandola), **I:** 253

"On the Discovery of a Lady's Painting" (Waller), **II:** 233

"On the English Novelists" (Hazlitt), **IV:** 136–137

"On the Feeling of Immortality in Youth" (Hazlitt), **IV:** 126

On the Frontier (Auden and Isherwood), **VII:** 312

"On the Genius and Character of Hogarth" (Lamb), **IV:** 80

"On the Head of a Stag" (Waller), **II:** 233

On the Herpetology of the Grand Duchy of Baden (Douglas), **VI:** 300, 305

"On the Influence of the Audience" (Bridges), **VI:** 83

"On the Knocking at the Gate in 'Macbeth' " (De Quincey), **IV:** 146, 149

"On the Living Poets" (Hazlitt), **IV:** 130

On the Margin (Huxley), **VII:** 201

"On the means of improving people" (Southey), **IV:** 102

"On the Medusa of Leonardo da Vinci in the Florentine Gallery" (Shelley), **III:** 337

"On the Morning of Christ's Nativity" (Milton), **II:** 199; **IV:** 222

"On the Origin of Beauty: A Platonic Dialogue" (Hopkins), **V:** 362

"On the Periodical Essayists" (Hazlitt), **IV:** 136

On the Place of Gilbert Chesterton in English Letters (Belloc), **VI:** 345

"On the Pleasure of Painting" (Hazlitt), **IV:** 137–138

"On the Profession of a Player" (Boswell), **III:** 248

"On the Receipt of My Mother's Picture" (Cowper), III: 208, 220

On the Rocks (Shaw), VI: 125, 126, 127

"On the Scotch Character" (Hazlitt), IV: 132

"On the Sea" (Keats), IV: 216

"On the Spirit of Monarchy" (Hazlitt), IV: 132

On the Study of Celtic Literature (Arnold), V: 203, 212, 216

On the Sublime and Beautiful (Burke), III: 195, 198, 205

On the Thermal Influence of Forests (Stevenson), V: 395

"On the Toilet Table of Queen Marie-Antoinette" (Nicholls), IV: 98

"On the Tragedies of Shakespeare . . . with Reference to . . . Stage-Representation" (Lamb), IV: 80

"On the Victory Obtained by Blake" (Marvell), II: 211

"On the Western Circuit" (Hardy), VI: 22

"On the Wounds of Our Crucified Lord" (Crashaw), II: 182

On Translating Homer (Arnold), V: xxii, 212, 215, 216

On Translating Homer: Last Words (Arnold), V: 214, 215, 216

"On Wit and Humour" (Hazlitt), II: 332

"On Wordsworth's Poetry" (De Quincey), IV: 146, 148

".007" (Kipling), VI: 170

Open Conspiracy, The, Blueprints for a World Revolution (Wells), VI: 240, 242

"Opening a Place of Social Prayer" (Cowper), III: 211

Open Letter to the Revd. Dr. Hyde in Defence of Father Damien, An (Stevenson), see *Father Damien*

Opium and the Romantic Imagination (Hayter), III: 338, 346; IV: 57

Oppenheim, E. Phillips, VI: 249

"Oracles, The" (Housman), VI: 161

Orage, A. R., VI: 247, 265; VII: 172

Orators, The (Auden), VII: 345, 380, 382

oratory, VI: 348–349, 356–358

"Orchards half the way, The" (Housman), VI: 159

Ordeal of George Meredith, The, A Biography (Stevenson), V: 230, 234

Ordeal of Gilbert Pinfold, The (Waugh), VII: 291, 293, 302–303

Ordeal of Richard Feveral, The (Meredith), V: xxii, 225, 226–227, 234

"Ordination, The" (Burns), III: 311, 319

Orford, fourth earl of, see Walpole, Horace

Orgel, Stephen, I: 237, 239

"Oriental Eclogues" (Collins), see "Persian Eclogues"

Orientations (Maugham), VI: 367

"Orient Ode" (Thompson), V: 448

Original and Progress of Satire, The (Dryden), II: 301

Original Letters &c of Sir John Falstaff (White and Lamb), IV: 79, 85

Original Poetry by Victor and Cazire (Shelley and Shelley), IV: 208

Origin, Nature, and Object of the New System of Education, The (Southey), IV: 71

Origin of Species, The (Darwin), V: xxii, 279, 287

Orlando (Woolf), VII: 21, 28, 35, 38

Orlando furioso (Ariosto), I: 131, 138

Orley Farm (Trollope), V: xxii, 100, 101

"Orpheus, or Philosophy" (Bacon), I: 267

Ortelius, Abraham, I: 282

Orthodoxy (Chesterton), VI: 336

Orwell, George, III: 341; V: 24, 31; VI: 240, 242; VII: xii, xx, **273–287**

Osborne, John, VI: 101

Osbourne, Lloyd, V: 384, 387, 393, 395, 396, 397

Oscar Wilde. Art and Egoism (Shewan), V: 409, 421

O'Shaughnessy, Arthur, VI: 158

Othello (Shakespeare), I: 316; II: 71, 79; III: 116

"Other Boat, The" (Forster), VI: 406, 411–412

Other House, The (James), VI: 48, 49, 67

"Other Kingdom" (Forster), VI: 399, 402

Otho the Great (Keats and Brown), IV: 231, 235

Otranto (Walpole), see *Castle of Otranto, The*

Our Betters (Maugham), VI: 368, 369

"Our Bias" (Auden), VII: 387

Our Corner (periodical), VI: 103

Our Exploits at West Poley (Hardy), **VI:** 20

Our Family (Hood), **IV:** 254, 259

Our Friend the Charlatan (Gissing), **V:** 437

"Our Hunting Fathers" (Auden), **VII:** 384

Our Mutual Friend (Dickens), **V:** xxiii, 42, 44, 55, 68–69, 72

Our Old Home (Hawthorne), **VI:** 34

"Our Parish" (Dickens), **V:** 43, 46

"Our Village—by a Villager" (Hood), **IV:** 257

Our Women: Chapters on the Sex-Discord (Bennett), **VI:** 267

"Outcast, The" (Tennyson), **IV:** 329

Outcast of the Islands, An (Conrad), **VI:** 136, 137, 148

Outcasts, The (Sitwell), **VII:** 138

Outcry, The (Julia), **VI:** 67

Outline of History, The: Being a Plain History of Life and Mankind (Wells), **VI:** 245

Out of India (Kipling), **VI:** 204

Out of the Picture (MacNeice), **VII:** 405

"Outpost of Progress, An" (Conrad), **VI:** 136, 148

"Outstation, The" (Maugham), **VI:** 370, 371, 380

Overbury, Sir Thomas, **IV:** 286

"Overcoat, The" (Gogol), **III:** 340, 345

Overruled (Shaw), **VI:** 129

Over the River (Galsworthy), **VI:** 272, 275

Over the River (Gregory), **VI:** 318

Ovid, **II:** 110$_n$, 185, 292, 304, 347; **III:** 54; **V:** 319, 321

Ovid's Art of Love Paraphrased (Fielding), **III:** 105

Ovid's Banquet of Sense (Chapman), **I:** 237–238

Owen, Wilfred, **VI:** xvi, 329, 416, 417, 419, 423, **443–460; VII:** xvi, 421; list of poems, **VI:** 458–459

"Owen Wingrave" (James), **VI:** 69

"Owl, The" (Thomas), **VI:** 424

"Owl and the Pussy-cat, The" (Lear), **V:** 83–84, 87

"O World of many Worlds" (Owen), **VI:** 445

"Oxen, The" (Hardy), **VI:** 16

Oxford Book of English Verse, The (ed. Quiller-Couch), **II:** 102, 121

Oxford Book of Modern Verse, The, **VI:** 219

Oxford Lectures on Poetry (Bradley), **IV:** 216, 236

Oxford movement, **V:** ix, xix, 62, 156, 248, 252, 253, 283, 292

"Oxford" papers (De Quincey), **IV:** 148

Oxford University Chest (Betjeman), **VII:** 356

"O Youth whose hope is high" (Bridges), **VI:** 159

P

Pacchiarotto and How He Worked in Distemper (Browning), **IV:** 359, 374; see also "Of Pacchiarotto"

Pacificator, The (Defoe), **III:** 12

pacifism, **VI:** 288

Packer, Lona Mosk, **V:** 251, 252–253, 260

"Pack Horse and the Carrier, The" (Gay), 59–60

Pagan Mysteries in the Renaissance (Wind), **V:** 317$_n$

Pagan Poems (Moore), **VI:** 98

Pageant and Other Poems, A (Rossetti), **V:** 251, 260

"Pageant of Knowledge" (Lydgate), **I:** 58

"Pageants" (Spenser), **I:** 123

Painful Adventures of Pericles, Prince of Tyre (Wilkins), **I:** 321

"Pains of Sleep, The" (Coleridge), **IV:** xvii, 48, 56

Painter, William, **I:** 297; **II:** 76

Painter of His Own Dishonour, The (tr. FitzGerald), **IV:** 344–345

Painter's Eye, The (James), **VI:** 67

Painting and the Fine Arts (Haydon and Hazlitt), **IV:** 140

Pair of Blue Eyes, A: A Novel (Hardy), **VI:** 3, 4, 20

"Palace of Art, The" (Tennyson), **IV:** 331

"Palace of Pan, The" (Swinburne), **V:** 328

Palace of Pleasure (Painter), **I:** 297, 313; **II:** 76

Paleface (Lewis), **VII:** 72, 75

Paley, William, **IV:** 144

Palgrave, Francis Turner, **II:** 208; **IV:** xxii, 196

Palicio (Bridges), **VI:** 83

Palladis Tamia (Meres), **I:** 296

"Palladium" (Arnold), **V:** 209

Palmer, John, **II:** 267, 271

Palmerin of England, **II:** 49; tr. Southey, **IV:** 71

"Palmer's 'Heroides' of Ovid" (Housman), **VI**: 156

Palmyra (Peacock), **IV**: 158, 169

Pamela (Richardson), **III**: 80, **82–85,** 92, 94, 95, 98

Pamphlet Against Anthelogies, A (Graves), **VI**: 207; **VII**: 260–261

"Pan and Pitys" (Landor), **IV**: 96

"Pan and Thalassius" (Swinburne), **V**: 328

"P. & O." (Maugham), **VI**: 370–371

"Pandora" (James), **VI**: 69

Pandosto (Greene), **I**: 165, 322

"Panegerick to Sir Lewis Pemberton, A" (Herrick), **II**: 110

Panegyrick to My Lord Protector, A (Waller), **II**: 238

Panegyric to Charles the Second, Presented . . . the Day of His Coronation . . . (Evelyn), **II**: 287

Panofsky, Erwin, **I**: 237

"Pan, or Nature" (Bacon), **I**: 267

"Panthea" (Wilde), **V**: 401

pantisocracy, **IV**: 43, 59, 61, 62

Paoli, Pasquale di, **III**: 235, 236, 243

Paper Money Lyrics, and Other Poems (Peacock), **IV**: 170

"Papers, The" (James), **VI**: 69

Papers by Mr. Yellowplush (Thackeray), see *Yellowplush Correspondence, The*

Paracelsus (Browning), **IV**: xix, 355, 365, 368, 373

Parade's End (Ford), **VI**: 321, 324, 328, 329–330; **VII**: xv

Paradise Lost (Milton), **I**: 188–189; **II**: 158, 161, **165–171,** 174, 176, 198, 294, 302; **III**: 118, 302; **IV**: 11–12, 15, 47, 88, 93, 95, 186, 200, 204, 229; ed. Bentley, **VI**: 153

Paradise Regained (Milton), **II**: 171–172, 174, 176

Parallel of the Antient Architecture with the Modern, An (tr. Evelyn), **II**: 287

pararhyme, **VI**: xvi, 446, 451$_n$

Parasitaster (Marston), see *Fawn, The*

Pardoner's Tale, The (Chaucer), **I**: 21, 42

Parents and Children (Compton-Burnett), **VII**: 62, 65, 66, 67

Parish Register, The (Crabbe), **III**: 275, 279, 283

Parisian Sketches (James), **VI**: 67

Parisina (Byron), **IV**: 173, 192

Paris Nights (Bennett), **VI**: 259, 264

Paris Sketch Book, The (Thackeray), **V**: 22, 37

Parker, Brian, **II**: 6

Parker, W. R., **II**: 165$_n$

Parkinson, T., **VI**: 220

Parlement of Foules (Chaucer), see *Parliament of Fowls, The*

Parleyings with Certain People of Importance in Their Day . . . (Browning), **IV**: 359, 374

Parliamentary Speeches of Lord Byron, The (Byron), **IV**: 193

Parliament of Birds (tr. FitzGerald), **IV**: 348–349, 353

Parliament of Fowls, The (Chaucer), **I**: 31, 38, 60

Parnassus plays, **I**: 191

Parnell, Thomas, **III**: 19

Parnell and His Island (Moore), **VI**: 86

parody, **VI**: 202, 239–240

Parr, Samuel, **IV**: 88

Parry, William, **IV**: 191, 193

Parson's Daughter, The (Trollope), **V**: 101

Parson's Tale, The (Chaucer), **I**: 34–35

Partial Portraits (James), **V**: 95, 97, 102; **VI**: x, 46

"Partie Fine, The" (Thackeray), **V**: 24, 38

"Partner, The" (Conrad), **VI**: 148

Part of the Seventh Epistle of the First Book of Horace Imitated (Swift), **III**: 35

Pascal, Blaise, **II**: 146, 244; **V**: 339

Pasiphaë: A Poem (Swinburne), **V**: 333

Pasquin (Fielding), **III**: 97, 98, 104, 105

Passages in the Life of an Individual (Brontë), see *Agnes Grey*

Passage to India, A (Forster), **VI**: 183, 397, 401, **408–410**; **VII**: xv

"Passer-by, A" (Bridges), **VI**: 78

"Passing Events" (Brontë), **V**: 122, 123, 151

Passing of the Essenes, The (Moore), **VI**: 96, 99

"Passing of the Shee, The" (Synge), **VI**: 314

"Passion, The" (Vaughan), **II**: 187

Passionate Century of Love (Watson), **I**: 193

"Passionate Man's Pilgrimage, The" (Ralegh), **I**: 148, 149

"Passionate Pilgrim, A" (James), **VI**: 69

Passionate Pilgrim, The, **I:** 291, 307

Passionate Pilgrim and Other Tales, A (James), **VI:** 67

Passionate Shepherd to His Love, The (Marlowe), **I:** 149, 284, 291; **IV:** 327

Passion Play, A (Shaw), **VI:** 107

Passion, Poison, and Petrification; or, The Fatal Gazogene (Shaw), **VI:** 129

"Passions, The" (Collins), **III:** 166, 168, 174

"Passions, The: An Ode. Set to Music" (Collins), **III:** 163, 175

Past and Present (Carlyle), **IV:** xx, 240, 244, 249, 250, 266$_n$, 301

"Paste" (James), **VI:** 69

pastoral elegy, **IV:** 205

Pastoral Lives of Daphnis and Chloë. Done into English (Moore), **VI:** 99

Pastorals (Blunden), **VI:** 427

Pastorals (Pope), **III:** 69

Pastorals of Virgil (tr. Thornton), **III:** 307

Pastors and Masters (Compton-Burnett), **VII:** 59, 65, 68

"Past ruin'd Ilion Helen lives" (Landor), **IV:** 99

"Patagonia, The" (James), **VI:** 49

Pater, Walter Horatio, **V:** xiii, xix, xxiv–xxvi, 286–287, 314, 323, 324, 329, **337–360,** 362, 400–401, 403, 408, 410, 411; **VI:** ix, 365

"Pater on Style" (Chandler), **V:** 359

"Path of Duty, The" (James), **VI:** 69

"Patience, hard thing!" (Hopkins), **V:** 375

Patmore, Coventry, **V:** 372, 379, 441

Patrician, The (Galsworthy), **VI:** 273, 278

Patriot (Johnson), **III:** 121

"Patrol: Buonomary" (Gutteridge), **VII:** 432–433

Pattern of Maugham, The (Curtis), **VI:** 379

Pattern of Painful Adventures, The (Twine), **I:** 321

Pauline: A Fragment of a Confession (Browning), **IV:** xix, 354, 355, 373

Paul's Departure and Crown (Bunyan), **II:** 253

Paul's Letters to His Kinsfolk (Scott), **IV:** 38

"Pavilion on the Links, The" (Stevenson), **V:** 395

"Pawnbroker's Shop, The" (Dickens), **V:** 45, 47, 48

Paying Guest, The (Gissing), **V:** 437

Payne, W. L., **III:** 41$_n$

"Peace" (Brooke), **VI:** 420

"Peace" (Collins), **III:** 166, 168

"Peace" (Hopkins), **V:** 370

"Peace" (Vaughan), **II:** 186, 187

Peaceable Principles and True (Bunyan), **II:** 253

Peace and the Protestant Succession, The (Trevelyan), **VI:** 392–393

Peace Conference Hints (Shaw), **VI:** 119, 129

Peace of the World, The (Wells), **VI:** 244

Peacock, Thomas Love, **III:** 336, 345; **IV:** xv, xvii–xix, xxii, **157–170,** 177, 198, 204, 306; **V:** 220; **VII:** 200, 211

Pearsall Smith, Logan, **VI:** 76

"Peasants, The" (Lewis), **VII:** 447

Peckham, Morse, **V:** 316, 335

Pedlar, The (Wordsworth), **IV:** 24

Peele, George, **I:** **191–211,** 278, 286, 305

"Peele Castle" (Wordsworth), see "Elegiac Stanzas, Suggested by a Picture of Peele Castle . . ."

"Peep into a Picture Book, A" (Brontë), **V:** 109

Pelican History of English Literature, The, **II:** 102

Pell, J. P., **V:** 161

Pelles, George, **VI:** 23

P.E.N. Club, **VI:** 273

Pendennis (Thackeray), see *History of Pendennis, The*

Penelope (Maugham), **VI:** 369

Penitential Psalms (Wyatt), **I:** 101–102, 108, 111

"Penny Plain and Twopence Coloured, A" (Stevenson), **V:** 385

Penny Whistles (Stevenson), see *Child's Garden of Verses, A*

"Pen, Pencil and Poison" (Wilde), **V:** 405, 407

Pen Portraits and Reviews (Shaw), **VI:** 129

"Penshurst, To" (Jonson), **II:** 223

"Pension Beaurepas, The" (James), **VI:** 69

Pentameron and Pentalogia, The (Landor), **IV:** 89, 90–91, 93, 100

Pentland Rising, The (Stevenson), **V:** 395

Pepys, Samuel, **II:** 145, 195, **273,** 274, 275, 278, **280–288,** 310

Per Amica Silentia Lunae (Yeats), **VI:** 209

Percy, Thomas, **III:** 36; **IV:** 28–29

Percy Bysshe Shelley (Swinburne), **V:** 333

Peregrine Pickle (Smollett), **III:** 149, 150, 152–153, 158

Perennial Philosophy, The (Huxley), **VII:** xviii, 206

"Perfect Critic, The" (Eliot), **VII:** 163

Perfect Wagnerite, The (Shaw) **VI:** 129

Pericles (Shakespeare), **I:** 321–322; **II:** 48

Pericles and Aspasia (Landor), **IV:** xix, 89, 92, 94–95, 100

Pericles and Other Studies (Swinburne), **V:** 333

Peripatetic, The (Thelwall), **IV:** 103

Perkins, Richard, **II:** 68

Perkin Warbeck (Ford), **II:** 89, 92, 96, 97, 100

Pernicious Consequences of the New Heresie of the Jesuites . . . , The (tr. Evelyn), **II:** 287

Peronnik the Fool (Moore), **VI:** 99

Perry, Thomas Sergeant, **VI:** 24

"Persian Eclogues" (Collins), **III:** 160, 164–165, 175

"Persian *Passion* Play, A" (Arnold), **V:** 216

Personal History, Adventures, Experience, and Observation of David Copperfield, The (Dickens), see *David Copperfield*

Personal Landscape (periodical), **VII:** 425, 443

Personal Record, A (Conrad), **VI:** 134, 148

Persons from Porlock (MacNeice), **VII:** 408

Persse, Jocelyn, **VI:** 55

Persuasion (Austen), **IV:** xvii, 106–109, 111, 113, 115–120, 122

"Pessimism in Literature" (Forster), **VI:** 410

Peter Bell (Wordsworth), **IV:** xviii, 2

Peter Bell the Third (Shelley), **IV:** 203, 207

"Peter Grimes" (Crabbe), **III:** 283, 284–285

Petrarch, **I:** 108–110, 115

Petrarchan sonnet, **I:** 97, 106–110; **IV:** 221

Petrarch's Seven Penitential Psalms (Chapman), **I:** 241–242

Peveril of the Peak (Scott), **IV:** xviii, 36, 37, 39

Phaedra (Seneca), **II:** 97

"Phaèthôn" (Meredith), **V:** 224

Phantasmagoria (Carroll), **V:** 270, 273

Pharos, pseud. of E. M. Forster

Pharos and Pharillon (Forster), **VI:** 408

Pharsalia (tr. Marlowe), **I:** 276, 291

Phases of Faith (Newman), **V:** 208$_n$

"Phebus and Cornide" (Gower), **I:** 55

phenomenalism, **V:** 343

Philanderer, The (Shaw), **VI:** 107, 109

Philaster (Beaumont and Fletcher), **II:** 45, 46, **52–54,** 55, 65

Philip (Thackeray), see *Adventures of Philip on His Way Through the World, The*

Philips, Ambrose, **III:** 56

Philips, Katherine, **II:** 185

Philip Sparrow (Skelton), **I:** 84, 86–88

Philip Webb and His Work (Lethaby), **V:** 291, 292, 296, 306

Phillipps, Sir Thomas, **II:** 103

Phillips, Edward, **II:** 347

"Phillis is my only Joy" (Sedley), **II:** 265

"Phillis, let's shun the common Fate" (Sedley), **II:** 263

Phillpotts, Eden, **VI:** 266

"Philosopher, The" (Brontë), **V:** 134

Philosophical Discourse of Earth, An, Relating to . . . Plants, &c. (Evelyn), **II:** 287

Philosophical Enquiry into the Origin of Our Ideas of the Sublime and Beautiful, A (Burke), see *On the Sublime and Beautiful*

Philosophical Lectures of S. T. Coleridge, The (ed. Coburn), **IV:** 52, 56

"Philosophical View of Reform, A" (Shelley), **IV:** 199, 209

"Philosophy of Herodotus" (De Quincey), **IV:** 147–148

Philosophy of Melancholy, The (Peacock), **IV:** 158, 169

Philosophy of Necessity, The (Bray), **V:** 188

Phineas Finn (Trollope), **V:** 96, 98, 101, 102

Phineas Redux (Trollope), **V:** 96, 98, 101, 102

Phoenix, The (Middleton), **II:** 21, 30

Phoenix and the Turtle, The (Shakespeare), **I:** 34, 313

Physicists, The (Snow), **VII:** 339–340

Physico-Theology (Derham), **III:** 49

Piccolomini, The, or, The First Part of Wallenstein (Coleridge), **IV:** 55–56

Pickering, John, **I:** 213, 216–218

Pickwick Papers (Dickens), **V:** xix, 9, 42, 46–47, 48, 52, 59, 62, 71

Pico della Mirandola, **II:** 146; **V:** 344

"Pictorial Rhapsody, A" (Thackeray), **V:** 37

"Pictor Ignotus, Florence 15—" (Browning), **IV:** 356, 361

Picture and Text (James), **VI:** 46, 67

Picture of Dorian Gray, The (Wilde), **III:** 334, 345; **V:** xxv, 339, 399, 410–411, 417, 419

"Picture of Little T.C. in a Prospect of Flowers, The" (Marvell), **II:** 211, 215

Pictures from Italy (Dickens), **V:** 71

Pictures in the Hallway (O'Casey), **VII:** 9, 12

Picturesque Landscape and English Romantic Poetry (Watson), **IV:** 26

"Pied Beauty" (Hopkins), **V:** 367

"Pied Piper of Hamelin, The" (Browning), **IV:** 356, 367

Pier-Glass, The (Graves), **VII:** 263–264

Piers Plowman (Langland), **I:** 1–18

Pigeon, The (Galsworthy), **VI:** 271, 274, 287–288

Pilgrim, The (Fletcher), **II:** 65

Pilgrim, The (Vanbrugh), **II:** 289, 305, 325, 336

"Pilgrimage of Pleasure, The" (Swinburne), **V:** 332

Pilgrimage of the Life of Man (Lydgate), **I:** 57

Pilgrims of Hope (Morris), **V:** 301, 306

Pilgrim's Progress, The (Bunyan), **I:** 16, 57; **II:** 240, 241, 243, 244, **245–250,** 253; **III:** 82; **V:** 27

Pilgrim to Compostella, The (Southey), **IV:** 71

Pillars of Society, The (Ibsen), **V:** xxiv, 414

Pindar, **II:** 198–199; **IV:** 95, 316

Pindaric Ode, A, Humbly Offer'd to the King . . . (Congreve), **II:** 350

Pindarique Ode on the Victorious Progress of Her Majesties Arms, A (Congreve), **II:** 350

Pindarique Odes (Cowley), **II:** 197, 199, 202

Pinero, Arthur Wing, **V:** 413; **VI:** 269, 368

Piozzi, Hester Lynch, **III:** 134, 246

Pippa Passes (Browning), **IV:** 356, 362–363, 370, 373

Piranesi, Giovanni Battista, **III:** 325, 338

Pirate, The (Scott), **IV:** 36, 39

"Pirate and the Apothecary, The" (Stevenson), **V:** 391

"Pit and the Pendulum, The" (Poe), **III:** 339

Pithy, Pleasant, and Profitable Works of John Skelton, The (ed. Stow), **I:** 94

"Pity" (Collins), **III:** 166

Pizarro (Sheridan), **III:** **267–270**

Plain-Dealer, The (Wycherley), **II:** 308, **318–320,** 321, 322, 343

Plaine Mans Path-Way to Heaven, The (Dent), **II:** 241, 246

Plain Man and His Plain Wife, The (Bennett), **VI:** 264, 267

"Plains, The" (Fuller), **VII:** 430

Plain Speaker, The (Hazlitt), **IV:** 131, 134, 136, 140

Plain Tales from the Hills (Kipling), **VI:** 168, 204

Plan of a Dictionary of the English Language, The (Johnson), **III:** 113, 121; see also *Dictionary of the English Language, A*

Plan of a Novel . . . With Opinions on "Mansfield Park" and "Emma" . . . (Austen), **IV:** 112, 122

Plan of the English Commerce, A (Defoe), **III:** 14

"Planter of Malata, The" (Conrad), **VI:** 148

Plato, **IV:** 47–48, 54; **V:** 339

Plato and Platonism (Pater), **V:** 339, 355, 356

"Platonic Love" (Cowley), **II:** 197

Playboy of the Western World, The (Synge), **VI:** xiv, 308, 309–310, 312–313, 316

Playground of Europe, The (Stephen), **V:** 282, 289

"Plays" (Landor), **IV:** 98

Plays for Puritans (Shaw), **VI:** 109

Plays of William Shakespeare, The (ed. Johnson), **III:** 115–117, 121

Plays: Pleasant and Unpleasant (Shaw), **VI:** ix, 104, **107–112**

Plea of the Midsummer Fairies, The (Hood), **IV:** 253, 255, 261, 267

Pleasant Notes upon Don Quixote (Gayton), **I:** 279

Pleasures of Poetry, The (Sitwell), **VII:** 129–130

Plebeian (periodical), **III:** 51, 53

Pléiade, **I:** 170

Plot Discovered, The (Coleridge), **IV:** 56

Plotinus, **III:** 291

Plough, The (Walker), **V:** 377

Plough and the Stars, The (O'Casey), **VI:** 214; **VII:** xviii, 5–6

Plumb, Sir John Harold, **IV:** 290; **VI:** xv, xxxiv, 391$_n$

Plumed Serpent, The (Lawrence), **VII:** 87–88, 91, **109–110,** 123

Plutarch, **II:** 185

Plutarch's Lives (tr. Goldsmith), **III:** 191

Plutarch's Lives. The translation called Dryden's . . . (ed. Clough), **V:** 157, 170

Plutus, the God of Riches (tr. Fielding), **III:** 105

Podro, Joshua, **VII:** 262

Poe, Edgar Allan, **III:** 329, 333, 334, 338–339, 340, 343, 345; **IV:** 311, 319; **V:** xvi, xx–xxi; **VI:** 371

Poemata et Epigrammata, . . . (Crashaw), **II:** 201

Poemata et inscriptiones (Landor), **IV:** 100

"Poem from the North" (Keyes), **VII:** 439

Poem in St. James's Park, A (Waller), **II:** 238

Poem on the Late Civil War, A (Cowley), **II:** 202

Poems [1853] (Arnold), **V:** xxi, 165, 209, 216

Poems [1854] (Arnold), **V:** 216

Poems [1855] (Arnold), **V:** 216

Poems [1857] (Arnold), **V:** 216

Poems (Bridges), **VI:** 83

Poems [1844] (Browning), **IV:** xx, 311, 313–314, 321, 356

Poems [1850] (Browning), **IV:** 311, 321

Poems (Byron), **IV:** 192

Poems (Carew), **II:** 238

Poems (Clough), **V:** 170

Poems (Cowley), **II:** 194, 198, 199, 202

Poems (Crabbe), **III:** 286

Poems (Eliot), **VII:** 146, 150

Poems (Gay), **III:** 55

Poems (Hood), **IV:** 252, 261, 266

Poems (Keats), **IV:** xvii, 211, 213–214, 216, 235

Poems (Lovell and Southey), **IV:** 71

Poems (Meredith), **V:** xxi, 219, 234

Poems (C. Rossetti), **V:** 260

Poems [1870] (D. G. Rossetti), **V:** xxiii, 237, 238, 245

Poems [1873] (D. G. Rossetti), **V:** 245

Poems [1881] (D. G. Rossetti), **V:** 238, 245

Poems (Ruskin), **V:** 184

Poems (Sassoon), **VI:** 429

Poems (Southey), **IV:** 71

Poems [1833] (Tennyson), **IV:** 326, 329, 338

Poems [1842] (Tennyson), **IV:** xx, 326, 333–334, 335, 338

Poems (Thompson), **V:** 439, 451

Poems (Waller), **II:** 238

Poems (Wilde), **V:** 401–402, 419

Poems, The (Landor), **IV:** xvi, 99

Poems, The (Swift), **III:** 15$_n$, 35

Poems and Ballads (Swinburne), **V:** xxiii, 309, 310, 313, **314–321,** 327, 330, 332

"Poems and Ballads of Goethe" (Clough), **V:** 170

Poems and Ballads: Second Series (Swinburne), **V:** xxiv, 314, 327, 332

Poems and Ballads: Third Series (Swinburne), **V:** 332

Poems and Letters of Bernard Barton (ed. FitzGerald), **IV:** 343–344, 353

Poems and Lyrics of the Joy of Earth (Meredith), **V:** 221, 224, 234

Poems and Metrical Tales (Southey), **IV:** 71

Poems and Prose Remains of A. H. Clough, The (ed. Clough and Symonds), **V:** 159, 170

Poems and Songs, The (Burns) **III:** 310$_n$, 322

Poems Before Congress (Browning), **IV:** 312, 315, 321

Poems by Alfred, Lord Tennyson (Lear), **V:** 78, 87

Poems by Currer, Ellis and Acton Bell (Brontës), **V:** xx, 131–134, 151

Poems by the Author of the Growth of Love (Bridges), **VI:** 83

Poems by the Way (Morris), **V:** 306

Poems by Two Brothers (Tennyson and Tennyson), **IV:** 337–338

Poems Chiefly in the Scottish Dialect (Burns), **III:** 315

Poems, Chiefly Lyrical (Tennyson), **IV:** xix, 326, 329, 331, 338

Poems Chiefly of Early and Late Years (Wordsworth), **IV:** xx, 25

Poems for Young Ladies (Goldsmith), **III:** 191

Poems from the Arabic and Persian (Landor), **IV:** 99

Poems from Villon, and Other Fragments (Swinburne), **V:** 333

Poems, in Two Volumes (Wordsworth), **IV:** 22, 24

Poems, 1930 (Auden), **VII:** xix

Poems 1938–1945 (Graves), **VII:** 267–268

Poems of Felicity (Traherne), **II:** 191, 202

Poems of Henry Vaughan, Silurist, The (ed. Chambers), **II:** 187

Poems of John Keats, The (ed. Allott), **IV:** 223$_n$, 224, 234–235

"Poems of 1912–13" (Hardy), **VI:** 14

Poems of Ossian, The (Macpherson), **III:** 336

Poems of Wit and Humour (Hood), **IV:** 257, 266

Poems on His Domestic Circumstances (Byron), **IV:** 192

Poems on the Death of Priscilla Farmer (Lloyd and Lamb), **IV:** 78, 85

Poems on Various Occasions (Byron), **IV:** 192

Poems on Various Subjects (Coleridge), **IV:** 43, 55, 78, 85

Poems Original and Translated (Byron), **IV:** 192

Poems Translated from the French of Madame de la Mothe Guion (tr. Cowper), **III:** 220

Poems, with the Tenth Satyre of Juvenal Englished (Vaughan), **II:** 184–185, 201

"Poem Upon the Death of O. C., A" (Marvell), **II:** 205, 211

"Poem with the Answer, A" (Suckling), **II:** 228

Poetaster (Jonson), **I:** 339, 340

"Poet Hood, The" (Blunden), **IV:** 267

Poetical Blossomes (Cowley), **II:** 194, 202

Poetical Calendar (Fawkes and Woty), **III:** 170$_n$

"Poetical Character, The" (Collins), **III:** 166, 168

Poetical Fragments (Swinburne), **V:** 333

Poetical Pieces (Lamb), **IV:** 74

Poetical Register (Jacob), **II:** 348

Poetical Sketches (Blake), **III:** 289, 290

Poetical Works (Bridges), **VI:** 83

Poetical Works, The, . . . (Traherne), **II:** 201–202

Poetical Works, The (Southey), **IV:** 71

Poetical Works of George Crabbe, The (ed. Carlyle and Carlyle), **III:** 272$_n$

Poetical Works of George Meredith, The (ed. Trevelyan), **V:** 223, 234

Poetical Works of Gray and Collins, The (ed. Poole and Stone), **III:** 161$_n$

Poetical Works of John Gay, The (ed. Faber), **III:** 66, 67

"Poetic Diction in English" (Bridges), **VI:** 73

Poetic Unreason (Graves), **VII:** 257, 260

poet laureateship, **IV:** 61, 310, 311, 324

Poetria nova (Geoffrey of Vinsauf), **I:** 59

poetry, form and techniques, **VII:** xii–xiii, 42, 131, 136, 145, 153–154; see also verse drama

"Poetry" [broadcast] (Bridges), **VI:** 83

"Poetry" (Moore), **IV:** 6

Poetry and Philosophy of George Meredith, The (Trevelyan), **VI:** 383

Poetry and Prose (ed. Sparrow), **VI:** 83

Poetry by the Author of Gebir (Landor), **IV:** 99

Poetry for Children (Lamb and Lamb), **IV:** 85

Poetry of Browning, The (Drew), **IV:** 375

Poetry of Ezra Pound, The (Kenner), **VI:** 333

Poetry of Meditation, The (Martz), **V:** 366, 382

Poetry of Nonsense, The (Cammaerts), **V:** 262, 274

"Poetry of Pope, The" (De Quincey), **IV:** 146

Poetry of the First World War (Hibberd), **VI:** 460

Poetry of Thomas Hardy, The (Day Lewis), **VI:** 21

"Poetry of W. B. Yeats, The" (Eliot), **VI:** 207$_n$, 223

Poetry of W. B. Yeats, The (MacNeice), **VII:** 404

"Poetry of Wordsworth, The" (De Quincey), **IV:** 146, 148

"Poetry Perpetuates the Poet" (Herrick), **II:** 115

Poet's Notebook, A (Sitwell), **VII:** 127, 139

Poets of the First World War (Stallworthy), **VI:** 441

Poets of World War I, **VI:** xvi, **415–441** (includes Lawrence Binyon, Edmund Blunden, Rupert Brooke, Ford Madox Ford, Julian Grenfell, Ivor Gurney, W. N. Hodgson, A. E. Housman, David Jones, Robert Nichols, Herbert Read, Isaac Rosenberg, Seigfried Sassoon, Charles Hamilton Sorley, Edward Thomas, Arthur

Poets of World War I (Cont.)
Graeme West); see separate articles on Wilfred Owen and Robert Graves

Poets of World War II, **VI:** 417; **VII:** 421–450 (includes John Bayliss, Norman Cameron, Roy Campbell, Charles Causley, Keith Douglas, Gavin Ewart, G. S. Fraser, Roy Fuller, Bernard Gutteridge, Hamish Henderson, Sidney Keyes, Alun Lewis, Edward Lowbury, John Manifold, F. T. Prince, Henry Read, Michael Riviere, Alan Ross, Vernon Scannell)

"Poet's Pilgrimage to Waterloo, The" (Southey), **IV:** 66, 71

"Poet's Vow, The" (Browning), **IV:** 313

Point Counter Point (Huxley), **VII:** xviii, 201, 202–204

"Point of It, The" (Forster), **V:** 208

Points of View (Maugham), **VI:** 374, 377

Polanski, Roman, **III:** 343

Polidori, John, **III:** 329, 334, 338

Polite Conversations (Swift), **III:** 36

Political Economy of Art, The (Ruskin), **V:** 184

Political Essays (Hazlitt), **IV:** 129, 139

Political History of the Devil, The (Defoe), **III:** 5, 14

Political Justice (Godwin), **IV:** 43

Political Romance, A (Sterne), **III:** 127, 135

Political Thought in England, 1848–1914 (Walker), **IV:** 304

Politicks of Laurence Sterne, The (Curtis), **III:** 127$_n$

"Politics vs. Literature" (Orwell), **VII:** 273, 282

Poliziano, Angelo, **I:** 240

Poll Degree from a Third Point of View, The (Stephen), **V:** 289

Polly (Gay), **III:** 55, 65–67

"Polonius" (FitzGerald), **IV:** 353

Polonius: A Collection of Wise Saws and Modern Instances (FitzGerald), **IV:** 344, 353

Polychronicon (Higden), **I:** 22

Pomes Penyeach (Joyce), **VII:** 42

Pomona (Evelyn), **II:** 287

Pompeii (Macaulay), **IV:** 290

Pompey the Great (tr. Dorset et al.), **II:** 270, 271

Poole, A. L., **III:** 161$_n$

Poole, Thomas, **IV:** 42, 43, 51

"Poor Man and the Lady, The" (Hardy), **VI:** 2, 20

Poor Man's Plea, The (Defoe), **III:** 2, 12

"Poor Mathias" (Arnold), **V:** 207

"Poor Richard" (James), **VI:** 69

Pope, Alexander, **I:** 326, 328; **II:** 195–197, 236, 259, 261, 263, 298, 308–309, 311, 321, 332, 335, 344; **III:** 1, 19, 20, 33, 46, 50, 54, 56, 60, 62, **68–79,** 95, 118, 167$_n$, 234, 278, 280–282, 288; **IV:** 104, 182, 187, 189–190, 280; **V:** 319

Popery: British and Foreign (Landor), **IV:** 100

"Poplar Field, The" (Cowper), **III:** 218

"Poppy grows upon the shore, A" (Bridges), **VI:** 78

Popular Education of France with Notices of that of Holland and Switzerland, The (Arnold), **V:** 216

"Popular Fallacies" (Lamb), **IV:** 82

"Pornography and Obscenity" (Lawrence), **VII:** 91, 101, 122

"Porphyria's Lover" (Browning), **IV:** 360; **V:** 315

Porson, Richard, **IV:** 63

"Portrait, The" (Gogol), **III:** 340, 345

"Portrait, The" (Rossetti), **V:** 239

Portrait, The (Swinburne), **V:** 333

"Portrait of a Grandfather, The" (Bridges), **VI:** 78

"Portrait of a Lady" (Eliot), **VII:** 144

Portrait of a Lady, The (James), **V:** xxiv, 51; **VI:** 25, 26, **35–38**

"Portrait of Mr. W. H., The" (Wilde), **V:** 405–406, 419

Portrait of Rossetti (Grylls), **V:** 247, 249, 260

Portrait of the Artist as a Young Man, A (Joyce), **VII:** xiv, 45–47; critical studies, **VII:** 57

Portraits Contemporains (Sainte-Beuve), **V:** 212

Portraits from Memory (Russell), **VI:** 170

Portraits of Places (James), **VI:** 67

Portugal History, The, or A Relation of the Troubles . . . in the Court of Portugal . . . (Pepys), **II:** 288

Positions (Mulcaster), **I:** 122

positivism, **V:** 428–429; **VII:** 240–241

Postal Problem, A (Carroll), **V:** 274

Posthumous Fragments of Margaret Nicholson . . . (ed. Shelley), **IV:** 208

Posthumous Papers of the Pickwick Club, The (Dickens), see *Pickwick Papers*

Posthumous Poems (Shelley), **IV:** 208

Posthumous Poems, The (Swinburne), **V:** 333

Posthumous Tales (Crabbe), **III:** 278, 286

"Postscript: for Gweno" (Lewis), **VII:** 444, 446

"Postscripts" (radio broadcasts), **VII:** 212

Pot of Broth, The (Yeats), **VI:** 218

Pottle, F. A., **III:** 234$_n$, 239, 240, 247, 249

Pound, Ezra, **I:** 98; **IV:** 323, 327, 329, 372; **V:** xxv, 304, 317$_n$; **VI:** 207, 216, 247, 323, 417; **VII:** xiii, xvi, 89, 148, 149

Pound on Demand, A (O'Casey), **VII:** 12

"Poussin" (MacNeice), **VII:** 411

Powell, Anthony, **VI:** 235; **VII:** xxi, **343–359**

Powell, Edgar, **VI:** 385

Powell, L. F., **III:** 234$_n$

Power in Men (Cary), **VII:** 186, 187

Power of Grace Illustrated (tr. Cowper), **III:** 220

Powys, T. F., **VII:** 21, 234

Practice of Piety, The (Bayly), **II:** 241

Praed, Winthrop Mackworth, **IV:** 269, 283; **V:** 14

Praeterita (Ruskin), **V:** 174, 175, 182, 184

"Praise for Mercies, Spiritual and Temporal" (Blake), **III:** 294

"Praise for the Fountain Opened" (Cowper), **III:** 211

"Praise of My Lady" (Morris), **V:** 295

"Praise of Pindar, The" (Cowley), **II:** 200

"Praise II" (Herbert), **II:** 129

Prater Violet (Isherwood), **VII:** 313–314

"Prayer Before Birth" (MacNeice), **VII:** 415

"Prayer for My Daughter, A" (Yeats), **VI:** 217, 220

"Prayer I" (Herbert), **II:** 122

Prayers Written at Vailima (Stevenson), **V:** 396

Praz, Mario, **I:** 146, 292, 354; **II:** 123; **III:** 329, 337, 344–345, 346; **V:** 412, 420; **VII:** 60, 62, 70

P.R.B.: An Essay on the Pre-Raphaelite Brotherhood 1847–1854 (Waugh), **VII:** 291

Predictions for the Year 1708 (Swift), **III:** 35

Pre-eminent Victorian, The: A Study of Tennyson (Richardson), **IV:** 339

"Preface: Mainly About Myself" (Shaw), **VI:** 129

Prefaces (Dryden), **IV:** 349

"Prefaces" (Housman), **VI:** 156

Preface to the Dramatic Works of Dryden (ed. Congreve), **II:** 348, 350

"Prefatory Letter on Reading the Bible for the First Time" (Moore), **VI:** 96

Prefatory Poem to My Brother's Sonnets" (Tennyson), **IV:** 327, 336

"Prelude" (Mansfield), **VII:** 177, 179, 180

"Prelude, A" (Lawrence), **VII:** 114

Prelude, The (Wordsworth), **IV:** ix–x, xxi, 1, 2, 3, 11–17, 24, 25, 43, 151, 315; **V:** 310

Premonition to Princes, A (Ralegh), **I:** 154

Pre-Raphaelite Brotherhood, **V:** xxi, 235–236, 248–249, 295

Pre-Raphaelite Imagination, The (Dixon Hunt), **VI:** 167

Pre-Raphaelite movement, **V:** xi–xii, xxi, 235–236, 248–249, 250, 252, 253, 295; **VI:** 103, 166, 167, 169–170, 209, 283; see also William Morris, Christina Rossetti, Dante Gabriel Rossetti, Algernon Charles Swinburne

Pre-Raphaelitism (Ruskin), **V:** 184

Prerogative of Parliaments, The (Ralegh), **I:** 157–158

"Presage of the Ruin of the Turkish Empire, A" (Waller), **II:** 233

Presbyterians' Plea of Merit, The (Swift), **III:** 36

Prescott, William H., **VI:** 394

Present and the Past, The (Compton-Burnett), **VII:** 61, 66

"Present and the Past, The: Eliot's Demonstration" (Leavis), **VII:** 237

Present Position of History, The (Trevelyan), **VI:** 383

Present State of All Nations, The (Smollett), **III:** 158

Present State of the Parties in Great Britain, The (Defoe), **III:** 13

Present State of Wit, The (Gay), **III:** 44, 67

"Present Time, The" (Carlyle), **IV:** 247–248

Press, John, **VI:** xvi, xxxiv; **VII:** xxii, xxxviii

Press Cuttings: A Topical Sketch (Shaw), **VI:** 115, 117, 118–119, 129

Preston, Thomas, **I:** 122, 213

Pretty Lady, The (Bennett), **VI:** 250, 251, 259

Prévost, Antoine, **III:** 333

Price, Alan, **VI:** 314

Price, Cecil, **III:** 258$_n$, 261, 264, 268, 271

Price, Cormell, **VI:** 166, 167

Price, Richard, **IV:** 126

Pride and Prejudice (Austen), **III:** 91, 336; **IV:** xvii, 103–104, 108–120, 122

Pride's Cure (Lamb), see *John Woodvie*

Priestley, J. B., **IV:** 160, 170; **V:** xxvi, 96; **VII:** xii, xviii, 60, **209–231**

Priestley, Joseph, **III:** 290

Priest to the Temple, A, or the Country Parson His Character etc. (Herbert), **II:** 120, 141

"Prime Minister" (Churchill), **VI:** 349

Prime Minister, The (Trollope), **V:** xxiv, 96, 97, 98–99, 101, 102

Primer, The, or Office of the B. Virgin Mary (Dryden), **II:** 304

Prince, F. T., **VII:** xxii, 422, 427

Prince Hohenstiel-Schwangau, Saviour of Society (Browning), **IV:** 358, 369, 374

Prince Otto (Stevenson), **V:** 386, 395

Prince Prolétaire (Swinburne), **V:** 333

"Prince Roman" (Conrad), **VI:** 148

"Prince's Progress, The" (Rossetti), **V:** 250, 258, 259

Prince's Progress and Other Poems, The (Rossetti), **V:** 250, 260

Princess, The (Tennyson), **IV:** xx, 323, 325, 328, 333–334, 336, 338

Princess Casamassima, The (James), **VI:** 27, 39, **41–43**, 67

Principles and Persuasions (West), **VI:** 241

Prior, Matthew, **II:** 265

Prioress's Prologue, The (Chaucer), **I:** 37

Prioress's Tale, The (Chaucer), **I:** 22, 34

"Prisoner, The" (Brontë), **V:** 142, 143, 254

"Prisoner, The" (Browning), **IV:** 313–314

Prisoner of Chillon, The (Byron), **IV:** 180, 192

Prisoner of Grace (Cary), **VII:** 186, 194–195

"Prisoner's Progress" (MacNeice), **VII:** 406

Pritchett, V. S., **IV:** 120, 298, 306

"Private Life, The" (James), **VI:** 48, 67, 69

Private Life of Henry Maitland, The (Roberts), **V:** 425, 427, 438

Private Papers of Henry Ryecroft, The (Gissing), **V:** 424, 425, 427, **430–432**, 436, 437

Private Papers of James Boswell . . . , The (ed. Pottle and Scott), **III:** 234$_n$, 247, 249

Privy Seal (Ford), **VI:** 324, 326

"Probable Future of Metaphysics, The" (Hopkins), **V:** 362

"Problem, The" (Swift), **III:** 32

problem novels, **VI:** 260

"Problem of Prose, The" (Leavis), **VII:** 248

problem play, **VI:** ix

Process of Real Freedom, The (Cary), **VII:** 186

"Procrastination" (Crabbe), **III:** 281, 285

"Proferred Love Rejected" (Suckling), **II:** 227

Professor, The (Brontë), **V:** xxii, 112, 122, 123, 125, 132, **134–137**, 148, 150, 151, 152

"Professor, The" (Thackeray), **V:** 21, 37

"Professor Fargo" (James), **VI:** 69

Profitable Meditations . . . (Bunyan), **II:** 253

Progress and Poverty (George), **VI:** viii

"Progress of Poesy" (Gray), **II:** 200; **III:** 140

"Progress of Poesy, The" (Arnold), **V:** 209

"Progress of the Soul, The" (Donne), **II:** 209

Project for the Advancement of Religion . . . , A (Swift), **III:** 26, 35, 46

Prometheus Bound (Aeschylus), **IV:** 199

Prometheus Bound, Translated from the Greek of Aeschylus (Browning), **IV:** 310, 321

Prometheus the Firegiver (Bridges), **VI:** 83

Prometheus Unbound (Shelley), **III:** 331; **IV:** xviii, 176, 179, 196, 198, **199–201**, 202, 207, 208; **VI:** 449–450

"Promise, The" (James), **VI:** 49

Promos and Cassandra (Whetstone), **I:** 313

Promus of Formularies and Elegancies, A (Bacon), **I:** 264, 271

"Propagation of Knowledge" (Kipling), **VI:** 200

Proper Studies (Huxley), **VII:** 198, 201

Prophecy (Seltzer), **III:** 345

Prophecy of Dante, The (Byron), **IV:** 193

Prophetess, The (Fletcher and Massinger), **II:** 55, 66

Pro populo anglicano defensio . . . (Milton), **II:** 176

Pro populo anglicano defensio secunda (Milton), **II:** 176

Proposal for Correcting . . . the English Tongue, A (Swift), **III:** 29, 35

Proposal for Giving Badges to the Beggars . . . of Dublin, A (Swift), **III:** 36

Proposal for Making an Effectual Provision for the Poor, A (Fielding), **III:** 105

Proposal for Putting Reform to the Vote, A (Shelley), **IV:** 208

Proposals for an Association of . . . Philanthropists . . . (Shelley), **IV:** 208

Proposals for Publishing Monthly . . . (Smollett), **III:** 148

Proposals for the Universal Use of Irish Manufacture . . . (Swift), **III:** 27–28, 35

Proposition for the Advancement of Experimental Philosophy, A (Cowley), **II:** 196, 202

Proserpine, The (Rossetti), **V:** 295

Prose Works, The (Swift), **III:** 15$_n$, 35

Prosody of "Paradise Lost" and "Samson Agonistes," The (Bridges), **VI:** 83

Protestant Ascendancy, **VI:** 209–210, 307

Protestant Monastery, The: or, A Complaint against the Brutality of the Present Age (Defoe), **III:** 14

"Proteus, or Matter" (Bacon), **I:** 267

Prothalamion (Spenser), **I:** 124, 131

"Proud word you never spoke, but you will speak" (Landor), **IV:** 99

Proust, Marcel, **V:** xxiv, 45, 174, 183

Provence (Ford), **VI:** 324

"Proverbs of Hell' (Blake), **III:** 298

"Providence and the Guitar" (Stevenson), **V:** 395

Provok'd Husband, The (Cibber), **II:** 326, 337

Provok'd Wife, The (Vanbrugh), **II:** 325, **329–332,** 334, 336, 360

Provost, The (Galt), **IV:** 35

Prussian Officer, The, and Other Stories (Lawrence), **VII:** 114

Pryce-Jones, Alan, **VII:** 70

Prynne, William, **II:** 339

Pseudodoxia Epidemica (Browne), **II:** 149–150, 151, 155, 156, 345$_n$

Pseudo-Martyr (Donne), **I:** 352–353, 362

Psyche Apocalypté, a Lyrical Drama (Browning and Horne), **IV:** 321

Psycho (film), **III:** 342–343

Psychoanalysis and the Unconscious (Lawrence), **VII:** 122

Public Address (Blake), **III:** 305

Publick Employment and an Active Life Prefer'd to Solitude (Evelyn), **II:** 287

Publick Spirit of the Whigs, The (Swift), **III:** 35

Public Ledger (periodical), **III:** 179, 188

Puck of Pook's Hill (Kipling), **VI:** viii, 169, 204

Pulci, Luigi, **IV:** 182, 188

Punch (periodical), **IV:** 263; **V:** xx, 19, 23, 24–25; **VI:** 367, 368

Punch's Prize Novelists (Thackeray), **V:** 22, 38

"Pupil, The" (James), **VI:** 49, 69

Purcell Commemoration Ode (Bridges), **VI:** 81

Purchas's Pilgrimage, **IV:** 46

Pure Poetry. An Anthology (Moore), **VI:** 99

Purgatorio II (Eliot), **VII:** 151

Purgatory (Yeats), **VI:** 219

Puritan, The, **I:** 194; **II:** 21

Puritan and the Papist, The (Cowley), **II:** 202

Puritanism, **I:** 178–184; **II:** 2

"Purple" (Owen), **VI:** 449

Purple Dust (O'Casey), **VII:** 7, 8

Pushkin, Aleksander, **III:** 339, 345

Put Out More Flags (Waugh), **VII:** 290, 297–298, 300, 313

Puttenham, George, **I:** 94, 114, 119, 146, 214

"Pygmalion" (Gower), **I:** 53–54

Pygmalion (Shaw), **VI:** xv, 108, 115, 116–117, 120

Pynson, Richard, **I:** 99

"Pyramus and Thisbe" (Gower), **I:** 53–54, 55

Q

"Qua cursum ventus" (Clough), **V:** 160

Quaritch, Bernard, **IV:** 343, 346, 348, 349

Quarles, Francis, **II:** 139, 246

Quarterly Review (periodical), **IV:** xvi, 60–61, 69, 133, 204–205, 269–270; **V:** 140

"Queen Annelida and False Arcite" (Browning), **IV:** 321

Queenhoo-Hall (Strutt), **IV:** 31

Queen Mab (Shelley), **IV:** xvii, 197, 201, 207, 208

Queen Mary (Tennyson), **IV:** 328, 338

Queen-Mother, The (Swinburne), **V:** 312, 313, 314, 330, 331, 332

Queen of Corinth, The (Field, Fletcher, Massinger), **II:** 66

"Queen of Spades, The" (Pushkin), **III:** 339–340, 345

Queen of the Air, The (Ruskin), **V:** 174, 180, 181, 184

Queen, The: or, The Excellency of Her Sex (Ford), **II:** 88, 89, 91, 96, 100

Queen's Tragedy, The (Swinburne), **V:** 333

Queen Yseult (Swinburne), **V:** 333

Queery Leary Nonsense (Lear), **V:** 87

Quennell, Peter, **V:** xii, xviii, 192, 193, 194; **VI:** 237

Quentin Durward (Scott), **IV:** xviii, 37, 39

"Question, A" (Synge), **VI:** 314

"Question, The" (Shelley), **IV:** 203

Question of Upbringing, A (Powell), **VII:** 343, 347, 350, 351

Questions about the . . . Seventh-Day Sabbath (Bunyan), **II:** 253

"Questions in a Wood" (Graves), **VII:** 268

Quest sonnets (Auden), **VII:** 380–381

"Qui laborat orat" (Clough), **V:** 160

Quiller-Couch, Sir Arthur, **II:** 121, 191; **V:** 384

Quillinan, Edward, **IV:** 143$_n$

Quinlan, M. J., **III:** 220

Quinn Manuscript, **VII:** 148

Quintessence of Ibsenism, The (Shaw), **VI:** 104, 106, 129

"Quip, The" (Herbert), **II:** 126

R

Rabelais, François, **III:** 24

Rachel Ray (Trollope), **V:** 101

Racine, Jean Baptiste, **II:** 98; **V:** 22

Radcliffe, Ann, **III:** 327, 331–332, 333, 335–338, 345; **IV:** xvi, 30, 35, 36, 111, 173, 218

Raffety, F. W., **III:** 199$_n$

Raiders' Dawn (Lewis), **VII:** 445, 448

Rain (Maugham), **VI:** 369

"Rain" (Thomas), **VI:** 424

Rainbow, The (Lawrence), **VI:** 232, 276, 283; **VII:** 88, 90, 93, **98–101**

Raine, Kathleen, **III:** 297, 308

Rain upon Godshill (Priestley), **VII:** 209, 210

Raj, the, see British Raj

"Rajah's Diamond, The" (Stevenson), **V:** 395

Rajan, B., **VI:** 219

Raknem, Ingwald, **VI:** 228

Ralegh, Sir Walter, **I:** **145–159**, 277, 278, 291; **II:** 138; **III:** 120, 122, 245

Raleigh, Sir Walter, see Ralegh, Sir Walter

Raleigh, Sir Walter Alexander, **VI:** 76, 157

Ralph the Heir (Trollope), **V:** 100, 102

Rambler (periodical), **II:** 142; **III:** 94, 110–111, 112, 119, 121

Rambles Among the Oases of Tunisia (Douglas), **VI:** 305

Ramillies and the Union with Scotland (Trevelyan), **VI:** 392–393

Ramsay, Allan, **III:** 312, 313; **IV:** 28

Ramsay, Andrew, **III:** 99, 100

Randall, H. S., **IV:** 275

Randolph, Thomas, **II:** 222, 237, 238

Ranke, Leopold von, **IV:** 288

Rape of Lucrece, The (Shakespeare), **I:** 306–307, 325; **II:** 3

Rape of the Lock, The (Pope), **III:** 70–71, 75, 77

Rape upon Rape (Fielding), **III:** 105

"Rapture, A" (Carew), **II:** 223

Rash Act, The (Ford), **VI:** 319, 331

Ratchford, Fannie, **V:** 133, 151, 152

Raven, The (Poe), **V:** xx, 409

"Ravenna" (Wilde), **V:** 401, 409

"Ravenswing, The" (Thackeray), **V:** 23, 35, 36

"Rawdon's Roof" (Lawrence), **VII:** 91

Rawley, William, **I:** 257

Ray, G. N., **V:** 37, 39

Raymond Asquith: Life and Letters (Jolliffe), **VI:** 428

Raysor, T. M., **IV:** 46, 51, 52, 56, 57

Razor's Edge, The (Maugham), **VI:** 374, 377–378

Read, Herbert, **III:** 134; **VI:** 416, 436–437; **VII:** 437

Reader (periodical), **III:** 50, 53

Reader's Guide to G. M. Hopkins, A (MacKenzie), **V:** 374, 382

Reader's Guide to Joseph Conrad, A (Karl), **VI:** 135

Readie & Easie Way to Establish a Free Commonwealth . . . (Milton), **II:** 176

Reading of Earth, A (Meredith), **V:** 221, 234

Reading of George Herbert, A (Tuve), **II:** 124, 130

Reading of Life, A, and Other Poems (Meredith), **V:** 234

Readings in Crabbe's "Tales of the Hall" (Fitzgerald), **IV:** 349, 353

realism, **VI:** 23, 169, 365, 366; **VII:** xiv, 96

realist movement, **V:** 424

Realists, The (Snow), **VII:** 338–339

Real Robert Louis Stevenson, The, and Other Critical Essays (Thompson), **V:** 450, 451

"Real Thing, The" (James), **VI:** 48, 69

"Rear-Guard, The" (Sassoon), **VI:** 431

Reasonable Life, The: Being Hints for Men and Women (Bennett), see *Mental Efficiency*

Reason and Sensuality (Lydgate), **I:** 57, 64

Reason of Church Government Urg'd Against Prelaty, The (Milton), **II:** 162, 175

"Reason our Foe, let us destroy" (Wycherley), **II:** 321

Reasons Against the Succession of the House of Hanover (Defoe), **III:** 13

Rebecca and Rowena: A Romance upon Romance (Thackeray), **V:** 38

"Recantation, A" (Kipling), **VI:** 192–193

"Receipt to Restore Stella's Youth . . . , A" (Swift), **III:** 32

"Recessional" (Kipling), **VI:** 203

"Recollections" (Pearsall Smith), **VI:** 76

Recollections of Christ's Hospital (Lamb), **IV:** 85

"Recollections of Solitude" (Bridges), **VI:** 74

Recollections of the Lake Poets (De Quincey), **IV:** 146$_n$, 155

"Reconcilement between Jacob Tonson and Mr. Congreve, The" (Rowe), **II:** 324

"Record of Badalia Herodsfoot, The" (Kipling), **VI:** 167, 168

Record of Friendship, A (Swinburne), **V:** 333

Record of Friendship and Criticism, A (Smith), **V:** 391, 396, 398

Records of a Family of Engineers (Stevenson), **V:** 387, 396

"Recovery, The" (Vaughan), **II:** 185

Recruiting Officer, The (Farquhar), **II:** 353, 358–359, 360, 361, 362, 364

Rectory Umbrella and Mischmasch, The (Carroll), **V:** 264, 273

Red Cotton Night-Cap Country (Browning), **IV:** 358, 369, 371, 374

"Redemption" (Herbert), **II:** 126–127

Redgauntlet (Scott), **IV:** xviii, 31, 35, 39

"Red, Red Rose, A" (Burns), **III:** 321

Red Roses for Me (O'Casey), **VII:** 9

Reed, Henry, **VII:** 422–423, 449

Reed, J. W., **III:** 249

"Reed, A" (Browning), **IV:** 313

Rees-Mogg, W., **II:** 288

Reeve, C., **III:** 345

Reeve, Clara, **III:** 80

Reeve's Tale, The (Chaucer), **I:** 37, 41

"Reflections on Leaving a Place of Retirement" (Coleridge), **IV:** 44

"Reflections on the Death of a Porcupine" (Lawrence), **VII:** 103–104, 110, 119

Reflections on the French Revolution (Burke), **III:** 195, 197, 201–205; **IV:** xv, 127

Reflections on the Late Alarming Bankruptcies in Scotland (Boswell), **III:** 248

Reflections upon Ancient and Modern Learning (Wotton), **III:** 23

Reflector (periodical), **IV:** 80

Reformation, **VI:** 337–338

Reformation of Manners (Defoe), **III:** 12

Refutation of Deism, in a Dialogue, A (Shelley), **IV:** 208

"Refutation of Philosophies" (Bacon), **I:** 263

"Regeneration" (Vaughan), **II:** 185, 187

Regent, The (Bennett), **VI:** 259, 267

Regicide, The (Smollett), **III:** 158

"Regina Cara" (Bridges), **VI:** 81

"Regret" (Swinburne), **V:** 332

Rehearsal, The (Buckingham), **II:** 206, 294

Rehearsal Transpros'd, The (Marvell), **II:** 205, 206–207, 209, 218, 219

Reid, J. C., **IV:** 254, 267

Rejected Address (Smith), **IV:** 253

"Relapse, The" (Vaughan), **II:** 187

Relapse, The: or, Virtue in Danger (Vanbrugh), **II:** 324, 326–329, 332, 334, 335, 336; **III:** 253, 261

Relation Between Michael Angelo and Tintoret, The (Ruskin), **V:** 184

Relationship of the Imprisonment of Mr. John Bunyan, A, (Bunyan), **II:** 253

Religio Laici, or a Layman's Faith (Dryden), **I:** 176, 189; **II:** 291, 299, 304

Religio Medici (Browne), **II:** 146–148, 150, 152, 156, 185; **III:** 40; **VII:** 29

"Religion" (Vaughan), **II:** 189

Religious Courtship: . . . Historical Discourses on . . . Marrying . . . (Defoe), **III:** 13

"Religious Musings" (Coleridge), **IV:** 43

Reliques of Ancient English Poetry (Percy), **III:** 336; **IV:** 28–29

Reliquiae Wottonianae, **II:** 142

"Remain, ah not in youth alone" (Landor), **IV:** 99

Remains of Sir Walter Ralegh, The, **I:** 146, 157

Remarks Upon a Late Disingenuous Discourse (Marvell), **II:** 219

"Remember" (Rossetti), **VII:** 64

Remembering Sion (Ryan), **VII:** 2

"Remember Me When I Am Gone Away" (Rossetti), **V:** 249

Remembrances of Words and Matter Against Richard Cholmeley, **I:** 277

Reminiscences (Carlyle), **IV:** 70_n, 239, 240, 245, 250

"Reminiscences of Charlotte Brontë" (Nussey), **V:** 108, 109, 152

Reminiscences of the Impressionistic Painters (Moore), **VI:** 99

Remorse (Coleridge), **IV:** 56

Remorse: A Study in Saffron (Wilde), **V:** 419

Renaissance, The: Studies in Art and Poetry (Pater), see *Studies in the History of the Renaissance*

Renan, Joseph Ernest, **II:** 244

Renegade Poet, A, And Other Essays (Thompson), **V:** 451

"Repentance" (Herbert), **II:** 128

"Rephan" (Browning), **IV:** 365

Replication (Skelton), **I:** 93

Reply to the Essay on Population, by the Rev. T. R. Malthus, A (Hazlitt), **IV:** 127, 139

"Reported Missing" (Scannell), **VII:** 424

"Report from Below, A" (Hood), **IV:** 258

"Report on Experience" (Blunden), **VI:** 428

Reports on Elementary Schools, 1852–1882 (Arnold), **V:** 216

Reprinted Pieces (Dickens), **V:** 72

Reprisal, The (Smollett), **III:** 149, 158

Reproof: A Satire (Smollett), **III:** 158

"Requiem" (Stevenson), **V:** 383

"Requiescat" (Arnold), **V:** 211

"Requiescat" (Wilde), **V:** 400

Rescue, The (Conrad), **VI:** 136, 147

"Resignation" (Arnold), **V:** 210

"Resolution and Independence" (Wordsworth), **IV:** 19–20, 22; **V:** 352

"Resound my voice, ye woods that hear me plain" (Wyatt), **I:** 110

Responsibilities (Yeats), **VI:** 213

"Resurrection, The" (Cowley), **II:** 200

Resurrection, The (Yeats), **VI:** xiv, 222

"Resurrection and Immortality" (Vaughan), **II:** 185, 186

Resurrection of the Dead, The, . . . (Bunyan), **II:** 253

"Retaliation" (Goldsmith), **III:** 181, 185, 191

"Retired Cat, The" (Cowper), **III:** 217

"Retirement" (Vaughan), **II:** 187, 188, 189

"Retreate, The" (Vaughan), **II:** 186, 188–189

"Retrospective Review" (Hood), **IV:** 255

"Return, The" (Conrad), **VI:** 148

Return from Parnassus, The, part II, **II:** 27

"Returning, We Hear the Larks" (Rosenberg), **VI:** 434–435

Return of the Druses, The (Browning), **IV:** 374

Return of the Native, The (Hardy), **V:** xxiv, 279; **VI:** 1–2, 5, 6, 7, 8

Return of Ulysses, The (Bridges), **VI:** 83

Return to Oasis (Durrell), **VII:** 425

Return to Yesterday (Ford), **VI:** 149

Revaluation (Leavis), **III:** 68; **VII:** 234, 236, 244–245

Revelations of Divine Love (Juliana of Norwich), **I:** 20–21

Revenge for Love, The (Lewis), **VII:** 72, 74, 81

Revenge Is Sweet: Two Short Stories (Hardy), **VI:** 20

Revenge of Bussy D'Ambois, The (Chapman), **I:** 251–252, 253; **II:** 37

revenge play, **I:** 284

Revenger's Tragedy, The, **II:** 1–2, 21, 29, **33–36**, 37, 39, 40, 41, 70, 97

Reverberator, The (James), **VI:** 67

"Reverie" (Browning), **IV:** 365

Reveries over Childhood and Youth (Yeats), **VI:** 222

Review (periodical), **II:** 325; **III:** 4, 13, 39, 41, 42, 51, 53

"Reviewer's ABC, A" (Aiken), **VII:** 149

Review of some poems by Alexander Smith and Matthew Arnold (Clough), **V:** 158

Review of the Affairs of France, A . . . (Defoe), **III:** 13

Revised Version of the Bible, **I:** 381–382

Revolt of Islam, The (Shelley), **IV:** xvii, 198, 203, 208; **VI:** 455

"Revolt of the Tartars" (De Quincey), **IV:** 149

"Revolution" (Housman), **VI:** 160

Revolutionary Epick, The (Disraeli), **IV:** 306, 308

Revolution in Tanner's Lane, The (Rutherford), **VI:** 240

Revue des Deux Mondes (Montégut), **V:** 102

"Reynard the Fox" (Masefield), **VI:** 338

Reynolds, G. W. M., **III:** 335

Reynolds, John, **II:** 14

Reynolds, John Hamilton, **IV:** 215, 221, 226, 228, 229, 232, 233, 253, 257, 259, 281

Reynolds, Sir Joshua, **II:** 336; **III:** 305

"Rhapsody of Life's Progress, A" (Browning), **IV:** 313

Rhetor (Harvey), **I:** 122

rhetoric, **IV:** 147, 148

"Rhetoric" (De Quincey), **IV:** 147

"Rhetoric and Poetic Drama" (Eliot), **VII:** 157

Rhoda Fleming (Meredith), **V:** xxiii, 227$_n$, 234

Rhododaphne (Peacock), **IV:** 158, 170

rhyme, **IV:** 316; **VI:** 454; **VII:** xii, 136

Rhyme? and Reason? (Carroll), **V:** 270, 273

rhyme royal, **I:** 58

Rhymers' Club, **V:** 439; **VI:** ix, 158, 216

"Ribblesdale" (Hopkins), **V:** 367, 372

Ribner, Irving, **I:** 287

Riccoboni, Luigi, **II:** 348

Riceyman Steps (Bennett), **VI:** 250, 252, 260–261

Rich, Barnaby, **I:** 312

"Richard Martin" (Hood), **IV:** 267

Richard Rolle of Hampole, **I:** 20

Richards, Grant, **VI:** 158

Richards, I. A., **III:** 324; **V:** 367, 381; **VI:** 207, 208; **VII:** xiii, 233, 239

Richardson, Dorothy, **VI:** 372; **VII:** 20

Richardson, Joanna, **IV:** xxv, 236; **V:** xi, xviii

Richardson, Samuel, **III:** **80–93**, 94, 98, 333; **VI:** 266

Richard II (Shakespeare), **I:** 286, 308

Richard III (Shakespeare), **I:** 285, 299–301

"Ride from Milan, The" (Swinburne), **V:** 325, 333

Riders to the Sea (Synge), **VI:** xvi, 308, 309, 310–311

Riding, Laura, **VI:** 207; **VII:** 258, 260, 261, 263, 269

Rigby, Elizabeth, **V:** 138

Right at Last and Other Tales (Gaskell), **V:** 15

Righter, Anne, **I:** 224, 269, 329

Rilke, Rainer Maria, **VI:** 215

"Rime of the Ancient Mariner, The" (Coleridge), see "Ancient Mariner, The"

Ring, The (Wagner), **V:** 300

Ring and the Book, The (Browning), **IV:** xxiii, 358, 362, 369, 373, 374

"R.I.P." (Gissing), **V:** 437

"Rise of Historical Criticism, The" (Wilde), **V:** 401, 419

Rise of Iskander, The (Disraeli), **IV:** 308

Rising of the Moon, The (Gregory), **VI:** 315, 316

Ritchie, Lady Anne, **V:** 10

Rival Ladies, The (Dryden), **II:** 293, 297, 305

Rivals, The (Sheridan), **III:** 253, **257–259,** 270

River Dudden, The, a Series of Sonnets (Wordsworth), **IV:** 24

River War, The (Churchill), **VI:** 351

Riviere, Michael, **VII:** 422, 424

R.L.S. and His Sine Qua Non (Boodle), **V:** 391, 393, 397

"Road from Colonus, The" (Forster), **VI:** 399

"Roads" (Stevenson), **V:** 386

Road to Wigan Pier, The (Orwell), **VII:** 274, 279–280

Road to Xanadu, The (Lowes), **IV:** 47, 57

"Road Uphill, The" (Maugham), **VI:** 377

Roaring Girl, The (Dekker and Middleton), **II:** 3, 21

Roaring Queen, The (Lewis), **VII:** 82

Robbery Under Law (Waugh), **VII:** 292, 294

Robe of Rosheen, The (O'Casey), **VII:** 12

Robert Bridges and Gerard Manley Hopkins (Ritz), **VI:** 83

Robert Bridges 1844–1930 (Thompson), **VI:** 83

"Robert Bridges: His Work on the English Language" (Daryush), **VI:** 76

Robert Browning (ed. Armstrong), **IV:** 375

Robert Browning (Chesterton), **VI:** 344

Robert Browning (Jack), **IV:** 375

Robert Browning: A Collection of Critical Essays (Drew), **IV:** 375

Robert Burns (Swinburne), **V:** 333

Robert Graves: His Life and Work (Seymour-Smith), **VII:** 272

Robert Louis Stevenson (Chesterton), **V:** 391, 393, 397; **VI:** 345

Robert Louis Stevenson (Cooper), **V:** 397, 398

Robert Louis Stevenson. An Essay (Stephen), **V:** 290

Robert Louis Stevenson: Man and Writer (Stewart), **V:** 393, 397

Robert Macaire (Stevenson), **V:** 396

Roberts, Michael, **VII:** xix, 411

Roberts, Morley, **V:** 425, 427, 428, 438

Robertson, Thomas, **V:** 330; **VI:** 269

Robert Southey and His Age (Carnall), **IV:** 72

Robin Hood: A Fragment, by the Late Robert Southey, and Caroline Southey, **IV:** 71

Robinson, Henry Crabb, **IV:** 11, 52, 56, 81

Robinson, Henry Morton, **VII:** 53

Robinson, Lennox, **VI:** 96

Robinson Crusoe (Defoe), **III:** 1, 5, 6, 7, 8, **10–12,** 13, 24, 42, 50, 95

Rob Roy (Scott), **IV:** xvii, 33, 34, 39

Rochester, earl of, **II:** 208$_n$, 255, 256, **257–261, 269–270**

Rock, The (Eliot), **VII:** 153

Roderick Hudson (James), **VI:** 24, **26–28,** 42, 67

Roderick Random (Smollett), **III:** **150–152,** 158

Roderick, the Last of the Goths (Southey), **IV:** 65–66, 68, 71

Rodker, John, **VI:** 327

Roe Head journals (Brontë), **V:** 119–122

"Roger Ascham and Lady Jane Grey" (Landor), **IV:** 92

Rogers, Charles, **III:** 249

Rogers, Woodes, **III:** 7

Rojas Zorilla, Francisco de, **II:** 325

Rokeby (Scott), **IV:** 38

"Rolling English Road, The" (Chesterton), **I:** 16

Rollins, Hyder, **IV:** 231, 232, 235

Rollo, Duke of Normandy (Chapman, Fletcher, Jonson, Massinger), **II:** 45, 66

romance, **IV:** 30

Romance (Conrad and Ford), **VI:** 146, 148, 321

"Romance" (Sitwell), **VII:** 132–133

"Romance of Certain Old Clothes, The" (James), **VI:** 69

Roman de la rose, **I:** 28, 49; tr. Chaucer, **I:** 28, 31

Roman de Troie (Benoît de Sainte-Maure), **I:** 53

Roman expérimental (Zola), **V:** 286

Roman Forgeries . . . (Traherne), **II:** 190, 191, 201

Roman History, The (Goldsmith), **III:** 180, 181, 191

Romantic Adventures of a Milkmaid, The (Hardy), **VI:** 20, 22

Romantic Agony, The (Praz), **III:** 337, 346; **V:** 412, 420

Romantic Image (Kermode), **V:** 344, 359, 412

romantic movement, **IV: vii–xxiii,** 77, 110; **VI:** viii

Romantic Poetry and the Fine Arts (Blunden), **IV:** 236

"Romaunt of Margaret, The" (Browning), **IV:** 313

Romeo and Juliet (Shakespeare), **I:** 229, 305–306, 320; **II:** 281; **IV:** 218

Romola (Eliot), **V:** xxii, 66, 194–195, 200

rondeau, **V:** 259

Rondeaux Parisiens (Swinburne), **V:** 333

Rookwood (Ainsworth), **V:** 47

Room of One's Own, A (Woolf), **VII:** 22–23, 25–26, 27, 38

Room with a View, A (Forster), **VI:** 398, 399, **403–404**

Rootham, Helen, **VII:** 129

"Roots of Honour, The" (Ruskin), **V:** 179–180

Roots of the Mountains, The (Morris), **V:** 302, 306

Roppen, G., **V:** 221$_n$

Rosalind and Helen (Shelley), **IV:** 208

Rosalynde (Lodge), **I:** 312

Rosamond, Queen of the Lombards (Swinburne), **V:** 312–314, 330, 331, 332, 333

"Rose, The" (Southey), **IV:** 64

Rose and Crown (O'Casey), **VII:** 13

Rose and the Ring, The (Thackeray), **V:** 38, 261

"Rose Mary" (Rossetti), **V:** 238, 244

Rosemary's Baby (film), **III:** 343

Rosenberg, Eleanor, **I:** 233

Rosenberg, Isaac, **VI:** xvi, 417, 420, **432–435; VII:** xvi

Rosenberg, John, **V:** 316, 334

Rosenfeld, S., **II:** 271

"Roses on the Terrace, The" (Tennyson), **IV:** 329, 336

"Rosiphelee" (Gower), **I:** 53–54

Ross, Alan, **VII:** xxii, 422, 433–434

Rossetti, Christina, **V:** xi–xii, xix, xxii, xxvi, **247–260**

Rossetti, Dante Gabriel, **IV:** 346; **V:** ix, xi, xii, xviii, xxiii–xxv, **235–246,** 247–253, 259, 293–296, 298, 299, 312–315, 320, 329, 355, 401; **VI:** 167

Rossetti, Maria, **V:** 251, 253

Rossetti, William, **V:** 235, 236, 245, 246, 248–249, 251–253, 260

Rossetti (Waugh), **VII:** 291

"Rossetti's Conception of the 'Poetic' " (Doughty), **V:** 246

Røstvig, Maren-Sofie, **I:** 237

"Rot, The" (Lewis), **VII:** 73

Rotting Hill (Lewis), **VII:** 72

Roundabout Papers (Thackeray), **V:** 34, 35, 38

Round Table, The (Hazlitt), **IV:** xvii, 129, 137, 139

Round Table, The, or, King Arthur's Feast (Peacock), **IV:** 170

Round the Sofa (Gaskell), **V:** 3, 15

Rousseau, Jean Jacques, **III:** 235, 236; **IV:** xiv, 207

Rover, The (Conrad), **VI:** 144, 147, 148

Rowe, Nicholas, **I:** 326

Rowley, William, **II:** 1, 3, 14, 15, 18, 21, 66, 69, 83, 89, 100

Roxana (Defoe), **III:** 8–9, 14

Royal Academy, **VI:** 167

Royal Academy, The (Moore), **VI:** 98

Royal Combat, The (Ford), **II:** 100

Royal Court Theatre, **VI:** 101

"Royal Man" (Muir), **I:** 247

Rubáiyát of Omar Khayyám, The (FitzGerald), **IV:** xxii, 342–343, **345–348,** 349, 352, 353; **V:** 318

Rudd, Margaret, **VI:** 209

Rude Assignment (Lewis), **VI:** 333; **VII:** xv, 72, 74, 76

Rudyard Kipling, Realist and Fabulist (Dobrée), **VI:** 200–203

Rudyard Kipling to Rider Haggard (ed. Cohen), **VI:** 204

Ruffhead, O., **III:** 69$_n$, 71

"Rugby Chapel" (Arnold), **V:** 203

"Ruined Cottage, The" (Wordsworth), **IV:** 23, 24

Ruins of Time, The (Spenser), **I:** 124

Rule a Wife and Have a Wife (Fletcher), **II:** 45, 65

"Rules and Lessons" (Vaughan), **II:** 187

Rules for Court Circular (Carroll), **V:** 274

Rural Minstrel, The (Brontë), **V:** 107, 151

Rural Sports: A Poem (Gay), **III:** 67

Ruskin, John, **IV:** 320, 346; **V:** xii, xviii, xx–xxii, xxvi, 3, 9, 17, 20, 85–86, **173–185**, 235, 236, 291–292, 345, 362, 400; **VI:** 167

Ruskin's Politics (Shaw), **VI:** 129

Russell, Bertrand, **VI:** xi, 170, 385; **VII:** 90

Russell, G. W. E., **IV:** 292, 304

Rusticus (Poliziano), **I:** 240

"Ruth" (Crabbe), **V:** 6

Ruth (Gaskell), **V:** xxi, 1, 6–7, 15

"Ruth" (Hood), **IV:** 255

Ryan, Desmond, **VII:** 2

Rymer, Thomas, **I:** 328

Ryskamp, C., **III:** 249

S

"Sabbath Morning at Sea, A" (Browning), **IV:** 313

Sackville, Charles, see Dorset, earl of

Sackville, Thomas, **I:** 169, 214

Sackville-West, Edward, **VII:** 35, 59

Sacred Flame, The (Maugham), **VI:** 369

Sacred Fount, The (James), **VI:** 56–57, 67

Sacred Wood, The (Eliot), **I:** 293; **V:** 310, 334; **VII:** 149, 164

"Sacrifice, The" (Herbert), **II:** 124, 128

"Sadak the Wanderer" (Shelley), **IV:** 209

Sade, marquis de, **V:** 316–317

Sadleir, Michael, **III:** 335, 346; **V:** 100, 101, 102

Sad One, The (Suckling), **II:** 226

Saga Library, The (Morris, Magnusson), **V:** 306

Sagar, Keith, **VII:** 104

"Sage to the Young Man, The" (Housman), **VI:** 159

"Sailor's Mother, The" (Wordsworth), **IV:** 21

"Sailor, What of the Isles?" (Sitwell), **VII:** 138

"Saint, The" (Maugham), **VI:** 377

"St. Alphonsus Rodriquez" (Hopkins), **V:** 376, 378

Sainte-Beuve, Charles, **III:** 226, 230; **V:** 212

"Sainte Mary Magdalene, or The Weeper" (Crashaw), see "Weeper, The"

St. Évremond, Charles de, **III:** 47

St. Francis of Assissi (Chesterton), **VI:** 341

Saint Ignatius Loyola (Thompson), **V:** 450, 451

St. Irvine (Shelley), **III:** 338

St. Irvyne or the Rosicrucian (Shelley), **IV:** 208

St. Ives (Stevenson and Quiller-Couch), **V:** 384, 387, 396

Saint Joan (Shaw), **VI:** xv, 120, **123–125**

St. Joan of the Stockyards (Brecht), **VI:** 123

St. Leon (Godwin), **III:** 332

"St. Martin's Summer" (Browning), **IV:** 369

"St. Mawr" (Lawrence), **VII:** 115

St. Patrick's Day (Sheridan), **III:** 253, 259, 270

St. Paul and Protestantism (Arnold), **V:** 216

St. Paul's boys' theater, **I:** 197

St. Ronan's Well (Scott), **IV:** 36, 37, 39

Saintsbury, George, **II:** 211; **IV:** 271, 282, 306; **V:** 31, 38; **VI:** 266

"St. Simeon Stylites" (Tennyson), **IV:** xx, 332

Saint's Knowledge of Christ's Love, The (Bunyan), **II:** 253

Saint's Privilege and Profit, The (Bunyan), **II:** 253

Saint's Progress (Galsworthy), **VI:** 272, 279, 280–281

St. Thomas Aquinas (Chesterton), **VI:** 341

St. Valentine's Day (Scott), **IV:** 39

"St. Winefred's Well" (Hopkins), **V:** 371

Salámón and Absál . . . Translated from . . . Jámí (FitzGerald), **IV:** 342, 345, 353

"Salisbury Plain" poems (Wordsworth), **IV:** 2, 3, 4, 5–6, 23, 24

Sally Bowles (Isherwood), **VII:** 311

Salomé (Wilde), **V:** xxvi, 412–413, 419

Salsette and Elephanta (Ruskin), **V:** 184

Salter, F. M., **I:** 82

"Salutation The" (Traherne), **II:** 191

"Salvation of Swithin Forsyte, The" (Galsworthy), **VI:** 274, 277

"Salvatore" (Maugham), **VI:** 370

Salve (Moore), **VI:** 99

Samson Agonistes (Milton), **II:** 165, 172–174, 176

Samuel Johnson (Krutch), **III:** 246

Samuel Johnson (Stephen), **V:** 281, 289

"Samuel Johnson and John Horne (Tooke)" (Landor), **IV:** 92

Samuel Pepys's Naval Minutes (ed. Tanner), **II:** 288

Samuel Pepys's "Penny Merriments": . . . Together with Comments . . . (ed. Thompson), **II:** 288

Samuel Taylor Coleridge: A Biographical Study (Chambers), **IV:** 41, 57

Samuel Titmarsh and the Great Hoggarty Diamond (Thackeray), see *Great Hoggarty Diamond, The*

Sánchez, Nellie, **V:** 393, 397

Sand, George, **V:** 22, 141, 207

Sandcastle, The (Murdoch), **VII:** 66

Sanders, M. F., **V:** 250, 260

Sanderson, Robert, **II:** 136–137, 140, 142

Sandison, Alan G., **VI:** xi, xxxiv

Sanditon (Austen), **IV:** 108, 110, 122

Sandra Belloni (Meredith), **V:** 226, 227, 234

"Sandro Botticelli" (Pater), **V:** 345, 348

Sanity of Art, The (Shaw), **VI:** 106–107, 129

Sapho and Phao (Lyly), **I:** 198, 201–202

"Sapphics" (Swinburne), **V:** 321

"Sappho to Phaon" (Ovid), **V:** 319

Sardanapalus (Byron), **IV:** xviii, 178–179, 193

Sartor Resartus (Carlyle), **IV:** xii, xix, 231, 239–240, 242–243, 249, 250

Sartre, Jean-Paul, **III:** 329, 345

Sassoon, Siegfried, **V:** 219, 234; **VI:** xvi, 416, **429–431,** 451, 454, 456–457; **VII:** xvi

Satan in Search of a Wife (Lamb), **IV:** 84, 85

Satire and Fiction (Lewis), **VII:** 72, 77

Satire on Satirists, A, and Admonition to Detractors (Landor), **IV:** 100

Satires (Donne), **I:** 361

Satires (Wyatt), **I:** 100, 101–102, 111

Satires of Circumstance (Hardy), **VI:** 14, 20

Satires of Circumstance (Sorley), **VI:** 421

"Saturday, or The Flights" (Gay), **III:** 56

Saturday Review (periodical), **V:** 279; **VI:** 103, 106, 366

"Satyr Against Mankind, A" (Rochester), **II:** 208$_n$, 256, 260–261, 270

"Satyrical Elegy on the Death of a Late Famous General, A" (Swift), **III:** 31

"Saul" (Browning), **IV:** 363

Saunders, Charles, **II:** 305

Sauter, Rudolf, **VI:** 284

Savage, Richard, **III:** 108

Savage Pilgrimage, The (Carswell), **VII:** 123

Saved By Grace (Bunyan), **II:** 253

Savile, George, see Halifax, marquess of

Saviour of Society, The (Swinburne), **V:** 333

Savonarola e il priore di San Marco (Landor), **IV:** 100

Savrola (Churchill), **VI:** 351

Sayers, Dorothy L., **III:** 341; **VI:** 345

"Say not of me that weakly I declined" (Stevenson), **V:** 390

"Say not the struggle nought availeth" (Clough), **V:** 158–159, 165, 166, 167

Scandal of Father Brown, The (Chesterton), **VI:** 338

Scannell, Vernon, **VII:** 422, 423–424

Scarlet Tree, The (Sitwell), **VII:** 128–129

Scarron, Paul, **II:** 354

"Scenes" (Dickens), **V:** 44–46

Scenes from Italy's War (Trevelyan), **VI:** 389

"Scenes from the Fall of Troy" (Morris), **V:** 297

Scenes of Clerical Life (Eliot), **V:** xxii, 2, 190–191, 200

Sceptick (Ralegh), **I:** 157

Scheme and Estimates for a National Theatre, A (Archer and Barker), **VI:** 104, 113

Schiller, Friedrich von, **IV:** xiv, xvi, 173, 241

Schlegel, A. W., **I:** 329; **IV:** vii, xvii; **V:** 62

Schneider, Elizabeth, **V:** 366, 382

"Scholar Gipsy, The" (Arnold), **V:** xxi, 209, 210, 211, 216

Scholasticism, **I:** 261

Schoolboy Verses (Kipling), **VI:** 200

School for Scandal, The (Sheridan), **III:** 97, 100, 253, **261–264,** 270

School of Abuse (Gosson), **I:** 161

School of Donne, The (Alvarez), **II:** 125$_n$

Schools and Universities on the Continent (Arnold), **V:** 216

Science and Poetry (Richards), **VI:** 207, 208

science fiction, **VI:** 226, 228–231, 233–234, 399; see also fantasy fiction

Science of Ethics, The (Stephen), **V:** 284–285, 289

"Science of History, The" (Froude), **IV:** 324

Science of Life, The (Wells), **VI:** 225

scientific romance, **VI:** 225

Scilla's Metamorphosis (Lodge), **I:** 306

"Scipio, Polybius, and Panaetius" (Landor), **IV:** 94

Scoop (Waugh), **VII:** 297

Scornful Lady, The (Beaumont and Fletcher), **II:** 65

"Scotch Drink" (Burns), **III:** 315

Scots Musical Museum (Johnson), **III:** 320, 322

Scott, Geoffrey, **III:** 234$_n$, 238, 249

Scott, John, **IV:** 252, 253

Scott, Robert Falcon, **II:** 273

Scott, Sir Walter, **II:** 276; **III:** 146, 157, 326, 335, 336, 338; **IV:** viii, xi, xiv, **27–40**, 45, 48, 102, 111, 122, 129, 133–136, 167, 168, 173, 254, 270, 281; **V:** 392; **VI:** 412

Scott-James, Rolfe Arnold, **VI:** x, xxxiv, 1

Scott-Kilvert, Ian Stanley, **VI:** xvi, xxxiv; **VII:** xxii

Scott-King's Modern Europe (Waugh), **VII:** 301

Scott Moncrieff, Charles, **VI:** 454, 455

Scotus, Duns, see Duns Scotus, John

Scourge of Villainy, The (Marston), **II:** 25, 26, 40

Scrapbook (Mansfield), **VII:** 181

Scriptorum illustrium maioris Britanniae catalogus (Bale), **I:** 1

Scrutiny (periodical), **VII:** 233, 238, 243, 251–252, 256

Scudéry, Georges de, **III:** 95

Sculptura: or The History . . . of Chalcography and Engraving in Copper (Evelyn), **II:** 287

Sea and Sardinia (Lawrence), **VII:** 116–117

Sea and the Mirror, The (Auden), **VII:** 379, 380, 388, 389

"Sea and the Skylark, The" (Hopkins), **V:** 367

"Sea Limits" (Rossetti), **V:** 241

"Sea-Mists of the Winter, The" (Lewis), **VII:** 84

Sean O'Casey: The Man Behind the Plays (Cowasjee), **VII:** 4

Search, The (Snow), **VII:** 321–322, 323–324

"Search, The" (Vaughan), **II:** 187

"Search After Happiness, The" (Brontë), **V:** 110

"Seaside Walk, A" (Browning), **IV:** 313

Seasonable Counsel: or, Advice to Sufferers (Bunyan), **II:** 253

Sea Voyage, The (Fletcher and Massinger), **II:** 43, 66

Seccombe, Thomas, **V:** 425, 437

"Second Best, The" (Arnold), **V:** 209

"Second Coming, The" (Yeats), **VI:** xiv

Second Defence of the People of England, The (Milton), **II:** 164

Second Funeral of Napoleon, The (Thackeray), **V:** 22, 38

Second Journal to Eliza, The, **III:** 135

Second Jungle Book, The (Kipling), **VI:** 204

Second Maiden's Tragedy, The (Middleton), **II:** 2, 3, **8–10**, 21

Second Mrs. Tanqueray, The (Pinero), **V:** 413

Second Nun's Tale, The (Chaucer), **I:** 31, 34, 43

Second Part of Mr. Waller's Poems, The (Waller), **II:** 238

Second Part of Pilgrim's Progress, The (T. S.), **II:** 248

Second Part of the Bloody Conquests of Mighty Tamburlaine, The (Marlowe), see *Tamburlaine*, Part 2

Second Satire (Wyatt), **I:** 111

Second World War, see World War II

Second World War (Churchill), **VI:** 359–360

Secord, Arthur Wellesley, **III:** 41

Secret Agent, The (Conrad), **VI: 143–144,** 148

Secret History of the White Staff, The, . . . (Defoe), **III:** 13

Secret Love, or the Maiden Queen (Dryden), **II:** 305

Secret of Father Brown, The (Chesterton), **VI:** 338

Secret Rose (Yeats), **VI:** 222

"Secret Sharer, The" (Conrad), **VI: 145–147**

Secular Lyrics of the XIVth and XVth Centuries (Robbins), **I:** 40

"Secular Masque, The" (Dryden), **II:** 289, 290, 305, 325

Sedley, Sir Charles, **II:** 255, 261, **263–266, 271**

"Seed Growing Secretly, The" (Vaughan), **II:** 189

Seek and Find (Rossetti), **V:** 260

Seicentismo e Marinismo in Inghilterra (Praz), **II:** 123

Sejanus (Jonson), **I:** 235, 242, 249, 345–346

Select British Poets, or New Elegant Extracts from Chaucer to the Present Time (Hazlitt), **IV:** 139

Select Collection of Original Scottish Airs (Thomson), **III:** 322

Select Conversations with an Uncle, Now Extinct . . . (Wells),

Selected Plays [of Lady Gregory] (ed. Coxhead), **VI:** 317

Selected Prose (Housman), **VI:** 154

Selected Speeches (Disraeli), **IV:** 308

Selection of Kipling's Verse (Eliot), **VI:** 202

Select Poets of Great Britain (Hazlitt), **IV:** 139

Self and Self-Management (Bennett), **VI:** 264

Self Condemned (Lewis), **VII:** 72, 74, 81–82

"Self-Unseeing, The" (Hardy), **VI:** 13

Selimus, **I:** 220

Seltzer, David, **III:** 343, 345

"Send-Off, The" (Owen), **VI:** 447, 452

Seneca, **I:** 214–215; **II:** 25, 28, 71, 97

Sense and Sensibility (Austen), **III:** 91, 336; **IV:** xvii, 108, 109, 111, 112, 114–122

Sense of the Past, The (James), **VI:** 64–65

"Sensitive Plant, The" (Shelley), **IV:** 203

Sentimental Journey, A (Sterne), **III:** 124, 127, 132–134, 135

Sentiments of a Church-of-England Man, The (Swift), **III:** 26

"Sentry, The" (Owen), **VI:** 448, 451

"Sepulchre" (Herbert), **II:** 128

Sequence of Sonnets on the Death of Robert Browning, A (Swinburne), **V:** 333

Serafino Aquilano, **I:** 103, 105, 110

"Seraphim, The" (Browning), **IV:** 312, 313

Seraphim, The, and Other Poems (Browning), **IV:** xix, 311, 312–313, 321

"Serenade" (Sitwell), **VII:** 135

Sergeant Lamb (Graves), **VII:** 258

serial publication, **VII:** 21, 349

Serious and Pathetical Contemplation of the Mercies of God, A . . . (Traherne), **II:** 201

Serious Reflections During . . . "Robinson Crusoe" (Defoe), **III:** 12, 13

Sermons (Donne), **I:** 364–366; **II:** 142

Sermons and Devotional Writings of Gerard Manley Hopkins, The (ed. Devlin), **V:** 372, 381

"Sermon to Our Later Prodigal Son" (Meredith), **V:** 223

"Serpent-Charm, The" (Gissing), **V:** 437

"Servant Girl Speaks, A" (Lawrence), **VII:** 118

Sesame and Lilies (Ruskin), **V:** 180, 184

"Session of the Poets, A" (Suckling), **II:** 229

"Sestina of the Tramp Royal" (Kipling), **VI:** 202, 203

Set of Six, A (Conrad), **VI:** 148

Seven Days in the New Crete (Graves), **VII:** 259

"Seven Good Germans" (Henderson), **VII:** 426

Seven Lamps of Architecture, The (Ruskin), **V:** xxi, 176, 184

Seven Lectures on Shakespeare and Milton (Coleridge), **IV:** 56

Seven Pillars of Wisdom (Lawrence), **VI:** 408

Seven Seas, The (Kipling), **VI:** 204

Seven Short Plays (Gregory), **VI:** 315

Seven Types of Ambiguity (Empson), **I:** 282; **II:** 124, 130; **VII:** 260

"Several Questions Answered" (Blake), **III:** 293

Severn and Somme (Gurney), **VI:** 425

"Sexton's Hero, The" (Gaskell), **V:** 15

sexuality, treatment of, **VI:** 258–259, 330, 411; **VII:** 87, 92–93, 97–98

Seymour-Smith, Martin, **VII:** xviii, xxxviii

Shabby Genteel Story, A (Thackeray), **V:** 21, 35, 37

Shadow Dance (Carter), **III:** 345

Shadow-Line, The: A Confession (Conrad), **VI:** 135, 146–147, 148

Shadow of a Gunman, The (O'Casey), **VI:** 316; **VII:** xviii, 3–4, 6, 12

Shadow of Cain, The (Sitwell), **VII:** xvii, 137

Shadow of Dante, A (Rossetti), **V:** 253$_n$

Shadow of Night (Chapman), **I**: 234, 237

Shadow of the Glen, The (Synge), **VI**: 308, 309, 310, 316

"Shadows" (Lawrence), **VII**: 119

"Shadows in the Water" (Traherne), **II**: 192

Shadowy Waters, The (Yeats), **VI**: 218, 222

Shadwell, Thomas, **I**: 327; **II**: 305, 359

"Shadwell Stair" (Owen), **VI**: 451

Shaftesbury, seventh earl of, **IV**: 62

Shaftesbury, third earl of, **III**: 44, 46, 198

Shakespear, Olivia, **VI**: 210, 212, 214

Shakespeare, William, **I**: 188, **295–334**; **II**: 87, 221, 281, 302; **III**: 115–117; **IV**: 149, 232, 352; **V**: 41, 328; and Collins, **IV**: 165, 165$_n$, 170; and Jonson, **I**: 335–337, **II**: 281; and Kyd, **I**: 228–229; and Marlowe, **I**: 275–279, 286; and Middleton, **IV**: 79–80; and Webster, **II**: 71–72, 74–75, 79; influence on English literature, **II**: 29, 42–43, 47, 48, 54–55, 79, 82, 84; **III**: 115–116, 167$_n$; **IV**: 35, 51–52; **V**: 405

Shakespeare (Swinburne), **V**: 333

"Shakespeare and Stage Costume" (Wilde), **V**: 407

Shakespeare and the Allegory of Evil (Spivack), **I**: 214

Shakespeare and the Idea of the Play (Righter), **I**: 224

"Shakespeare and the Stoicism of Seneca" (Eliot), **I**: 275

Shakespearean sonnet, **IV**: 221

"Shakespeare as a Man" (Stephen), **V**: 287

Shakes Versus Shav (Shaw), **VI**: 130

Shamela (Fielding), **III**: 84, 98, 105

Shape of Things to Come, The (Wells), **VI**: 228, 241

Sharp, William, **IV**: 370

Sharrock, Roger, **II**: 246, 254

Shaving of Shagpot, The (Meredith), **V**: 225, 234

Shaw, George Bernard, **III**: 263; **V**: xxii, xxv, xxvi, 284, 301, 305–306, 423, 433; **VI**: viii, ix, xiv–xv, **101–132**, 147, 343

Shaw Gives Himself Away: An Autobiographical Miscellany (Shaw), **VI**: 129

Shaw-Stewart, Patrick, **VI**: 418–419, 420

Shelley, Mary Wollstonecraft, **III**: **329–331**, 336, 341, 342, 345; **IV**: xvii, 197, 201, 202, 203

Shelley, Percy Bysshe, **II**: 102, 200; **III**: 329, 330, 333, 336–338; **IV**: vii–xii, 63, 132, 158–159, 161, 163, 164, 168–169, 172, 176–179, 182, **195–210**, 217, 234, 281, 299, 349, 354, 357, 366, 372; **V**: 214, 330, 401, 403; **VI**: 453

Shelley (Swinburne), **V**: 333

Shelley (Thompson), **V**: 450, 451

Shelley: A Life Story (Blunden), **IV**: 210

Shelley and Keats as They Struck Their Contemporaries (Blunden), **IV**: 210

Shelley's Idols of the Cave (Butler), **IV**: 210

Shepheardes Calendar (Spenser), see *Shepherd's Calendar, The*

Shepheards Oracles, The (Quarles), **II**: 139

Shepherd, Ettriek, pseud. of James Hogg

"Shepherd and the Nymph, The" (Landor), **IV**: 96

Shepherd of the Giant Mountains, The (tr. Smedley), **V**: 265

"Shepherd's Brow, The" (Hopkins), **V**: 376, 378$_n$

Shepherd's Calendar, The (Spenser), **I**: 97, 121, 123, 124–128, 162

Shepherd's Life, A (Hudson), **V**: 429

Shepherd's Week, The (Gay), **III**: 55, 56, 67

Sheppey (Maugham), **VI**: 377

Sherburn, George, **III**: 73, 78

Sheridan, Richard Brinsley, **II**: 334, 336; **III**: 32, 97, 101, **252–271**

"She's all my fancy painted him" (Carroll), **V**: 264

She Stoops to Conquer (Goldsmith), **II**: 362; **III**: 177, 181, 183, 188, 191, 256

Shewan, R., **V**: 409$_n$, 421

Shewing-Up of Blanco Posnet, The: A Sermon in Crude Melodrama (Shaw), **VI**: 115, 117, 124, 129

She Wou'd if She Cou'd (Etherege), **II**: 266, 268, 271

"Shield of Achilles, The" (Auden), **VII**: 388, 390–391, 397–398

Shining, The (King), **III**: 345

Shipman's Tale, The (Chaucer), **I**: 36

"Ship That Found Herself, The" (Kipling), **VI**: 170

Shirley, James, **II**: 44, 66, 87

Shirley (Brontë), **V**: xxi, 12, 106, 112, **145–147**, 152

Shoemaker's Holiday, The (Dekker), **II**: 89

"Shooting an Elephant" (Orwell), **VII:** 273, 276, 282

Shooting Niagara—And After? (Carlyle), **IV:** xxii, 240, 247, 250

Short Account of a Late Short Administration, A (Burke), **III:** 205

Short Character of . . . [the Earl of Wharton], A (Swift), **III:** 35

Shortened History of England, A (Trevelyan), **VI:** 395

Shorter, Clement, **V:** 150, 151–153

Shorter Poems (Bridges), **VI:** 72, 73, 81

Shortest Way to Peace and Union, The (Defoe), **III:** 13

Shortest Way with the Dissenters, The (Defoe), **III:** 2, 3, 12–13

Short Historical Essay . . . , A (Marvell), **II:** 219

Short History of the English People (Green), **VI:** 390

Short Stories, Scraps, and Shavings (Shaw), **VI:** 129

short story, **VI:** 369–370; **VII:** xvii, 178–181

Short View of the Immorality and Profaneness of the English Stage, A (Collier), **II:** 303, 325, 338, 340, 356; **III:** 44

Short View of the State of Ireland, A (Swift), **III:** 28, 35

Short Vindication of "The Relapse" and "The Provok'd Wife," A, . . . by the Author (Vanbrugh), **II:** 332, 336

Shout, The (Graves), **VII:** 259

"Show me, dear Christ, thy spouse" (Donne), **I:** 367, 368

Shropshire Lad, A (Housman), **VI:** ix, xv, 157, 158–160, 164

"Shrove Tuesday in Paris" (Thackeray), **V:** 22, 38

"Sibylla Palmifera" (Rossetti), **V:** 237

Sibylline Leaves (Coleridge), **IV:** 56

Sicilian Romance, A (Radcliffe), **III:** 338

"Sick King in Bokhara, The" (Arnold), **V:** 210

Sidgwick, Henry, **V:** 284, 285

Sidley, Sir Charles, see Sedley, Sir Charles

Sidney, Sir Philip, **I:** 123, **160–175**; **II:** 46, 48, 53, 80, 158, 221, 339; **III:** 95

Siege of Corinth, The (Byron), **IV:** 172, 192; see also Turkish tales

Siege of London, The (James), **VI:** 67

Siege of Thebes, The (Lydgate), **I:** 57, 61, 65

"Siena" (Swinburne), **V:** 325, 332

"Sighs and Grones" (Herbert), **II:** 128

Sign of the Cross, The (Barrett), **VI:** 124

Signs of Change (Morris), **V:** 306

"Signs of the Times" (Carlyle), **IV:** 241–242, 243, 249, 324; **V:** viii

Sigurd the Volsung (Morris), see *Story of Sigurd the Volsung and the Fall of the Niblungs, The*

Silas Marner (Eliot), **V:** xxii, 194, 200

"Silent One, The" (Gurney), **VI:** 427

"Silent Voices, The" (Tennyson), **IV:** 329

Silex Scintillans: . . . (Vaughan), **II:** 184, 185, 186, 201

Silverado Squatters, The (Stevenson), **V:** 386, 395

Silver Box, The (Galsworthy), **VI:** 273, 284–285

Silver Spoon, The (Galsworthy), **VI:** 275

Silver Tassie, The (O'Casey), **VII:** 6–7

"Silvia" (Etherege), **II:** 267

Simenon, Georges, **III:** 341

Simmons, Ernest, **V:** 46

Simonidea (Landor), **IV:** 100

"Simon Lee" (Wordsworth), **IV:** 7, 8–9, 10

Simple and Religious Consultation (Bucer), **I:** 177

Simpleton of the Unexpected Isles, The (Shaw), **VI:** 125, 126, 127, 129

"Simplicity" (Collins), **III:** 166

"Simplify Me When I'm Dead" (Douglas), **VII:** 440

Simpson, Percy, **I:** 279

Simpson, Richard, **IV:** 107, 122

"Sincerest Critick of My Prose, or Rhime" (Congreve), **II:** 349

"Since thou, O fondest and truest" (Bridges), **VI:** 74, 77

Singer, S. W., **III:** 69

Single Man, A (Isherwood), **VII:** 309, 316–317

Sing-Song (Rossetti), **V:** 251, 255, 260

Singular Preference, The (Quennell), **VI:** 237, 245

Sinjohn, John, pseud. of John Galsworthy

Sins of the Fathers and Other Tales (Gissing), **V:** 437

Sir Charles Grandison (Richardson), **III:** 80, 90–91, 92; **IV:** 124

"Sir Dominick Ferrand" (James), **VI:** 69

"Sire de Maletroit's Door, The" (Stevenson), **V:** 395

"Sir Edmund Orme" (James), **VI:** 69

Siren Land (Douglas), **VI:** 293, 294, 295, 297, 305

"Sirens, The" (Manifold), **VII:** 426

"Sir Eustace Grey" (Crabbe), **III:** 282

Sir Gawain and the Carl of Carlisle, **I:** 71

Sir Gawain and the Green Knight, **I:** 2, 28, 69, 71

Sir George Otto Trevelyan: A Memoir (Trevelyan), **VI:** 383, 391

Sir Harry Hotspur of Humblethwaite (Trollope), **V:** 100, 102

Sir Harry Wildair, Being the Sequel of "The Trip to the Jubilee" (Farquhar), **II:** 352, 357, 364

Sir Hornbook: or, Childe Launcelot's Expedition (Peacock), **IV:** 169

Sir John Vanbrugh's Justification of . . . the Duke of Marlborough's Late Tryal (Vanbrugh), **II:** 336

Sir Launcelot Greaves (Smollett), **III:** 149, 153, 158

Sir Martin Mar-All or the Feign'd Innocence (Dryden), **II:** 305

Sir Proteus, a Satirical Ballad (Peacock), **IV:** 169

Sir Thomas More, **I:** 325

Sir Thomas More: or, Colloquies on the Progress and Prospects of Society (Southey), **IV:** 69, 70, 71, 280

Sir Thomas Wyatt (Dekker and Webster), **II:** 68

Sir Tristrem (Thomas the Rhymer), **IV:** 29

"Sir Walter Scott" (Carlyle), **IV:** 38

Sir Walter Scott: The Great Unknown (Johnson), **IV:** 40

Sisson, C. J., **I:** 178*n*, 326

"Sister Helen" (Rossetti), **IV:** 313; **V:** 239, 245

"Sister Maude" (Rossetti), **V:** 259

Sisters, The (Conrad), **VI:** 148

Sisters, The (Swinburne), **V:** 330, 333

Sister Songs (Thompson), **V:** 443, 449, 450, 451

Sister Teresa (Moore), **VI:** 87, 92, 98

Sitwell, Edith, **I:** 83; **III:** 73, 78; **VI:** 454; **VII:** xv–xvii, **127–141**

Sitwell, Osbert, **V:** 230, 234; **VII:** xvi, 128, 130, 135

Sitwell, Sacheverell, **VII:** xvi, 128

Six Distinguishing Characters of a Parliament-Man, The (Defoe), **III:** 12

Six Dramas of Calderón. Freely Translated (FitzGerald), **IV:** 342, 344–345, 353

"Six o'clock in Princes Street" (Owen), **VI:** 451

Six of Calais, The (Shaw), **VI:** 129

"Sixpence" (Mansfield), **VII:** 175, 177

Six Stories Written in the First Person Singular (Maugham), **VI:** 374

Sixteen Self Sketches (Shaw), **VI:** 102, 129

"Six Weeks at Heppenheim" (Gaskell), **V:** 14, 15

"Six Years After" (Mansfield), **VII:** 176

Skeat, W. W., **I:** 17

Skelton, John, **I:** **81–96**

Skeltonic verse, **I:** 86

"Sketch, A" (Rossetti), **V:** 250

Sketch Book (Irving), **III:** 54

Sketches and Essays (Hazlitt), **IV:** 140

Sketches and Reviews (Pater), **V:** 357

Sketches and Travels in London (Thackeray), **V:** 38

Sketches by Boz (Dickens), **V:** xix, 42, 43–46, 47, 52, 71

Sketches from Cambridge, by a Don (Stephen), **V:** 289

Sketches of the Principal Picture-Galleries in England (Hazlitt), **IV:** 132, 139

"Sketch from Private Life, A" (Byron), **IV:** 192

Skin Game, The (Galsworthy), **VI:** 275, 280, 288

"Sleep" (Cowley), **II:** 196

"Sleep, The" (Browning), **IV:** 312

"Sleep and Poetry" (Keats), **IV:** 214–215, 217, 228, 231

"Sleeping at Last" (Rossetti), **V:** 251–252, 259

Sleeping Beauty, The (Sitwell), **VII:** 132

Sleeping Fires (Gissing), **V:** 437

Sleep of Reason, The (Snow), **VII:** 324, 331–332

"Slough" (Betjeman), **VII:** 366

"Slumber Did My Spirit Seal, A" (Wordsworth), **IV:** 18

Small Boy and Others, A (James), **VI:** 65

Small House at Allington, The (Trollope), **V:** xxiii, 101

Smeaton, O., **III:** 229*n*

"Smile of Fortune, A" (Conrad), **VI:** 148

Smiles, Samuel, **VI:** 264

Smith, Adam, **IV:** xiv, 144–145; **V:** viii

Smith, Alexander, **IV:** 320; **V:** 158

Smith, Edmund, **III:** 118

Smith, George, **V:** 13, 131, 132, 147, 149, 150, 279–280

Smith, Henry Nash, **VI:** 24

Smith, James, **IV:** 253

Smith, Janet Adam, **V:** 391, 393, 395–398

Smith, Nichol, **III:** 21

Smith, Sydney, **IV:** 268, 272

Smith (Maugham), **VI:** 368

Smith, Elder & Co. (publishers), **V:** 131, 140, 145, 150; see also Smith, George

Smithers, Peter, **III:** 42, 53

Smollett, Tobias, **III: 146–159; V:** xiv, 52

"Snake" (Lawrence), **VII:** 119

"Snap-dragon" (Lawrence), **VII:** 118

"Snayl, The" (Lovelace), **II:** 231

Snobs of England, The (Thackeray), see *Book of Snobs, The*

Snodgrass, Chris, **V:** 314

Snooty Baronet (Lewis), **VII:** 77

Snow, C. P., **VI:** 235; **VII:** xii, xxi, 235, **321–341**

"Snow" (MacNeice), **VII:** 412

social commentary, **VI:** 227, 240–243, 250–251, 257, 269, 273–274; **VII:** 76, 277

Social Democratic Federation, **VI:** 168

social history, **VI:** 390–391, 393

Socialism, **VI:** viii, 241 **VII:** 89, 210, 274

Socialism and the Family (Wells), **VI:** 244

Socialism: Its Growth and Outcome (Morris and Box), **V:** 306

"Socialism: Principles and Outlook" (Shaw), **VI:** 129

socialist pacifism, **VI:** 241

"Social Life in Roman Britain" (Trevelyan), **VI:** 393

social realism, see realism

Social Rights and Duties (Stephen), **V:** 289

social satire, **VII:** 37

Society for Pure English, **VI:** 76

Society for Pure English Tracts, **VI:** 83

"Sociological Cure for Shellshock, A" (Hibberd), **VI:** 460

"So crewell prison howe could betyde, alas" (Surrey), **I:** 113

Soft Side, The (James), **VI:** 67

"Sohrab and Rustum" (Arnold), **V:** xxi, 208, 209, 210, 216

"Soldier, The" (Brooke), **VI:** 420, 421

"Soldier, The" (Hopkins), **V:** 372

Soldier and a Scholar, A (Swift), **III:** 36

Soldier of Humour (ed. Rosenthal), **VII:** 73

Soldier's Art, The (Powell), **VII:** 349

"Soldiers Bathing" (Prince), **VII:** xxii, 427

"Soldiers of the Queen" (Kipling), **VI:** 417

Soldiers Three (Kipling), **VI:** 204

"Solid Objects" (Woolf), **VII:** 31

"Soliloquy of the Spanish Cloister" (Browning), **IV:** 356, 360, 367

Soliman and Perseda, **I:** 220

"Solitary Reaper, The" (Wordsworth), **IV:** 22

"Solitude" (Carroll), **V:** 263

"Solitude" (Traherne), **II:** 192

Solomon, Simeon, **V:** 312, 314, 320

Solomon's Temple Spiritualized (Bunyan), **II:** 253

Solon, **II:** 70

Solstices (MacNeice), **VII:** 416

"Solution, The" (James), **VI:** 69

Some Advice . . . to the Members of the October Club (Swift), **III:** 35

Some Arguments Against Enlarging the Power of the Bishop (Swift), **III:** 35

Some Do Not (Ford), **VI:** 319

Some Early Impressions (Stephen), **V:** 278, 281, 290

Some Free Thoughts upon the Present State of Affairs (Swift), **III:** 27, 36

Some Gospel-Truths Opened According to the Scriptures (Bunyan), **II:** 253

Some Observations upon a Paper (Swift), **III:** 35

Some Papers Proper to Be Read Before the Royal Society (Fielding), **III:** 105

Some Passages in the Life of Major Gahagan (Thackeray), see *Tremendous Adventures of Major Gahagan, The*

Some Popular Fallacies About Vivisection (Carroll), **V:** 273

Some Reasons Against the . . . Tyth of Hemp . . . (Swift), **III:** 36

Some Reasons to Prove That No Person Is Obliged . . . as a Whig, etc. (Swift), **III:** 35

Some Remarks on the Barrier Treaty (Swift), **III:** 35

Some Remarks upon a Pamphlet (Swift), **III:** 35

Some Reminiscences (Conrad), **VI:** 148

Somerset Maugham (Brander), **VI:** 379

Somerset Maugham (Curtis), **VI:** 379

Somervell, Robert, **VI:** 385

Something Childish, and Other Stories (Mansfield), **VII:** 171

"Something Else" (Priestley), **VII:** 212–213

"Sometime I fled the fire that me brent" (Wyatt), **I:** 103–104

Somnium Scipionis (Cicero), **IV:** 189

"Sonatas in Silence" (Owen), **VI:** 449, 451, 454

"Song" (Blake), **III:** 290

"Song" (Collins), **III:** 170

"Song" (two poems, Congreve), **II:** 347–348

"Song" (Goldsmith), **III:** 184–185

"Song" (Lewis), **VII:** 446

"Song" (Tennyson), **IV:** 329

"Song, A" (Rochester), **II:** 258

Songes and Sonnettes . . . (pub. Tottel), see *Tottel's Miscellany*

Song for St. Cecelia's Day, A (Dryden), **II:** 304

"Song for Simeon, A" (Eliot), **VII:** 152

"Song from Cymbeline, A" (Collins), **III:** 163, 169–170

"Song in Storm, A" (Kipling), **VI:** 201

"Song in the Songless" (Meredith), **V:** 223

Song of Hylas (Morris), **VII:** 164

Song of Italy, A (Swinburne), **V:** 313, 332

Song of Liberty, A (Blake), **III:** 307

Song of Los, The (Blake), **III:** 307

"Song of Poplars" (Huxley), **VII:** 199

"Song of Rahero, The" (Stevenson), **V:** 396

Song of Roland, **I:** 69

"Song of the Bower" (Rossetti), **V:** 243

Song of the Cold, The (Sitwell), **VII:** 132, 136, 137

"Song of the Militant Romance, The" (Lewis), **VII:** 79

"Song of the Shirt, The" (Hood), **IV:** 252, 261, 263–264

Songs, The (Burns), **III:** 322

Songs and Sonnets (Donne), **I:** 357, 358, 360, 368

Songs Before Sunrise (Swinburne), **V:** xxiii, 313, 314, 324–325, 331, 332

"Songs for Strangers and Pilgrims" (Rossetti), **V:** 251, 254*n*, 260

"Songs in a Cornfield" (Rossetti), **V:** 258

Songs of Chaos (Read), **VI:** 436

Songs of Experience (Blake), **III:** 292, 293, 294, 297

Songs of Innocence (Blake), **III:** 292, 297, 307

Songs of Innocence and of Experience (Blake), **III:** 290, 299, 307; **V:** xv, 330

Songs of the Springtides (Swinburne), **V:** 332

Songs of Travel (Stevenson), **V:** 385, 396

Songs of Two Nations (Swinburne), **V:** 332

Songs Wing to Wing (Thompson), see *Sister Songs*

"Song Written at Sea . . ." (Dorset), **II:** 261–262, 270

"Sonnet, 1940" (Ewart), **VII:** 423

"Sonnet on the Death of Richard West" (Gray), **III:** 137

sonnets (Bridges), **VI:** 81

sonnets (Shakespeare), **I:** 307–308

"Sonnets from the Portuguese" (Browning), **IV:** xxi, 311, 314, 320, 321

Sonnets of William Wordsworth, The, **IV:** 25

Sonnets to Fanny Kelly (Lamb), **IV:** 81, 83

"Sonnet to Henry Lawes" (Milton), **II:** 175

"Sonnet to Liberty" (Wilde), **V:** 401

"Sonnet to Mr. Cyriack Skinner Upon His Blindness" (Milton), **II:** 164

"Sonnet to my Friend with an identity disc" (Owen), **VI:** 449

Son of Frankenstein (film), **III:** 342

Sons and Lovers (Lawrence), **VII:** 88, 89, 91, 92, **95–98**

"Son's Veto, The" (Hardy), **VI:** 22

"So On He Fares" (Moore), **VI:** 93

Sophonisba (Marston), see *Wonder of Women, The*

Sordello (Browning), **IV:** xix, 355, 371, 373

Sorel, Georges, **VI:** 170

Sorley, Charles Hamilton, **VI:** xvi, 415, 417, 420, **421–422**

Sorrows of Young Werther, The (Goethe), **IV:** xiv, 59

"Sospetto d'Herode" (Crashaw), **II:** 180, 183–184

"So sweet love seemed that April morn" (Bridges), **VI:** 77

Sotheby, William, **IV:** 50

Soul of Man Under Socialism, The (Wilde), **V:** 409, 413, 415, 419

"Soul's Beauty" (Rossetti), **V:** 237

"Soul's Expression, The" (Browning), **IV:** 313

"Soul's Travelling, The" (Browning), **IV:** 313

South Africa (Trollope), **V:** 102

Southam, Brian Charles, **IV:** xi, xiii, xxv, 122, 124, 337

Southern, Thomas, **II:** 305

"Southern Night, A" (Arnold), **V:** 210

Southey, Cuthbert, **IV:** 62, 72

Southey, Robert, **III:** 276, 335; **IV:** viii–ix, xiv, xvii, 43, 45, 52, **58–72**, 85, 88, 89, 92, 102, 128, 129, 162, 168, 184–187, 270, 276, 280; **V:** xx, 105, 121

"Southey and Landor" (Landor), **IV:** 93

"Southey and Porson" (Landor), **IV:** 93, 97

"Southey's *Colloquies*" (Macaulay), **IV:** 280

Southey's Common-place Book (ed. Warter), **IV:** 71

"South-Sea House, The" (Lamb), **IV:** 81–82

South Seas, The (Stevenson), **V:** 396

"South-Wester, The" (Meredith), **V:** 223

South Wind (Douglas), **VI:** 293, 294, 300–302, 304, 305; **VII:** 200

Space Vampires (Wilson), **III:** 341

"Spain 1937" (Auden), **VII:** 384

Spanish Civil War, **VII:** xix, 280–281

Spanish Curate, The (Fletcher and Massinger), **II:** 66

Spanish Fryar, The: Or, the Double Discovery (Dryden), **II:** 305

Spanish Gipsy, The (Middleton and Rowley), **II:** 100

Spanish Gypsy, The (Eliot), **V:** 198, 200

"Spanish Military Nun, The" (De Quincey), **IV:** 149

Spanish Tragedy, The (Kyd), **I:** 212, 213, 218, 220, **221–229; II:** 25, 28–29, 69

Sparrow, John, **VI:** xv, xxxiv; **VII:** 355, 363

Spasmodie School, **IV:** 313

Speak, Parrot (Skelton), **I:** 83, 90–91

Speaker (periodical), **VI:** 87, 335

Speaking Likenesses (Rossetti), **V:** 260

"Speak to Me" (Tennyson), **IV:** 332

"Special Type, The" (James), **VI:** 69

"Specimen of an Induction to a Poem" (Keats), **IV:** 214

Specimens of English Dramatic Poets (Lamb), **IV:** xvi, 79, 85

Specimens of German Romance (Carlyle), **IV:** 250

Specimens of Modern Poets: The Heptalogia . . . (Swinburne), **V:** 332

Speckled Bird, The (Yeats), **VI:** 222

Spectator (periodical), **III:** 39, 41, 44, **46–50**, 52, 53; **V:** 86, 238; **VI:** 87

"Spectre of the Real, The" (Hardy), **VI:** 20

Speculum hominis (Gower), **I:** 48

Speculum meditantis (Gower), **I:** 48

Speculum Principis (Skelton), **I:** 84

Spedding, James, **I:** 257$_n$, 259, 264, 324

Speech Against Prelates Innovations (Waller), **II:** 238

Speech . . . Against Warren Hastings (Sheridan), **III:** 270

Speeches on Parliamentary Reform (Disraeli), **IV:** 308

Speeches on the Conservative Policy of the Last Thirty Years (Disraeli), **IV:** 308

Speeches, Parliamentary and Miscellaneous (Macaulay), **IV:** 291

Speech . . . for the Better Security of the Independence of Parliament (Burke), **III:** 205

Speech, 4 July 1643 (Waller), **II:** 238

Speech . . . in Bristol upon . . . His Parliamentary Conduct, A (Burke), **III:** 205

Speech on American Taxation (Burke), **III:** 205

Speech . . . on Mr. Fox's East India Bill (Burke), **III:** 205

Speech on Moving His Resolutions for Conciliation with the Colonies (Burke), **III:** 205

Speech on Parliamentary Reform (Macaulay), **IV:** 274

Speech on the Anatomy Bill (Macaulay), **IV:** 277

Speech on the Army Estimates (Burke), **III:** 205

Speech on the Edinburgh Election (Macaulay), **IV:** 274

Speech on the People's Charter (Macaulay), **IV:** 274

Speech on the Ten Hours Bill (Macaulay), **IV:** 276–277

Speech Relative to the Nabob of Arcot's Debts (Burke), **III:** 205

Speech to the Electors of Bristol (Burke), **III:** 205

Speedy Post, A (Webster), **II:** 69, 85

Spell, The: An Extravaganza (Brontë), **V:** 151

"Spelt from Sybil's Leaves" (Hopkins), **V:** 372–373

Spence, Joseph, **II:** 261; **III:** 69, 86$_n$

Spencer, Herbert, **V:** 182, 189, 284

Spender, Stephen, **VII:** 153, 382, 410

Spenser, Edmund, **I: 121–144,** 146; **II:** 50, 302; **III:** 167$_n$; **IV:** 59, 61, 93, 205; **V:** 318

Spenserian stanza, **I:** 133–134

"Sphinx, The" (Rossetti), **V:** 241

Sphinx, The (Wilde), **V:** 409–410, 415, 419

"Sphinx, or Science" (Bacon), **I:** 267

Spielmann, M. H., **V:** 137, 152

Spiess, Johann, **III:** 344

Spingarn, J. E., **II:** 256$_n$

"Spinster Sweet-Arts, The" (Tennyson), **IV:** 327

Spirit of Man, The (ed. Bridges), **II:** 160; **VI:** 76, 83

Spirit of the Age, The (Hazlitt), **III:** 276; **IV:** xi, 39, 129, 131, 132–134, 137, 139

Spirit of Whiggism, The (Disraeli), **IV:** 308

Spiritual Exercises (Loyola), **V:** 362, 367, 371, 373$_n$

"Spite of thy hap hap hath well happed" (Wyatt), **I:** 103

Spitzer, L., **IV:** 323$_n$, 339

Spivack, Bernard, **I:** 214

Spoils of Poynton, The (James), **VI: 49–50**

Spottiswoode, John, **II:** 142

Sprat, Thomas, **II:** 195, 196, 198, 200, 202, 294; **III:** 29

Spreading the News (Gregory), **VI:** 309, 315, 316

"Sprig of Lime, The" (Nichols), **VI:** 419

"Spring" (Hopkins), **V:** 368

"Spring, The" (Carew), **II:** 225

"Spring, The" (Cowley), **II:** 197

"Spring and Fall" (Hopkins), **V:** 371–372, 381

Spring Days (Moore), **VI:** 87, 91

"Spring 1942" (Fuller), **VII:** 429

"Spring Offensive" (Owen), **VI:** 455, 456, 458

sprung rhythm, **V:** 363, 365, 367, 374, 376, 379, 380

spy novels, see espionage stories

Squire, J. C., **VII:** xvi

"Squire Petrick's Lady" (Hardy), **VI:** 22

Squire's Tale, The (Chaucer), **I:** 23, 24

Squire Trelooby (Congreve, Vanbrugh, Walsh) **II:** 325, 336, 339, 347, 350

"Staff and Scrip, The" (Rossetti), **V:** 240

Staffordshire Sentinel (periodical), **VI:** 248

Stage Coach, The, **II:** 353, 358, 364

Stalky & Co. (Kipling), **VI:** 204

Stallworthy, Jon, **VI:** 220, 438

Stallybrass, Oliver, **VI:** 397

Stanley, Arthur, **V:** 13, 349

Stans puer ad mensam (Lydgate), **I:** 58

"Stanzas" (Hood), **IV:** 263

"Stanzas from the Grande Chartreuse" (Arnold), **V:** 210

"Stanzas in Memory of the Author of 'Oberman'" (Arnold), **V:** 206

"Stanzas Written in Dejection" (Shelley), **IV:** 201

Star (periodical), **VI:** 103

"Stare's Nest by My Window, The" (Yeats), **VI:** 212

"Starlight Night, The" (Hopkins), **V:** 366–367

"Stars" (Brontë), **V:** 133, 142

Star Turns Red, The (O'Casey), **VII:** 7–8

State of France, The, . . . in the IXth Year of . . . , Lewis XIII (Evelyn), **II:** 287

State of Innocence, The (Dryden), **II:** 290, 294, 305

Statesman's Manual, The (Coleridge), **IV:** 56

"Statue and the Bust, The" (Browning), **IV:** 366

"Statue in Stocks-Market, The" (Marvell), **II:** 218

"Statues, The" (Yeats), **VI:** 215

S. T. Coleridge (ed. Brett), **IV:** 57

"Steam Washing Co., The" (Hood), **IV:** 267

Steele, Richard, **II:** 359; **III:** 7, 18, 19, **38–53**

Steel Glass, The (Gascoigne), **I:** 149

Steevens, George, **I:** 326

Steevens, G. W., **VI:** 351

Steffan, Truman Guy, **IV:** 179, 193

Stein, Gertrude, **VI:** 252; **VII:** 83

"Stella at Wood-Park" (Swift), **III:** 32

"Stella's Birthday . . . A.D. 1720–21" (Swift), **III:** 32

"Stella's Birthday, March 13, 1727" (Swift), **III:** 32

Stella's Birth-Days: A Poem (Swift), **III:** 36

"Stella's Birth Day, 1725" (Swift), **III:** 32

Step by Step (Churchill), **VI:** 356

Stephen, Janus K., **IV:** 10–11, 268

Stephen, Leslie, **II:** 156, 157; **III:** 42; **IV:** 301, 304, 306; **V:** xix, xxv, xxvi, **227–290**, 386; **VII:** xxii, 17, 238

Stephen Hero (Joyce), **VII:** 45–46, 48

Stephens, Frederick, **V:** 235, 236

Stephens, James, **VI:** 88

Steps to the Temple. Sacred Poems, with Other Delights of the Muses (Crashaw), **II:** 179, 180, 184, 201

Sterling, John, **IV:** 54

Stern, Gladys Bronwen, **IV:** 123; **V:** xiii, xxviii, 395

Sterne, J. B., **I:** 291

Sterne, Laurence, **III:** **124–135,** 150, 153, 155, 157; **IV:** 79, 183; **VII:** 20

Steuart, J. A., **V:** 392, 397

Stevens, Wallace, **V:** 412

Stevenson, L., **V:** 230, 234

Stevenson, Robert Louis, **I:** 1; **II:** 153; **III:** 330, 334, 345; **V:** xiii, xxi, xxv, xxvi, 219, 233, **383–398**

Stevenson and Edinburgh: A Centenary Study (MacLaren), **V:** 393, 398

Stevenson Companion, The (ed. Hampden), **V:** 393, 395

Stevensoniana (ed. Hammerton), **V:** 393, 397

Stewart, J.I.M., **I:** 329; **IV:** xxv; **VII:** xiv, xxxviii

"Still Falls the Rain" (Sitwell), **VII:** xvii, 135, 137

Stirling, William Alexander, earl of, see Alexander, William

"Stoic, A" (Galsworthy), **VI:** 275, 284

Stoker, Bram, **III:** 334, 342, 343, 344, 345

Stokes, John, **V:** xiii, xxviii

Stolen Bacillus, The (Wells), **VI:** 226

Stolen Bacillus, The, and Other Incidents (Wells), **VI:** 243

Stone, C., **III:** 161_n

Stones of Venice, The (Ruskin), **V:** xxi, 173, 176–177, 180, 184, 292

Storey, Graham, **V:** xi, xxviii, 381

Stories from "Black and White" (Hardy), **VI:** 20

Stories of Red Hanrahan (Yeats), **VI:** 222

"Storm" (Owen), **VI:** 449

"Storm is over, the land hushes to rest, The" (Bridges), **VI:** 79

Storm, The: or, A Collection of . . . Casualties and Disasters . . . (Defoe), **III:** 13

"Story in It, The" (James), **VI:** 69

"Story of a Masterpiece, The" (James), **VI:** 69

"Story of a Panic, The" (Forster), **VI:** 399

"Story of a Year, The" (James), **VI:** 69

Story of Fabian Socialism, The (Cole), **VI:** 131

Story of Grettir the Strong, The (Morris and Magnusson), **V:** 306

Story of Rimini, The (Hunt), **IV:** 214

Story of San Michele, The (Munthe), **VI:** 265

Story of Sigurd the Volsung and the Fall of the Niblungs, The (Morris), **V:** xxiv, 299–300, 304, 306

Story of the Glittering Plain, The (Morris), **V:** 306

Story of the Injured Lady, The (Swift), **III:** 27

Story of the Malakand Field Force (Churchill), **VI:** 351

Story of the Sundering Flood, The (Morris), **V:** 306

"Story of the Three Bears, The" (Southey), **IV:** 58, 67

"Story of the Unknown Church, The" (Morris), **V:** 293, 303

Story of the Volsungs and . . . Songs from the Elder Edda, The (Morris and Magnusson), **V:** 299, 306

Story-Teller's Holiday, A (Moore), **VI:** 88, 95, 99

Stowe, Harriet Beecher, **V:** xxi, 3

Strachey, J. St. Loe, **V:** 75, 86, 87

Strachey, Lytton, **III:** 21, 28; **IV:** 292; **V:** 13, 157, 170, 277; **VI:** 155, 247, 372, 407; **VII:** 34, 35

Strado, Famiano, **II:** 90

Strafford: An Historical Tragedy (Browning), **IV:** 373

Strait Gate, The . . . (Bunyan), **II:** 253

Strange Case of Dr. Jekyll and Mr. Hyde, The (Stevenson), **III:** 330, 342, 345; **V:** xxv, 383, 387, 388, 395; **VI:** 106

"Strange Meeting" (Owen), **VI:** 444, 445, 449, 454, 457–458

Stranger, The (Kotzebue), **III:** 268

"Strange Ride of Morrowbie Jukes, The" (Kipling), **VI: 175–178**

Strange Ride of Rudyard Kipling, The (Wilson), **VI:** 165

Strangers and Brothers cycle (Snow), **VII:** xxi, 322, **324–336**

"Stratton Water" (Rossetti), **V:** 239

Strayed Reveller, The (Arnold), **V:** xxi, 209, 216

stream of consciousness, **VII:** 19–20, 74, 225–226; see also interior monologue

Street Songs (Sitwell), **VII:** 135

"Strephon and Chloe" (Swift), **III:** 32

Strickland, Agnes, **I:** 84

Strictures on "Coningsby" (Disraeli), **IV:** 308

"Strictures on Pictures" (Thackeray), **V:** 37

Strife (Galsworthy), **VI:** xiii, 269, 285–286

Strike at Arlingford, The (Moore), **VI:** 95

Stringham, Charles, **IV:** 372

Strings Are False, The (MacNeice), **VII:** 406

Strode, Ralph, **I:** 49

Strong, Roy, **I:** 237

structuralism, **VII:** 249

Structure in Four Novels by H. G. Wells (Newell), **VI:** 245, 246

Struggles of Brown, Jones and Robinson, The (Trollope), **V:** 102

Strutt, Joseph, **IV:** 31

Struwwelpeter (Hoffman), **I:** 25

Stuart, D. M., **V:** 247, 256, 260

"Stubb's Calendar" (Thackeray), see "Fatal Boots, The"

Studies in Classic American Literature (Lawrence), **VII:** 90

Studies in Prose and Poetry (Swinburne), **II:** 102; **V:** 333

Studies in Song (Swinburne), **V:** 332

Studies in the History of the Renaissance (Pater), **V:** xxiv, 286–287, 323, 338–339, **341–348,** 351, 355–356, 400, 411

Studies in the Prose Style of Joseph Addison (Lannering), **III:** 52

Studies of a Biographer (Stephen), **V:** 280, 285, 287, 289

Study of Ben Jonson, A (Swinburne), **V:** 332

Study of Shakespeare, A (Swinburne), **V:** 328, 332

"Study of Thomas Hardy" (Lawrence), **VI:** 20

Study of Victor Hugo, A (Swinburne), **V:** 332

"Style" (Pater), **V:** 339, 347, 353–355

Substance of the Speeches for the Retrenchment of Public Expenses (Burke), **III:** 205

Substance of the Speech . . . in Answer to . . . the Report of the Committee of Managers (Burke), **III:** 205

"Such nights as these in England . . ." (Swinburne), **V:** 310

Such Stuff as Dreams Are Made On (tr. FitzGerald), **IV:** 349, 353

Such, Such Were the Joys (Orwell), **VII:** 275, 282

Such Was My Singing (Nichols), **VI:** 419

Suckling, Sir John, **I:** 337; **II:** 222, 223, **226–229**

"Sudden Light" (Rossetti), **V:** 241, 242

Sue, Eugène, **VI:** 228

"Suicide Club, The" (Stevenson), **V:** 395

Sultry Month, A: Scenes of London Literary Life in 1846 (Hayter), **IV:** 322

Summer Day's Dream (Priestley), **VII:** 229

"Summerhouse on the Mound, The" (Bridges), **VI:** 74

Summer Islands (Douglas), **VI:** 295, 305

Summers, M., **III:** 345

Summing Up, The (Maugham), **VI:** 364, 374

Summoned by Bells (Betjeman), **VII:** 355, 356, 361, 373–374

"Sundew, The" (Swinburne), **V:** 315, 332

"Sunlight on the Garden" (MacNeice), **VII:** 413

"Sunne Rising, The" (Donne), **II:** 127

"Sunrise, A" (Owen), **VI:** 449

Sun's Darling, The (Dekker and Ford), **II:** 89, 100

Sunset and Evening Star (O'Casey), **VII:** 13

"Sunset on Mount Blanc" (Stephen), **V:** 282

"Sunsets" (Aldington), **VI:** 416

"Superannuated Man, The" (Lamb), **IV:** 83

"Super Flumina Babylonis" (Swinburne), **V:** 325

supernatural, **VI:** 193–196, 207, 214

Supernatural Horror in Literature (Lovecraft), **III:** 340

Supernatural Omnibus, The (Summers), **III:** 345

"Superstition" (Bacon), **III:** 39

"Superstitious Man's Story, The" (Hardy), **VI:** 22

"Supports, The" (Kipling), **VI:** 189

"Supposed Confessions of a Second-rate Sensitive Mind in Dejection" (Owen), **VI:** 445

Supposes (Gascoigne), **I:** 298, 303

Surgeon's Daughter, The (Scott), **IV:** 34–35, 39

Surrey, Henry Howard, earl of, **I:** 97, 98, **113–120**

Survey of Experimental Philosophy, A (Goldsmith), **III:** 189, 191

Survey of Modernist Poetry, A (Graves), **VII:** 260

"Surview" (Hardy), **VI:** 13

"Survivors" (Ross), **VII:** 433

Suspense (Conrad), **VI:** 147

"Suspiria de Profundis" (De Quincey), **IV:** 148, 153, 154

"Swallow, The" (Cowley), **II:** 198

Swan Song (Galsworthy), **VI:** 275

Swearer's Bank, The (Swift), **III:** 35

Swedenborg, Emanuel, **III:** 292, 297

Sweeney Agonistes (Eliot), **VII:** 157–158

"Sweeney Among the Nightingales" (Eliot), **VII:** xiii, 145

"Sweeney Erect" (Eliot), **VII:** 145

Sweeney poems (Eliot), **VII:** 145–146; see also "Sweeney Among the Nightingales," "Sweeney Erect"

"Sweetheart of M. Brisieux, The" (James), **VI:** 69

"Sweet William's Farewell to Black-ey'd Susan" (Gay), **III:** 58

Swift, Jonathan, **II:** 240, 259, 261, 269, 273, 335; **III:** **15–37**, 39, 44, 53, 55, 76; **IV:** 160, 257, 258; **VII:** 127

"Swift has sailed into his rest" (Yeats), **III:** 21

Swinburne, Algernon Charles, **II:** 102; **III:** 174; **IV:** 90, 337, 346, 370; **V:** xi, xii, 236, 284, 286, 298–299, **309–335**, 346, 355, 365, 401

Swinburne: The Portrait of a Poet (Henderson), **V:** 335

"Swing of the Pendulum, The" (Mansfield), **VII:** 172

Swinnerton, Frank, **VI:** 247, 268; **VII:** 223

Sword of Honour trilogy (Waugh), **VII:** xx–xxi, 303–306; see also *Men at Arms, Officers and Gentlemen, Unconditional Surrender*

Sybil (Disraeli), **IV:** xii, xx, 296, 300, 301–302, 305, 307, 308; **V:** viii, x, 2, 4

Sykes Davies, Hugh, **IV:** xii, xxv; **V:** x, xxviii, 103

Sylva (Cowley), **II:** 202

Sylvae (ed. Dryden), **II:** 301, 304

Sylva, or A Discourse of Forest-Trees (Evelyn), **II:** 275, 287

Sylva sylvarum (Bacon), **I:** 259, 263, 273

Sylvia's Lovers (Gaskell), **V:** 1, 4, 6, 7–8, 12, 15

Sylvie and Bruno (Carroll), **V:** 270–271, 273

Sylvie and Bruno Concluded (Carroll), **V:** 271, 273

Symbolic Logic (Carroll), **V:** 271, 274

symbolism, **IV:** 46, 53; **VI:** viii–ix, 208, 215; **VII:** xii, xiv, 128

Symbolist Movement in Literature, The (Symons), **VI:** ix

symbolist poetry, **VI:** 215; **VII:** 128

Symonds, John Addington, **V:** 83

Symons, Arthur, **VI:** ix

Synge, John Millington, **II:** 258; **VI:** xiv, **307–314**, 317; **VII:** 3, 42

Synge and Anglo-Irish Drama (Price), **VI:** 317

Synge and the Ireland of His Time (Yeats), **VI:** 222, 317

Syrie Maugham (Fisher), **VI:** 379

Systema medicinae hermeticae generale (Nollius), **II:** 201

System of Logic (Mill), **V:** 279

System of Magick, A: or, A History of the Black Art (Defoe), **III:** 14

Syzygies and Lanrick (Carroll), **V:** 273–274

T

Table Book (Hone), **IV:** 255

Tables Turned, The (Morris), **V:** 306

"Tables Turned, The" (Wordsworth), **IV:** 7, 225

Table Talk (Hazlitt), **IV:** xviii, 131, 137, 139

Table Talk, and Other Poems (Cowper), **III:** 220

Taken Care of (Sitwell), **VII:** 128, 132

Talbert, E. W., **I:** 224

"Tale, The" (Conrad), **VI:** 148

Tale of a Town, The (Martyn), **VI:** 95

"Tale of a Trumpet, A" (Hood), **IV:** 258

Tale of a Tub, A (Swift), **II:** 259, 269; **III:** 17, 19, **21–23,** 35

Tale of Balen, The (Swinburne), **V:** 333

Tale of Beowulf, Done out of the Old English Tongue, The (Morris, Wyatt), **V:** 306

Tale of King Arthur, The (Malory), **I:** 68

Tale of Paraguay, A (Southey), **IV:** 66–67, 68, 71

Tale of Rosamund Gray and Old Blind Margaret, A (Lamb), **IV:** 79, 85

Tale of Sir Gareth of Orkeney that was called Bewmaynes, The (Malory), **I:** 72, 73

Tale of Sir Thopas, The (Chaucer), **I:** 67, 71

Tale of the House of the Wolflings, A (Morris), **V:** 302, 306

Tale of the Noble King Arthur that was Emperor himself through Dignity of his Hands (Malory), **I:** 69, 72, 77–79

Tale of the Sankgreal, The (Malory), **I:** 69

Tale of the Sea, A (Conrad), **VI:** 148

Tale of Two Cities, A (Dickens), **V:** xxii, 41, 42, 57, 63, 66, 72

Tales (Crabbe), **III:** 278, 285, 286; see also *Tales in Verse; Tales of the Hall; Posthumous Tales*

"Tales" (Dickens), **V:** 46

Tales and Sketches (Disraeli), **IV:** 308

Tales from Angria (Brontë), **V:** 151

Tales from Shakespeare (Lamb and Lamb), **IV:** xvi, 80, 85

Tales in Verse (Crabbe), **III:** 275, 278, 279, 281, 286

Tales of a Grandfather (Scott), **IV:** 38

Tales of All Countries (Trollope), **V:** 101

Tales of Good and Evil (Gogol), **III:** 345

Tales of Hearsay (Conrad), **VI:** 148

Tales of Hoffmann (Hoffmann), **III:** 334, 345

Tales of Mean Streets (Morrison), **VI:** 365

Tales of My Landlord (Scott), **IV:** 39

Tales of Sir Gareth (Malory), **I:** 68

Tales of the Crusaders (Scott), **IV:** 39

Tales of the Five Towns (Bennett), **VI:** 253

Tales of the Hall (Crabbe), **III:** 278, 285, 286; **V:** xvii, 6

"Tales of the Islanders" (Brontë), **V:** 107, 114, 135

Tales of Three Cities (James), **VI:** 67

Tales of Unrest (Conrad), **VI:** 148

Talfourd, Field, **IV:** 311

Talisman, The (Scott), **IV:** 39

Talking of Jane Austen (Kaye-Smith and Stern), **IV:** 123

Tamburlaine the Great (Marlowe), **I:** 212, 243, 276, 278, 279–280, **281–282; II:** 69, 305

Tamburlaine, Part 2 (Marlowe), **I:** 281–282, 283

Taming of the Shrew, The (Shakespeare), **I:** 298, 302–303, 327; **II:** 68

"Tam o' Shanter" (Burns), **III:** 320

Tancred (Disraeli), **IV:** 294, 297, 300, 302–303, 307, 308

Tancred and Gismund (Wilmot), **I:** 216

Tangier Papers of Samuel Pepys, The (ed. Chappell), **II:** 288

Tangled Tale, A (Carroll), **V:** 273

Tanner, Anthony, **VI:** x, xxxiv

Tanner, J. R., **II:** 288

Tanner, Tony, **VI:** x

Tannhäuser and Other Poems (Clarke), **V:** 318$_n$

"Tapestry Trees" (Morris), **V:** 304–305

"Tardy Spring" (Meredith), **V:** 223

Tarr (Lewis), **VII:** xv, 72

"Tarry delight, so seldom met" (Housman), **VI:** 161

Task, The (Cowper), **III:** 208, **212–217,** 220; **IV:** xv, 184

Tasso, Torquato, **II:** 49; **III:** 171

Tate, Nahum, **I:** 327; **II:** 305

Tatler (periodical), **II:** 339; **III:** 18, 29, 30, 35, 39, **41–45,** 46, 51, 52, 53

Tawney, R. H., **I:** 253

Taxation No Tyranny (Johnson), **III:** 121

Taylor, A.J.P., **IV:** 290, 303

Taylor, A. L., **V:** 270, 272, 274

Taylor, Henry, **IV:** 62$_n$

Taylor, John, **IV:** 231, 233, 253

Taylor, Mary, **V:** 117

Taylor, Thomas, **III:** 291

Taylor, Tom, **V:** 330

Teapots and Quails (Lear), **V:** 87

"Teare, The" (Crashaw), **II:** 183

"Tears" (Thomas), **VI:** 424

"Tears" (Vaughan), **II:** 187

"Tears, Idle Tears" (Hough), **IV:** 323$_n$, 339

"Tears, Idle Tears" (Tennyson), **IV:** 329–330, 334

" 'Tears, Idle Tears' Again" (Spitzer), **IV:** 323$_n$, 339

Tears of Amaryllis for Amyntas, The: A Pastoral. (Congreve), **II:** 350

Tears of Peace, The (Chapman), **I:** 240–241

Tea-Table (periodical), **III:** 50

Tea-Table Miscellany, The (Ramsay), **III:** 312; **IV:** 28–29

" 'Teem' " (Kipling), **VI:** 169, 189

Tellers and Listeners: The Narrative of Imagination (Hardy), **V:** 73

Tellers of Tales (Maugham), **VI:** 372

"Tell me, Dorinda, why so gay" (Dorset), **II:** 262–263

"Tell me not here, it needs not saying" (Housman), **VI:** 160

"Tell me what means that sigh" (Landor), **IV:** 98

"Temper, The" (Herbert), **II:** 125

Tempest, The (Shakespeare), **I:** 323–324; **II:** 55; **III:** 117

Tempest or the Enchanted Island, The (Dryden), **II:** 305

Temple, Sir William, **III:** 16, 19, 23, 40, 190

Temple, The (Herbert), **II:** 119, 121–125, 128, 129, 184

"Temple, The" (Herrick), **II:** 113

Temple Bar (Forster), **VI:** 399

Temple Beau, The (Fielding), **III:** 96, 98, 105

Temple of Fame, The (Pope), **III:** 71, 77

Temple of Glass, The (Lydgate), **I:** 57, 62, 65

Temporary Kings (Powell), **VII:** 352

Tenant of Wildfell Hall, The (Brontë), **V:** xxi, 130, 153

ten Brink, Bernard, **I:** 98

Ten Burnt Offerings (MacNeice), **VII:** 415

"Ten Lines a Day" (Boswell), **III:** 237

Tenniel, John, **V:** 266, 267

Ten Novels and Their Authors (Maugham), **VI:** 363–364

Tennyson, Alfred, Lord, **II:** 200, 208; **IV:** viii, xii–xiii, 196, 240, 292, 310, 313, **323–339,** 341, 344, 351, 352, 371; **V:** ix, 77–79, 85, 182, 285, 299, 311, 327, 330, 365, 401; **VI:** 455–456

Tennyson, Emily, **V:** 81

Tennyson, Frederic, **IV:** 350, 351

Tennyson, Hallam, **IV:** 324, 329, 332, 338

"Tennyson and Picturesque Poetry" (McLuhan), **IV:** 323$_n$, 338, 339

"Tennyson and the Romantic Epic" (McLuhan), **IV:** 323$_n$, 339

Tennyson: Poet and Prophet (Henderson), **IV:** 339

"Ten O'Clock Lecture" (Whistler), **V:** 407; **VI:** 103

Tenure of Kings and Magistrates, The (Milton), **II:** 176

Teresa of Watling Street (Bennett), **VI:** 249

"Tereus" (Gower), **I:** 54

Terminations (James), **VI:** 49, 67

"Terminus" (Emerson), **IV:** 81

"Terra Incognita" (Lawrence), **VII:** 119

Terry, Ellen, **VI:** 104

Terry Hogan, an Eclogue (Landor), **IV:** 100

Teseide (Boccaccio), **I:** 30

Tess of the d'Urbervilles: A Pure Woman Faithfully Presented (Hardy), **VI:** 5, 9, 20

Testament (Lydgate), **I:** 65

Testament of Beauty, The (Bridges), **VI:** 72, 73, 74, 75, 82

Testament of Love, The (Usk), **I:** 2

"Test of Manhood, The" (Meredith), **V:** 222

Tetrachordon: . . . (Milton), **II:** 175

Texts and Pretexts (Huxley), **VII:** 204

T. Fisher Unwin (publisher), **VI:** 373

Thackeray, Anne Isabella, **VI:** 4

Thackeray, William Makepeace, **II:** 363; **III:** 124, 125, 146; **IV:** 240, 251, 254, 257, 266, 272, 301, 306, 340; **V:** ix, **17–39,** 56, 62, 68, 69, 139, 140, 147, 179, 191, 279

Thackeray (Trollope), **V:** 102

Thackeray: Prodigal Genius (Carey), **V:** 39

Thalaba the Destroyer (Southey), **III:** 335; **IV:** 64, 65, 71, 197, 217

"Thalassius" (Swinburne), **V:** 327

Thalia Rediviva (Vaughan), **II:** 185, 201

Thanksgiving Ode, 18 January 1816 (Wordsworth), **IV:** 24

Thanksgivings (Traherne), **II:** 190–191

"That Nature Is a Heraclitean Fire" (Hopkins), **V:** 376, 377

"That Now Is Hay Some-tyme Was Grase" (Lydgate), **I:** 57

Thealma and Clearchus (Chalkhill), **II:** 133

Theatre (periodical), **III:** 50, 53

Theatrical Companion to Maugham (Mander and Mitchenson), **VI:** 379

Theatrum Orbis Terrarum (Ortelius), **I:** 282

Theatrum Poetarum (Phillips), **II:** 347

"Their Finest Hour" (Churchill), **VI:** 358

"Their Lonely Betters" (Auden), **VII:** 387

"Their Very Memory" (Blunden), **VI:** 428

Thelwall, John, **IV:** 103

Themes and Conventions of Elizabethan Tragedy (Bradbrook), **I:** 293; **II:** 78

"Then dawns the Invisible . . ." (Brontë), **V:** 143; see also "Prisoner, The"

Theobald, Lewis, **I:** 324, 326; **II:** 66, 87; **III:** 51

"Theodolinde" (James), **VI:** 69

Theodore (Boyle), **III:** 95

Théophile (Swinburne), **V:** 333

Theophrastus, **II:** 68, 81; **III:** 50

Theory of the Leisure Class, The (Veblen), **VI:** 283

theosophy, **VI:** 249

"There is a hill beside the silver Thames" (Bridges), **VI:** 78

"There Is a House Not Made with Hands" (Watts), **III:** 288

There Is No Natural Religion (Blake), **III:** 292, 307

"There Is Nothing" (Gurney), **VI:** 426–427

"There was an old Derry down Derry" (Lear), **V:** 82

"There Was an Old Man in a Barge" (Lear), **V:** 83

"There Was an Old Man of Blackheath" (Lear), **V:** 86

"There Was an Old Man of Three Bridges" (Lear), **V:** 86

"There was never nothing more me pained" (Wyatt), **I:** 103

"These *Summer-Birds* did with thy Master stay" (Herrick), **II:** 103

These Twain (Bennett), **VI:** 258

Thespian Magazine (periodical), **III:** 263

"They" (Kipling), **VI:** 199

"They" (Sassoon), **VI:** 430

"They Are All Gone into the World of Light!" (Vaughan), **II:** 188

They Came to a City (Priestley), **VII:** 210, 227

"They flee from me" (Wyatt), **I:** 102

They Walk in the City (Priestley), **VII:** 217

They Went (Douglas), **VI:** 303, 304, 305

"Thief" (Graves), **VII:** 267

Thierry and Theodoret (Beaumont, Fletcher, Massinger), **II:** 66

Things That Have Interested Me (Bennett), **VI:** 267

Things That Interested Me (Bennett), **VI:** 267

Things Which Have Interested Me (Bennett), **VI:** 267

"Third Person, The" (James), **VI:** 69

Third Satire (Wyatt), **I:** 111

"This Is No Case of Petty Right or Wrong" (Thomas), **VI:** 424

This Life I've Loved (Field), **V:** 393, 397

"This Lime Tree Bower My Prison" (Coleridge), **IV:** 41, 44

This Misery of Boots (Wells), **VI:** 244

"This was for youth, Strength, Mirth and wit that Time" (Walton), **II:** 141

Thomas, Dylan, **II:** 156

Thomas, Edward, **IV:** 218; **V:** 313, 334, 355, 358; **VI:** 420–421, **423–425; VII:** xvi, 382

Thomas Carlyle (Campbell), **IV:** 250

Thomas Carlyle (Froude), **IV:** 238–239, 250

Thomas De Quincey: A Biography (Eaton), **IV:** 142, 156

Thomas De Quincey: His Life and Writings (Page), **IV:** 152, 155

"Thomas Gray" (Arnold), **III:** 277

Thomas Hardy: A Bibliographical Study (Purdy), **VI:** 19

Thomas Hobbes (Stephen), **V:** 289

Thomas Hood (Reid), **IV:** 267

Thomas Hood and Charles Lamb (ed. Jerrold), **IV:** 252, 253, 267

Thomas Hood: His Life and Times (Jerrold), **IV:** 267

Thomas Love Peacock (Priestley), **IV:** 159–160, 170

Thomas Nabbes (Swinburne), **V:** 333

Thomas Stevenson, Civil Engineer (Stevenson), **V:** 395

Thomas the Rhymer, **IV:** 29, 219

Thomism, **VI:** 341

Thompson, Francis, **III:** 338; **V:** xxii, xxvi, **439–452**

Thompson, R., **II:** 288

Thomson, George, **III:** 322

Thomson, James, **III:** 162, 171, 312

"Thorn, The" (Wordsworth), **IV:** 6, 7

Thornton, R. K. R., **V:** 377, 382

Thornton, Robert, **III:** 307

Thorsler, Jr., P. L., **IV:** 173, 194

Those Barren Leaves (Huxley), **VII:** 79, 199, 202

"Thou art an Atheist, *Quintus,* and a Wit" (Sedley), **II:** 265–266

"Thou art fair and few are fairer" (Shelley), **IV:** 203

"Thou art indeed just, Lord" (Hopkins), **V:** 376, 378

"Thou damn'd Antipodes to Common sense" (Dorset), **II:** 263

"Though, Phillis, your prevailing charms," **II:** 257

"Thought" (Lawrence), **VII:** 119

"Though this the port and I thy servant true" (Wyatt), **I:** 106

Thought Power (Besant), **VI:** 249

Thoughts and Details on Scarcity . . . (Burke), **III:** 205

Thoughts in the Wilderness (Priestley), **VII:** 212

"Thoughts of a Suicide" (Tennyson), see "Two Voices, The"

"Thoughts on Criticism, by a Critic" (Stephen), **V:** 286

Thoughts on the Cause of the Present Discontents (Burke), **III:** 197

Thoughts on the . . . Falkland's Islands (Johnson), **III:** 121

"Thou that know'st for whom I mourne" (Vaughan), **II:** 187

Thrale, Hester, see Piozzi, Hester Lynch

"Thrawn Janet" (Stevenson), **V:** 395

Three Clerks, The (Trollope), **V:** 101

Three Friends (Bridges), **VI:** 72, 83

Three Guineas (Woolf), **VII:** 22, 25, 27, 29, 38

Three Hours After Marriage (Gay), **III:** 60, 67

Three Letters, Written in Spain, to D. Francisco Riguelme (Landor), **IV:** 100

Three Memorials on French Affairs . . . (Burke), **III:** 205

Three Men in New Suits (Priestley), **VII:** 218

Three Northern Love Stories (Morris and Magnusson), **V:** 306

Three of Them (Douglas), **VI:** 300, 305

Three Plays for Puritans (Shaw), **VI:** 104, 112, 129

Three proper, and witty, familiar Letters (Spenser), **I:** 123

Three Sermons (Swift), **III:** 36

"Three Strangers, The" (Hardy), **VI:** 20, 22

Three Sunsets and Other Poems (Carroll), **V:** 274

Three Voices of Poetry, The (Eliot), **VII:** 161, 162

Three Wayfarers, The: A Pastoral Play in One Act (Hardy), **VI:** 20

Three Years in a Curatorship (Carroll), **V:** 274

Threnodia Augustalis (Goldsmith), **III:** 191

Threnodia Augustalis: A Funeral . . . Poem to . . . King Charles II (Dryden), **II:** 304

"Through the Looking Glass" (Auden), **VII:** 381

Through the Looking-Glass and What Alice Found There (Carroll), **V:** xxiii, 261, 262, 264, 265, 267–269, 270–273

"Through These Pale Gold Days" (Rosenberg), **VI:** 435

"Thrush in February, The" (Meredith), **V:** 222

"Thursday, or The Spell" (Gay), **III:** 56

Thus to Revisit (Ford), **VI:** 321, 323

Thyestes (Seneca), **I:** 215; **II:** 71

"Thyrsis" (Arnold), **V:** 157–158, 159, 165, 209, 210, 211; **VI:** 73

Thyrza (Gissing), **V:** 437

Tickell, Thomas, **III:** 50

Ticonderoga (Stevenson), **V:** 395

Tietjens tetralogy (Ford), **VI:** xii, 319, **328–331; VII:** xxi; see also *Some Do Not, No More Parades, A Man Could Stand Up, Last Post*

"Tiger! Tiger!" (Kipling), **VI:** 199

Tillotson, Kathleen, **IV:** 34; **V:** 73

Timbuctoo (Tennyson), **IV:** 338

Time and the Conways (Priestley), **VII:** 212, 224–225

Time and Tide by Weare and Tyne (Ruskin), **V:** 184

Time and Western Man (Lewis), **VII:** 72, 74, 75, 83, 262

Time Flies: A Reading Diary (Rossetti), **V:** 260

Time Machine, The: An Invention (Wells), **VI:** ix, xii, 226, 229–230

Time Must Have a Stop (Huxley), **VII:** 205

Time of Hope (Snow), **VII:** xxi, 321, 324–325

Time of the Angels, The (Murdoch), **III:** 341, 345

"Time of Waiting, A" (Graves), **VII:** 269

Times (periodical), **IV:** xv, 272, 278; **V:** 93, 279

Time's Laughingstocks and other Verses (Hardy), **VI:** 20

"Time the Tiger" (Lewis), **VII:** 74

Time to Go, A (O'Casey), **VII:** 12

Time Traveller, The: The Life of H. G. Wells (MacKenzie and MacKenzie), **VI:** 228, 246

Timon of Athens (Shakespeare), **I:** 318–319, 321; **II:** 70

Tinker, C. B., **III:** 234ₙ, 249, 250

"Tinker, The" (Wordsworth), **IV:** 21

Tinker's Wedding, The (Synge), **VI:** 311, 313–314

"Tintern Abbey" (Wordsworth), see "Lines Composed a Few Miles Above Tintern Abbey"

Tireless Traveller, The (Trollope), **V:** 102

"Tiresias" (Tennyson), **IV:** 328, 332–334, 338

"Tiriel" (Blake), **III:** 298, 302

"Tirocinium: or A Review of Schools" (Cowper), **III:** 208

'Tis Pity She's a Whore (Ford), **II:** 57, 88, 89, 90, 92–93, 99, 100

Tit-Bits (periodical), **VI:** 135, 248

"Tithon" (Tennyson), **IV:** 332–334; see also "Tithonus"

"Tithonus" (Tennyson), **IV:** 328, 333

Title, The (Bennett), **VI:** 250, 264

Title and Pedigree of Henry VI (Lydgate), **I:** 58

Titmarsh, Michael Angelo, pseud. of William Makepeace Thackeray

Titus Andronicus (Shakespeare), **I:** 279, 305; **II:** 69

"To a Black Greyhound" (Grenfell), **VI:** 418

"To a Butterfly" (Wordsworth), **IV:** 21

"To a Cold Beauty" (Hood), **IV:** 255

"To a Comrade in Flanders" (Owen), **VI:** 452

"To a Devout Young Gentlewoman" (Sedley), **II:** 264

"To a *Fine Singer,* who had gotten a *Cold; . . .*" (Wycherley), **II:** 320

"To a fine Young *Woman . . .*" (Wycherley), **II:** 320

"To A. L." (Carew), **II:** 224–225

"To a Lady in a Letter" (Rochester), **II:** 258

To a Lady More Cruel Than Fair (Vanbrugh), **II:** 336

"To a Lady on Her Passion for Old China" (Gay), **III:** 58, 67

"To a Lady on the Death of Colonel Ross . . ." (Collins), **III:** 166, 169

"To a Louse" (Burns), **III:** 315, 317–318

"To Althea from Prison" (Lovelace), **II:** 231, 232

"To Amarantha, That She Would Dishevell Her Haire" (Lovelace), **II:** 230

"To Amoret Gone from Him" (Vaughan), **II:** 185

"To Amoret, of the Difference 'twixt Him, . . ." (Vaughan), **II:** 185

"To a Mountain Daisy" (Burns), **III:** 313, 315, 317, 318

"To a Mouse" (Burns), **III:** 315, 317, 318

"To a Nightingale" (Coleridge), **IV:** 222

"To Anthea" (Herrick), **II:** 105–106, 108

"To Any Dead Officer" (Sassoon), **VI:** 431

"To a Skylark" (Shelley), **III:** 337

"To Autumn" (Keats), **IV:** 221, 226–227, 228, 232

"To a Very Young Lady" (Etherege), **II:** 267

To Be a Pilgrim (Cary), **VII:** 186, 187, 191, 192–194

"To Be Less Philosophical" (Graves), **VII:** 266

"To Blossoms" (Herrick), **II:** 112

"To cause accord or to agree" (Wyatt), **I:** 109

"Toccata of Galuppi's, A" (Browning), **IV:** 357

"To Celia" (Johnson), **IV:** 327

"To Charles Cowden Clarke" (Keats), **IV:** 214, 215

"To Constantia Singing" (Shelley), **IV:** 209

"To Daffodills" (Herrick), **II:** 112

To-Day (periodical), **VI:** 103

"To Deanbourn" (Herrick), **II:** 103

Todhunter, John, **V:** 325

"To Dianeme" (Herrick), **II:** 107, 112

"To Edward Thomas" (Lewis), **VII:** 445

"To E. Fitzgerald" (Tennyson), **IV:** 336

"To Electra" (Herrick), **II:** 105

"To E.L., on his Travels in Greece" (Tennyson), **V:** 79

"To Everlasting Oblivion" (Marston), **II:** 25

"To Fanny" (Keats), **IV:** 220–221

"To George Felton Mathew" (Keats), **IV:** 214

"To Germany" (Sorley), **VI:** 421

Together (Douglas), **VI:** 299–300, 304, 305

"To God" (Gurney), **VI:** 426

"To His Coy Mistress" (Marvell), **II:** 197, 198, 208–209, 211, 214–215

"To His Love" (Gurney), **VI:** 426

"To His Lovely Mistresses" (Herrick), **II:** 113

To His Sacred Majesty, a Panegyrick on His Coronation (Dryden), **II:** 304

"To His Sweet Savior" (Herrick), **II:** 114

"To Julia, the Flaminica Dialis, or Queen-Priest" (Herrick), **II:** 113

To Keep the Ball Rolling (Powell), **VII:** 351

"To King Henry IV, in Praise of Peace" (Gower), **I:** 56

To Let (Galsworthy), **VI:** 272, 274, 275, 282

"To Live Merrily, and to Trust to Good Verses" (Herrick), **II:** 115

To Live with Little (Chapman), **I:** 254

"To Lizbie Browne" (Hardy), **VI:** 16

"To Lord Stanhope" (Coleridge), **IV:** 43

"To Lucasta, Going to the Warres" (Lovelace), **II:** 229

"To Marguerite—Continued" (Arnold), **V:** 211

"To Mary Boyle" (Tennyson), **IV:** 329, 336

Tom Brown's Schooldays (Hughes), **V:** xxii, 157, 170

"To Mr. Dryden" (Congreve), **II:** 338

To Mr. Harriot (Chapman), **I:** 241

"To Mr. Hobs" (Cowley), **II:** 196, 198

To Mistress Anne (Skelton), **I:** 83

Tom Jones (Fielding), **III:** 95, 96–97, 100–102, 105

Tomlin, Eric Walter Frederick, **VII:** xv, xxxviii

"Tomlinson" (Kipling), **VI:** 202

"Tomorrow" (Conrad), **VI:** 148

"Tom's Garland" (Hopkins), **V:** 376

Tom Thumb (Fielding), **III:** 96, 105

"To My Brother George" (Keats), **IV:** 214

"To My Brothers" (Keats), **IV:** 215

"To My Friend, Mr. *Pope*, . . ." (Wycherley), **II:** 322

"To My Inconstant Mistris" (Carew), **II:** 225

To My Lady Morton (Waller), **II:** 238

To My Lord Chancellor . . . (Dryden), **II:** 304

"To My Lord Northumberland Upon the Death of His Lady" (Waller), **II:** 233

To My Mother on the Anniversary of Her Birth, April 27, 1842 (Rossetti), **V:** 260

"To My Sister" (Wordsworth), **IV:** 8

"Tone of Time, The" (James), **VI:** 69

"To Night" (Lovelace), **II:** 231

"To Nobodaddy" (Blake), **III:** 299

Tono-Bungay (Wells), **VI:** xii, 237–238, 244

Tonson, Jacob, **II:** 323; **III:** 69

"Tony Kytes, the Arch-Deceiver" (Hardy), **VI:** 22

"Too Dearly Bought" (Gissing), **V:** 437

Too Good to Be True (Shaw), **VI:** 125, 127, 129

"Too Late" (Browning), **V:** 366, 369

Too Many Husbands (Maugham), **VI:** 368–369

"To One Who Was with Me in the War" (Sassoon), **VI:** 431

"To Perilla" (Herrick), **II:** 113

"To Please His Wife" (Hardy), **VI:** 20, 22

"To R.B." (Hopkins), **V:** 376, 378

"To Rilke" (Lewis), **VII:** 446

Tortoises (Lawrence), **VII:** 118

Tortoises, Terrapins and Turtles (Sowerby and Lear), **V:** 76, 87

"To Saxham" (Carew), **III:** 223

"To seek each where, where man doth live" (Wyatt), **I:** 110

"To seem the stranger lies my lot" (Hopkins), **V:** 374–375

"To Sleep" (Graves), **VII:** 267

"To Sleep" (Keats), **IV:** 221

"To Solitude" (Keats), **IV:** 213–214

"To Stella, Visiting Me in My Sickness" (Swift), **III:** 31

"To Stella, Who Collected and Transcribed His Poems" (Swift), **III:** 31

"To Stella . . . Written on the Day of Her Birth . . ." (Swift), **III:** 32

"To the King" (Waller), **II:** 233

To the King, upon His . . . Happy Return (Waller), **II:** 238

To the Lighthouse (Woolf), **V:** 281; **VI:** 275, 278; **VII:** xv, 18, 21, 26, 27, 28–29, 36, 38

"To the Master of Balliol" (Tennyson), **IV:** 336

To the Memory of Charles Lamb (Wordsworth), **IV:** 86

"To the Muses" (Blake), **III:** 289

"To the Name of Jesus" (Crashaw), **II:** 180

"To the Queen" (Tennyson), **IV:** 337

To the Queen, upon Her . . . Birthday (Waller), **II:** 238

"To the Reader" (Webster), **I:** 246

"To the Reverend Shade of His Religious Father" (Herrick), **II:** 113

"To the Rev. W. H. Brookfield" (Tennyson), **IV:** 329

"To the Royal Society" (Cowley), **II:** 196, 198

"To the Shade of Elliston" (Lamb), **IV:** 82–83

"To the Small Celandine" (Wordsworth), **IV:** 21

"To the Virgins, to Make Much of Time" (Herrick), **II:** 108–109

Tottel's Miscellany, **I:** 97–98, 114

Touch and Go (Lawrence), **VII:** 120, 121

Tourneur, Cyril, **II:** 24, 33, **36–41**, 70, 72, 85, 97

Tour Thro' the Whole Island of Great Britain (Defoe), **III:** 5, 13

Tour to the Hebrides, A (Boswell), see *Journal of a Tour to the Hebrides*

"To Vandyk" (Waller), **II:** 233

"To Virgil" (Tennyson), **IV:** 327

"Towards an Artless Society" (Lewis), **VII:** 76

Tower, The (Yeats), **VI:** 207, 216, 220

"To wet your eye withouten tear" (Wyatt), **I:** 105–106

"To what serves Mortal Beauty?" (Hopkins), **V:** 372, 373

"To William Godwin" (Coleridge), **IV:** 43

Town (periodical), **V:** 22

"Town and Country" (Brooke), **VI:** 420

Townley plays, **I:** 20

Townsend, Aurelian, **II:** 222, 237

Townsend Warner, George, **VI:** 385

Town-Talk (periodical), **III:** 50, 53

Tractarian movement, see Oxford movement

"Tradition and the Individual Talent" (Eliot), **VII:** 155, 156, 163, 164

"Tradition of Eighteen Hundred and Four, A" (Hardy), **VI:** 22

Traffics and Discoveries (Kipling), **VI:** 204

"Tragedy and the Essay, The" (Brontë), **V:** 135

Tragedy of Brennoralt, The (Suckling), **II:** 226

Tragedy of Byron, The (Chapman), **I:** 233, 234, 241$_n$, 251

Tragedy of Count Alarcos, The (Disraeli), **IV:** 306, 308

"Tragedy of Error, A" (James), **VI:** 25

Tragedy of Sir John Van Olden Barnavelt, The (Fletcher and Massinger), **II:** 66

Tragedy of the Duchess of Malfi, The (Webster), see *Duchess of Malfi, The*

Tragedy of Tragedies, The: or, The Life . . . of Tom Thumb (Fielding), see *Tom Thumb*

"Tragedy of Two Ambitions, A" (Hardy), **VI:** 22

Tragical History of Dr. Faustus, The (Marlowe), **III:** 344

Tragic Comedians, The (Meredith), **V:** 228, 234

Tragic History of Romeus and Juliet, The (Brooke), **I:** 305–306

Tragic Muse, The (James), **VI:** 39, **43–45,** 67

"Tragic Theatre, The" (Yeats), **VI:** 218

Traherne, Thomas, **II:** 123, **189–194, 201–203**

Traill, H. D., **III:** 80

Trained for Genius (Goldring), **VI:** 333

Traité du poeme épique (Le Bossu), **III:** 103

"Trampwoman's Tragedy, The" (Hardy), **VI:** 15

transatlantic review (periodical), **VI:** 324

Transatlantic Sketches (James), **VI:** 67

Transformed Metamorphosis, The (Tourneur), **II:** 37, 41

Translations and Tomfooleries (Shaw), **VI:** 129

Traulus (Swift), **III:** 36

Traveller, The (Goldsmith), **III:** 177, 179, 180, 185–186, 191

"Travelling Companions" (James), **VI:** 25, 69

"Travelling Letters" (Dickens), **V:** 71

Travelling Sketches (Trollope), **V:** 101

Travels in Italy (Addison), **III:** 18

Travels Through France and Italy (Smollett), **III:** 147, **153–155,** 158

Travels with a Donkey in the Cevennes (Stevenson), **V:** 389, 395

travel writing, **VI:** 295, 296–297

Treasure Island (Stevenson), **V:** xxv, 383, 385, 386, 394, 395

"Treasure of Franchard, The" (Stevenson), **V:** 395

"Treatise for Laundresses" (Lydgate), **I:** 58

Treatise of Civil Power in Ecclesiastical Causes . . . , The (Milton), **II:** 176

Treatise of Human Nature, A (Hume), **IV:** 138

Treatise of the Fear of God, A (Bunyan), **II:** 253

Treatise of the Soul, A (Ralegh), **I:** 157

Treatise on Method (Coleridge), **IV:** 56

Treatise on the Astrolabe, A (Chaucer), **I:** 31

Trebitsch, Siegfried, **VI:** 115

"Tree of Knowledge, The" (James), **VI:** 69

Trelawny, Edward, **IV:** xiv, 203, 207, 209

Tremaine (Ward), **IV:** 293

Trembling of the Veil, The (Yeats), **VI:** 210

Tremendous Adventures of Major Gahagan, The (Thackeray), **V:** 22, 37

Trespasser, The (Lawrence), **VII:** 89, 91, **93–95**

Trevelyan, G. M., **I:** 375; **V:** xxiv, 223, 227, 234; **VI:** xv, 347, **383–396;** list of works, **VI:** 394–396

Trial, The (Kafka), **III:** 340

Trial of the Honourable Augustus Keppel, The (Burke), **III:** 205

Trick to Catch the Old One, A (Middleton), **II:** 3, 4–5, 21

Trinity College (Trevelyan), **VI:** 383, 393

Triple Thinkers, The (Wilson), **VI:** 164

Trip to Scarborough, A (Sheridan), **II:** 334, 336; **III:** 253, 261, 270

"Tristram and Iseult" (Arnold), **V:** 210

"Tristram and Iseult: Prelude of an Unfinished Poem" (Swinburne), **V:** 332

Tristram Shandy (Sterne), **III:** 124, 126, **127–132,** 135, 150, 153; **IV:** 183

"Triumphal March" (Eliot), **VII:** 152–153

Triumph and Tragedy (Churchill), **VI:** 361

Triumph of Death (Fletcher), **II:** 66

Triumph of Gloriana, The (Swinburne), **V:** 333

Triumph of Honour (Field), **II:** 66

"Triumph of Life, The" (Shelley), **IV:** xi, 197, 206–207, 209

Triumph of Love (Field), **II:** 66

Triumph of Time (Fletcher), **II:** 66

"Triumph of Time, The" (Swinburne), **V:** 311, 313, 318–319, 331

"Triumphs of Odin, The" (Gray), **III:** 142

Triumphs of Truth, The (Middleton), **II:** 3

Triumphs of Wealth and Prosperity, The (Middleton), **II:** 3

Trivia: or, The Art of Walking the Streets of London (Gay), **III:** 55, 57, 67

Troilus and Cressida (Dryden), **II:** 293, 305

Troilus and Cressida (Shakespeare), **I:** 313, 314; **II:** 47, 70; **IV:** 225; **V:** 328

Troilus and Criseyde (Chaucer), **I:** 24, 30, 31, 32–34, 41, 43, 44; **IV:** 189

Trollope, Anthony, **II:** 172–173; **IV:** 306; **V:** x, xvii, xxii–xxv, 11, **89–103**; **VII:** xxi

Trollope, Frances, **V:** 89

Trollope: A Commentary (Sadleir), **V:** 100, 102

"Trollope and His Style" (Sykes Davies), **V:** 103

"Troopship in the Tropics, A" (Lewis), **VII:** 446

Troubled Eden, A, Nature and Society in the Works of George Meredith (Kelvin), **V:** 221, 234

Troublesome Reign of John, King of England, The, **I:** 301

Troy-book (Lydgate), **I:** 57, 58, 59–65, 280

Troy Park (Sitwell), **VII:** 138

"Truce of the Bear, The" (Kipling), **VI:** 203

True-Born Englishman, The (Defoe), **III:** 3, 12

True History (Lucian), **III:** 24

True Patriot, The (Fielding), **III:** 105

True Relation of the Apparition of . . . Mrs. Veal . . . to . . . Mrs. Bargrave . . . (Defoe), **III:** 13

True State of the Case of Bosavern Penlez, A (Fielding), **III:** 105

True Widow, The (Shadwell), **II:** 305

Trumpet-Major, The: A Tale (Hardy), **VI:** 5, 6–7, 20

"Truth" (Bacon), **III:** 39

"Truth" (Cowper), **III:** 212

Truth About an Author (Bennett), **VI:** 264–265

"Truthful Adventure, A" (Mansfield), **VII:** 172

"Truth of Masks, The" (Wilde), see "Shakespeare and Stage Costume"

"Tryst at an Ancient Earthwork, A" (Hardy), **VI:** 22

Trystram of Lyonesse (Swinburne), **V:** 299, 300, 314, 327–328, 332

T. S. Eliot (Bergonzi), **VII:** 169

"T. S. Eliot" (Forster), **VII:** 144

"T. S. Eliot as Critic" (Leavis), **VII:** 233

Tucker, Abraham, pseud. of William Hazlitt

Tudor trilogy (Ford), **VI:** 319, 323, **325–327;** see also *The Fifth Queen, Privy Seal, The Fifth Queen Crowned*

"Tuesday, or The Ditty" (Gay), **III:** 56

Tumble-down Dick (Fielding), **III:** 105

Tunning of Elinour Rumming, The (Skelton), **I:** 82, 86–87, 92

Turkish Mahomet and Hiren the Fair Greek (Peele), **I:** 205

Turkish tales (Byron), **IV:** x, 172, **173–175**

Turner, J. M. W., **V:** xix, xx, 174–175, 178

Turn of the Screw, The (James), **III:** 334, 340, 345; **V:** xxvi, 14; **VI:** 39, **52–53,** 69

Tutchin, John, **III:** 3

Tuve, Rosamund, **II:** 124, 130

"Twa Dogs, The" (Burns), **III:** 315, 316

"Twa Herds, The" (Burns), **III:** 311, 319

Twain, Mark, **IV:** 106; **V:** xix, xxiv–xxv

Twelfth Night (Shakespeare), **I:** 312, 320

Twelve Adventurers and Other Stories (Brontë), **V:** 151

Twelve Months in a Curatorship (Carroll), **V:** 274

"Twelve Songs" (Auden), **VII:** 383, 386

Twenty-five (Gregory), **VI:** 309

"Twenty Pounds" (Gissing), **V:** 437

Twilight in Italy (Lawrence), **VII:** 116

Twine, Laurence, **I:** 321

Twin Rivals, The (Farquhar), **II:** 353, 357–358, 364

'Twixt Land and Sea: Tales (Conrad), **VI:** 148

Two Cheers for Democracy (Forster), **VI:** 397, 411

"Two Countries" (James), **VI:** 69

Two Drovers, The (Scott), **IV:** 39

"Two Early French Stories" (Pater), **V:** 344

"Two Faces, The" (James), **VI:** 69

Two Foscari, The (Byron), **IV:** xviii, 178, 193

"Two Fusiliers" (Graves), **VI:** 452

"Two Gallants" (Joyce), **VII:** 44

Two Generals, The (FitzGerald), **IV:** 353

Two Gentlemen of Verona (Shakespeare), **I:** 302, 311–312

Two Great Questions Consider'd, The (Defoe), **III:** 12

Two Guardians, The (Yonge), **V:** 253

Two Heroines of Plumplington, The (Trollope), **V:** 102

"Two in the Campagna" (Browning), **IV:** 357, 369

"Two Kitchen Songs" (Sitwell), **VII:** 130–131

"Two Knights, The" (Swinburne), **V:** 315, 333

Two Letters on the Conduct of Our Domestic Parties (Burke), **III:** 205

Two Letters on the French Revolution (Burke), **III:** 205

Two Letters . . . on the Proposals for Peace (Burke), **III:** 205

Two Letters . . . to Gentlemen in the City of Bristol . . . (Burke), **III:** 205

Two Magics, The (James), **VI:** 52, 69

Two Noble Kinsmen, The (Shakespeare), **I:** 324, 325; **II:** 43, 66, 87

Two on a Tower: A Romance (Hardy), **VI:** 4, 5, 20

Two or Three Graces (Huxley), **VII:** 201

Two-Part Inventions (Howard), **V:** 418

"Two-Party System in English Political History, The" (Trevelyan), **VI:** 392

Two Paths, The (Ruskin), **V:** 180, 184

"Two Peacocks of Bedfont, The" (Hood), **IV:** 256, 267

"Two Races of Men, The" (Lamb), **IV:** 82

"Two-Sided Man, The" (Kipling), **VI:** 201

"Two Spirits, The" (Shelley), **IV:** 196

"Two Voices, The" (Tennyson), **IV:** 329

Two Worlds and Their Ways (Compton-Burnett), **VII:** 65, 66, 67, 69

"Tyger, The" (Blake), **III:** 296

Tyler, F. W., **I:** 275$_n$

Tylney Hall (Hood), **IV:** 254, 256, 259, 267

Tynan, Katherine, **V:** 441

Tyndale, William, **I:** 375–377

"Typhoon" (Conrad), **VI:** 136, 148

Tyrannick Love, or the Royal Martyr (Dryden), **II:** 290, 294, 305

"Tyronic Dialogues" (Lewis), **VII:** 82

U

Udolpho (Radcliffe), see *Mysteries of Udolpho, The*

Ulick and Soracha (Moore), **VI:** 89, 95, 99

"Ultima" (Thompson), **V:** 441

Ulysses (Joyce), **IV:** 189; **VII:** xv, 42, 46–47, 48–52; critical studies, **VII:** 57–58

"Ulysses" (Tennyson), **IV:** xx, 324, 328, 332–334

"Unarmed Combat" (Reed), **VII:** 422–423

Unclassed, The (Gissing), **V:** 437

Uncle Silas (Le Fanu), **III:** 345

Uncollected Essays (Pater), **V:** 357

Uncollected Verse (Thompson), **V:** 451

Uncommercial Traveller, The (Dickens), **V:** 72

Unconditional Surrender (Waugh), **VII:** 303, 304; see also *Sword of Honour* trilogy

"Uncovenanted Mercies" (Kipling), **VI:** 175

"Under a Lady's Picture" (Waller), **II:** 234–235

"Under Ben Bulben" (Yeats), **VI:** 215, 219–220

Undergraduate Sonnets (Swinburne), **V:** 333

Under the Greenwood Tree: A Rural Painting of the Dutch School (Hardy), **VI:** 1, 2–3, 5, 20

Under the Hill (Beardsley), **VII:** 292

Under the Microscope (Swinburne), **IV:** 337; **V:** 329, 332, 333

Undertones of War (Blunden), **VI:** 428, 429

Under Western Eyes (Conrad), **VI:** 134, **144–145,** 148

" 'Under Which King, Bezonian?' " (Leavis), **VII:** 242

Underwood, Dale, **II:** 256$_n$

Underwoods (Stevenson), **V:** 390$_n$, 395

Undying Fire, The (Wells), **VI:** 242

"Unfortunate Lover, The" (Marvell), **II:** 211

Unfortunate Traveller, The (Nashe), **I:** 114, 281

"Ungratefulnesse" (Herbert), **II:** 127

Unhappy Favorite, The (Banks), **II:** 305

Unholy Trade, The (Findlater), **VII:** 8–9, 14

Unicorn, The (Murdoch), **III:** 341, 345

Unicorn, The (Rosenberg), **VI:** 433

Unicorn from the Stars, The (Yeats and Gregory), **VI:** 318

Union of the Two Noble and Illustre Families of Lancaster and York, The (Hall), **I:** 299

Universal Chronicle (periodical), **III:** 111

Universal Gallant, The (Fielding), **III:** 105

"University Feud, The: A Row at the Oxford Arms" (Hood), **IV:** 258

university wits, **I:** 191, 192, 194, 336

Unjust War: An Address to the Working-men of England (Morris), **V:** 305

Unknown, The (Maugham), **VI:** 369

Unprofessional Tales (Douglas), **VI:** 293, 305

Unpublished Early Poems (Tennyson), **IV:** 338

Unrelenting Struggle, The (Churchill), **VI:** 356

Unsocial Socialist, An (Shaw), **VI:** 103, 104, 105, 106, 129

"Unstable dream" (Wyatt), **I:** 103, 109

Untilled Field, The (Moore), **VI:** 88, 93, 98

Unto This Last (Ruskin), **V:** xii, xxii, 20, 179–180, 184

"Up at a Villa—Down in the City" (Browning), **IV:** 360

"Upon a Child That Dyed" (Herrick), **II:** 115

"Upon a Cloke Lent Him by Mr. J. Ridsley" (Vaughan), **II:** 184

Upon a Dead Man's Head (Skelton), **I:** 84

"Upon Ancient and Modern Learning" (Temple), **III:** 40

"Upon Appleton House" (Marvell), **II:** 208, 209–210, 211, 212–213

Upon Cromwell's Return from Ireland (Marvell), **II:** 199

Upon Her Majesty's New Buildings (Waller), **II:** 238

"Upon Heroick Virtue" (Temple), **III:** 40

"Upon Julia's Clothes" (Herrick), **II:** 107

"Upon Julia's Fall" (Herrick), **II:** 107

"Upon Julia's Unlacing Herself" (Herrick), **II:** 106

"Upon Julia's Voice" (Herrick), **II:** 107

"Upon Nothing" (Rochester), **II:** 259, 270

"Upon Our Late Loss of the Duke of Cambridge" (Waller), **II:** 233

"Upon Poetry" (Temple), **III:** 40

"Upon the Death of a Gentleman" (Crashaw), **II:** 183

"Upon the Death of Mr. R. W . . . ." (Vaughan), **II:** 184

"Upon the Earl of Roscommon's Translation of Horace" (Waller), **II:** 234

"Upon the Gardens of Epicurus" (Temple), **III:** 40

Upon the Late Storme, and of the Death of His Highnesse (Waller), **II:** 238

"Upon the Lonely Moor" (Carroll), **V:** 265, 267

Up the Rhine (Hood), **IV:** 254, 259, 267

Up to Midnight (Meredith), **V:** 234

Upton, John, **I:** 121

Ure, Peter, **VI:** 220

Useful and Instructive Poetry (Carroll), **V:** 263, 264, 273

Use of Poetry and the Use of Criticism, The (Eliot), **VII:** 153, 158, 164

Usk, Thomas, **I:** 2

utilitarianism, **IV:** xii, 133; **V:** viii, 288–289

Utopia (More), **III:** 24

utopian literature, **VI:** 225, 227, 241; **VII:** xviii, 200, 204, 206; see also dystopian literature

"Utter Rim, The" (Graves), **VII:** 270

V

Vagrant Mood, The (Maugham), **VI:** 374

Vailima Letters (Stevenson), **V:** 391, 396

Vain Fortune (Moore), **VI:** 87, 91

Vala, Or the Four Zoas (Blake), see *Four Zoas, The*

Val D'Arno (Ruskin), **V:** 184

Vale (Moore), **VI:** 99

"Valediction, A: Forbidding Mourning" (Donne), **II:** 185, 197

"Valediction, A: Of Weeping" (Donne), **II:** 196

Valentinian (Fletcher), **II:** 45, **58–60,** 65

Valentinian: A Tragedy . . . (Rochester), **II:** 270

Valiant Scot, The (Webster), **II:** 69, 85

Valley of Bones, The (Powell), **VII:** 349

"Valley of Couteretz" (Tennyson), **IV:** 330

Vampirella (Carter), **III:** 341

Vampyre, The (Polidori), **III:** 329, 334

Vanbrugh, Sir John, **II:** 289, **323–337,** 339, 347, 360; **III:** 253, 261

"Vanitie" (Herbert), **II:** 127

Vanity Fair (Thackeray), **IV:** 301; **V:** xxi, 17, 19, 20, 23, **25–28,** 30, 31, 35, 38

"Vanity of Human Wishes, The" (Johnson), **III:** 109–110, 121, 280, 281; **IV:** 188

"Vanity of Spirit" (Vaughan), **II:** 185

Variation of Public Opinion and Feelings . . . , The (Crabbe), **III:** 286

Varieties of Parable (MacNeice), **VII:** 405

Varma, D. P., **III:** 338, 346

Vasari, Georgio, **V:** 346

"Vastness" (Tennyson), **IV:** 329, 330

Vathek (Beckford), **III: 327–329,** 345; **IV:** xv, 230

Vaughan, Henry, **II:** 123, 126, **184–189,** 190, **201–203,** 221

Vaughan, Thomas, **II:** 184, 185

"Vauxhall Gardens by Day" (Dickens), **V:** 47$_n$

"Velvet Glove, The" (James), **VI:** 69

Venables, Robert, **II:** 131, 137

Venerable Bede, the, **I:** 374–375

Venetia (Disraeli), **IV:** xix, 298, 299, 307, 308

Veni, Creator Spiritus (Dryden), **II:** 300

Venus and Adonis (Shakespeare), **I:** 291, 306, 325; **IV:** 256

Venus and Tannhäuser (Beardsley), **V:** 318$_n$

Venusberg (Powell), **VII:** 344, 345

Veranilda (Gissing), **V:** 435, 437

Vera; or, The Nihilists (Wilde), **V:** 401, 419

Vergil, **II:** 292, 300, 304; **III:** 222, 311, 312; **IV:** 327

Vergil's Gnat (Spenser), **I:** 123

Vérité de la religion Chrétienne (tr. Sidney), **I:** 161

Verlaine, Paul, **V:** 404, 405

vernacular speech, **VI:** 200, 203

Verne, Jules, **III:** 341; **VI:** 229

Veronese, Paolo, **V:** 179

verse drama, **VII:** 153

Verses (Rossetti), **V:** 260

Verses, in the Character of a Corsican . . . (Boswell), **III:** 248

Verses Lately Written upon Several Occasions (Cowley), **II:** 202

Verses on the Death of Dr. Swift (Swift), **III:** 21, 32, 36

"Verses . . . to Sir Thomas Hanmer" (Collins), **III:** 160, 175

Very Woman, A (Fletcher and Massinger), **II:** 66

Vexilla Regis (Skelton), **I:** 84

"Vicar, The" (Praed), **V:** 14

Vicar of Bullhampton, The (Trollope), **V:** 102

Vicar of Wakefield, The (Goldsmith), **III:** 177, 178, 179, 180, **181–184,** 185, 188, 191

Victim of Circumstances, A, and Other Stories (Gissing), **V:** 437

"Victor Hugo" (Swinburne), **V:** 333

Victoria, queen of England, **IV:** 303–304, 305; **V:** xvii, xix, xxv–xxvi, 77, 114, 117

Victorian Age in Literature (Chesterton), **VI:** 337

Victorian and Edwardian London from Old Photographs (Betjeman), **VII:** 358

Victorian era, **VI:** viii

Victorian Lady Travellers (Middleton), **V:** 253

Victorian Ode for Jubilee Day, 1897 (Thompson), **V:** 451

Victorian Romantic, A: D. G. Rossetti (Doughty), **V:** 246, 297$_n$, 307

Victory (Conrad), **VI:** 144, 146, 148

View of the Edinburgh Theatre . . . , A (Boswell), **III:** 247

View of the English Stage, A (Hazlitt), **IV:** 129, 139

View of the Present State of Ireland (Spenser), **I:** 139

Views and Reviews (James), **VI:** 67

Views in Rome and its Environs (Lear), **V:** 76, 87

Views in the Seven Ionian Islands (Lear), **V:** 87

Vigny, Alfred de, **IV:** 176

Vile Bodies (Waugh), **VII:** 289, 290–291

Village, The (Crabbe), **III:** 273, 274, 275, 277–278, 283, 286

Village Wooing (Shaw), **VI:** 127, 129

Villainy of Stock-Jobbers Detected, The (Defoe), **III:** 12

Villa Rubein (Galsworthy), **VI:** 277

Villette (Brontë), **V:** xxi, 112, 125–126, 130, 132, 136, 145, **147–150,** 152

Villiers, George, see Buckingham, duke of

Villon, François, **V:** 327, 384

Vindication &c., The (Dryden), **II:** 305

Vindication of a Natural Diet . . . , A (Shelley), **IV:** 208

Vindication of . . . Lord Carteret, A (Swift), **III:** 35–36

Vindication of Natural Society, A (Burke), **III:** 195, 198, 205

Vindication of . . . Some Gospel-Truths, A (Bunyan), **II:** 253

Vindication of Some Passages in . . . the Decline and Fall . . . , A (Gibbon), **III:** 233

Vindication of the English Constitution (Disraeli), **IV:** 298, 308

Vindication of the Rights of Women, A (Wollstonecraft), **IV:** xv, 118

Vindiciae Ecclesiae Anglicanae: Letters to Charles Butler . . . (Southey), **IV:** 71

Vintage London (Betjeman), **VII:** 358–359

"Vintage to the Dungeon, The" (Lovelace), **II:** 231

Violent Effigy, The: A Study of Dickens's Imagination (Carey), **V:** 73

Viper and Her Brood, The (Middleton), **II:** 3, 33

Virchow, Rudolf, **V:** 348

Virgidemiarum (Hall), **II:** 25

Virgil, see Vergil

Virgin and the Gipsy, The (Lawrence), **VII:** 91, 115

Virginians, The (Thackeray), **V:** 29, **31–33**, 38

Virginia Woolf: A Biography (Bell), **VII:** 38

Virginibus Puerisque and Other Papers (Stevenson), **V:** 395

"Virgin Mary to the Child Jesus, The" (Browning), **IV:** 313

Vision, A (Yeats), **VI:** 209, 213, 214, 222

"Vision, The" (Burns), **III:** 315

Vision of Bags, A (Swinburne), **V:** 333

Vision of Don Roderick, The (Scott), **IV:** 38

Vision of Judgement, A (Southey), **IV:** 61, 71, 184–187

Vision of Judgment, The (Byron), **IV:** xviii, 58, 61–62, 132, 172, 178, **184–187**, 193

"Vision of Poets, A" (Browning), **IV:** 316

"Vision of the Last Judgment, A" (Blake), **III:** 299

"Vision of the Mermaids, A" (Hopkins), **V:** 361, 381

Vision of the Three T's, The (Carroll), **V:** 274

Vision of William Concerning Piers the Plowman . . . , The (ed. Skeat), **I:** 17

Visions of the Daughters of Albion (Blake), **III:** 307

Visitations (MacNeice), **VII:** 416

"Visits, The" (James), **VI:** 49, 69

"Vitai Lampada" (Newbolt), **VI:** 417

Vita Nuova (tr. Rossetti), **V:** 238

Vittoria (Meredith), **V:** 227–228, 234

Vivian Grey (Disraeli), **IV:** xvii, 293–294, 297, 299, 308

Vizetelly (publisher), **VI:** 86

"Voice, The" (Hardy), **VI:** 18

"Voice of Nature, The" (Bridges), **VI:** 79

Volpone (Jonson), **I:** 339, 343–344, 348; **II:** 4, 45, 70, 79; **V:** 56

Voltaire, **II:** 261, 348; **III:** 149, 235, 236, 327; **IV:** xiv, 290, 295, 346

"Volunteer, The" (Asquith), **VI:** 417

Vonnegut, Kurt, Jr., **III:** 341

Vorticist movement, **VII:** xii, 75–76, 77

Voss (White), **VII:** 31

Votive Tablets (Blunden), **IV:** 86

Vox clamantis (Gower), **I:** 48, 49–50

Voyage of Captain Popanilla, The (Disraeli), **IV:** 294–295, 308

Voyage Out, The (Woolf), **VII:** 20, 27, 37

Voyages (Hakluyt), **I:** 150, 267; **III:** 7

Voyage to Abyssinia, A (tr. Johnson), **III:** 107, 112, 121

Voyage to New Holland, A (Dampier), **III:** 24

Vulgar Errors (Browne), see *Pseudodoxia Epidemica*

"Vulgarity in Literature" (Huxley), **V:** 53

Vulgarity in Literature (Huxley), **VII:** 198

Vulgar Streak, The (Lewis), **VII:** 72, 77

W

Waagen, Gustav Friedrich, **III:** 328

Wager, William, **I:** 213

Waggoner, The (Wordsworth), **IV:** 24, 73

Wagner the Werewolf (Reynolds), **III:** 335

Wagstaff, Simon, pseud. of Jonathan Swift

Waif Woman, The (Stevenson), **V:** 396

Wain, John, **VI**: 209

Wainewright, Thomas, **V**: 405

Waingrow, W., **III**: 249

Waith, Eugene, **II**: 51, 64

"Waiting at the Station" (Thackeray), **V**: 25

Waiting for Godot (Beckett), **I**: 16–17

"Waiting Supper, The" (Hardy), **VI**: 22

Wakefield Plays, **I**: 20

Waldegrave, Frances, **V**: 77, 80, 81

Walker, Ernest, **IV**: 304

Walker, R. S., **III**: 249

Walk in Chamounix, A, and Other Poems (Ruskin), **V**: 184

"Walking with God" (Cowper), **III**: 212

"Walking Wounded" (Scannell), **VII**: 423

Waller, Edmund, **II**: 138, 222, **232–236**, 256, 271

Walpole, Horace, **III**: 324, **325–327**, 336, 345

Walpole, Hugh, **VI**: 55; **VI**: 247, 377; **VII**: 211

"Walrus, The, and the Carpenter" (Carroll), **V**: 268

Walsh, William, **II**: 325, 337, 339, 347

Walter Pater: A Critical Study (Thomas), **V**: 355, 358; **VI**: 424

Walter Pater: The Idea in Nature (Ward), **V**: 347, 359

Walter Savage Landor: A Biography (Forster), **IV**: 87, 100

Walton, Izaak, **I**: 178; **II**: 118, 119, 130, **131–144**

Walton, William, **VII**: xv

Waltz: An Apostrophic Hymn by Horace Hornem, Esq. (Byron), **IV**: 192

Wanderer, The (Auden), **VII**: 380

Wandering Jew, The (Shelley), **IV**: 209

Wanderings of Oisin, The (Yeats), **IV**: 216; **VI**: 220, 221

War and Common Sense (Wells), **VI**: 244

Ward, A. C., **V**: xiii, xxviii, 85, 86, 347, 348, 349

Ward, Edward, **III**: 41

Ward, Mrs. Humphry, **VI**: 387

Ward, R. P., **IV**: 293

Warden, The (Trollope), **V**: xxii, 92, 93, 101

"Warden's Daughter, The" (Gissing), **V**: 437

Ware the Hawk (Skelton), **I**: 88

"Waring" (Browning), **IV**: 356

War in Samoa (Stevenson), **V**: 396

War in the Air . . . , The (Wells), **VI**: 234, 244

War Issues for Irishmen (Shaw), **VI**: 119

"Warning to Children" (Graves), **VII**: 265

War of the Worlds, The (Wells), **VI**: 226, 233–234

war poets, see Poets of World War I, Poets of World War II, Robert Graves, Wilfred Owen

Warren, Austin, **II**: 155, 332$_n$

"Warrior's Soul, The" (Conrad), **VI**: 148

War's Embers (Gurney), **VI**: 425

war songs, **VI**: 435–436

War Speeches (Churchill), **VI**: 361

"War That Will End War, The" (Wells), **VI**: 227, 244

Warton, Joseph, **III**: 162, 170$_n$

Washington Square (James), **VI**: **32–33**

Wasp in a Wig, The (Carroll), **V**: 274

"Waste Land, The" (Eliot), **VI**: 137, 158; **VII**: xv, 143, **147–150**

Watch and Ward (James), **VI**: 24, 26, 67

Watchman, The (periodical), **IV**: 43, 55, 56

"Water Lady, The" (Hood), **IV**: 255

Water of Life, The (Bunyan), **II**: 253

Water of the Wondrous Isles, The (Morris), **V**: 306

Watson, George L., **VI**: 152

Watson, John Richard, **IV**: ix, xxv, 26, 375

Watson, Richard, **III**: 301

Watson, Thomas, **I**: 193, 276

Watson, Sir William, **VI**: 415

Watsons, The (Austen), **IV**: 108, 122

Watt, Ian, **VI**: 144

Watts, Isaac, **III**: 118, 211, 288, 294, 299, 300

Watts-Dunton, Theodore, **V**: 314, 334

Wat Tyler (Southey), **IV**: 59, 62, 66, 71, 185

Waugh, Evelyn, **V**: 33; **VII**: xviii, xx–xxi, **289–308**

Waverly novels (Scott), **IV**: 28, 30–34, 38

Waverly: or, 'Tis Sixty Years Since (Scott), **III**: 335; **IV**: xvii, 28, 30–31, 37, 38

Waves, The (Woolf), **VI**: 262; **VII**: xv, 18, 22, 27, 38

"Way It Came, The" (James) **VI**: 69

Way of All Flesh, The (Butler), **VI**: ix

"Way of Imperfection, The" (Thompson), **V**: 451

Way of the World, The (Congreve), **II:** 339, **343–346,** 347, 350

Way We Live Now, The (Trollope), **IV:** 307; **V:** xxiv, 98–99, 100, 102

W. B. Yeats, Man and Poet (Jeffares), **VI:** 223

W. B. Yeats: The Critical Heritage (Jeffares), **VI:** 224

Wealth of Mr. Waddy, The (Wells), see *Kipps*

Wealth of Nations, The (Smith), see *Inquiry into the Nature & Causes of the Wealth of Nations*

"We Are Seven" (Wordsworth), **IV:** 8, 10

Wearieswa': A Ballad (Swinburne), **V:** 333

Webb, Beatrice, **VI:** 227, 241

Webb, Philip, **V:** 291, 296

Webb, Sidney, **VI:** 102

Webster, John, **II:** 21, 31, 33, **68–86,** 89, 97, 100

Webster: "The Dutchess of Malfi" (Leech), **II:** 90$_n$

Wedd, Nathaniel, **VI:** 398, 399

Wedding-Day, The (Fielding), **III:** 105

"Wedding Gown, The" (Moore), **VI:** 93

Wedgwood, Tom, **IV:** 127–128

"Wednesday, or The Dumps" (Gay), **III:** 56

Weekly Journal (newspaper), **III:** 7

"Weeper, The" (Crashaw), **II:** 180, 181, 183

Wee Willie Winkie (Kipling), **VI:** 204

"We have a pritty witty king" (Rochester), **II:** 259

Weir of Hermiston, The (Stevenson), **V:** 383, 384, 387, 390, 392, 396

Weis, C. McC., **III:** 249

"Welcome, The" (Cowley), **II:** 196

"Welcome to Sack, The" (Herrick), **II:** 111

Well at the World's End, The (Morris), **V:** 306

Well-Beloved, The: A Sketch of a Temperament (Hardy), **VI:** 14, 20

Well of Loneliness, The (Hall), **VI:** 411

"Well of Pen-Morta, The" (Gaskell), **V:** 15

Well of the Saints, The (Synge), **VI:** 308, 311, 312–313

Wells, H. G., **III:** 341; **V:** xxiii, xxvi, 388, 426–427, 429, 438; **VI:** x–xiii, 102, **225–246,** 287; **VII:** xiv, 197; list of works and letters, **VI:** 243–246

"Wells, Hitler, and the World State" (Orwell), **VII:** 274

Well-Wrought Urn, The (Brooks), **IV:** 323$_n$, 339

Welsh Ambassador, The, **II:** 100

Welsh Opera, The (Fielding), **III:** 105

Werner, J., **III:** 249

Werner: A Tragedy (Byron), **IV:** 193

Werther (Goethe), see *Sorrows of Young Werther, The*

Wesker, Arnold, **VI:** 101

Wesley, Charles, **III:** 211

Wesley, John, **II:** 273

Wessex Poems (Hardy), **VI:** 14

Wessex Tales: Strange, Lively and Commonplace (Hardy), **VI:** 20

West, Anthony, **VI:** 241, 242

West, Arthur Graeme, **VI:** 423

West, Rebecca, **VI:** 226, 227, 252, 371

"West Indies, The" (Macaulay), **IV:** 278

West Indies and the Spanish Main, The (Trollope), **V:** 101

"Westland Well" (Swinburne), **V:** 333

"Westminster Abbey" (Arnold), **V:** 208–209

Westminster Review, The (periodical), **V:** xviii, 189

Westward Ho! (Dekker and Webster), **II:** 68, 85

"What Does It Matter?" (Forster), **VI:** 411

What D'Ye Call It, The (Gay), **III:** 58, 60, 67

Whately, Richard, **IV:** 102, 122

What I Really Wrote About the War (Shaw), **VI:** 129

What Is He? (Disraeli), **IV:** 308

"What Is There to Discuss?" (Ramsey), **VII:** 240

What Maisie Knew (James), **VI: 50–52,** 67

"What meaneth this?" (Wyatt), **I:** 104

"What rage is this" (Wyatt), **I:** 104

What's Become of Waring? (Powell), **VII:** 346, 353

What the Public Wants (Bennett), **VI:** 263–264

"What the Shepherd Saw" (Hardy), **VI:** 22

"What the Thrush Said" (Keats), **IV:** 225

What You Will (Marston), **II:** 29–30, 40

"Wheel of Time, The" (James), **VI:** 69

Wheels of Chance, The: A Holiday Adventure (Wells), **VI:** 231–232, 244

"When a Beau Goes In" (Ewart), **VII:** 423

"When Earth's Last Picture Is Painted" (Kipling), **VI:** 169

"When I Am Dead, My Dearest" (Rossetti), **V:** 249

"When I Have Fears" (Keats), **IV:** 221

"When Israel came out of Egypt" (Clough), **V:** 160

When the Moon Has Set (Synge), **VI:** 310$_n$

When the Sleeper Wakes (Wells), **VI:** 234

When the Wicked Man (Ford), **VI:** 319, 332

When We Dead Awaken (Ibsen), **VI:** 269

"When we that were dear . . ." (Henley), **V:** 392

"When Windsor walles sustained my wearied arm" (Surrey), **I:** 113

"When you see millions of the mouthless dead" (Sorley), **VI:** 422

Where Angels Fear to Tread (Forster), **VI:** 400–401

"Whereto Art Thou Come" (Thompson), **V:** 444

Whetstone, George, **I:** 282, 313

Whibley, Charles, **II:** 259

Whig Examiner (periodical), **III:** 51, 53

Whig Interpretations of History, The (Butterfield), **IV:** 291

Whims and Oddities (Hood), **IV:** 253, 255, 257, 267

Whimsicalities (Hood), **IV:** 254, 267

Whirlpool, The (Gissing), **V:** 437

"Whispers" (Tennyson), **IV:** 332

"Whispers of Immortality" (Eliot), **VII:** 145

Whistlecraft (Frere), **IV:** 182–183

Whistler, James McNeill, **V:** 238, 245, 320, 407

White, James, **IV:** 79

White, Norman, **V:** 379$_n$

White Cockade, The (Gregory), **VI:** 315

White Devil, The (Webster), **I:** 246; **II:** 68, 70, 72, **73–75,** 76, 79, 80–85, 97

White Doe of Rylstone, The (Wordsworth), **IV:** xvii, 24

White Goddess, The (Graves), **VII:** xviii, 257, 259, 261–262

Whitehall, Harold, **V:** 365, 382

"White Island, The: or Place of the Blest" (Herrick), **II:** 113

White Monkey, The (Galsworthy), **VI:** 274

White Peacock, The (Lawrence), **VII:** 88, 89, **91–93**

"White Ship, The" (Rossetti), **V:** 238, 244

"White Stocking, The" (Lawrence), **VII:** 114

Whitman, Walt, **IV:** 332; **V:** 418; **VI:** 55, 63

"Whitsunday" (Herbert), **II:** 125

"Whitsunday in Kirchstetten" (Auden), **VII:** 396, 397

Whole Duty of Man, The (Allestree), **III:** 82

Whole Works of Homer, The (Chapman), **I:** 235

"Whoso list to hunt" (Wyatt), **I:** 101, 109

Why Come Ye Not to Court? (Skelton), **I:** 92–93

Why Frau Frohmann Raised Her Prices and Other Stories (Trollope), **V:** 102

"Why Not Take Pater Seriously?" (Fletcher), **V:** 359

"Why She Would Not" (Shaw), **VI:** 130

"Why the Novel Matters" (Lawrence), **VII:** 122

"Wicked Tunge Wille Sey Amys, A" (Lydgate), **I:** 57

Widow, The (Middleton), **II:** 3, 21

Widowers' Houses (Shaw), **VI:** 104, 107, 108, 129

Widowing of Mrs. Holroyd, The (Lawrence), **VII:** 120, 121

Widow Ranter, The (Belin), **II:** 305

Widow's Tears, The (Chapman), **I:** 243–244, 245–246

Wiene, Robert, **III:** 342

Wife for a Month (Fletcher), **II:** 65

Wife of Bath, The (Gay), **III:** 60, 67

Wife of Bath's Prologue, The (Chaucer), **I:** 24, 34, 39, 40

Wife of Bath's Tale, The (Chaucer), **I:** 27, 35–36

Wilberforce, William, **IV:** 133, 268; **V:** 277

Wild Ass's Skin, The (Balzac), **III:** 339, 345

"Wild Boar and the Ram, The" (Gay), **III:** 59

Wild Body, The (Lewis), **VII:** 72, 77, 78, 79

Wild Duck, The (Ibsen), **VI:** ix

Wilde, Oscar, **III:** 334, 345; **V:** xiii, xxi, xxv, xxvi, 53, 339, **399–422**; **VI:** ix, 365; **VII:** 83

Wilder Hope, The: Essays on Future Punishment . . . (De Quincey), **IV:** 155

"Wilderness, The" (Keyes), **VII:** 439

"Wild Flowers" (Howard), **V:** 48

Wild Gallant, The (Dryden), **II:** 305

Wild Goose Chase, The (Fletcher), **II:** 45, 61–62, 65, 352, 357

Wild Knight, The (Chesterton), **VI:** 336

Wild Swans at Coole, The (Yeats), **VI**: 207, 213, 214, 217

"Wild with All Regrets" (Owen), **VI**: 446, 452, 453

"Wilfred Owen and the Georgians" (Hibberd), **VI**: 460

"Wilfred Owen's Letters" (Hibberd), **VI**: 460

Wilfred Owen: War Poems and Others (Hibberd), **VI**: 446, 459

Wilhelm Meister (Goethe), **IV**: 241; **V**: 214

Wilhelm Meister's Apprenticeship (tr. Carlyle), **IV**: 241, 250

Wilkes, John, **IV**: 61, 185

Wilkes, Thomas, **II**: 351, 363

Wilkie, David, **IV**: 37

Wilkins, George, **I**: 321

Will Drew and Phil Crewe and Frank Fane . . . (Swinburne), **V**: 333

Willey, B., **II**: 145, 157

William Blake (Chesterton), **VI**: 344

William Blake (Swinburne), **V**: 313, 314, 317, 329–330, 332

William B. Yeats: The Poet in Contemporary Ireland (Hone), **VI**: 223

William Cobbett (Chesterton), **VI**: 341, 345

"William Congreve" (Swinburne), **V**: 332

William Morris (Bloomfield), **V**: 306

William Morris, Artist, Writer, Socialist (Morris), **V**: 301, 305

"William Morris as I Knew Him" (Shaw), **VI**: 129

William Pitt . . . an Excellent New Ballad . . . (Boswell), **III**: 248

Williams, Basil, **VI**: 234

Williams, H., **III**: 15$_n$, 35

Williams, Iolo, **VII**: 37

William Wetmore Story and His Friends (James), **VI**: 67

"William Wordsworth" (De Quincey), **IV**: 146

William Wordsworth: A Biography (Moorman), **IV**: 4, 25

Willis, W., **III**: 199$_n$

"Will o' the Mill" (Stevenson), **V**: 395

"Willowwood" sonnets (Rossetti), **V**: 243, 259

Will Warburton (Gissing), **V**: 435, 437

Wilmot, John, see Rochester, earl of

Wilson, Sir Angus, **V**: 43, 72; **VI**: 165

Wilson, Colin, **III**: 341

Wilson, Dover, see Wilson, J. Dover

Wilson, Edmund, **IV**: 27; **V**: 66, 69, 72; **VI**: 56, 62, 363; **VII**: 53

Wilson, F. A. C., **VI**: 208, 220

Wilson, F. P., **I**: 286

Wilson, J. Dover, **I**: 326; **III**: 116$_n$; **V**: 287, 290

Wilson, J. H., **II**: 257, 271

Wilson, John, **IV**: 11

Wilson, Rae, **IV**: 262

Wimsatt, M. K., Jr., **III**: 249

Winckelmann, Johann, **V**: 341, 343, 344

"Winckelmann" (Pater), **V**: 341, 343, 344

Wind, Edgar, **I**: 237; **V**: 317$_n$

Wind Among the Reeds, The (Yeats), **VI**: 211, 222

"Windhover, The" (Hopkins), **V**: 366, 367

"Window, The" (Moore), **VI**: 93

Window in Thrums, A (Barrie), **V**: 392

Windows (Galsworthy), **VI**: 269

"Wind's on the World, The" (Morris), **V**: 305

Windsor Forest (Pope), **III**: 70, 77

Wine: A Poem (Gay), **III**: 67

Wine, Water and Song (Chesterton), **VI**: 340

Wings of the Dove, The (James), **VI**: 32, 55, **59–60**; **VI**: 320

Winkworth, Catherine, **V**: 149

Winnowers, The" (Bridges), **VI**: 78

"Winter" (Brontë), **V**: 107

Winter Fuel (Millais), **V**: 379

"Winter, My Secret" (Rossetti), **V**: 256

Winters, Yvor, **VI**: 219

"Winters and the Palmleys, The" (Hardy), **VI**: 22

Winterslow: Essays and Characters Written There (Hazlitt), **IV**: 140

Winter's Tale, The (Chaucer), **I**: 25

Winter's Tale, The (Shakespeare), **I**: 166$_n$, 302, 322–323, 327

"Winter with the Gulf Stream" (Hopkins), **V**: 361, 381

Winter Words, in Various Moods and Metres (Hardy), **VI:** 20

Wisdom of Father Brown, The (Chesterton), **VI:** 338

Wisdom of Solomon Paraphrased, The (Middleton), **II:** 2

Wisdom of the Ancients (Bacon), see *De sapientia veterum*

Wise, T. J., **V:** 150, 151

"Wish, The" (Cowley), **II:** 195, 198

"Wishes to His (Supposed) Mistresse" (Crashaw), **II:** 180

"Wish House, The" (Kipling), **VI:** 169, 193, 196, **197–199**

Wit at Several Weapons, **II:** 21, 66

Witch, The (Middleton), **II:** 3, 21; **IV:** 79

"Witch of Atlas, The" (Shelley), **IV:** 196, 204

Witch of Edmonton, The (Dekker, Ford, Rowley), **II:** 89, 100

Wither, George, **IV:** 81

"Withered Arm, The" (Hardy), **VI:** 22

Within the Gates (O'Casey), **VII:** 7

Within the Tides: Tales (Conrad), **VI:** 148

"Without Benefit of Clergy" (Kipling), **VI:** **180– 183**

Wit's Treasury (Meres), **I:** 296

Wit Without Money (Fletcher), **II:** 66

Wives and Daughters (Gaskell), **V:** xxiii, 1–4, 8, 11–13, 14, 15

"W. Kitchener" (Hood), **IV:** 267

Woefully Arrayed (Skelton), **I:** 84

Wolf, Friedrich, **IV:** 316–317

Wolf, Lucien, **IV:** 293

Wolff, S. L., **I:** 164

Wolf Leader, The (Dumas *père*), **III:** 339

Wollstonecraft, Mary, **IV:** xv, xvi, 118, 197

Wolves and the Lamb, The (Thackeray), **V:** 35

Woman (periodical), **VI:** 249

"Woman at the Shore, The" (Mansfield), **VII:** 173

Woman-Captain, The (Shadwell), **II:** 359

Woman Hater, The (Beaumont and Fletcher), **II:** 46, 65

Womanhood, Wanton, Ye Want (Skelton), **I:** 83

"Woman in His Life, The" (Kipling), **VI:** 193

Woman in the Moon, The (Lyly), **I:** 204–205

Woman in White, The (Collins), **III:** 340, 345

Woman Killed With Kindness, A (Heywood), **II:** 19

woman novelists, **VII:** 20

Woman of No Importance, A (Wilde), **V:** xxvi, 414, 419

Woman Pleased (Fletcher), **II:** 45, 65

"Woman's Last Word, A" (Browning), **IV:** 367

Woman's Prize, The, or the Tamer Tamed (Fletcher), **II:** 43, 45, 65

Woman's World (periodical), **V:** 404

"Woman Who Rode Away, The" (Lawrence), **VII:** 87–88, 91, 115

Women Beware Women (Middleton), **II:** 1, 3, 8, **10–14,** 19

Women in Love (Lawrence), **IV:** 119; **VI:** 276; **VII:** 87–88, 89, 91, 98, **101–104**

women poets, **VII:** 127

women's suffrage, **VI:** 274

"Wonder" (Traherne), **II:** 191

Wonderful Visit, The (Wells), **VI:** 226, 228, 230, 243

Wonder of Women, The: or The Tragedie of Sophonisba (Marston), **II:** 25, 30–31, 40, 305

Wondrous Tale of Alroy, The (Disraeli), see *Alroy*

Wood, Anthony à, **II:** 185

Wood Beyond the World, The (Morris), **V:** 306

Woodhouse, Richard, **IV:** 230, 232, 233

Woodlanders, The (Hardy), **VI:** 1, 5, 7, 8, 9

"Woods of Westermain, The" (Meredith), **V:** 221

"Woodspurge, The" (Rossetti), **V:** 241, 242, 314– 315

Woodstock (Scott), **IV:** xviii, 27, 39

Woodward, Benjamin, **V:** 178

Woolf, Leonard, **VI:** 415; **VII:** 17

Woolf, Virginia, **I:** 169; **IV:** 107, 320, 322; **V:** xxv, 226, 256, 260, 281, 290; **VI:** 243, 252, 275, 411; **VII:** xii, xiv–xv, **17–39**

Word for the Navy, A (Swinburne), **V:** 332

Word-Links (Carroll), **V:** 274

Words upon the Window Pane, The (Yeats), **VI:** 219, 222

Wordsworth, Dorothy, **II:** 273; **IV:** 1–4, 10, 19, 49, 128, 143, 146

Wordsworth, William, **II:** 188–189; **III:** 174; **IV:** viii–xi, **1–26,** 33, 70, 73, 95–96, 111, 137, 178,

Wordsworth, William (Cont.)
214, 215, 281, 311, 351, 352; **V**: 287, 311, 331, 351–352; **VI**: 1; and Coleridge, **IV**: 43–45, 50, 51, 54; and DeQuincey, **IV**: 141–143, 146, 154; and Hazlitt, **IV**: 126–130, 133–134, 137, 138; and Keats, **IV**: 214, 215, 225, 233; and Shelley, **IV**: 198, 203, 207; and Tennyson, **IV**: 326, 329, 336; literary style, **III**: 304, 338; **IV**: 95–96, 154, 336; verse forms, **II**: 200; **V**: 224

"Wordsworth" (Pater), **V**: 351–352

"Wordsworth and Byron" (Swinburne), **V**: 332

"Wordsworth's Ethics" (Stephen), **V**: 287

"Work" (Lamb), **IV**: 83

Workers in the Dawn (Gissing), **V**: 424, 435, 437

Workes of Edmund Waller in This Parliament, The (Waller), **II**: 238

"Workhouse Clock, The" (Hood), **IV**: 261, 264

Workhouse Ward, The (Gregory), **VI**: 315, 316

Working Novelist, The (Pritchett), **VI**: 290

Workmen's Neutrality Demonstration, **VI**: 168

Works (Congreve), **II**: 348

Works (Cowley), **II**: 195

Works (Swift), **III**: 24

Works of Art and Artists in England (Waagen), **III**: 328

Works of Charles Lamb, The, **IV**: 73, 81, 85

Works of Henry Fielding, The (ed. Stephen), **V**: 290

Works of Henry Vaughan, The (Martin), **II**: 184

Works of Morris and Yeats in Relation to Early Saga Literature, The (Hoare), **V**: 299, 306

Works of Samuel Johnson, The, **III**: 108$_n$, 121

Works of Sir John Vanbrugh, The (ed. Dobrée and Webb), **II**: 323$_n$

Works of Sir Thomas Malory, The (ed. Vinavier), **I**: 70, 80

Works of Thomas Lodge, The (Tyler), **VI**: 102

Works of Virgil, The (tr. Dryden), **II**: 304

Works of William Blake, The (ed. Yeats), **VI**: 222

Work Suspended (Waugh), **VII**: 298–299

Work, Wealth and Happiness of Mankind, The (Wells), **VI**: 225

World (periodical), **VI**: 103, 104

"World, The" (Vaughan), **II**: 185, 186, 188

World Crisis, The (Churchill), **VI**: 353–354

world government, **VI**: 227

World in the Evening, The (Isherwood), **VII**: 309, 314–315

Worldliness (Moore), **VI**: 95, 98

World of Light, The (Huxley), **VII**: 201

World Set Free, The: A Story of Mankind (Wells), **VI**: 227, 244

World War I, effects on English literature, **VI**: 250, 352–354, 389, 415; **VII**: xv–xvi, xviii, xix, 108, 211

World War I, poets of, see Poets of World War I

World War II, effects on English literature, **VI**: 347, 349, 357; **VII**: xix, xxii, 137

World War II, poets of, see Poets of World War II

Worm of Spindlestonheugh, The (Swinburne), **V**: 333

"Worst of It, The" (Browning), **IV**: 369

Worthies of England (Fuller), **II**: 45

Wotton, Sir Henry, **II**: 132, 133, 134, 138, 140, 141, 142, 166

Wotton, William, **III**: 23

Wotton Reinfred (Carlyle), **IV**: 250

Woty, W., **III**: 170$_n$

Wrecker, The (Stevenson), **V**: 383, 387, 396

"Wreck of the Deutschland, The" (Hopkins), **V**: 361, 362, **363–366,** 367, 369, 370, 375, 379, 380, 381

"Wreck of the Deutschland, The": A New Reading (Schneider), **V**: 366, 382

Wrens, The (Gregory), **VI**: 315–316

"Wrestling" (Rossetti), **V**: 260

Wright, William Aldis, **IV**: 343, 353

Writer and the Absolute, The (Lewis), **VII**: xv, 71, 72, 73–74, 76

Writers and Their Work series, **VII**: xi, xxii

Writer's Diary, A (Woolf), **V**: 226

Writer's Notebook, A (Maugham), **VI**: 365, 366

"Written After the Death of Charles Lamb" (Wordsworth), **IV**: 73

"Written in My Lady Speke's Singing Book" (Waller), **II**: 234

Wrong Box, The (Stevenson and Osbourne), **V:** 387, 396

W. Somerset Maugham and the Quest for Freedom (Calder), **VI:** 376$_n$

Wuthering Heights (Brontë), **III:** 333, 338, 344, 345; **V:** xx, 113, 114, 127, 128, 131, 133–135, 140, **141–145,** 254

Wyatt, Sir Thomas, **I: 97–112,** 113, 115

"Wyatt resteth here, that quick could never rest" (Surrey), **I:** 115

Wycherley, William, **II: 307–322,** 343, 352, 360

Wycliffe, John, **I:** 375

Wymer, T. L., **V:** 324, 335

Wyndham Lewis: A Memoir (Eliot), **VII:** 77

Wyndham Lewis: His Theory of Art and Communication (McLuhan), **VII:** 71$_n$

Y

"Yardley Oak" (Cowper), **III:** 218

Yarrow Revisited, and Other Poems (Wordsworth), **IV:** 25

Yates, Edmund, **V:** 20

Yates, Frances M., **I:** 237

Years, The (Woolf), **VII:** 18, 22, 24, 27, 28, 36, 38

Years Between, The (Kipling), **VI:** 204

Yeast (Kingsley), **V:** 4

Yeats, William Butler, **II:** 78; **III:** 21, 36, 184; **IV:** 196, 216, 323, 329; **V:** xxiii, xxv, xxvi, 301, 304, 306, 311, 318, 329–330, 355, 356, 404; **VI:** ix, xiii–xiv, 55–56, 86, 88, **207–224,** 307, 308, 309, 314; **VII:** 1, 3, 42, 404

"Ye happy youths, whose hearts are free" (Etherege), **II:** 267

Yellow Book (periodical), **VI:** 248, 365

"Yellow Girl, The" (Sitwell), **VII:** 138

Yellowplush Correspondence, The (Thackeray), **V:** 21, 22, 37

"Yellow Streak, The" (Maugham), **VI:** 371

"Yongy-Bonghy-Bo" (Lear), **V:** 84–86

Yorkshire Tragedy, The, **II:** 3, 21

You Never Can Tell (Shaw), **VI:** 109, 111–112

Young, Edward, **III:** 302, 307, 336

Young, G. M., **IV:** 277, 290, 291, 295; **V:** 228, 262

Young, Kenneth, **IV:** xii, xxv; **VI:** xi–xii, xiii, xxxiv; **VII:** xviii, xxxix

Young, Richard B., **I:** 170

"Young Dragon, The" (Southey), **IV:** 67

Young Duke, The (Disraeli), **IV:** 293, 295–296, 308

"Young King, The" (Wilde), **V:** 406

"Young Love Lies Sleeping" (Rossetti), **V:** 249

"Young Parson Richards" (Shelley), **IV:** 209

Young Samuel Johnson (Clifford), **III:** 244$_n$

"Young Soldier with Bloody Spurs, The" (Lawrence), **VII:** 118

Young Visitors, The (Ashford), **V:** 111, 262

"You praise the firm restraint with which they write" (Campbell), **IV:** 320

Your Five Gallants (Middleton), **II:** 3, 21

Youth (Conrad), **VI:** 135, 137

Youth (Rosenberg), **VI:** 432

"Youth" (Tennyson), **IV:** 329

"Youth and Art" (Browning), **IV:** 369

"You that in love find luck and abundance" (Wyatt), **I:** 104

"Youth in Memory" (Meredith), **V:** 222, 234

"Youth of Man, The" (Arnold), **V:** 210

"Youth of Nature, The" (Arnold), **V:** 210

Z

Zapolya (Coleridge), **IV:** 56

Zastrozzi: A Romance (Shelley), **III:** 338; **IV:** 208

Zola, Émile, **V:** xxiv–xxvi, 286; **VI:** viii

Zoo (MacNeice), **VII:** 403